A HISTORY OF CHRISTIAN EDUCATION

JAMES E. REED
RONNIE PREVOST

LINCOLN CHRISTIAN COLLEGE AND SEMINARY

BROADMAN
& HOLMAN
PUBLISHERS

Nashville, Tennessee

4265-86

ISBN: 0-8054-6586-3

Dewey Decimal Classification: 268.09
Subject Heading: RELIGIOUS EDUCATION - HISTORY
Library of Congress Catalog Number: 91-38526
Printed in the United States of America

Library of Congress Cataloging-in-Publication Data

Reed, James E., 1944-
    A history of Christian education / James E. Reed, Ronald F.
Prevost.
        p.   cm.
    Includes bibliographical references and index.
    ISBN 0-8054-6586-3
    1. Christian Education—History. 2. Education, Ancient.
I. Prevost, Ronald F., 1949- . II. Title.
BV1465.R44 1992
268'.09—dc20   91-38526
                                                                                    CIP

To William B. Rogers, Jr.

mentor, friend, and colleague

Contents

Part 5: The Beginnings of Modern Christian Education

Part 6: Americans and Christian Education

Part 7: Christian Education in the Twentieth Century

Foreword

Writing history is an important and difficult undertaking. History gives a sense of identity to a person, people, or nation. It enables one to get in touch with one's roots. A person with amnesia struggles intensely to recall or learn about his or her past, otherwise that individual has no sense of identity. Some of us are old enough to remember the two-hundredth anniversary of the birth of our nation. Small children waved flags. Bands marched and played stirring music. Adults lined the streets and cheered. Speakers told stories of the founders of our nation. Recalling and reliving our history gave us a sense of identity.

Knowing history also aids in choosing direction for our future. As Santayana, the Spanish philosopher, is reported to have said, "He who does not know history is doomed to repeat it." We do not want every generation to have to reinvent the wheel. We desire progress. We do not want to repeat the mistakes of the past. If Santayana is correct, knowing history is a "must."

Writing history is exceedingly difficult because it involves the complex task of interpretation. Writing history is not simply a matter of recording what is supposed to have happened or what was reputed to have been said. Writing history involves the use of sources, either primary or secondary. Artifacts, letters, committee reports, transcripts, and eyewitness testimony are examples of *primary sources*. These are direct testimonies and evidences of history. Later, however, others tell and retell the story. Their reports are *secondary sources*.

Historians use both primary and secondary sources, but both of these have limitations. A secondary source reflects the interpretive judgment of the writer. The historian who uses primary sources must evaluate the authenticity of the source and interpret the dynamics in the situation that led the person to say or write at that particular time in history. The farther back into history one goes, the more difficult interpretation becomes.

Even with those still living, interpretation continues to be necessary. A few years ago I taught a course in the philosophy of Christian education. I carefully studied the writings of leaders in the field and sought to share their views with students. At times I role-played a particular scholar, being confident that I understood his or her writings. Later a few of these scholars came on campus to give a series of lectures. These men and women lectured in chapel and various classes. I was amazed at how often I had failed to understand what these leaders had meant by what they had written. I had interpreted them through my mind-set and preconceived perspectives. I was seeking to interpret "current history," to say nothing of seeking to understand the dynamics and meaning of what transpired centuries ago.

This task places an awesome responsibility of interpretation upon the historian. The impetus of human thought is the dynamic interaction of family, culture, and special events that are happening all the time. For Christians, God is also at work. These factors provide the milieu that influences what an individual becomes in his or her inner being in terms of feelings, insights, ideas, and convictions. Likewise, it is the dynamic interaction of the culture, life and times, and current events taking place around individuals at a particular phase of history that influenced them to do, say, or write what they did. To understand these dynamics as clearly as possible and to interpret their depth and reality for the modern mind is an awesome task.

The authors recognize the interpretative factor in their work by using the indefinite article in the title: A History of Christian Education. They invite rebuttal because they recognize that others will approach movements, councils, events, and writings from their own perspectives and thus may come to differing conclusions. They believe that interaction and dialogue will be beneficial to all who are involved.

The authors also recognize that they face the factor of selectivity. They undertake neither to give a serious study of the Christian faith nor of the broad field of education. In dealing with the much more specific area of Christian education, inevitably they have had to be highly selective in the material they used.

A number of things impressed me about this book. First and foremost, I am greatly impressed by the extensiveness of this volume. This is most obvious to the naked eye by its size. Far more than that, this book gives a comprehensiveness and depth to the study of the history of Christian education that is rare indeed.

Second, I am deeply impressed with the scope and quality of the research these writers have done. They have used primary sources or the translations of primary sources extensively. They also make excellent use of scholarly and recent works to give insights.

A third area that impressed me was the strong emphasis they placed on the life and work of persons to give meaning and dynamic to differing points of view, councils, and movements. I am aware of the differing points of view in social theory concerning how much difference one person or even a group of persons can make in changing the direction of history or a movement within history. However, in my more mature years, I am coming to believe more and more that persons under God can make a difference. These writers with their emphasis on the life and contribution of persons make the study of Christian history come alive. They make historical events take on a sense of reality as they point out the interaction of outstanding leaders and their influence on the development of significant events.

In six of the seven parts, the writers have a chapter on women in education. Part 7 has a brief section on the women's movement. In the Introduction, the authors indicate that lifting out the education of women for special attention might be interpreted by some as being "segregation" or a type of sexism. Like the authors I feel it is important to give this special attention to the education of women so that it will not be overlooked, as has often been the case in the past.

My assessment of this work is easy to state. I think it will become a classic in its field. Although the history of Christian education was not my teaching responsibility, I certainly thought I had an adequate knowledge of the field. However, in reading the manuscript in preparation for writing this Foreword, I was introduced to information, ideas, insights, persons, and relationships I knew nothing about. The chapter dealing with the beginnings of the Sunday School movement is illustrative of this point. If there was one area I thought I knew, this was it. In reading this chapter, I became so excited with the new information given and the dynamic interrelationships involved, I felt I was reading it for the first time.

I am not a prophet or the son of a prophet, but I predict this will become the standard work for the study of the history of Christian education for decades to come.

Findley B. Edge
Winter Park, Florida

Acknowledgments

In the fall of 1985 Ronnie Prevost and I decided to write a history of Christian education. Since our initial meeting, a host of competent and caring individuals have given their encouragement and expertise for the fruition of this book. Colleagues in Christian education and other disciplines at The Southern Baptist Theological Seminary and New Orleans Baptist Theological Seminary have enhanced this publication with their support and insightful critiques. The administrators of these schools have provided assistance and sabbatical leave for this project.

While on the seminary faculty at New Orleans, I benefited greatly from serving as a team-teacher with Ferris Jordan and Bart Neal in the course "Historical Foundations of Christian Education." I am grateful for their friendship and professionalism. Over a period of years, Bob Mathis, Jeanine Bozeman, Jim Minton, and Jerry Pounds have patiently dialogued with me about several subjects in this textbook. Their support and advice leaves me indebted to them.

Observations and questions from our students at New Orleans Seminary, Southern Seminary, Samford University, Mississippi College, and/or Gardner-Webb College are present throughout the pages of this history. Fortunately for Ronnie and me, some of the most capable seminary students served as our graduate assistants. Israel Galindo, Bayne Pounds, John Gibson, and Cary Hanks spent countless hours at New Orleans writing seminar papers, grading assignments, and engaging in critical thought about educational history. Tim Brock, Bob Brocious, David Cassady, and Mark McElroy contributed by similar means for Ronnie at Louisville.

The preparation of this manuscript would have been impossible without efficient secretaries. In New Orleans, Caroline Humphreys, Cathy Minton, Judy Robertson, and Jeralyn Pander typed notes, checked citations, and assisted in other ways that directly or indirectly appear in this text. During the final two years of preparation, Martha Strong faithfully interpreted difficult handwriting, typed and retyped the manuscript, and guarded the "original documents" from her absentminded professor. In 1991, at First Baptist Church in Dothan, Alabama, Shirley McInnis and Beverly Karwan typed the final draft. Ronnie and I owe a debt of gratitude to these competent and kind secretaries.

Several other critics, advisors, editors, and professors have significantly contributed to the betterment of this manuscript. Larry Garner, minister of adult education at First Baptist Church in Dothan, Alabama; Fred Grissom, professor of church history at Southeastern Baptist Theological Seminary in Wake Forest, North Carolina; Philip Wise, pastor of First Baptist Church in Dothan, Alabama; John Landers, academic editor of Broadman & Holman; and James Loder, professor of the philosophy of Christian education at Princeton Theological Seminary, improved the quality of this book by carefully reading portions of the manuscript, questioning some of the conclusions, and evoking changes in the earlier drafts. At the same time, of course, responsibility for shortcomings belongs solely with the authors.

Finally, we wish to express deepest appreciation to our families. Peggy Prevost (wife), William Prevost, Jane Reed (wife), David Reed, and Amanda Reed provided assistance, encouragement, and family time toward the completion of this goal.

James E. Reed
First Baptist Church
Dothan, Alabama

Introduction

By design, the title of this volume is *A History of Christian Education,* not *The History of Christian Education.* While the authors carefully selected events, personalities, and movements for consideration, an even larger body of historical information remains excluded. The writers acknowledge that their choices must leave room for the readers' perspectives about educational history and, for this reason, they welcome the opportunity for rebuttal. For example, in each of the first six parts of this history, the writers have included a chapter specifically about women in Christian education. Some readers may perceive this as segregation, but the authors' intention is to make certain the inclusion of women.

The perception of historical events will vary with the writer, who preserves a record of events; the teacher, who projects his or her commentary on human happenings; and the student, who ideally internalizes the content of the writer with the commentary of the teacher. This process creates critique whenever perceived as well as real differences abound. As students write and teach, this process continues from one academic generation to another.

A history of Christian education appropriately begins with the Hebrews, not the Sunday School movement. To be valid, such a construction of history must synthesize Christian education with biblical, theological, philosophical, cultural, political, and social perspectives.

Because of our common humanity, many problems in the Christian church today resemble the difficulties Christ's followers faced in the first century. In the early 1980s, T. B. Maston (1897–1988) correctly analyzed the twentieth-century predicament of many evangelical churches. Although addressing primarily the perceived ills of his own constituency, Maston's reflections also identify universal concerns about ministerial leadership. Serious students of Christian educational history will discover various examples of Maston's observations.

The authors of this volume have combined their own interpretations of Maston's outlook with commentary from such insightful leaders as Findley Edge, Bill Rogers, Larry Richards, Lyle Schaller, and Jim Loder. These observations are grouped under three headings, and examples of each abound throughout the history of the church.

Success Syndrome Versus Servant Life-style

Materialism has hindered the church from its inception. Congregations often perceive ministerial effectiveness as a numbers game. By equating bigness with greatness, this "nickels and noses" mentality has frequently diverted the attention of the church and her ministers from faithful service. The servant motivation in Christian ministry has given way to grasping for prestige and power. As Christians have drifted away from the simple life-style of the New Testament toward the pursuit of materialistic success, the church's inconsistency has scrambled its message of care.

Superficial Evangelism Versus Nurture

Christ plainly teaches His followers to rejoice when another person enters the kingdom. However, manipulative efforts credited to the Holy Spirit in the name of evangelism dishonor God and shame His church. Christian history includes positive growth movements like Methodism. In the first century Jesus commanded Christians to grow both in number and nurture. Christ's inclusive ideal for both has not changed and never will.

Throughout history new converts to the Christian faith have received too little and too shallow instructional training and organic nurture for Christian living. Homogeneous training, designed by several Christian groups to evangelize the lost, has created serious inconsistencies with the teachings of the New Testament concerning classes, colors, and cultures. These and other concerns in evangelism and nurture indicate that many Christians have directed their attention more toward an orthodoxy of belief than an orthodoxy of life.

Institutional Form Versus Individual Faith

As the simple faith of the New Testament became increasingly institutionalized, organizations within the medieval church often energized self-serving "ministries" designed to perpetuate ecclesiastical control. During the Middle Ages, the art of politics consumed much of the spiritual potential within Christianity. Unwilling to tolerate diversity in belief and function, church and state joined forces to demand religious conformity. In this process the form of religion solidified, but vital faith stagnated.

Although the Reformation brought change and great hope, in time a new set of institutions developed. The names of institutions often changed more than their true nature.

Findley Edge, Bill Rogers, and others have described a cyclic process of institutionalism. First, as a reaction to errors, abuses, and injustices, a movement is born in a time of great stress. Second, the new movement must organize its own institutions to survive. Third, society rejects the growing movement as a hated sect. Fourth, the movement passes from rejection to toleration to acceptance by society. Fourth, once the movement's dogma has become accepted, either an individual or the group itself demands conformity. Thus the cycle repeats itself.

In contrast, individual faith stresses a direct relationship between God and humans. Such radical faith has almost always met persecution. Jesus' crucifixion provides the supreme example of this truth. In reality, the church as the living body of Christ is much more than a structured institution.

During the past twenty centuries, representatives of the church have disagreed in their purposes for education. In many cases they have shared both ignorance and truth. Yet the Christian church has served as civilization's primary means of education despite great faults. During the Medieval period, the church carried nearly the entire educational load in Christendom.

The past masters of nurture and instruction did not finish the educational job, for this task is never completed. Human life moves in a congruent trilogy from past to present into the future. None of these three stands alone or casts a shadow over another. Each inseparably defines and refines the others.

Richard E. Gross has identified some essentials of educational history. Although not inclusive, his list includes the considerations of theorists and practitioners throughout history. Students of Christian education should recognize the contrasting emphases of master teachers of the past. The history of education reveals the following contrasting movements, among others:

- Education for an elite clientele versus education for all;
- Education for private purposes versus education for public purposes;
- Education for the individual versus education for the society or state;
- Education for religious aims versus education for secular purposes;
- Education for intellectual development versus education for utility;
- Education for liberal ends versus education for vocational goals;
- Education for knowledge as an end in itself versus education as a means;
- Education for what to think versus education for how to think;
- Education for discipline, control, and conformity versus education for freedom;
- Education for adult purposes versus education for children's needs;
- Education for training the mind versus education for applying the mind;
- Education for former or other societies versus education for a given people, currently indigenous.[1]

By studying the dilemmas of Christian education in history and the methods devised to solve these problems, today's minister can more adequately serve the church's current needs and prepare for the challenges of tomorrow. In this process the analytic student will often discover that newfangled solutions are not really new.

Note

1. Richard E. Gross, ed., *Heritage of American Education* (Boston: Allyn and Bacon, 1962), 13-14.

PART 1

Education in Ancient Societies

1

Education
in Greece

Every ancient society must have had, by some definition, a system of education. None of these, however, has had such an impact on Christian education as that of the Greeks. Although Christianity found much of its content in its Jewish origins, the Greeks contributed much to Christian educational philosophy, curriculum structure, and methodology.

Greek civilization began during the Iron Age. In their beginnings the Greeks existed as a loose-knit group of independent city-states. These city-states developed differing and varied approaches to life and, so, to education. Two of the best examples of this variety in education are the city-states of Sparta and Athens.

Sparta

Sparta was located in the south central area of the Peloponnesus, a peninsula joined to the southern end of Greece by the Isthmus of Corinth. The city emerged during the eighth century B.C. as Lacedaemon but soon became known as Sparta.[1]

The citizens of Sparta shared their society with two other classes: the Perioeci, free, dependent subjects of Sparta who lived in the surrounding villages; and the Helots, slaves owned by the state. Most of the Helots were Messenians from the valley of Pamissus, a short distance to the west of Sparta. Sparta first conquered Messenia by war in about 753 B.C.; the Messenians revolted about sixty years later, but the Spartans prevailed.

Because of constant fear of insurrection, citizens of Sparta sought to secure their military and civic supremacy over the other two classes, especially the Helots. The Spartan system of education developed from their struggle to maintain supremacy.

The Spartans shared much with other Greeks, including literature, religion, and language, but Spartan education was primarily physical, military, and moral. Obligation to the Spartan system of education was taken so seriously that it excluded from citizenship anyone who did not accept the approved discipline.[2]

Plutarch attributed much of the structure and stridency of Spartan education to Lycurgus, a legendary ruler of ancient Sparta:

> [Lycurgus] trained the citizens to have neither the desire nor the capacity to live by themselves; but like bees to make themselves always one with the community, clustering together about their leader, forgetting themselves in their enthusiasm and ambition and devotion to their country.[3]

Education began early in the life of a Spartan child. Only healthy children were trained for citizenship; others were exposed to die, though some were adopted by the subject classes.

If a child was allowed to live, the mother had charge of her boy until the age seven or of her girl a few years longer. At age seven, a Spartan boy was transferred to a public barrack, where he received instruction in physical activity and the Spartan virtues. Each barrack was controlled by a *paidonomos,* a leader or ruler of boys.

Provisions at the schools were scant: the bed was hard; food was meager (to accustom the boy to endure hunger in war); clothing was skimpy; blankets and sandals were nonexistent. Students were encouraged to steal in order to learn the cunning necessary in war. Such cunning was necessary because boys caught stealing were flogged.[4]

After some ten years of barrack training an eighteen-year-old Spartan received two years of military training. The years between the ages of twenty and thirty were spent in military duty on some frontier post. After age thirty a Spartan man was compelled to marry and produce more children (preferably male children) for Sparta.

Intellectual stimulation was relatively unimportant to the Spartans. They were concerned with functional literacy. Spartan reading was usually restricted to Homer or Pindar. The young Spartan memorized the laws of Lycurgus and a little of Homer and listened to the war stories of older men. Spartans prized short, pithy sayings and tried to speak succinctly and precisely. They gave their name to *laconic* wit.

The Spartan system demanded that the individual unconditionally subjugate himself to the will of the community—education by the

Spartan system was characterized by total subservience of the individual to the group, education by force, and schooling for the sake of technique only. The curriculum of physical and military training underscored the Spartan aims of strength, endurance, patriotism, obedience, and military efficiency.

Athens

Athens was a Greek city-state that arose, with Sparta, above the others. Although Athens was only about a day's journey from Sparta, the two cities were separated by differing views of the nature of persons.

From 1000 to 600 B.C. Athens was the principal city of Attica, just across the Isthmus of Corinth from the Peloponnisos. Until 500 B.C., the population subsisted primarily on agriculture. The poor soil and low productivity, along with reforms instituted by the Athenian magistrate, Solon, influenced the development of commerce and industry.

By 500 B.C., Athens had an estimated population of 200,000, including 80,000 slaves, 20,000 *metics* (foreign traders and manufacturers), and 100,000 citizens. At this time, some social and economic equality existed because of the system of democracy developed under Cleisthenes. This system did away with most political and class distinction among Athenian males, though some disparity existed between the rich and the poor.

Athenians codified their laws under the leadership of Solon in about 594 B.C. The laws of Solon required the appointment of a supervisor of schools and regulated the size of classes, hours, and admission standards of schools. The law required that parents see to it that their sons could read, write, and swim. The state paid to private schools the tuition of boys whose fathers had died in battle defending Athens.

Athenian children remained at home and received no formal education until age six. At this time, boys from well-to-do families entered school; other boys entered school one or two years later.

Basically four types of schools existed: elementary schools for boys aged six to thirteen or fourteen; secondary schools for boys aged thirteen to eighteen; schools for higher education; and military schools for boys aged eighteen to twenty. Athenian higher education was limited not by age, as were the others, but by ability and interest.

Schoolboys were given over to the care of a *paidagogos*, or pedagogue. The pedagogue functioned as a chaperone, butler, tutor, and bodyguard. He was in many cases an active slave, unable to do hard labor. He escorted the boy to and from school and often sat with him in the classroom. He was also a moral advisor.

Little indicates that the Athenian government owned or supported schools. All early Athenian education was probably private. These private schools were usually run by liberated slaves whom the Athenians held in low esteem. Since nearly everyone was able to finance at least a few years of elementary school for their sons, tuitions must have been modest.

Athenians had three types of elementary schools. Each boy was trained in a particular subject area, and the instruction in each had a specific title. The physical training school or *palaestra* was an open air school in which boys were taught by the *paidotribes*. Instruction was given in wrestling, boxing, running, jumping, and other sports. In the music schools, called the *didascaleua,* the *kitharistes* taught the boys vocal and instrumental music. A letters school was sometimes also called the *didascaleum,* and the instructors were called *grammatistes*. An Athenian boy normally attended these three schools each day, though at varying times of the day.[5]

Literacy was important to the Athenians. Learning to read was difficult because of the form of early Greek writing. The writing had no small letters or punctuation, and letters and words were strung together: ITLOOKEDLIKETHISANDSURELYMADEFORVERYDIF-FICULTREADING. No picture books aided the new reader. Pupils learned to write by first copying individual letters, then combining the letters into syllables, and, finally, into words. Each boy later developed reading and writing skills by studying the classical poetry of Homer and Hesiod. This reading was meant to develop high ideals, thoughts, and virtue.

Musical training developed a sense of rhythm and melody, preparing the boy to participate in Athenian civic and religious feasts and festivals. Physical education developed grace, stamina, and health habits. Winning was of little importance in athletic endeavors at this stage; exercise and training were the prime considerations.

Secondary schools were basically private. Poorer parents often apprenticed their sons to a trade at age thirteen. Those who could afford tuition sent their sons to more advanced schools. Most schools were temporary because teachers wandered from city to city. After a teacher had recruited enough students, he rented a lecture hall and charged admission. If the clientele fell off, he moved to another city.

The state provided facilities for the physical training of boys ages thirteen to eighteen. These gymnasiums were usually located just outside the city and were well equipped with steam rooms, rubdown parlors, and arenas for competition. Athletic competition was much more intense and severe than in the elementary schools.

Higher education centered in the *ephebia,* or ephebic school. Ephebic training consisted of two or three years of public military training. During this period, the cadets, or ephebi, were probationary citizens. The first year of ephebic training was spent learning the basics of military life. The second year was spent in civil service such as rural police. At the end of ephebic training the young men vowed allegiance to the state, pledging bravery and declaring loyalty to the gods and civil magistrates. A tour of regular military duty in the service of Athens followed.

In the fifth century B.C., the **Sophists** began to influence the Athenian cultural and educational scene. The Athenian aristocracy patronized these foreign teachers because of their knowledge and skill in argument. Sophists were often looked down on because their professionalism frequently led them to grossly exaggerated claims, yet they helped accelerate social, cultural, and intellectual growth. They systematized Greek and other languages, making deeper language study possible. For example, two Sophists, Protagoras and Hippias of Elis, led in the scientific study of grammar.

The Sophists were concerned with more than grammar. They taught a broad range of subjects including arithmetic, geometry, astronomy, natural history, ethics, mythology, political science, the arts, military science, and rhetoric. Their liberal education sought to meet the needs of freemen.

Normally, the Sophists taught only a few students at a time, holding sessions in an area convenient—at the marketplace, by the roadside, in an inn. Their teaching methods were surprisingly methodical. Isocrates, a Sophist known as the foremost teacher of oratory and rhetoric, is an example. His teaching method had three basic parts: instruction in ideas (thought elements, speaking style, and theories and composition of speech); presentation and analysis of exemplary speeches; and weaving together what was learned in the first two parts to produce an appropriate speech.[6]

Some include **Socrates** (ca. 470-399 B.C.) among the Sophists, though he was a native Athenian and refused to accept fees. Little is known of his life outside the writings of Xenophon and Plato. Socrates

developed a teaching method that remains in use today. Some regard
him as the most important figure in ancient education.

Born in Athens at the end of the Persian Wars, Socrates took up the
craft of his father, a sculptor. Socrates was probably educated in the
manner customary for young Athenians of the time. Possibly he studied under the Anaxagoras and Archelaus.[7]

Aristotle attributed to Socrates two major contributions to human
knowledge: universal definition and dialectical argument. *Universal
definition* is the definition of values that would be true under all
conditions. *Dialectic argument* refers to the Socratic method comprised of questions and answers. Socrates' emphasis on universal
definition and classification encouraged the further study of grammar.
The Socratic method gave impetus to the Greek analysis of thought
processes known as logic.

Socrates believed that the first task of a teacher was to awaken the
student through self-examination and self-criticism. This in itself set
Socrates apart from the Sophists, teachers of eloquence and rhetoric,
who often claimed to know all. His aim in education was to expose
error and, in so doing, discover truth.[8]

Another Athenian who had particular influence on education was
Plato (ca. 428-348 B.C.). Born to a prominent Athenian family, Plato
became a student of Socrates. The apparently false charges that led to
Socrates's death may have turned Plato against the civic career for
which he, being of distinguished background, would have been groomed.

Plato

Lived: 429-348 B.C. in Athens, Greece

Writings that dealt with education: *Republic*; dialogues

Views related to education:
- the tripartite nature of the state is similar to that of persons
  (rational, emotional, and desiring, and the purpose of education is to equip persons to function as citizens in one of three
  classes (philosophers, warriors, laborers) that are manifes-
  tations of this nature
- education was integral to developing the ideal state as outlined
  in *Republic*
- the goal of education was to bring the potential of the person
  to be manifested in outward life, morally and socially

Plato's career included both teaching and writing. He established the Academy in Athens in 387 B.C. and numbered Aristotle among his students.

Plato's philosophy of education is found in three of his dialogues: *Protagoras, Republic,* and *Laws.* For Plato, education should unify the individual with society. He emphasized the need for interaction between body and mind as the basis for education. The four virtues (wisdom, temperance, courage, and justice) were the points of union between the individual and society.

According to Plato, the soul possesses three kinds of abilities: reason, spirit, and appetite. Reason enables humans to discern truth. Spirit translates wisdom into action. Appetite relates to bodily functions. His method of education was designed to instruct humans by leading their souls toward the four virtues.[9]

Plato held that the beginning is the most important part of education. In childhood the character is being formed and impressions are most easily made. In *Laws,* Plato argues that children should be educated through play that imitates skills necessary in the adult world.[10]

Plato recommended various levels of education. The first level (from birth to the time at which a child is capable of mental training) was a time of informal instruction in proper social and health practices. The second (from six to eighteen years) included formal instruction in what comprised the "good life" and how one might develop sound character. The third level (from eighteen to twenty) was a time of intensive physical and military training. The fourth level (from twenty to thirty) was a period of advanced scientific study. The fifth level (from thirty to thirty-five) was devoted to study of the dialectical method. At the fifth level (from thirty-five to fifty) those successful in dialectical education assumed low posts in government.[11]

At each level, Plato considered the potential contribution of the individual to society. One who was to govern was required to train in all areas because his decisions would affect all. Artisans, on the other hand, ceased training after the first level, because at that point they already possessed the modicum of culture that most concerned them.

Aristotle (384-322 B.C.) was the last outstanding Athenian educator. For Aristotle, society is a natural institution, and the state is the highest achievement of nature and humans. He viewed slavery as a natural institution, since he believed nature makes one person superior to another. Aristotle agreed with Plato that each person should find a place in society according to those gifts endowed by nature. Aristotle would exclude slaves, artists, and merchants from citizenship because their work would deprive them of leisure for self-improvement. He believed that the goal of the individual and that of society should be the same.

Education, according to Aristotle, involved a process of self-realization for a person as a rational being. He discerned three developmental periods: one of primarily physical growth, then a period of the emergence of the irrational, and, finally, a period dominated by reason.

In *Politics* Aristotle expressed concern for prenatal education. He believed a mother's physical and mental condition affected her unborn infant. He believed that only well-informed children should be allowed to live. Until the age of seven children should be educated at home, exercising and listening to traditional poetry.[12]

The first period of formal education lasted from age seven until puberty. During these years the child would be trained in reading, writing, gymnastics, music, and drawing. What was learned was to be put immediately into daily practice, because it was for the enhancement of life, and not for vocation.[13]

The second period of education was to last from puberty to age twenty-one. But, Aristotle did not describe this period upon Aristotle's own school, the Lyceum, was devoted to the intellectual growth of young adults of the third period (eighteen to twenty).

Aristotle was a major figure in many areas of human thought and knowledge. His personality remained dominant, and many of his teachings became established educational methods and approaches during the Hellenistic era. His eclectic and comprehensive approach to learning led to the growth of the seven liberal arts that have influenced education even to the present.[14]

The Athenians, like the Spartans, were concerned with the survival of the state. Being less isolated than Spartans, the Athenians had more exposure to other cultures and ways of thought. Perhaps this exposure led Athenians to a different view of what would strengthen the state and help it survive. A strong state required citizens strong in every area of life: the intellectual, aesthetic, political, and physical. Athenian educational methods sought to form these citizens.

The Hellenistic Empire

Toward the end of the fourth century B.C., Alexander the Great forged a multinational empire. He ushered in a new age of amalgamation dominated by Greek culture. The result was Hellenistic culture. Much of what was expressed as Greek reflected Aristotle's influence in the life of Alexander.

These cultural developments are seen in Hellenistic education. Municipally controlled elementary school systems arose during the third and second centuries. These were often endowed by private individuals. For instance, a certain Eudemus gave Leletus such an endowment in 210 B.C. These schools were usually located in cities and provided free education. Freedmen living in or near these cities were normally expected to send their children, sometimes both boys and girls, to the elementary school there.[15]

Hellenistic education followed the Athenian pattern of five stages: home education (birth to seven years); elementary school (seven years to fourteen); grammar school (fourteen years to eighteen); ephebic service (eighteen years to twenty); and higher education (twenty years to as long as they could afford). Reading and writing were taught through oral recitations and drills and the copying of passages and maxims from the classical authors and poets. Discipline was severe and learning was slow.[16]

The Education of Children, an essay possibly written by Plutarch, reveals much of the Hellenistic ideal of education. The whole of the environment—both at home and school—should teach morality by precept and example. *The Education of Children* is a significant departure from ancient Greek tradition, for it stresses, not the political view of the common good, but the personal worth of intrinsic moral values and education.[17]

Notes

1. James Bowen, *The Ancient World: Orient and Mediterranean (200 B.C.-A.D. 1054),* vol. 1 in *A History of Western Education* (New York: St. Martin's Press, 1972), 50.

2. James Mulhern, *A History of Education: A Social Interpretation,* 2d ed. (New York: Ronald Press, 1959), 134.

3. Plutarch, *Lycurgus* 25.3.3; *Plutarch: Selected Lives and Essays,* trans. Louise R. Loomis (Roslyn, N.Y.: Walter J. Black, 1951).

4. Elmer H. Wilds and Kenneth V. Lottich, *The Foundations of Modern Education,* 4th ed. (New York: Holt, Rinehart and Winston, 1970), 95.

5. R. Freeman Butts, *The Education of the West: A Formative Chapter in the History of Civilization* (New York: McGraw-Hill, 1973), 88.

6. Adolph E. Meyer, *An Educational History of the Western World,* 2d ed. (New York: McGraw-Hill, 1972), 22-23.

7. Jean Brun, *Socrates,* trans. Louise R. Loomis (New York: Walker and Co., 1962), 6.

8. Butts, 92.

9. Robert Ulich, *History of Educational Thought*, rev. ed. (New York: American Book Co., 1968), 5-9.

10. Plato, *The Dialogues of Plato*, vol. 7 in *Great Books*, trans. Benjamin Jowett (Chicago: William Benton, 1952), 1.643.

11. E. H. Gwynne-Thomas, *A Concise History of Education to 1900 A.D.* (Lanham, Md.: University Press of America, 1981), 11-12.

12. *Aristotle, vol. II, Politics*, vol. 9 in *Great Books*, trans. Benjamin Jowett (Chicago: William Benton, 1952), 7.16.

13. Ibid., 7.17.

14. Bowen, 128-29.

15. Christopher J. Lucas, *Our Western Educational Heritage* (New York: The Macmillan Co., 1972), 97.

16. Bowen, 152.

17. Ibid., 162-65.

2

Education
in Rome

The impact of Rome on Christian education can hardly be overstated. In the Roman Empire, Christians first developed their views, tools, methods of education, and curriculum.

The history of Rome is often divided into periods based on political or military events, but for our purposes it is better to follow the lead of James Mulhern, who distinguishes four periods in the history of Roman education. The first of these was the Native Roman Period, which itself embraced two segments: the first ended about 600 B.C., when Rome had an alphabet of obscure origin; and the second ended in 250 B.C., when Livius Andronicus translated Homer's *Odyssey* into Latin. The second period was the Transition Period, during which the educational ideals and practices of the Greeks were introduced to Rome. This period ended about 55 B.C., when Cicero wrote *De Oratore*, approving the new modes of education. The Hellenized Roman Period saw education take on a distinctly Greek form with a Roman spirit. Education in this period expanded greatly but ended about A.D. 200. The decline of the Roman Empire brought Roman education into the fourth period, a Period of Decline. The climax of this period is found in Justinian's dissolution of the university in Athens in 529 B.C.[1]

The Native Roman Period

Early Rome was agricultural, and its approach to life was somewhat like that of the Spartans. Romans were concerned with survival of their way of life in the face of what they perceived as a hostile environment. This environment included the Etruscans, who lived in Italy. While Romans eyed Etruscans with particular suspicion,

Etruscans influenced the Romans more than the Romans were willing to admit.

The purpose of education in early Rome was to mold young people to the community ideals of *virtus* and *pietas*. *Virtus* was that quality evidenced by unquestioned loyalty and strength of character (and for young men consciousness of virility). *Pietas* was awareness of and reverence for those unseen but powerful forces that gave rise to sacred mores and demanded scrupulous observance and obedience. *Pietas* was the religious and cultic aspect of life. Roman education sought to develop persons who would be responsible and loyal to both the seen (civil) and unseen (spiritual) forces that affected their lives.

The family was the primary agent of education for the early Romans. The mother cared for the child and equipped the child with the knowledge essential to a Roman citizen. The father was head of the household. His authority was complete although his role in his son's education was more subjective than that of the mother. The father was to discipline his son. He was an example to his son of the skills and duties required of a Roman man. (Mothers were role models for their daughters, but this will be covered in a later chapter.)

The religious and moral training of a Roman boy normally involved attending, with his father, local rituals and ceremonial functions. There he would hear great orators, observe priests and other religious dignitaries perform Roman cultic activities, and learn from these as well as his father's communion with them.

Vocational education began about age seven. The economy of early Rome was primarily agrarian. Most boys learned farming skills as apprentices to their fathers. Little is known about the training of artisans in early Rome, but evidence suggest the existence of guilds. These guilds trained the young in particular crafts—probably by a system of apprenticeships. This same method taught boys the work of government.[2]

At age sixteen a boy passed through the ritual symbolizing his entrance into manhood. His *toga praetexta*, boyish clothing, was exchanged for the clothing of a full-grown man, the *toga virilis*. At this point a kinsman or friend of the family became responsible for educating him. Patricians, the privileged class, would see that their sons, now young men, studied reading, writing, history, and weaponry and learned gymnastics. By the third century, young men customarily spent three years in informal preparation for military service.

The publication of *Laws of the Twelve Tables* (ca. 450 B.C.) marked a turning point in early Rome and its system of education. These laws outlined the Roman legal system. Before the circulation of the *Twelve Tables*, lower-class plebeians had known less about the conduct of lawsuits than the upper-class patricians; as Roman literary education developed, however, both patrician and plebeian boys memorized and studied the *Twelve Tables*. This strengthened awareness of personal rights among the plebeians. A class struggle resulted in the restructuring of Roman rule in 287 B.C.[3]

The earliest period of Roman educational history evidences little formal schooling. The only institutions approximating schools were the *tabernae*, which existed by 305 B.C. These were described by Livy as places where slaves or freemen taught basic grammar.[4]

The Transition Period

Hellenistic culture was firmly established by 300 B.C., and Greek scholars were founding and teaching schools at hundreds of population centers in the Mediterranean world. Rome soon came under the Hellenistic spell. Rome and Greece had considerable commerce for some time. Nevertheless, Rome resisted Greek influence until its conquest of a Greek city in Italy, Tarentum, in 270 B.C.

The victors brought the vanquished back to Rome as slaves. Many of these were later freed and subsequently began translating Greek classics into Latin. One of the first of these was the translation of Homer's *Odyssey* by Livius Andronicus, who had been taken captive in Tarentum. Roman interest in the *Odyssey* was predictable since it deals with the Trojan War and its aftermath. Aeneas was a legendary hero, a Trojan who left Troy after its fall and whose travels were later recounted by the Roman poet, Publius Vergil (70-19 B.C.), in his *Aeneid*.

Other translations followed, spurring growth in the study and appreciation of literature. Roman education began to include the study of Greek drama and literature as well as the burgeoning Roman literature.

This new Greek learning altered the structure of Roman education. Roman fathers began to turn more of the responsibility for educating their sons over to *litteratores*, individuals—usually Greek slaves—who were the Roman equivalents of the Greek *grammatistes*. Some wealthy Romans used *litteratores* just as the Greeks had employed the *paidagogos*. Poorer Romans sent their sons to private schools taught by *litteratores*.[5]

The Roman elementary school, or *ludus* (which means "play" or "game"), became the agent of both literary and moral education. These schools were for Roman boys seven to twelve years old. Methods were built on the Greek model, and discipline was severe.

Roman secondary education centered in grammar schools for young men ages twelve to sixteen. The educational ideals expressed by the Romans in these schools were similar to the Greek concept of liberal education. They included the study of Greek and Latin grammar, but the curriculum also included history, geography, mythology, and Greek and Roman literature.

Little honor was accorded teachers in either the *ludus* or grammar school in Rome. There were no academic requirements for the elementary teachers. On the other hand, a teacher of grammar, or *grammaticus*, was required to be skilled and knowledgeable in grammar, literature, and other fields. The Romans prized education but did not value educators, regardless of credentials.[6]

Some Romans, such as Marcus **Cato** (234-149 B.C.), also known as Cato the Censor, feared the corruption that Greek learning might bring. Cato brought Chilon, a Greek slave-poet, from Sardinia in 204 B.C. Cato made money by renting Chilon to other families, but he would not allow Chilon to teach his own son.[7] In 161 B.C. Cato, then a senator, sponsored legislation to expel all philosophers and rhetoricians from Rome. The Greeks remained, however, and even Cato began to study Greek in later life.[8]

Roman higher education also came under Greek influence. As the Roman government became more complex, Rome became more susceptible to the cajoling of Greek rhetoric. The Romans became the object of the subtlety of Greek rhetoricians and adopted those aspects of rhetoric congenial to Roman life-style.[9]

Thus, Roman higher education consisted primarily of the study of rhetoric. Students were generally ages sixteen to twenty and were trained in public address, politics, and public service. They were drilled in oratory, declamation, and debate and studied logic, ethics, literature, grammar, arithmetic, geometry, philosophy, and astronomy. Students studied these so that they would be equipped with a variety of knowledge for the sake of ease of discourse on any subject.[10]

Physical training continued during the Transition Period. Physical exercise was to improve health and service to the state. This is somewhat similar to the emphasis on physical training in Sparta and differs from the Athenian ideal of self-fulfillment. Roman scholars also included military training, gymnastics, and athletics. However, the *gym-*

nasium, the Roman physical training facility, was independent and not connected with formal schools.

Dominating the Transition Period in Roman education is the figure of Marcus Tullius **Cicero** (106-43 B.C.). Cicero, unlike Cato the Censor, was a product of Hellenistic culture. Cicero was born to an upper-class family near Arpinum, in the Volscian mountains southeast of Rome, at a time when Greek educational ideas and culture were widely accepted among the Romans. His father, a studious man himself, was concerned for the education of his son. Being acquainted with leading citizens of Rome, he was able to make available to Cicero the best the city had to offer.[11]

Cicero was a brilliant student. Like most Roman boys of his time, he memorized the *Twelve Tables* and the Latin translation of the *Odyssey* and studied Greek and Roman drama, literature, and rhetoric. After receiving his *toga virilis*, he studied law under Quintus Mucius Scaevola the Augur, one of Rome's foremost legal experts. Cicero later befriended a young relative of the Augur, Scaevola the Pontifex Maximus, head of the state religion. Cicero also developed an interest in Greek philosophy.

Cicero was a prolific writer. He dealt with education primarily in his treatises concerning rhetoric. Among the most notable of these was his *De Oratore* (On the Education of an Orator).

In *De Oratore*, Cicero did not deal with elementary schools, because he was Roman enough to agree in theory with Cato that the education of the child was the parent's duty. His emphasis in education began with the schools of grammar and rhetoric. The curriculum of the grammar school should include the study of philosophy, mathematics, music, literature, rhetoric, geometry, and astronomy (the seven liberal arts of the Middle Ages).[12] Cicero was concerned with the quality of Roman education and recommended that a teacher of rhetoric be required to have a higher education.[13]

Cicero's concern for the education of orators was related to his patriotism. As he saw it, orators would influence Roman law and government. For the good of the state, orators must be men whose intelligence, virtue, integrity, and loyalty to Rome were beyond question.[14] The education needed to produce an orator demanded literary instruction and personal development, unifying the good speaker and deep thinker—the rhetorician and philosopher. *De Oratore* treated history, philosophy, and law, supposing that the other disciplines had already been taught in the lower schools. Cicero believed that knowledge of law was necessary for cultural growth. He sought to distinguish between legal and literary studies. He believed that an orator should be well-versed in law by the very nature of his profession and that he should exercise wisdom in individual thought as well as in the choice of words, gestures, and rhythm in speaking.[15]

The development of ethical character, called *humanitas*, was Cicero's ideal in education. Leaders must be well-educated, honest, unselfish, and of sound mind and body: "Nature herself has stamped on us a character in excellence greatly surpassing the rest of animal creation . . . as nature herself has cast to us our parts in constancy, moderation, temperance, and modesty."[16]

The Hellenized Period

The educational traditions that evolved during the Transition Period became fixed in the Hellenized Period, when Rome built its greatest monuments and developed its distinctive art. Great writers such as Seneca, Ovid, Livy, Petronius, Apuleius, Juvenal, and Tacitus arose along with the philosophers Epictetus and Marcus Aurelius. Strangely enough, it was also a time of violence and moral decay.[17]

Education became more formalized, and the number of grammar and rhetorical schools grew. Interest in literature also increased because of increased literacy and the development of the codex, the prototype of the modern book (as opposed to the commonly used papyrus or parchment scroll).[18]

The Roman republic had not regulated education. A Roman governmental policy on education began to develop during the first century of the Roman Empire. School attendance was not compulsory, nor were schools free. Gradually cities began assuming responsibility for elementary education. Julius Caesar offered Roman citizenship to teachers of the liberal arts in order to encourage them to remain in the city of Rome. During the great famine of A.D. 6, Augustus expelled from Rome all foreigners except physicians and teachers. In A.D. 74, Vespasian exempted freed schoolmasters from local taxation. He also established salaries for Latin and Greek teachers of rhetoric to be paid from public coffers. The emperors Domitian and Trajan were known as patrons of higher education. Teachers were in greater demand and were much more respected than before. Little emphasis was placed on early childhood education, but the writers of this period had much to say about grammatical studies and higher education.[19]

Seneca (4 B.C.-A.D. 65) was a Roman Stoic who believed in natural law. He stressed the importance of individual freedom for education but criticized education that was not applicable to life:

> We dull our fine edge by such superfluous pursuits; these things make men clever, but not good. Wisdom is a plainer thing than that; nay, it is clearly better to use literature for the improvement of the mind, instead of wasting philosophy itself as we waste other efforts on superfluous things. Just as we suffer from excess in all things, so we suffer from excess in literature; thus we learn our lessons, not for life, but for the lecture-room.[20]

Quintilian (ca. A.D. 35-96) was, arguably, the most important figure in Roman education during the Hellenistic Period. He was born Marcus Fabius Quintilianus in Calagurris, Spain. His father was well educated but not of the aristocracy. Quintilian probably received his elementary education at home, but by A.D. 57 he was in Rome studying rhetoric. After completing his education he returned to Spain to practice law in the provincial courts. He later moved to Rome to practice law and eventually founded a rhetorical school.[21]

The emperor Vespasian established Quintilian as the first professor of Latin rhetoric in Rome, thus placing him at the head of his profession. Quintilian taught for twenty years and then retired from the bar as well as from education.

In retirement Quintilian wrote his most significant work, *De Institutio Oratoria* (On the Education of an Orator). Early in A.D. 95, Domitian, whose heirs he had been teaching, gave Quintilian an honorary award. However, Quintilian was executed in September of that same year, convicted of a religious charge. According to George Kennedy, Quintilian may have been leaning toward Christianity.[22]

Quintilian divided oratorical education into three stages: early education (to be attained at home until age seven), grammatical education, and rhetorical education. He emphasized the importance of a father's concern for education. He believed that reasoning was a natural faculty for every normal individual but acknowledged that there were varying levels of talent.

Quintilian's first concern for elementary education was for the nurse who would be in charge of the child's education during the first three years. The nurse should be eloquent, for the child would first imitate the sounds of the nurse. Quintilian recognized differences among developmental age groups but believed that the child should be taught to read as early as possible. Greek should be learned first with Latin soon to follow; then the two languages were to be studied jointly. Quintilian had sympathy for children and wanted education to be interesting:

> Above all things we must take care that the child, who is not yet old enough to love his studies, does not come to hate them and dread the bitterness which he once tasted even when the years of infancy are left behind. His studies must be made an amusement; he must be questioned and praised and taught to rejoice when he has done well . . . at times also he must be engaged in competition and should be allowed to believe himself successful more often than not, while he should be encouraged to do his best by such rewards as may appeal to his tender years.[23]

The alphabet was to be learned first by the shapes of the letters and then in order. He stressed the use of memory and repetition in learning to read and write.

After the nurse, the child was to be turned over to a pedagogue until beginning grammatical instruction. The pedagogue would teach for only a few years, following the pattern of the Greek *paidagogos* as the child's companion and counselors.

The teacher should ascertain the boy's character and ability, using praise as well as rebuke in teaching. Flogging was not to be employed as any educational method.

Quintilian commended the study of literature. He proposed to train the student to speak correctly and to interpret the poets. Literature was studied through reading aloud and analyzing vocabulary. Also necessary to the study of literature was the study of music (to learn of meter and rhythm), astronomy (because poets alluded to time through references to stars), and philosophy (because poetry is often based on the intricacies of philosophy).

Socialization of the student was important. Quintilian wanted schoolwork to mirror the realities of life outside the school. Education in rhetoric was to include memorization of passages from great speeches and the study of declamation and judicial themes. However, he urged that the subject of a student's theme should come from daily life; speeches should deal with topics of current public interest, and judicial cases tried in moot courts should be of the type actually tried in courts.[24]

Plutarch (ca. A.D. 46-120) was another writer of the Hellenized Period of Roman education. Like Quintilian, Plutarch was neither creative nor innovative. He was a moralist who stressed tradition, habit, reason, physical exercise, and environment as essential elements of education. His ideas came mostly from Plato, Aristotle, the Stoics, and the Epicureans. Thus, Plutarch's educational theory was based to a great extent on preserving those values discovered and tested by experience.[25]

The Period of Decline

During the Period of Decline (A.D. 200-259), Roman rhetoric became an end in itself. Imperial edicts killed freedom of speech. Moral training dissolved as moral qualities increasingly became topics for discussion rather than virtues to be incorporated into life. Indeed, many of the schoolmaster's life-styles were morally questionable.[26]

State control over schools continued. Emperors Theodosius I and Valentinian I prohibited the opening of a school without state permission. Roman higher education came to an end for all intents and purposes in A.D. 529, when Justinian closed the schools of philosophy and law in Athens and all schools of higher learning in Rome except the law schools.[27]

Notes

1. James Mulhern, *A History of Education: A Social Interpretation*, 2d ed. (New York: Ronald Press, 1959), 178.

2. Ibid., 191.

3. A. H. McDonald, *Republican Rome* (New York: Frederick A. Praeger, 1966), 46-47.

4. Livy, *From the Founding of the City*, vol. 2 in *Livy*, trans. B. O. Foster (London: William Heinemann, 1922), 3.44.6.

5. James Bowen, *A History of Western Education*, The Ancient World: Orient and Mediterranean (200 B.C.-A.D. 1054), vol. 1 (New York: St. Martin's Press, 1972), 175.

6. Edward J. Power, *Main Currents in the History of Education*, 2d ed. (New York: McGraw-Hill Book Co., 1970), 159.

7. Harry G. Good and James D. Teller, *A History of Western Education*, 3d ed. (London: The Macmillan Co./Collier-Macmillan Limited, 1969), 46.

8. S. E. Frost, Jr., and Kenneth P. Bailey, *Historical and Philosophical Foundations of Western Education*, 2d ed. (Columbus, Ohio: Charles E. Merrill Publishing Co., 1973), 87.

9. George Kennedy, *The Art of Rhetoric in the Roman World: 300 B.C.-A.D. 300* (Princeton, N.J.: Princeton University Press, 1972), 4.

10. Adolph E. Meyer, *An Educational History of the Western World*, 2d ed. (New York: McGraw-Hill Book Co., 1972), 44-45.

11. H. J. Haskell, *This Was Cicero* (Greenwich, Conn.: Fawcett Publications, 1942), 32-38.

12. Aubrey Gwynn, *Roman Education from Cicero to Quintilian* (1926; reprint, New York: Russell and Russell Publishers, 1964), 83-84.

13. Ibid., 82.

14. Christopher J. Lucas, *Our Western Educational Heritage* (New York: Macmillan, 1972), 127.

15. Power, *Main Currents*, 176-78.

16. Cicero, *The Offices*, from *Three Books of Offices*, or *Moral Duties*, trans. Cyrus R. Edmonds (New York: Harper and Brothers, 1855), 1.28.

17. Lucas, 122.

18. Bowen, 191-93.

19. Ibid., 197-99.

20. Seneca, *Letters to Lucillius*, vol. 3 in *Ad Lucilium Epistulae Morales*, trans. Richard M. Gummare (London: William Meinemann, 1925), 106.12.

21. George Kennedy, *Quintilian* (New York: Twayne Publishers, Inc., 1969), 18-19.

22. Kennedy, *The Art of Rhetoric in the Roman World*, 493-94.

23. Quintilian, *De Institutione Oratoria*, vol. 1 in *The Institutio Oratoria of Quintilian*, trans. H. E. Butler (Cambridge, Mass.: Harvard University Press, 1953), 1.1.20.

24. Luella Cole, *A History of Education: From Socrates to Montessori* (New York: Holt, Rinehart and Winston), 54.

25. Robert Ulich, *History of Educational Thought*, rev. ed. (New York: American Book Co., 1968), 44-49.

26. Mulhern, 208.

27. Power, 167.

3

Hebrew and
Jewish Education

Understanding the history of Christian education, especially its origins, requires an examination of Jewish education because Christian education is, in many ways, an extension of Jewish education.

The history of the Jews is a record of their relationship with God as expressed in covenant. Their educational system arose as an instrument to pass on that relationship to subsequent generations. It also was an act of obedience to God's commands within the covenant. The Jews believed that, as God had chosen them, God was concerned with the means by which they should educate and be educated.

Many historical events shaped the covenant people. The Babylonian exile modified and shifted expressions of the covenant relationship between God and His people. The covenant people were generally called "Hebrews" before the exile, but they were known as "Jews" after the exile. Thus, our discussion will be divided into two parts: Hebrew Education and Jewish Education.

Hebrew Education

In Genesis, God is quoted in reference to His covenant with Abraham: "For I have chosen him, so that he will direct his children and his household after him to keep the way of the Lord by doing what is right and just, so that the Lord will bring about for Abraham what he has promised him" (Gen. 18:19).

Abraham and the other Hebrew patriarchs were nomadic. Their life-style precluded the founding of permanent schools. Education was natural and informal, including all aspects of life. The children were taught by example. They learned vocational responsibilities by watching and following the parents as they saw to their duties. Children learned about their particular cultic and covenant responsibilities to God as the parents built altars and led in rituals such as sacrifices and circumcision.

After the patriarchal era, the Hebrews received, in the Mosaic law, not only a system of laws by which to conduct their individual and corporate lives, but also a plan by which to teach the laws and their way of life. The family was the primary educational institution of the Hebrews. The *Shema*, which was foundational to all Hebrew/Jewish belief, is found in Deuteronomy and speaks not only to the nature of God but to the importance and place of education:

> Hear, O Israel: The Lord our God, the Lord is one. Love the Lord your God with all your heart and with all your soul and with all your strength. These commandments that I give you today are to be upon your hearts. Impress them on your children. Talk about them when you sit at home and when you walk along the road, when you lie down and when you get up. Tie them as symbols on your hands and bind them on your foreheads. Write them on the door frames of your houses and on your gates (Deut. 6:4-9).

The mother was to teach the children while performing her household duties. Mothers were to obey dietary restrictions as well as other restrictions that dealt with the household so that their children would be familiar with these laws. The mothers also related stories of the patriarchs and other national heroes and of the acts of God in Hebrew history.

Hebrew fathers considered their responsibility for teaching their children their most important task. Much attention was given to memorizing the Mosaic law and oral traditions of the people of God. Knowledge of these matters was considered to be the ability to repeat it unerringly. Although Hebrew education was almost totally "religious" education, the father was to teach his son a trade.[1]

Hebrew family education also placed demands upon the child. The call to obedience was reflected in the command, "Honor your father and your mother, so that you may live long in the land the Lord your God is giving you" (Ex. 20:12). Later the Proverbs urged, "My son, keep your father's commands / and do not forsake your mother's teaching" (6:20).

The home did not carry the sole responsibility for education. The priestly tribe of Levi was commanded to go before the people at the

Feast of Tabernacles "so they can listen and learn to fear the Lord your God and follow carefully all the words of this law" (Deut. 31:12).

The Levites were not conscripted for military service. They were given no land to farm, nor were they to have any other vocation than that of priest. They were to be supported by the tithes of the other Hebrew tribes. As priests they would be the nation's educators.

The educational role of the priests was expressed in two ways. First, they were to train the priests who were to follow in the ritual observances required by the law. Second, they were to train the people in the law, especially in the law concerning worship, sacrifices, festivals, and other religious duties. In these rituals and other religious observances the priests were to teach the people regarding beliefs and concepts about God.

The priests also had to teach the people how to live together. They gave advice and interpreted God's will for the people in practical terms, particularly concerning ethical and civil duties.

The priests remained the primary public educators of the nation until the exile. They were generally held in high regard by the people and were amply relied upon for instruction.[2]

After the Hebrews settled in Canaan, prophets began teaching the people. The prophets were not so much predictors of what was to come as "stern guardians of individual and national conduct, the living Hebrew conscience, the poets of statesmanship."[3]

The themes of prophetic teaching were many. Among these were God's justice, mercy, judgment, holiness, repentance, faith, and obedience. These themes were intended to be taught not only to the children but also to all the people, particularly the leaders.

The Old Testament mentions groups or "processions" of prophets known as "schools of prophets."[4] In these groups, prophets learned how to be prophets, practiced ecstasy, and may have preserved prophetic traditions. Some believe that participants "studied the Law and its interpretation, made copies of it, and became teachers and preachers who denounced national, family, and personal sins."[5] In fact, the purpose of these bands is unclear, although instruction may have taken place within them.[6] Little can be proven regarding these schools of prophets, but there was probably some form of training available for prophets.[7]

The Hebrew word *yada* is translated "know" and sheds light on Hebrew concepts of knowledge and education. *Yada* implies involvement with that which is being known, for one can know, in this sense, only by experiencing. This concept was reflected by the Jewish historian Josephus (ca. A.D. 37-100) in his treatise *Against Apion*:

> For our legislator, [Moses] . . . very carefully joined the two methods
> of instruction together; for he neither left these practical exercises to go
> on without verbal instruction, nor did he permit the hearing of the Law
> to proceed without the exercises for practice.[8]

The experiential and practical education called for by the Hebrew concept of knowledge was expressed in religious feasts and festivals. Sabbath observances (not just the Sabbath Day, but also the Sabbath and jubilee years) taught about the creation as well as responsibility and stewardship toward God. The Passover celebrated and taught the people regarding the exodus. Similarly, the Feast of Tabernacles recalled the Hebrew wilderness experience. The expiatory ritual of the Day of Atonement taught the people about God's continuing mercy, justice, and deliverance.

These celebrations taught the people—especially the children—to relive, or reexperience to some degree, these important events in their national history. These feasts and festivals included informal conversation involving the family: "As the child asked questions about the meaning of the ceremonies, the parents' answers were to be informative and instructive."[9]

Hebrew educational methods included memorization and repetition. Repetition was particularly important in teaching a child to read. As Scripture developed and the importance of maintaining the oral traditions waned, learning to read became more necessary. Isaiah implied that not everyone could read (29:11-12).

The Hebrew prophets also communicated their messages through prophetic acts or object lessons. Jeremiah frequently employed this methodology; examples are his burying the loin cloth (13:1-7), visiting the potter (18:1-10), smashing the clay jar (19:1-13), and wearing the yoke (28:10-14).

Hebrew education was concerned with teaching the child not only early in life but also as early in the day as possible. It was then that their minds would be fresh and most capable of learning. Children were to be taught a little at a time. The child first learned the letters of the alphabet. Even wisdom was taught in small doses in the form of proverbs. Moral teaching was designed to teach truth when the learner was resistant to overt instruction. Nathan's parable in 2 Samuel 12:1-13 convicted David of his sin with Bathsheba.[10]

Jewish Education

The Babylonian exile followed the collapse of the southern Hebrew kingdom of Judah (ca. 586 B.C.). During this period most Jews remained in Judah, though some emigrated to Egypt and others were taken to Babylon. This was an era of rapid change. Judaism (as it evolved from the Hebrew religion) took shape during these years. New liturgical forms were introduced, new traditions began, the synagogue developed, and education took on a different meaning and purpose.[11]

The Jews (as they were now known, most being from the tribe of Judah) at last rejected idolatry and placed new emphasis on religious education. They developed a system of schools led by exalted teachers. These new developments gave Judaism a strong organizational and institutional basis. During the exile, the Jews had no religious center; as a result, local Jewish communities developed their own places for meeting. The impetus for these meeting places appears to have been Jeremiah's urging the captives to pray for the city of their captivity (29:7).[12] As the captives gathered to pray, a natural extension was fellowship and study. This community meeting place became the synagogue.[13]

The primary purpose of the **synagogue** was instruction and study of the law. Even Sabbath services at the synagogue were specifically for instruction as well as for worship and devotion. In the synagogue services, the law was read consecutively and was interpreted. Further lessons included treatment of the prophetic writings by means of a similar method.[14]

The synagogue did not operate in competition with the Jewish temple. The temple was for worship; the synagogue for study. In the days of Jesus, the temple even had a room that was used as a synagogue.[15]

The Jews were concerned that their children receive instruction at the synagogues (after instruction at home until age six). Attendance was not compulsory until A.D. 64, when it was ordered by Joshua ben Gamala, the Jewish high priest during the last days of the temple. He required that Jewish parents send their boys to a synagogue school for religious education. Free instruction made elementary education available to all regardless of economic standing.[16]

The synagogue school was governed by rules known as *bet has-seper* (house of the book). It was not to be located in densely populated areas. School hours were regulated for the students' comfort. Class size was regulated as were faculty-student ratios. The students sat on the ground at the teacher's feet. Teaching was conducted by repetition and memorization. Boys learned to read in order to read the Torah in the synagogue. Instruction included basic arithmetic, and some students learned to write. The students were expected to master the *Shema*, the *Hallel* (a series of psalms), the creation story, and the Levitical law.[17] The law had precedence even over national history; this is evidenced by the choice of the Book of Leviticus as the first subject to be taught from the Bible.[18]

The Jewish boy began to study the Mishnah at age ten.[19] The Mishnah was a textbook for study of the oral law. It was concerned with agricultural laws, festivals and feasts, marriage and divorce, civil and criminal law, the temple, and laws of purity and impurity.

Skillful students were sent to rabbinical academies when they reached the age of fifteen to study the Talmud. The Talmud was a unit comprised of the Mishnah and the Gemara. It distinguished between written law and oral law, though both were seen as expressions of the same Divine law. The Gemara was a commentary on the Mishnah.[20]

Adult education was also a responsibility of the synagogue. The *Beth Hamidrash* (house of study) arose adjunct to the synagogue. It was a place where Jewish men could read, contemplate, and discuss the law.[21] The synagogue became so important to Jewish education that one was found in almost every city with ten Jewish males. These synagogues were important to the spread of Christianity in the Roman world of the first century. Repeatedly, Paul went into the synagogues to plant the seeds of Christian faith. One of the best examples of this is found in Acts 17: "Now the Bereans were of more noble character than the Thessalonians, for they received the message with great eagerness and examined the Scriptures every day to see if what Paul said was true" (v. 11). In the Berean synagogue, as in all synagogues, Paul found hearers who knew the Old Testament and could discuss messianic themes with intelligence. The synagogues provided fertile soil for the early church because of their emphasis upon the study of the Scriptures. Leadership in Jewish education, especially in the synagogues, was vested in **scribes and rabbis**.

The Babylonian exile separated the Jews from Jerusalem and their temple. The temple was the center of their sacral religion, and the priests were the mediators between them and Yahweh. The separation was traumatic for the exiles. In Babylon the synagogues developed as worship and study. Along with the place, a leadership developed—the scribes. Apparently the scribes arose out of the families of the priests and Levites and became, as their predecessors, the guardians of the law.

The importance of the scribes grew as the Jews, after the exile, became increasingly concerned with the written law. Scribes were copiers and interpreters of Jewish books. They were a class of teachers who helped fill the role held by the sages of the earlier era.[22] Scribes often devoted themselves fully to scholarly pursuits and frequently made legal judgments (based on their understanding of the Torah).[23]

Growing out of the scribal tradition were the rabbis of postexilic Judaism. The term *rabbi* comes from the Hebrew word for *great* and is normally used to denote a master or teacher. Rabbis were not usually salaried by the community.[24] Most Jews felt that religious teaching was to be done without charging a fee: "Here thou hast learned that everyone who makes profit from the words of the Torah removes his life from the world."[25] Rabbis were highly respected, often more so than parents.[26] Rabbinical influence grew and, as might be expected, supplanted that of the priests after the final destruction of the temple (A.D. 70).

Jewish education retained many of the components of preexilic, or Hebrew, education. All teaching still began in the home. It was a place not only of first instruction but of the daily living out of that which was learned. The national/religious feasts and festivals of the Jews continued to serve educational functions. More recent events in Jewish history were reflected in new celebrations. For example, the Feast of Purim commemorated the deliverance of the Jews as recorded in the Book of Esther.

Finally, after the exile, the Jews found themselves scattered more or less permanently. In this Diaspora they interacted with non-Jewish cultures. During biblical times, the most prominent of these was Hellenism. Especially in areas with both strong Hellenism and a large Jewish population, such as Alexandria, Egypt, the tendency was to adopt or adapt Greek educational practices.[27]

Notes

1. William Barclay, *Educational Ideals in the Ancient World* (Grand Rapids, Mich.: Baker Book House, 1974), 16-17.

2. C. B. Eavey, *History of Christian Education* (Chicago: Moody Press, 1964), 55-56.

3. Abram L. Sachar, *A History of the Jews*, 5th ed. rev. (New York: Alfred A. Knopf, 1965), 61.

4. Compare 1 Samuel 10:5; 19:20.

5. Clarence H. Benson, *A Popular History of Christian Education* (Chicago: Moody Press, 1943), 22.

6. Eavey, 62.

7. J. Kaster, "Education, OT," vol. 2 in *Interpreters Dictionary of the Bible*, ed. G. A. Buttrick (Nashville: Abingdon Press, 1962), 31.

8. Titus Flavius Josephus, "Against Apion," *Complete Works of Flavius Josephus*, trans. William Whitson (Grand Rapids, Mich.: Kregel Publications, 1960), 2:18.

9. Eavey, 53.

10. Kaster, 33-34.

11. Sachar, 78-81.

12. J. A. Sanders, "Dispersion," *Interpreters Dictionary of the Bible* (Nashville: Abingdon Press, 1962), 1:855.

13. Benson, 24-25.

14. Eavey, 64.

15. Azriel Eisenberg, *The Synagogue Through the Ages* (New York: Block Publishing Co., 1974), 41.

16. Nathan Drazin, *History of Jewish Education from 515 B.C.E. to 220 C.E.* (New York: Arno Press, 1979), 46.

17. Barclay, 39-43.

18. Eavey, 64.

19. Alfred Edersheim, *Sketches of Jewish Social Life in the Days of Christ* (Grand Rapids, Mich.: Wm. B. Eerdmans Publishing Co., 1953), 136.

20. R. J. Zwierblowsky and Geoffrey Wigoder, eds., "Talmud," *The Encyclopedia of the Jewish Religion* (London: Phoenix House, 1965), 373-74.

21. Isaac Levy, *The Synagogue: Its History and Function* (London: Vallentine, Mitchell, and Co., 1963), 19.

22. George Buchanan Gray, *Sacrifice in the Old Testament: Its Theory and Practice*, The Library of Biblical Studies, ed. Harry M. Orlinsky (New York: KTAV Publishing House, 1971), 307.

23. Martin Hengel, *Judaism and Hellenism: Studies in Their Encounter in Palestine during the Early Hellenistic Period*, trans. John Bowden, 2 vols. (Philadelphia: Fortress Press, 1974), 1:78-80.

24. Eisenberg, 137.

25. R. Travers Herford, ed. and trans., *The Ethics of the Talmud: Sayings of the Fathers* (New York: Schocken Books, 1962), 4:7.

26. Edersheim, 128.

27. D. F. Payne, "Education," *New Bible Dictionary*, ed. J. D. Douglas et al., 2d ed. (Wheaton, Ill.: Inter-Varsity Press, 1982), 300.

4

Women in Education: The Ancient World

Women played a minimal role in ancient education, whether as teachers or students. Cultures reveal their concepts of education not only in their formal and informal educational structures but also by excluding certain persons from aspects of the educational process.

Greece

Although the Greeks were among the most enlightened peoples of their time, they assigned to women a second-class humanity. Plato differed from most Greeks in defending the general equality of women, but even he admitted feminine inferiority.[1]

The Spartan system of education relegated women to birthing healthy babies (preferably male babies for the standing army). Young Spartans underwent vigorous physical training in running, wrestling, gymnastics, and throwing the discus and javelin. Patriotic fervor encouraged women to give up their young boys to the state.[2] Plutarch attributed expressions of the patriotic and militaristic spirit to Spartan women:

> Another [Spartan mother], as she handed her son his shield, exhorted him saying, "Either this or on this." Another, as her son was going forth to war, said, as she gave the shield into his hands, "This shield your father kept always safe for you; do you, therefore, keep it safe, or cease to live."[3]

Even so, women may have had a higher place in Sparta than in Athens. Because of Sparta's militarism and its ample supply of slaves, Spartan women may have been free from some characteristically femi-

nine duties and allowed to assume additional duties, including management of their husband's affairs. Spartan women had a stronger voice in
their own affairs than did their counterparts in Athens.[4] Since little
evidence exists of formal education in Sparta beyond quasi-military
and physical education, it may be assumed that women learned the
skills they needed from their mothers.

Athenian women were not citizens. They were restricted to domestic
duties and their lot was only slightly better than that of slaves. Barred
from classroom education, an Athenian girl was given informal instruction that prepared her for motherhood and a life of service to her
husband. Nevertheless, many women in Athens were literate and a few
had some higher education.[5]

Plato, outlining his utopian state in *Republic*, assented to the principle of equal social, political, and educational rights for women. Although this was rather revolutionary and visionary for his context,
Plato was far from being a feminist. He considered women to be in
some way inferior to men. Some have inferred that Plato would have
allowed women to advance in his republic as far as their capacities
allowed, but he would expect few exceptional women to advance very
far.[6]

Women were given more opportunities for formal education in the
Hellenistic Period than in earlier periods. Freemen often sent their
daughters to endowed elementary schools in the cities.[7]

Rome

In ancient Rome as in ancient Greece, women found little identity
apart from their fathers or husbands. Women were normally seen
almost as property. Cato spoke in opposition to the repeal of a law
which restricted women's dress, barred women from riding in carri-
ages within a mile of the city, and limited the amount of gold women
could carry. The historian Livy included the following quote from
Cato's speech in his *History of Rome:*

> Our ancestors permitted no woman to conduct even personal business
> without a guardian on her behalf; they wished them to be under the
> control of fathers, brothers, husbands; we (Heaven help us!) allow them
> now even to interfere in public affairs, yes, and to visit the Forum and
> our formal and informal sessions. What else are they doing now on the
> streets and at the corners except urging the bill of the tribunes and

voting for the repeal of the law? Give loose rein to their uncontrollable nature and to this untrained creature and expect that they will themselves set bounds to their licence; unless you act, this is the least of things enjoined upon women by custom or law and to which they submit a feeling of injustice. It is complete liberty, or, rather, if we wish to speak the truth, complete licence, they desire.

If they win this, what will they not attempt? Review all the laws with which your forefathers restrained their licence and made them subject to their husbands; even with all these bonds you can scarcely control them. What of this? If you suffer them to seize these bonds one by one and wrench themselves free and finally be placed on a parity with their husbands, do you think you will be able to endure them? The moment they begin to be your equals, they will be your superiors.[8]

A Roman woman was to aid her husband, run the household, teach her children Roman virtues, and teach her daughters those skills proper to the Roman wife and mother. These duties could be learned in an informal way from her mother, or perhaps from a female slave given duties of instruction. Nevertheless, there were schools for Roman girls during the late republic.[9] Also, during the Republican Period some women were allowed to conduct business and practice medicine and midwifery.[10] Such activity probably required a form of education resembling an apprenticeship.

Judaism

Superficially, Judaism reflects the Greek and the Roman view of women. Jewish Scripture taught that woman was created out of man as his aid (Gen. 2:18-22) and led man into his sinful estate (3:1-6). Women were the source of temptation and their public conduct was of particular concern both before and after the exile. Josephus notes that women were not allowed to testify in Jewish courts because of "the levity and boldness of their sex"[11]; he quotes Scripture, incorrectly, to prove the inferiority of women.[12] Although women were second-class citizens and their role was perceived primarily in domestic terms, Jewish women enjoyed a higher level of security and protection than other women in the ancient world.

This somewhat elevated position of women developed slowly. Although Jewish Law had always protected women, the Talmud developed this even more. There was a running battle between two schools of rabbinic thought, one more "feminist," the other more "anti-feminist."[13]

The rabbinic debate regarding the place of women in Jewish life included education. Women had always taught their children, particularly their daughters, in and through their domestic duties. Jewish laws were lessons in obedience and piety. In later Judaism, the mother often had a more formal role in the literary education of her children, and her domestic role was interpreted in terms of freeing her husband to study the law. Some Jewish women gave generous financial support to scholars and scholarly activities. They attained varying degrees of education and some were well-known as scholars.[14] Formal education for most Jewish women was, however, limited. The typical Jewish girl was taught by her mother regarding her womanly, wifely, and motherly duties under the law. From her mother she had access to basic schooling in reading and writing and perhaps to some training from her father or a local synagogue school. Further education was generally perceived as unnecessary and, perhaps, dangerous.

Notes

1. Plato, *Republic*, v. 455. *The Republic of Plato: A New Version Founded on Basic English*, trans. I. A. Richards (New York: W. W. Norton and Co., Inc., 1942), 95-96.

2. Plutarch, "Lycurgus," *Selected Lives and Essays*, trans. Louise R. Loomis (Roslyn, N.Y.: Walter J. Black, 1951), 13-17.

3. Plutarch, *Sayings of Spartan Women*, in *Moralia*, III.241F.16-17, *Plutarch's Moralia*, trans. Frank Cole Babbitt (London: William Heinemann, Ltd., 1931), 465.

4. Vern L. Bullough and Bonnie Bullough, *The Subordinate Sex: A History of Attitudes toward Women* (Urbana, Ill.: University of Illinois Press, 1973), 68.

5. Ibid., 66.

6. Ibid., 60-61.

7. Christopher Lucas, *Our Western Educational Heritage* (New York: The Macmillan Co., 1972), 97.

8. Livy, XXXIV.ii.12—iii.3, *Livy*, trans. Evan T. Sage, vol. 9 (Cambridge, Mass.: Harvard University Press, 1936), 417-19.

9. Charles Alexander Robinson, Jr., *Ancient History: From Prehistoric Times to the Death of Justinian*, ed. Alan L. Boegehold, 2d ed. (London: The Macmillan Co., 1967), 539.

10. Bullough and Bullough, 95.

11. Titus Flavius Josephus, *Antiquities of the Jews*, IV.viii.15, *Complete Works of Flavius Josephus*, trans. William Whitson (Grand Rapids, Mich.: Kregel Publications, 1960), 97.

12. Josephus, II.25, 632.

13. Salo W. Baron, *A Social and Religious History of the Jews*, 2d ed. rev. (New York: Columbia University Press, 1952), 2:235-41.

14. Ibid., 239-40.

Synopsis
of Part 1

In both ancient and more modern technological societies, survival is basic. The educational system that it develops best illustrates society's understanding of what is necessary to survive and the role of persons in helping the society survive. The ancient societies covered in the previous chapters serve as clear examples of this process at work.

Both Sparta and Athens seemed to view their people as natural resources, much as they did their soil or water. Both understood that there was a relationship between their image of the individual and the composition of their society. Their educational systems demonstrate a significant difference between the two regarding the nature of that relationship.

Sparta's system of education demonstrated an understanding of the person as a cog on the wheel. Each individual had a particular place of service, and each was trained narrowly to serve in just that position. Spartans were taught that their identity and relationship to each other were in and through the city-state. Thus, their schooling had little need for exercises in reflective thinking and advanced communication skills. Spartans taught obedience, loyalty, and the warrior spirit, which they believed necessary to Sparta's survival.

Athens, on the other hand, viewed the individual as a microcosm of society. Athenians recognized that, for their city-state to survive, youth needed to be equipped in relational, communication, and reflective skills, not only in military subjects. After all, being commercial and seafaring people with the nearby port of Piraeus, the Athenians found that understanding other cultures was imperative to their survival as a city-state. This understanding of relationships external to their city-state carried over to their perception of internal relationships. Athenians were more broadly educated than their Spartan neighbors because they were expected to function in relationship with each other much like their city-state did with other societies.

The Romans were like both the Spartans and the Athenians. As a republic, Rome required an approach to education similar to that of Athens for similar reasons. The Roman republic evolved into the Roman Empire, requiring elements of Spartan education (a strong military being necessary to expand and protect the boundaries of the empire) while maintaining elements of Athenian education (to provide for cultural integration, keep peace in the provinces with minimal need for military intervention, and provide a system by which to administer a large and diverse empire). To accomplish this the Roman curricula included rhetoric and engineering in addition to subjects taught by the Greeks.

Religious beliefs and gods of the Greeks and Romans were related to their civil existences and identities. However, the Jews saw virtually no distinction between their existence as a nation and their identity as the people of God. They perceived that their survival depended on their corporate relationship with God. Their system of education not only came from God but was structured to maintain this essence of their existence. At the risk of oversimplification, survival meant for the Hebrews (preexilic Israel) keeping the covenant and for the Jews (postexilic Israel) observing the law. While the lines of distinction between the two concepts may be fine (and their relationship is much more complex than can be dealt with here), curricula, methods, and institutions of education in preexilic and postexilic Israel give one a feeling for their differences.

PART 2

Ancient Christian Education

5

Jesus
the Teacher

Jesus of Nazareth is the central figure of the Christian religion. Christians regard Him as Lord, the God-Man, the Christ, and Redeemer. The celebrations of His birth, death, and resurrection mark the holiest days of the Christian calendar. However, Christians also regard Jesus as the master teacher. Certainly the effect of the method and content of Jesus' teachings have had a great impact on the Christian faith and education.

The New Testament Gospels witness to the teaching ministry of Jesus. Robert H. Stein has pointed out that, of all the titles used for Jesus in the Gospels, the one most frequently used was *Teacher*. This title was used forty-five times and the particular title *Rabbi* was used fourteen times.[1] Of course, the Gospels are our source of information regarding Jesus as a teacher. One must keep in mind, however, that each evangelist had his own particular purpose in mind and, therefore, expressed facets of Jesus' life and teachings differently from the other evangelists. Although specific examples of Jesus the Teacher can be cited, one must look at the Gospels as a whole to receive the true and complete picture.

The Education of Jesus

Some believe Jesus' expertise as a teacher was inherent in His divinity. If these skills were acquired, where did Jesus learn them? Although the general answer to this question is rather simple, specific answers may be open to conjecture. Jesus was born into a devout Jewish home. In light of this and the miraculous circumstances surrounding His birth, Joseph and Mary made available the best education that their circumstances would allow to the boy Jesus.

Young Jesus was exposed in His home to the rituals and feasts
required by the law. Luke 2:21-39 tells of Jesus' circumcision and
consecration as well as Mary's postpartum purification. Immediately
following, in the same chapter, Luke told of the twelve-year-old Jesus'
going with His parents to the Passover at Jerusalem. There the young
man began to take His place "in the temple courts, sitting among the
teachers, listening to them and asking them questions" (Luke 2:46).
Luke further commented on the people's wonder at Jesus' exceptional
abilities at such a tender age.

The young Jesus received the basic synagogue education. In the
synagogue school and at home He was taught to read and write. He
learned of Moses, the prophets, and the other great leaders of Israel.
He learned Hebrew poetry and proverbs. He was taught the history of
the Jewish people during what we know today as the intertestamental
period. Almost certainly, Joseph taught Jesus the family trade of
carpentry.

Some have surmised that Jesus had further educational opportunities. Some claim Jesus was taught and influenced by a community of
Essenes, a monastic Jewish sect of the intertestamental and New
Testament periods.[2] Although there were similarities between the
teachings and terminology of Jesus and those of the Essenes, there
were also significant differences. Others propose that Jesus was a pupil
of John the Baptist, about whom stronger evidence indicates some
connection with the Essenes.[3] Almost certainly, there was a personal
relationship between John and Jesus before their first recorded meeting. However, the Gospels provide little indication and no development of the teachings of John the Baptist (in contrast to the treatment
of the teachings of Jesus). Therefore, there is little evidence for such a
scenario.[4]

The Teaching Roles of Jesus

To understand Jesus the Teacher one must understand the role
models He had and how these models manifested themselves in His
life. Remember that Jesus was not born in a vacuum but was influenced by what He was taught. The methodology of those who taught
Him was influenced by the great teachers in Jewish history.

In His teaching ministry, Jesus often functioned as a **prophet,** or
nabhi. In this role as moral messenger, Jesus sometimes illustrated His
message with an object lesson as did Jeremiah. This was one interpre-

tation of Jesus' actions in the temple as recorded in Matthew 21:12-13, Mark 11:15-18, and Luke 19:45-47. Although incensed over the lack of reverence held by the business community for the temple, Jesus may also have been pointing to these people as an illustration of what He saw the Jews doing; rather than bringing "all nations" to worship God, the Jews' exclusiveness and prejudice had caused them to become thieves, stealing God from "all nations." According to the verse preceding Matthew's account of this incident, Jesus was referred to as a prophet by the crowd (see Matt. 21:11). The lament of Jesus on the eve of His crucifixion suggests that Jesus saw Himself in the role of prophet (23:37). He specifically compared Himself to the prophet Jonah in Luke 11:30-31.

Jesus also compared Himself to wise King Solomon and, by implication, to the other wise men or **sages** in the same passage. This aspect of Jesus' teaching ministry is often overlooked, despite numerous instances of His use of Jewish wisdom literature from the Old Testament to the Apocrypha for both form and content.[5]

Notice the following pairs of similar passages:

> Look at the birds of the air; they do not sow or reap or store away in barns, and yet your heavenly Father feeds them. Are you not much more valuable than they? (Matt. 6:26).
> Who provides food for the raven / when its young cry out to God and wander about for lack of food? (Job 38:41).
> He said to them, "You are the ones who justify yourselves in the eyes of men, but God knows your hearts. What is highly valued among men is detestable in God's sight" (Luke 16:15).
> All a man's ways seem innocent to him, / but motives are weighed by the Lord (Prov. 16:2).
> Give us today our daily bread (Matt. 6:11).
> Keep falsehood and lies far from me; / give me neither poverty nor riches, but give me only my daily bread (Prov. 30:8).

Jesus' familiarity with extrabiblical Jewish wisdom literature is indicated by these examples of His sayings and their parallels in Apocryphal writings:

> Give to the one who asks you, and do not turn away from the one who wants to borrow from you (Matt. 5:42).
> Do not refuse a suppliant in his trouble, / and do not avert your face from the poor (Sirach 4:4)[6]

> Do to others as you would have them do to you (Luke 6:31).
> Do not do to anyone else what you hate (Tobit 4:15).

As **rabbi,** Jesus may be contrasted with other rabbis of first-century Palestine. He probably did not receive the more structured schooling expected of a rabbi. However, Jesus taught in the synagogues (Luke 4:16), was often found asking and answering questions regarding the law (Matt. 15:1-9), gathered disciples to Himself (4:18), and taught people regarding ethics (6:1-7,28).

People of His day noted a difference between Jesus and other rabbis. Matthew 7:28-29 indicates that they saw in Jesus a primary source of rabbinic teaching. This would be seen in contrast with other rabbis, who belonged to "schools" of rabbinic tradition. They functioned somewhat as keepers of that which had been taught them by the rabbi of whom they had been disciples. The rabbis merely repeated what they had been taught. Jesus taught as one of primary authority.

Of course, Jesus' "school" was unstructured in every sense of the term. He taught wherever people were willing to listen and learn: on a mountain (Matt. 5:1 *ff.*); along the seaside (13:1 *ff.*); in countryside (Luke 9:10-12); and in Jerusalem (Mark 11:1 *ff.*). Jesus had many disciples, not only the inner circle of the twelve. Anyone who cared to learn received instruction from Him. He taught persons from all walks of life and levels of society. He taught a member of the ruling council of the Jews named Nicodemus and, shortly later, an outcast of outcasts, the Samaritan woman. He encouraged women to learn; for instance, Mary, the sister of Lazarus and Martha, was approved for listening to His teachings. He taught individuals like Zacchaeus, the tax collector, as well as crowds of thousands. Most of those who followed Jesus were common people. In fact, it was Jesus' disposition to associate with what the Jews considered the dregs of society that so often resulted in opposition to Him.

Jesus' traveling school was composed of all types and included both men and women. According to Luke, Jesus traveled about from one town and village to another, proclaiming the good news of the kingdom of God. The twelve were with Him, and also some women who had been cured of evil spirits and diseases: Mary (called Magdalene) from whom seven demons had come out; Joanna, the wife of Chuza, the manager of Herod's household; Susanna; and many others. These women helped to support Jesus and the twelve from their own means (8:1-3).

The Teaching Methods of Jesus

As a Master Teacher, Jesus used a wide variety of teaching methods. These methods arose from teaching He experienced and were not peculiar to Him. Nevertheless, what follows is a summary of how He taught with a brief definition of each method.

Parables are, perhaps, the best known of Jesus' instructional methods. The parables of the good Samaritan (Luke 10:25-37) and the prodigal son (15:11-32) have given rise to terms commonly used in casual conversation, even by persons not particularly familiar with their specific content or origin. Most of the Gospels records of Jesus' teaching is in the form of parables.

Parables are stories used to illustrate a central truth. Generally fictitious, they were at least plausible and were drawn from familiar life situations with which the learner was somewhat familiar. While similar to allegories, parables are different. An allegory is filled with symbols, each of which must be interpreted; a parable is to be interpreted much more in summary, teaching the one principle it was intended to demonstrate.

For instance, Jesus used the parable of the prodigal son to respond to the Pharisees' attacks against Him for associating with sinners. The central lesson of the parable is that a repentant sinner is welcomed by God and should be welcomed by others. Various Christian interpreters, using an allegorical method, later choose to understand the major characters of this parable symbolically: the faithful father (God), the son who remained (the Jews), and the wayward son (the "sinners"). Some interpret the distant country, the pigs, and the pods the pigs were eating symbolically. Such allegorizing obscures the message of the parable.

Jesus used parables to help His students. Parables gave concrete expression to abstract principles. At the same time, they required the learner to reflect on their meaning. They were wonderful aids to the memories of the learners. Perhaps that was why the Gospel writers remembered, and why we remember, Jesus' teaching in parables more than the other forms He used.

Jesus also used *object lessons*. In fact, some of Christianity's most importance ordinances and symbols came from His object lessons. At the last supper (Mark 14:12-26) Jesus used the bread and wine as symbols of His body and blood. Jesus used a drink of water to teach a Samaritan woman about true worship and His role as the Christ (John

4:26). Children were an object lesson in Matthew 19:13-15, as was the coin in Mark 12:13-17 and the widow in Mark 12:41-44.

Jesus acted out object lessons. As He washed His disciples' feet (John 13:1-17), Jesus taught humility and servanthood. His driving the money changers out of the temple (Mark 11:12-18) can be seen as an object lesson.

In many ways, the whole life of Jesus can be seen as an object lesson. In every sense of the term Jesus was, and is, an example—an object lesson—of how we should live in relationship with others and God (see Heb. 12:2-3).

Dialogue was often used by rabbis to discuss the law and, so, came naturally to Jesus as a teaching tool. Although the Gospels contain many examples of this, perhaps the best example is found in John 3:1-15. Jesus challenged the Pharisee Nicodemus to consider a creative way of relating to God. In this interesting dialogue, Jesus can be found asking and answering questions. He looked beyond the superficial, saw the basic question, and helped the learner find the answer.

Sometimes Jesus' questions or answers took the form of riddles. In John 2:12-18, after Jesus cleansed the temple, He was asked for a sign to prove His authority. Jesus replied with a riddle: "Destroy this temple, and I will raise it again in three days" (v. 19). The answer to a riddle is relatively obscure. The task for the learner is to uncover the hidden meaning by reflection.

Jesus also taught by *comparisons*. His comparisons took the form of parables, object lessons, similes, and metaphors. Similes are figures of speech in which two otherwise unlike things are compared explicitly. In a simile the comparison is usually suggested by using a word such as *like* or *as*. Jesus' application of simile can be found in such passages as Matthew 13:40: "As weeds are pulled up and burned in the fire, so it will be at the end of the age." Metaphors are figures of speech in which two otherwise unlike things are compared implicitly. Jesus also made extensive use of metaphors. A well-known example is: "You are the light of the world. A city on a hill cannot be hidden" (Matt. 5:14).

Jesus also utilized *poetry* to teach. Jewish poetry of Jesus' day was not based on rhyme but on rhythm and parallelism. The educational effectiveness of ancient poetry lies in its repetitive nature the repetition of the rhythmic beat or of parallel thoughts.

Parallelism in Jewish poetry involved the relationship between successive lines. The two lines may be synonymous or a restatement of thought: "Do not judge, and you will not be judged. Do not condemn, and you will not be condemned'' (Luke 6:37). The two lines may be antithetical, a contrasting thought: "Likewise every good tree bears good fruit, but a bad tree bears bad fruit'' (Matt. 7:17). Sometimes the second line builds on the first and is a completion of thought: "Whoever welcomes one of these little children in my name welcomes me; and whoever welcomes me does not welcome me but the one who sent me'' (Mark 9:37).

A teaching method of Jesus that raises difficulties of interpretation is overstatement or *hyperbole*. Certainly hyperbole seized the learner's attention. Sometimes Jesus' use of hyperbole is evident, as in Matthew 7:3, "Why do you look at the speck of sawdust in your brother's eye and pay no attention to the plank in your own eye?''

However, in some passages the line between command and overstatement may not be so clear. Some disfigured themselves because they interpreted Jesus' remarks in Matthew 5:29-30 as a command to be taken literally. Most Christians probably understand this as overstatement. Even more unclear is the intent of other teachings such as Matthew 5:38-42 in which Jesus spoke of turning "the other cheek.'' It has been suggested that this challenge to right living is another example of Jesus' use of overstatement. While Jesus' use of overstatement was obvious to His listeners, sometimes it poses difficult hermeneutical questions today.

Jesus also used *puns*. These plays on words are not usually evident in English, and they may not be evident in the Greek New Testament. However, when one retranslates the Greek into Aramaic (Jesus' mother tongue) the puns become more obvious. Such a play on words can be found in Matthew 23:24: "You blind guides! You strain out a gnat but swallow a camel.'' In English and Greek this seems to be a simple hyperbole. However, in Aramaic the word for gnat is *galma* while the word for camel is *gamla*. The similar sounding of the words added to the humor of the image of the hyperbole and made for a memorable lesson.[7]

Jesus was creative in His use of methods to teaching a wide variety of persons in an equally wide variety of situations. Though creative, He maintained an educational balance between the traditions of His people and the more complete revelation of God's will for humankind. Jesus was, indeed, a master teacher.

Notes

1. Robert H. Stein, *The Method and Message of Jesus' Teaching* (Philadelphia: Westminster Press, 1978), 1.

2. Charles Francis Potter, *The Lost Years of Jesus Revealed*, rev. ed. (Greenwich, Conn.: Fawcett Publications, 1962), 42.

3. Otto Betz, "Dead Sea Scrolls" in *The Interpreter's Dictionary of the Bible*, ed. George A. Buttrick, vol. 1 (New York: Abingdon Press, 1962), 801-02.

4. Paul Johnson, *A History of Christianity* (New York: Atheneum Press, 1976), 20-21.

5. Stein, 2-3.

6. This and subsequent citations of Old Testament Apocrypha is from *The Apocrypha: An American Translation*, trans. Edgar J. Goodspeed (New York: Vintage Books, 1959).

7. Stein, 13.

6

Education in the Apostolic Church

The earliest Christian community is often referred to as the apostolic church. It was comprised of three groups:

- the twelve whom Jesus Himself selected and who were viewed as the nucleus of the believers;
- the apostles, missionaries whose numbers included the twelve;
- remaining adherents of Jesus' ministry.

(After the death of Judas Iscariot, the eleven restored their number by election.)

At its beginning the church was almost exclusively Jewish but became increasingly Gentile. In fact, this aspect of the church's evolving nature became the source of controversy and many questions. Some of Paul's writings—his letter to the Galatian churches, for example—dealt with this struggle.

Apparently, the earliest Christians saw themselves as still basically Jewish. They worshiped and lived as Jews, observing the holy days and rituals of Judaism. Peter preached the first Christian sermon in the temple on the Jewish holy day of Pentecost (Acts 2:14-41). Baptism had roots in Judaism but received new meaning in Christianity. Christians accepted the Jewish Scripture—basically the Old Testament. Peter's response to the vision on Simon the tanner's rooftop (Acts 10:9-23) indicated a continued concern for adherence to Jewish dietary laws. The Epistle to the Galatians evidences a continued practice of the Jewish ritual of circumcision. In the synagogue the early Christians worshiped, prayed, read Scripture, and exercised freedom of speech.[1] In summary, education in the earliest church was basically Jewish.

However, the church slowly became distinctively Christian. This evolution can be seen and understood in the changing role of the apostles in the life of the church, hence characterizing the church at this stage as apostolic. The term *apostle* can be understood in a number of ways. It comes from the Greek *apostellein* meaning "to send out." The word sometimes refers to the twelve—those men originally sent out by Jesus. *Apostle* is also used to refer to leaders and teachers such as Paul, Barnabas, and Mark.[2]

Apostles and Other Teachers

The twelve apostles led the Jerusalem church, though Acts tells of Peter's missionary activity and some traditions and apocryphal sources suggest missionary activity on the part of others of the twelve. Apostles in the latter sense were primarily missionaries.

The apostles held a special place in the early church. As the church began the process of reidentification as an entity separate from Judaism, it looked to the apostles to teach and settle disputes. The apostles were not always in agreement but were apparently used as sources of authority among the first Christians (see 1 Cor. 1:12). As the apostolic church began to realize its distinctive nature, it needed a source of definition for its teachings, ceremonies, and polity that distinguished it from Judaism as well as a source for redefining its relationship with Judaism. The apostles' role in the church, then, was basically educational.

The role of the apostles as educators in the primitive church was obviously important as well as formative. Luke recorded that, following Pentecost, those who believed "devoted themselves to the apostles' teaching" (Acts 2:42). The first major crisis faced by the Jerusalem church in Acts 6 gives further clues to this teaching ministry of the apostles. A complaint arose from the Grecian Jews that their widows were being neglected in the daily distribution of food. "So the Twelve gathered all the disciples together and said, 'It would not be right for us to neglect the ministry of the word of God in order to wait on tables'" (Acts 6:2). The first order of priority for the twelve was their teaching ministry.

The role of teachers in general (of which, it may be argued, the apostles were the most prominent) was critical to the life of the church as it expanded. Many of the New Testament books, particularly the Pauline and Johannine writings, report issues regarding teachings and teachers. Paul believed teachers were specially gifted of God for their specific function. In 1 Corinthians 12:28, Ephesians 4:11, and Romans 12:7, Paul discussed the charismatic nature of teachers and their importance to the health of the church as a body. He commended those who had obeyed the teachers to which they were entrusted (Rom. 6:17), but he chided those who would make too much of the responsibility of the student to the teacher (1 Cor. 1:10-17).

This seeming contradiction may be simply explained. The most important duty of the teachers may have been to educate the new converts—primarily in anticipation of baptism. If new converts followed the Jewish model of the rabbi/disciple relationship, they might make too much of who was their teacher rather than being intent on following Jesus.[3]

Teachers were concerned with transmitting truths regarding Jesus Christ. This was done primarily in the training of baptismal candidates, or *catechumenoi*. Early baptismal creeds or confessions were almost certainly used in this instruction. An example of a rudimentary creed is 1 Corinthians 12:3: "Jesus is Lord." Paul used what may be an example of a more developed creed in 1 Corinthians 15:3-6:

> For what I received I passed on to you as of first importance: that Christ died for our sins according to the Scriptures, that he was buried, that he was raised on the third day . . . and that he appeared to Peter, and then to the Twelve. After that, he appeared to more than five hundred of the brothers at the same time, most of whom are still living, though some have fallen asleep.

The earliest confessions were still simple because a distinctively Christian system of doctrine and tradition had not yet developed. In fact, the Scriptures to which Paul alluded in 1 Corinthians 15 probably refer to Old Testament prophecies about the suffering Messiah. The Gospels were probably written after Paul (although, of course, many of the oral traditions used as sources by the Gospel writers may have been in circulation before Paul).[4] It is doubtful that Paul considered his own writings to be canonical Scripture, but he considered his writings God-led and somewhat authoritative because of his apostolic office. Paul stated in 1 Corinthians 7:25 that he had no particular direction from God on the subject of virgins. By implication, he believed his other directives were inspired by God. He seemed to indicate those areas in which no special revelation was given. Before the close of the apostolic era, Paul's writings had taken on the weight of Scripture. Peter indicated this in his Second Epistle:

Bear in mind that our Lord's patience means salvation, just as our dear brother Paul also wrote you with the wisdom that God gave him. He writes the same way in all his letters, speaking in them of these matters. His letters contain some things that are hard to understand, which ignorant and unstable people distort, as they do the other Scriptures, to their own destruction (2 Pet. 3:15-16).

Christian Writings

Early Christian writings other than those of Paul were circulated within the apostolic church and, like Paul's letters, some later came to be regarded as canon. The New Testament books served varying purposes. Obviously, some New Testament writings dealt with particular doctrinal, ethical, or ecclesiastical controversies. They involved the relationship of Judaism to the Christian church (Galatians), dealt with heresies as gnosticism (1 John, Colossians), sought to heal church divisions (1 Corinthians), and sometimes sought to isolate false teachers and troublemakers (2 and 3 John). The Gospels and Acts, recorded and interpreted the foundations of Christian tradition regarding the person of Jesus and the beginnings of the church. Still others, such as Revelation, were primarily to encourage persecuted churches.

Whatever their varying purposes, Christian writings of the apostolic era, both canonical and noncanonical, had both implicit and explicit educational value; some were intended to instruct a particular individual, group or groups, but many received wider distribution and circulation than may have been originally intended. Paul's comment to Timothy reflected an application of Scripture: "All Scripture is God-breathed and is useful for teaching, rebuking, correcting and training in righteousness, so that the man of God may be thoroughly equipped for every good work" (2 Tim. 3:16-17). Most definitely Paul meant the Old Testament Scriptures, but the same is true of the New Testament. His audience was Timothy, but his words are relevant to every Christian.

Methods of Teaching

The particular methods by which these writings were taught or employed is not totally clear. Written materials were relatively scarce and the church was poor. Many of the earliest Christians came from the lower socioeconomic and less-educated classes. Keeping, teaching, and copying the church's writings were necessarily entrusted to a few.

Memorization (as in Judaism) was undoubtedly relied upon heavily.

The apostolic church taught implicitly through baptism and the Lord's Supper. Earliest Christian baptism may have been interpreted by the primarily Jewish church in terms of Jewish baptism as expressed by John the Baptist. However, it was also seen in a new light: as a proclamation of the Christ-event, identifying the individual with Christ and His body, the church (Rom. 6:1-14).

In the New Testament, baptism almost immediately followed Christian conversion (Acts 8:30-38; 10:44-48; 16:11-15) and seemed to have little instructional use other than the symbolism and proclamation mentioned above. However, the perspective of the time of Luke—Acts was not that of twentieth-century persons and, so, a time of instruction preceding baptism even in Acts cannot be ruled out. Philip's encounter with and subsequent baptism of the Ethiopian eunuch involved a time of instruction the length of which is not established (Acts 8:30-38).

The union of Christians with Jesus Christ and His sacrifice were (and are) the core instructional themes of the Lord's Supper. In 1 Corinthians 10:14-17 and 11:23-34, Paul taught regarding these two themes as well as decorum during the observance of the Supper and its significance to the unity of the church. (He also promised further instructions upon his arrival.)

Worship itself was instructional in the apostolic church. Again, because of the earliest Christians' Jewish roots, their worship resembled the Jewish worship with which they were familiar. It involved the reading of Scripture, singing, and praying. In early years, the Scripture reading was exclusively from the Old Testament, but what sermonizing and teaching was done would have taken a particularly Christian flavor and perspective. Later, some of the existing New Testament writings would have been read for their instructional value. Paul's comment at the end of his Letter to the Colossians may indicate these new directions for the church. "After this letter has been read to you, see that it is also read in the church of the Laodiceans and that you in turn read the letter from Laodicea" (Col. 4:16).

Teaching was a major consideration in the apostolic church. Paul, Peter, John, and Jude all wrote about false teachers (both Judaizers and Gnostics) warning believers to beware of heretical teachings. James echoed the teachings of Jesus by cautioning teachers of their great responsibility: "Not many of you should presume to be teachers, my brothers, because you know that we who teach will be judged more strictly" (3:1).

Paul added to the portrait of instruction in the early church by his directions to Titus, his pastoral assistant stationed on Crete. Apparently Judaistic teachers were persuading some Christians to depart from the truth. Titus was told to "teach what is in accord with sound doctrine" (2:1). Paul then specified various groups in the church needing instruction. He also outlined what was to be taught to those groups. At the end of the section of instruction Paul concluded, "These, then, are the things you should teach. Encourage and rebuke with all authority. Do not let anyone despise you" (2:15). The ability to teach was required in pastoral leadership. Paul gave both Timothy and Titus lists of qualifications of a bishop or pastor. One of the major differences in the qualities required in a pastor and those of a deacon was the ability to teach (1 Tim. 3:2). When Paul listed the four gifted leaders for the churches in Ephesians 4:11, he identified one of the four as pastor-teacher. These church leaders had responsibility to equip believers for their ministries. This meant helping them "grow in the grace and knowledge of our Lord and Savior Jesus Christ" (2 Pet. 3:18). The teaching ministry of the church has always been an integral part of God's plan for spreading the gospel and changing lives. Paul's closing words to Timothy capture this concept: "The things you have heard me say in the presence of many witnesses entrust to reliable men who will also be qualified to teach others" (2 Tim. 2:2).

Notes

1. A. E. Welsford, *Life in the Early Church: A.D. 33 to 313* (London: National Society, 1955), 32.

2. Robert A. Spivey and D. Moody Smith, *Anatomy of the New Testament: A Guide to Its Structure and Meaning,* 3d ed. (New York: The Macmillan Publishing Co., 1982), 280-81.

3. Joseph A. Grassi, *Teaching the Way: Jesus, the Early Church and Today* (Lanham, Md.: University Press of America, 1982), 130-31.

4. Norman Perrin and Dennis C. Culling, *The New Testament: An Introduction,* 2d ed. (New York: Harcourt, Brace, Jovanovich, 1982), 42-43.

7

Education in the Postapostolic Church

Christianity encountered persecution and internal conflict during the second century. In response to these difficulties, church practices and beliefs hardened into a system, but this institutionalization meant the loss of some of the flexibility of the apostolic era. Clement of Rome, in his first letter to the Corinthian church, called for unity: "We must preserve our Christian body... in its entirety."[1]

Characteristic of this institutionalization of the church was the development of the monarchical episcopate (defined by Kurt Aland as "the leadership of a congregation by one bishop, to whom the other officeholders are subordinate").[2] Such a central authority figure was needed to fill the gap left by the passing of the apostolic generation.

The issue of apostolic authority was still important. (Note the number of second-century writings that claim apostolic authorship.) In this milieu developed the doctrine of apostolic succession, which enhanced the authority of the bishop, particularly in the area of education.

The *Didache,* or Teaching of the Twelve Apostles, appeared during this same period. This early manual of Christian morals and church discipline claims authorship by Jesus and the twelve, but the manual in its present form probably dates from about A.D. 140. Even so, it preserves some early and even primitive church traditions.

The moral instructions of the *Didache* show the influence of Proverbs and the ethical teachings of Jesus, especially of the Sermon on the Mount. The manual contains instructions regarding fasting, prayer, baptism, the Lord's Supper, false teachers, church officers, the Lord's Day, and church fellowship. Because of its content and structure as well as the variety of languages of the ancient manuscripts in which it is found (Greek, Syriac, Latin, Coptic, and Arabic), it may safely be inferred that the *Didache* was widely used as an catechetical manual in the early church. It primarily served as an instructional manual for baptismal candidates.

The Apologists

Other noncanonical writings of the postapostolic church were probably used in its teaching ministry. Prominent among these were the works of the apologists.

The unity which Clement of Rome sought resulted from persecution. Christians encountered persecution for many reasons: political, religious, economic, and social. Politically, Christians were considered anarchists whose concern for the kingdom of God was at cross-purposes with Roman patriotism. Refusal to participate in state festivals raised further question about the loyalty of Christians. Religiously, Christians were thought to be "atheists" who would not worship the emperor nor the other gods of Rome. Also, because of misunderstandings regarding Christian teachings on the Lord's Supper, it was rumored that Christians were cannibals. Corrupt views of love led to charges of incest. Economically, Christians were despised because they did not buy products from the makers of pagan objects. They were even blamed for the onset of various natural calamities. Finally, Christians represented a new order that threatened the upper class.[3]

Persecution continued from place to place. **Apologists** wrote in response to these persecutions and to rumors regarding Christian faith and practice. The apologists were literary defenders of the faith who appealed to the intellect. The most important were Aristides (ca. 140), Justin (ca. 153), and Athenagoras (ca. 175).

These and other apologists argued that Christianity taught the highest moral standards. Their writings quoted the Greco-Roman poets and philosophers, using the Greek rhetorical form. The apologists usually addressed their work to the sitting Roman emperor, though some may have presented their pleas to the emperor in person.[4] They were careful not to insult him, but they defended their faith from persecution with every conceivable argument, and they sought, at the same time, to win people to Christ.

The apologists had relatively little impact on the pagan world. Most of their readers were educated Christians who almost certainly used their writings to teach other Christians. These writings were sources for instruction in theology, church practice, and defense of the faith.[5]

Many uneducated Christians had their first contact with classical and rhetorical literature from contact with these writings.

Doctrinal Development

Attacks on the postapostolic church in the form of heresies arose. Of course, it is evident from the New Testament that even very early in the life of the church doctrinal controversies and aberrations developed. In the postapostolic church, one or two steps removed from sources of doctrinal authority (Jesus and the apostles), these heresies were deeper, more numerous, and more threatening to the church.

The struggle with heresy raised the question of authority. Who had authority to define and ferret out heresy? This authority was eventually vested in the office of the **monarchical episcopate** or bishop. Eusebius of Caesarea (ca. A.D. 325) referred to Clement (ca. A.D. 96) as bishop of Rome and ascribed to Clement certain rights of authority that would be given to a monarchical bishop:

> Of this Clement there is one epistle extant, acknowledged as genuine, of considerable length and of great merit, which he wrote in the name of the church at Rome, to that of Corinth, at the time when there was dissension in the latter. This we know to have been publicly read for common benefit, in most of the churches, both in former times and in our own; and that at the time mentioned a sedition did take place at Corinth, is abundantly attested by Hegesippus.[6]

This letter makes clear Clement's intention to be heard and obeyed as a monarchical bishop. In the latter part of the letter he wrote, "If, on the other hand, there be some who fail to obey what God has told them through us, they must realize that they will enmesh themselves in sin and in no insignificant danger."[7]

In this period of persecution, heresies, and a search for church unity as a means to survival, the monarchical bishop became more than a leader and high priest: he became the doctrinal authority. One whose knowledge pretended to go beyond the limits set by the bishop was lost. The bishop held the teaching chair or cathedra. This made him responsible for the education of candidates for church membership. The churches had teachers to instruct the catechumens, and the right and responsibility to supervise these teachers became significant, both as a source of future controversy and for the further entrenchment of episcopal authority. Implicit in authority over candidates for the clergy was the charge of their education and training.

In the postapostolic church, baptism and the Lord's Supper grew in importance. The canon of Scripture continued to develop with the involvement of such bishops as Clement of Rome and in response to heretical movements. Creeds became increasingly important.

Converts, especially those from paganism, required instruction in their newfound faith. Later writers continued developing confessions like those in the New Testament. Ignatius made extensive use of **creeds** and confessions in his writings. For example, he included such a statement in his letter to the church at Smyrna:

> Son of God according to God's will and power, actually born of a virgin; baptized by John, that "all righteousness might be fulfilled by him," and actually crucified for us in the flesh, under Pontius Pilate and Herod the Tetrarch. (We are part of His fruit which grew out of his most blessed passion.) And this, by his resurrection, he raised a standard to rally his saints and faithful forever—whether Jews or Gentiles—in one body of his church. For it was for our sakes that he suffered all this to save us.[8]

The old Roman symbol is a creed that some have traced to A.D. 100 and out of which may have developed the Apostles' Creed. This symbol, that of Ignatius, and others like them gradually changed in purpose—although they were still in many senses educational. They became not so much tools to teach baptismal candidates but guides to orthodoxy. In keeping with the times, control of the creeds was increasingly in the hands of the bishops.

Education in the postapostolic church attempted to instruct new converts and to equip church leaders. For various reasons little attention was given to teaching Christians in "worldly" things. The majority of early Christians were from the lower, less-educated social classes and, so, the education of the Greco-Roman world little interested them. Many early Christians—even those of the postapostolic era—anticipated the immediate return of Christ. If Jesus were, indeed, to return so soon, a secular education was deemed unnecessary and superfluous. Moreover, the Christian community was so concerned with the survival of its doctrines and traditions that the church had little time for education, which most Christians perceived as being outside the realm of the church. Finally, early Christians were suspicious of Greek and Roman literature.

Tertullian of Carthage (ca. A.D. 225) exemplifies these attitudes toward the Greek and Roman culture. Born in the middle of the second century, he became a well-educated lawyer before his conversion to Christianity at about age forty. He was so important as a Christian polemicist that he is known as the father of Latin theology, even though he eventually joined the Montanists, an early schismatic group. In spite of his learning (perhaps he would say because of it), Tertullian derided the philosophers. He believed that their search for truth was pointless: "For by whom has the truth ever been discovered without God? . . . For it is really better for us not to know a thing because He has not revealed it to us, than to know it according to man's wisdom, because *he* has been bold enough to assume it."[9]

Tertullian favored a radical break between Christians and secular culture. He did moderate somewhat at the point of school attendance. He believed Christians should not be schoolmasters, but he allowed Christian children to attend secular schools.

The most common method of teaching in the postapostolic church was oral instruction. Oral traditions played an important part in the developing and preserving the New Testament canon, particularly the Gospels. The creeds were transmitted orally and were to be memorized. Instruction in the creeds followed the question-answer form of catechism. Worship was not only an end in itself but a means of education.

Oral instruction was necessary; few Christians could read, and writing materials were beyond the reach of even most literate Christians. Yet maintaining an oral tradition in the faith instilled a certain "life," rather than the message being relegated to the pages of a book, the message *lived* within the heart, mind, and life of the Christian.

Notes

1. First Clement 38:1 in *Early Christian Fathers,* ed. Cyril C. Richardson (Philadelphia: Westminster Press, 1953), 61.

2. Kurt Aland, *A History of Christianity,* trans. James L. Schaaf, vol. 1 (Philadelphia: Fortress Press, 1985), 123.

3. Charles L. Whaley, *Outlines of Christian History* (Fukuoka, Japan: Seinan Gakuin University, 1987), 44-45.

4. Leslie W. Barnard, *Athenagoras: A Study in Second Century Apologetic* (Paris: Beauchesne, 1972), 11-12.

5. Aland, 140.

6. Eusebius, *Ecclesiastical History,* trans. C. F. Cruse, 9th ed. (New York: Stanford and Swords, 1976), 3:16.

7. First Clement 59:1 in *Early Christian Fathers*, ed. Cyril C. Richardson (Philadelphia: Westminster Press, 1953), 70.

8. Ignatius, *To the Smyrnaeans* 1:1-2 in *Early Christian Fathers*, ed. Cyril C. Richardson (Philadelphia: Westminster Press, 1953), 113.

9. Tertullian, "A Treatise on the Soul," in *The Ante-Nicene Fathers*, ed. Alexander Roberts and James Donaldson, vol. 3 (Grand Rapids: Eerdmans, 1950), 181-82.

8

The Alexandrian
Catechetical School

Alexandria was founded on the Mediterranean coast of Egypt by Alexander the Great in 331 B.C. It became a center of Greek culture, education, commerce, and religion. The Alexandrian educational system was based on the Greco-Roman gymnasiums and ephebic schools. The city contained two state libraries, a museum, and one of the great universities of the ancient Mediterranean world.

Alexandrian education emphasized the Greek language. Some scholars of Alexandria developed a system of accents to guide pronunciation. Study included mathematics, astronomy, geography, biology, textual and literary criticism, and rhetoric. The rhetorical school in Alexandria was one of the finest in the world—on a level with those in Tarsus, Athens, and Rome.

Alexandria, with its large Jewish community, also became a center of Jewish learning. The Septuagint, the Greek translation of the Old Testament, was completed there in the third century B.C. The Jewish philosopher Philo (ca. 20 B.C.-A.D. 50) lived, wrote, and taught in Alexandria. He led in applying Platonic philosophy to the Old Testament through allegory. This Philonic synthesis later influenced the development of Christian theology.

Not much is known regarding the history of Alexandrian Christianity before A.D. 180. Tradition has it that Mark brought the gospel to the city. The Jewish community in Alexandria could have received the gospel from those returning from pilgrimages and other trips to Judea and Jerusalem.

The church in Alexandria almost certainly developed a ministry of catechetical instruction from the beginning. The first mention of a Christian school in Alexandria dates from the second century.[1] As with other catechumenal schools, the one in Alexandria developed adjunct to the church, and the bishop had increasing control over it.

Pantaenus

In A.D. 179, Pantaenus (ca. 180-200), a converted Stoic, became the head of the Alexandrian church's catechumenal school. He broadened its curriculum so that it became a school of religious and secular learning.

The Alexandrian catechetical school proved pivotal in the development of Christian education. Christians of all ages and both sexes were given an education that grounded them in the doctrine and traditions of the church. Students confronted Greco-Roman classics, philosophers, and academic disciplines. They were equipped to converse with the most educated non-Christians. Such conversation was necessary to the propagation and preservation of the gospel. They were taught that there was nothing to fear from open and honest inquiry into all thought and that such inquiry could serve a missionary and apologetic purpose.

Clement of Alexandria

Clement of Alexandria (ca. 150-215) succeeded Pantaenus as the head of the school between A.D. 190 and 200. He was born to pagan parents in either Athens or Alexandria. He received the standard education typical of a relatively wealthy boy and young man of the day. Converted while in his teens, he spent several years on a series of journeys searching for Christian scholars from whose discourses he could develop a better understanding of Christianity.[2] His travels took him to southern Italy, Palestine, Greece, and the Near East before he settled in Alexandria. In his longest work, *Stromateis* (Miscellanies), he describes his travels and mentions an Ionian, thought by some to be the apologist Athenagoras.

Pantaenus influenced Clement to take up residence in Alexandria. They worked together until Pantaenus's death, after which Clement assumed leadership of the school. Clement added rhetoric to the curriculum and probably lived from voluntary fees and the offerings of wealthy patrons. Clement was ordained to the priesthood but was under less supervision by the bishop than those who succeeded him; this may have been because the bishop of Alexandria, Demetrius, was younger than Clement and became bishop after Clement had estab-

---

Clement of Alexandria

Lived: A.D. 215 in Alexandria, Egypt

Career: developed and taught in the catechetical school of the Alexandrian church

Writings dealing with education: *Stromateis* ("Miscellanies"); *Paidagogos* ("Christ the Teacher"); *Protreptikos* ("Exhortations")

Views related to education:
- education in philosophy and other "secular" subjects could be reconciled with Christian education
- Christian educators could use philosophy as a means by which to draw their students closer to Christ

---

lished himself. Although Demetrius generally allowed Clement to follow his own lead, he did not encourage Clement to return to Alexandria once he had left.

Clement left Alexandria in A.D. 202 during the persecution under Severus. Other than the mention by Eusebius, Rufinus, and Jerome, little evidence exists that Clement was well-known among later Christians. Nothing is known for certain regarding his fate. It may be inferred from Eusebius' *Ecclesiastical History* (6:11,14) that Clement later served and perhaps died in Antioch.[3]

Clement's attitude toward philosophy was certainly influenced by the fact that he came to Christianity by way of philosophy. In *Stromateis* 1:5, he wrote:

Philosophy was necessary to the Greeks for righteousness. And now it becomes conducive to piety; being a kind of preparatory training to those who attain faith through demonstration. "For thy foot," it is said, "will not stumble, if thou refer what is good, whether belonging to the Greeks or to us, to Providence." For God is the cause of all good things; but of some primarily, as of the Old and the New Testament; and of others by consequences, as philosophy. Perchance, too, philosophy was given to the Greeks directly and primarily, till the Lord should call the Greeks. For this was a schoolmaster to bring "the Hellenic mind," as the law, the Hebrews, "to Christ." Philosophy, therefore, was a preparation, paving the way for him who is perfected in Christ.[4]

What remains of Clement's writings consist primarily of three works: *Protreptikus* (Exhortation to the Heathen—ca. A.D. 195), *Paidagogos*

(The Instructor—ca. A.D. 197), and *Stromateis* (Miscellanies—ca. A.D. 199). In *Protreptikus* Clement heaped invective upon the religion and mystery cults of the pagans. A prominent metaphor for Jesus in this work of Clement is "light." He declared that Jesus dispels darkness (ignorance) and encourages people to be "illuminated by Him."[5] *Paidagogos* depicts Jesus as "The Teacher" to whom the Christian must look for instruction regarding right living.

In *Stromateis* Clement suggested a relationship between Greco-Roman philosophy and Judeo-Christian thought. Clement cited Paul's speech to the Greeks in Athens (Acts 17:22-32) to support his thesis.[6] Clement freely cited Christian, Jew, Greek, and Roman alike in making his various points.

For Clement, knowledge was not necessary to faith, but he believed ". . . it is impossible for a man without learning to comprehend the things which are declared in the faith."[7]

On the other hand, faith is basic to the true search for knowledge: "For that investigation, which accords with faith, which builds, on the foundation of faith, the august knowledge of the truth, we know to be the best."[8]

Clement believed the purpose of humankind was to rediscover the lost relationship of unity, perfection, and fulfillment with God. Since God's image in persons was reflected in their rational nature, knowledge was both an end in itself and a means to an end.

Clement went into exile during the Severian persecution of A.D. 202. Origen, one of his students, succeeded him as leader of the catechetical school.

Origen

Most of our biographical knowledge of Origen (184?-254?) comes from his own extensive writings and from the *Ecclesiastical History* of Eusebius (ca. A.D. 325). He produced a compilation of Old Testament translations (the *Hexapla*), commentaries and homilies on most biblical books, and several major theological works and letters. Some additional information regarding Origen, particularly his approach to education, can be gleaned from contemporary writers, such as Gregory Thaumaturgus, who mentioned him.

Origen was one of the first Christian theologians born and reared in a Christian home. From a young age he was diligent in studying Scripture, attacking heresy, and yearning for martyrdom. Besides Clement, Origen's teachers included at least one pagan, Ammonius Saccas, whom some consider the founder of Neoplatonism.[9]

When Origen was seventeen, his father, Leonidas, was beheaded during the Severian persecution. Origen wished to follow his father in martyrdom. After he rebuffed his mother's appeals to reconsider, she hid his clothes to keep him at home. His father's property was confiscated by the imperial government, so Origen's family (including six younger brothers) was reduced to poverty. Their situation was relieved, however, by a local "lady of great wealth and distinction."[10]

Bishop Demetrius appointed Origen to lead the school. His efforts in teaching and preaching were so successful that some pagans took steps to inhibit him. Many of his students became martyrs.

Origen lived an ascetic life. He limited his possessions to one coat and no shoes because of his understanding of the teachings of Jesus. He frequently fasted and slept on the bare ground. Origen castrated himself to avoid slander concerning his relationship with female students and in keeping with his interpretation of the statement of Jesus concerning eunuchs for the sake of the kingdom (Matt. 19:12). Upon learning of Origen's self-castration, Demetrius commended him for the ardor of his faith and encouraged him to continue teaching. Later, Demetrius (motivated by jealousy of Origen's success, according to Eusebius) wrote a letter to other bishops attacking Origen's act as foolish.

During a time of persecution, Origen fled to Caesarea, where he preached at the request of local bishops even though he was not ordained. His conflict with Demetrius continued, and he settled in Caesarea and established a school. Known for his prolific writings and his evangelistic fervor, Origen died a martyr's death during the Decian persecution (ca. A.D. 254).

Origen emphasized the importance of Greco-Roman learning in Christian education. In his "Letter to Gregory," he wrote:

A natural readiness of comprehension, as you well know, may, if practice be added, contribute somewhat to the contingent end, if I may so call it, of that which any one wishes to practise. Thus your natural good parts might make of you a finished Roman lawyer or a Greek philosopher, so to speak, of one of the schools in high reputation. But I am anxious that you should devote all the strength of your natural good parts to Christianity for your end; and in order to this, I wish to ask you to extract from the philosophy of the Greeks what may serve as a course of study or a preparation for Christianity, and from geometry and

astronomy what will serve to explain the Scriptures, in order that all that
the sons of the philosophers are wont to say about geometry and music,
grammar, rhetoric, and astronomy, as fellow-helpers to philosophy, we
may say about philosophy itself, in relation to Christianity.[11]

Origen held the intellect in highest regard. To him the "soul" was
simply fallen understanding and, once "repaired and corrected, it
returned to the condition of the understanding."[12] However, the purpose of "understanding"—the use of rational, logical thinking—was
not merely speculative knowledge but reasoned faith that would lead to
right doctrine and morality. Again, he argued that reason without God
was insufficient.

Origen divided his students into elementary and advanced groups.
He appointed his student Heraclas to teach less-advanced students. (It
was this Heraclas who later succeeded Demetrius as bishop in Alexandria.)
He taught men and women from all over the Mediterranean world and
was highly regarded even by non-Christian teachers.

Origen began his teaching by pointing out the relationship between
genuine Christianity and philosophy. As one of his students, Gregory
Thaumaturgus, stated:

He asserted further that there could be no genuine piety towards the
Lord of all in the man who despised the gift of philosophy . . . but his
desire was, with a benignant, and affectionate, and most benevolent
mind, to save us, and make us partakers in the blessings that flow from
philosophy.[13]

Gregory indicated that Origen took his students beyond basic instruction in philosophy; geometry, astronomy, and physics were also
part of the curriculum. The Christian should avoid only the writings of
atheists in search for truth. Yet to establish Christian doctrine, Christians should devote themselves "to God alone and to the prophets."[14]
Origen believed that atheists had lapsed from human intelligence in
their denial of a God or providence.

Gregory described Origen as a teacher who taught by example,
contemplation, and observation. His lectures also included questions
and answers, and some of the many writings may be transcripts of his
lectures.

Notes

1. Robert W. Smith, *The Art of Rhetoric in Alexandria* (The Hague: Martinus Nijhoff, 1974), 141.

2. Henri Daniel-Rops, *The Church of the Apostles and Martyrs*, trans. Audrey Butler (London: J. M. Dent and Sons, Ltd., 1960), 343.

3. Eusebius, *Ecclesiastical History*, trans. C. F. Cruse, 9th ed. (New York: Stanford and Swords, 1976), 230,234.

4. Clement of Alexandria, "The Stromata, or Miscellanies," in *The Ante-Nicene Fathers*, ed. Alexander Roberts and James Donaldson, vol. 2 (Grand Rapids: Eerdmans, 1950), 305.

5. Clement of Alexandria, "Exhortation to the Heathen," in *The Ante-Nicene Fathers*, ed. Alexander Roberts and James Donaldson, vol. 2 (Grand Rapids: Eerdmans, 1950), 203.

6. Clement, "The Stromata, or Miscellanies" (1:19), 2:321.

7. Ibid., (1:6), 2:307.

8. Ibid., (5:1), 2:445.

9. "Origen," in *Oxford Dictionary of the Christian Church*, eds. F. L. Cross and E. A. Livingstone, 2d ed. (London: Oxford University Press, 1983), 1008.

10. Eusebius, *Ecclesiastical History*, 6:2.

11. Origen, "A Letter from Origen to Gregory," sec. 1 in *The Ante-Nicene Fathers*, vol. 4, (Grand Rapids: Eerdmans, 1950), 393.

12. Origen, "Origen de Principiis," 2.8.3. in *Ante-Nicene Fathers*, vol. 4 (Grand Rapids: Eerdmans, 1950), 288.

13. Gregory Thaumaturgus, "Oration and Panegyric Addressed to Origen," Argument 4 in *The Ante-Nicene Fathers*, vol. 6 (Grand Rapids: Eerdmans, 1950), 27-28.

14. Ibid., Argument 15, 36.

9

Post-Nicene Christian Fathers and Education

The most important developments in the history of the Christian church in the West during the fourth century were the Edict of Milan in A.D. 313, the events that led to it, and those events it influenced. Persecution of Christians had continued under third- and early fourth-century Roman emperors, particularly Decius, Valerian, and Diocletian. The coemperors Constantius Chlorus and Galerius succeeded Diocletian. Soon a struggle developed for control of the empire that continued under their successors, Constantine (Constantius Chlorus's son), Licinius, and Maxentius (son of Maximian, a crony of Diocletian).

Christianity had grown to the point that efforts to subdue it were futile. Most persecution of Christians had ended in the west by A.D. 306. An edict of toleration, the Edict of Nicomedia, was issued in A.D. 311 by Galerius, Constantine, and Licinius. It stated, according to Eusebius, that:

> There may be Christians again, and that they may restore their houses in which they were accustomed to assemble, so that nothing be done by them contrary to their profession . . . they are obligated to implore their God for our safety, as well as that of the people and their own. That in every place the public welfare may be preserved, and they may live unmolested in their respective homes and fire-hearths.[1]

Galerius died soon after the issue of this edict. The fight for the empire soon pitted Constantine and Licinius against Maxentius and Maximianus I, a protege of Galerius. The night before one particular battle, Constantine was purported to have had a dream in which he saw the first two letters of the name *Christ* and the words *By this sign thou shalt conquer.* Constantine had a monogram with the first two letters of the name *Christ* emblazoned on the shields of his army and won the Battle of the Mulvian Bridge in 312. He attributed his victory to the strength of the God of the Christians.

This victory led Constantine and Licinius to issue the Edict of Milan. Although it may not have been formally published, it went a step further than the Edict of Nicomedia by giving Christians equal footing with pagans, full freedom of conscience, and the return of church property taken during a previous persecution.[2] Whether or not the Edict of Milan was original with Constantine and Licinius or a republication of earlier edicts of toleration is a matter of debate.[3] However, its issue or republication by Constantine is important to the history of the church in light of Constantine's later use of the church and his direct intervention in Christian doctrinal controversy.

Christians soon changed from a persecuted underclass to a favored group that was to join the government in oppressing other faiths. Constantine believed that Christianity could be the force to keep his empire from fragmenting.

Once Christianity's institutional survival seemed secure, the church was free to examine and debate the finer details of doctrine. In about 320 a controversy over the nature of the Christ arose in Alexandria between Arius, a presbyter, and Alexander, the bishop. The Arian controversy grew to seriously threaten church unity. Concerned that disunity in the church would lead to a split in the empire, Constantine called the first general council of the church. The council gathered bishops from throughout the empire in Nicaea in 325. The Council of Nicaea rejected the doctrines of Arius and published a creed to define Christological orthodoxy.

The legalization of Christianity had a significant impact on Christian education. As Christianity became more pervasive through society, so did its educational institutions and functionaries. Christian education and the church itself become intertwined with the government, at times influencing the government, at other times being influenced by the government. Emperor Theodosius (379-395) issued a series of edicts that established Christianity as the religion of the empire. Many more people aligned themselves with the church and, so, were affected by Christian education.

During this era, many Christian writers emerged to influence the developing character of Christian education. Most of these are best known as theologians, but they had much to say about the church's teaching ministry in their roles as bishops, presbyters, and other leaders in the church. Some of the more significant of these individuals are Gregory of Nyssa, Jerome, Ambrose, John Chrysostom, and Augustine of Hippo.

Gregory of Nyssa

One of the foremost writers and leaders of the fourth-century church was Gregory of Nyssa (ca. 335-394). He was born into a wealthy family of ten children, possibly in Caesarea of Cappadocia. His family was strongly Christian. His older brother, Basil, became bishop of Caesarea and a leader of considerable influence in ecclesiastical affairs. A younger brother, Peter, became bishop of Sebaste. Another brother, Nectarius, followed in the footsteps of their father and became a rhetorician. The family was wealthy enough to provide advanced education for these (and certainly the other children) despite the early death of the father. A sickly child, Gregory probably received most of his early education at home. His elder brother Basil, being well-educated in Athens, apparently had a significant part in the higher education of Gregory.

Gregory was baptized after he was confronted by Christian martyrs in a dream. Upon his baptism he became a reader in the church but later gave up that office to become a rhetorician. Because of family influences, he later returned to a life more connected to the church and entered his brother's monastery, where he studied the Bible and the writings of Origen.

Gregory was deposed as bishop after a few years in office and falsely charged with embezzlement of church funds. The emperor Valens exiled him to Seleucia in 376. After Valens died, Gregory returned to his office of bishop. He was held in high esteem by Emperor Theodosius and was one of the bishops to comprise the Second Ecumenical Council in Constantinople in A.D. 381.[4]

Gregory's instructional theory proceeded from his doctrine of creation in the image of God. While the two natures—the Divine and incorporeal nature, and the irrational life of brutes—are separated from each other as extremes, human nature is the mean between them:

> For in the compound nature of man we may behold a part of each of the natures I have mentioned—of the Divine, the rational and intelligent

element, which does not admit the distinction of male and female; of the irrational, our bodily form and structure, divided into male and female: for each of these elements is certainly to be found in all that partakes of human life. . . . The language of Scripture therefore expresses it concisely by a comprehensive phrase, in saying that man was made "in the image of God": for this is the same as to say that He made human nature participant in all good.[5]

Gregory affirmed the intelligence and rational nature of human beings as part of their being created in God's image, and he linked this with participation in God's goodness.[6] For Gregory, education was necessary to bring this image of God to fruition. In his instruction to teachers, *The Great Catechism*, Gregory set the intellect in opposition to the senses in terms of how the world is perceived and noted that they are both necessary to a well-rounded view of the world. Nonetheless, he seemed to consider the preexistent intellect as greater than the senses.

In *The Great Catechism*, Gregory gave some practical instruction to those who would teach:

The presiding ministers of the "mystery of godliness" have need of a system in their instructions, in order that the Church may be replenished by the accession of such as should be saved, through the teaching of the word of Faith being brought home to the hearing of unbelievers. Not that the same method of instruction will be suitable in the case of all who approach the word. The catechism must be adapted to the diversities of their religious worship; with an eye, indeed, to the one aim an end of the system, but not using the same method of preparation in each individual case.[7]

The link between Gregory's theology and his concept of education is important. He believed that goodness is inherent in the intellect; thus, he affirmed a variety of teaching methods to reach students of diverse religious backgrounds. Education was important in evangelism and in the search for orthodoxy and church unity.[8]

Gregory valued the teacher. The teacher should be well versed in doctrine, logic, and other skills of reasoning and should also be an able rhetorician, capable of discerning the weaknesses in heretical arguments. The capable teacher understands the student's former religion and life.

Jerome

Sophronius Eusebius Hieronymus, better known as Jerome (ca. 347-420), was born to Christian parents in Strido, a town in what is now Croatia/Dalmtia. In Rome, where he was baptized in 360, he distinguished himself as a scholar. He settled in Aquileia, in northeastern Italy, but traveled widely, seeking to know scholars throughout the world. One of his trips took him through Antioch, where he became seriously ill. In the course of this illness he had a vision of Christ who took him to task for his zeal for classical literature. In response to the vision, Jerome devoted himself to studying the Scripture, religious writing, and monastic living.[9]

Jerome is known for his translation of the Bible from Hebrew and Greek into Latin. This translation, the *Vulgate,* gained wide acceptance in the West and was given official status by the Council of Trent in 1546. Jerome also became involved with the struggle against the Pelagians, who taught that there was no original sin, that baptism was unnecessary for salvation, and that persons were capable of doing good completely under their own power.[10]

In *Against the Pelagians,* Jerome proposed a dialogue (after the style of Plato) in which Atticus, the defender of orthodoxy stated that knowledge can be divided into three areas: *dogma* (teaching), *methodos* (method), and *empeiria* (practice). Persons can learn these God-given truths but Cicero correctly stated the limits of human knowledge— nobody can be learned in everything. Atticus calls for the affirmation of personally held knowledge, limited though it may be:

[God] also gave different precepts and various virtues, but we cannot possess all of them at the same time. And so it comes that one virtue, that is primarily and wholly cultivated by one individual, is cultivated in part by another individual; and yet, he who does not possess all virtues should not be considered at fault, nor should he be condemned for what he does not possess, but rather should be justified for what he does possess.[11]

Yet Jerome distrusted secular learning. This may have resulted from his dramatic vision. In a letter to Pope Damasus, Jerome commented on the parable of the prodigal:

We may also interpret the husks in another fashion. The food of the demons is the songs of poets, secular wisdom, the display of rhetorical language . . . they afford their readers nothing more than empty sound and the hubbub of words. No satisfaction of truth, no refreshment of justice is found. They who are zealous for these things continue to hunger for truth, to lack value.[12]

Despite such warnings, Jerome frequently quoted Roman classics in his own writing. His warning attempted to alert others to the folly of secular wisdom for its own sake.

Jerome underscored the teaching role of the bishop. Commenting on Paul's qualifications for bishops in 1 Timothy 3:1-7, Jerome wrote:

> [Paul] suggests that you should look for a man who is "married but once, reserved, prudent, of good conduct, hospitable"; and as for the following virtue, that he be *didaktikos*, "one who can teach," and not *docilis*, "one who is teachable," as it is translated literally in Latin.[13]

Yet Jerome did not consider biblical study the sole qualification of the teacher. In his letter to Eustochium, Jerome stated that the teacher's moral and ethical behavior commends him to be heard. Jerome wrote to Nepotian, bishop of Altinium concerning the duties of the clergy: "Learn so that you may teach."[14] Jerome took his own advice and sought instruction in the Hebrew from Jews so that he could become a more adequate translator.[15]

Thoroughly convinced of the necessity of biblical learning, Jerome argued that Scripture could be understood by study:

> Let not the simplicity of the Scripture or the poorness of its vocabulary offend you; . . . for in this way it is better fitted for the instruction of an unlettered congregation as the educated person can take one meaning and the uneducated another from the same sentence.[16]

Ambrose

Ambrose (330-397) was born in Treves (now Trier, Germany). His father, Ambrosius, was a government official and his family was prominent. When in his early teens, Ambrose moved to Rome with his mother, older brother, and sister (his father had died). Ambrose studied law and advanced rapidly in the legal profession. In 370 he was appointed governor of the provinces of Liguris and Aemilia with headquarters in Milan. He became a respected judge. When Auxentius, bishop of Milan, died, Ambrose was soon named to replace him though Ambrose was still a catechumen. He was baptized and, eight days later, installed as bishop.[17]

Ambrose immediately dedicated himself to theological study. He made significant contributions to practical theology and hymnology. His commitment to faith as expressed in the Nicene Creed soon brought conflict with Empress Justina, an Arian sympathizer. Jerome also opposed the construction of an "Altar to Victory" in the senate chamber in Rome and successfully challenged Emperor Theodosius to repent publicly of ordering the killing of many Thessalonians in 390.[18]

Ambrose considered the bishop's role as teacher to be a serious burden after that of Christ and the apostles. He confessed his lack of theological preparation for the bishopric, but he determined to learn as he taught:

> For I was carried off from the judgment seat, and the garb of office, to enter the priesthood, and began to teach you, what I myself had not yet learnt. So it happened that I began to teach before I began to learn. Therefore I must learn and teach at the same time, since I had no leisure to learn before.[19]

Another incident that Ambrose records sheds some light on his educational practice:

> The day after, which was Sunday, after the lessons and the sermon, when the Catechumens were dismissed, I was teaching the creed to certain candidates in the baptistry of the basilica . . . I, however, remained at my ministrations, and began to celebrate mass.[20]

That the instruction was taking place in the baptistry does not necessarily indicate that teaching usually happened there. Possibly Ambrose was teaching baptism that day. Whatever the case, the students learned through sermons, Scripture lessons, ritual, and creeds (probably in the form of catechism). By this time two levels of students had developed in the church: catechumens and *competentes*. The *competentes* were catechumens who had requested baptism. In anticipation of their baptism, they were given extra instruction. (This offers another explanation of why Ambrose taught in the baptistry.)

Bishop Ambrose was concerned to instruct catechumens about the sacraments. Two of his important works are "On the Sacraments" and "On the Mysteries." In these he described the meaning and form of the liturgy. The liturgy was a salvation drama and a salvific act that the participant should understand. Ambrose was concerned that instruction and discussion be practical and understandable:

> Let us have a reason for beginning, and let our end be within due limits. For a speech that is wearisome only stirs up anger . . . The treatment also of such subjects as the teaching of faith, instruction on self-restraint, discussion on justice, exhortation to activity, must not be taken up by us and fully gone into all at one time . . . The address should be plain and simple, clear and evident, full of dignity and weight; it should not be studied or too refined, nor yet, on the other hand, be unpleasing and rough in style.[21]

John Chrysostom

John Chrysostom (ca. 347-407), the most influential father of the Eastern church, was born in Antioch of Syria. Chrysostom's father died when he was very young. His pious mother, Anthusa, shaped his life and provided for him a quality education in rhetoric. His teacher was Libanius, an advocate of a return to the Roman gods, but Anthusa had already grounded Chrysostom in the Christian faith.

John Chrysostom was baptized after he had become a successful lawyer. He had became disillusioned with the legal profession and prospects of a career in politics. He undertook a catechumenate of three years and was baptized around 369. He soon became a reader in the church and was dissuaded from a monastic life only by his mother's dramatic pleas. Even so, Chrysostom practiced asceticism and supported monasticism.

After his mother's death, John became, in succession, a monk, deacon, priest, and presbyter. He was an effective and charismatic preacher (his surname, Chrysostom, meaning "golden mouth," was given to him later, probably after his death). In 398 he succeeded Nectarius as patriarch of Constantinople. He soon clashed with Empress Eudoxia, who conspired with Bishop Theophilus of Alexandria to banish Chrysostom from Constantinople twice. The first banishment was short; the people rebelled against their popular prelate's exile, and an earthquake in the city was seen as a sign of God's displeasure with those who had deposed him. He died in 407, however, on a journey to the intended place of his second exile. He was buried at his place of death, the chapel of Basilicus near Comana, but was reinterred in Constantinople in 438.[22]

John Chrysostom's works on Christian education and related issues include *Baptismal Instructions, On Vainglory and the Right Way for Parents to Bring Up Their Children,* and *Homilies on the Statues.* The latter is a collection of sermons issued in response to the desecration of statues of Theodosius and his deceased wife Flacilla.

John Chrysostom believed that humans are rational in order that they might be righteousness: "For this reason men have the power of thinking; that they may avoid sin."[23] Knowledge and wisdom were to be practical and utilized outside the place of instruction. What is to be aimed at is not that we be lovers of wisdom here only, but that when we depart, we may take this reverence out with us, where we especially need it."[24]

In his thirteenth homily on the statues, Chrysostom contrasts between teachers and craftsmen:

> It is not with the office of teaching, as it is with other arts. For the silversmith, when he has fabricated a vessel of any kind, and laid it aside, will find it on the morrow just as he left it . . . But it is not so with us, but altogether the reverse; for we have not lifeless vessels to forge, but reasonable souls. Therefore we do not find you such as we leave you, . . . [but] the urgency of business, besetting you from every side, again perverts you, and causes us increased difficulty.[25]

Baptismal Instructions reflects a similar concern for teachers who feel that their work is futile. "When the teacher sees that, after he has shown great care and taught unceasingly, his disciples continue in the same negligence, he could never deliver his spiritual instruction with the same zeal."[26] The teacher is to develop skills to ward off the evils of the world.[27] Students so equipped would "shine forth for us with a brilliance more radiant than the very stars."[28]

The teaching process was at times intimidating. In the sixteenth homily, John spoke of children who cried to their mothers about fear of their teachers. In *Baptismal Instructions* (9:28-29), he compared the training of a catechumen to that of a wrestler. Wrestling in the school was combative and rigorous but safe; it prepared the student for real combat (encounter with worldly forces).

Chrysostom's most important treatise about Christian education is

On Vainglory and the Right Way for Parents to Bring Up Their Children. In this work he declared the importance of the family in the proper education of a young man. He wrote of the tragedy of a father who was more concerned to give his son material goods than godly wisdom. It was imperative that parents, particularly the father, discipline a boy from his earliest years. He compared parenting to the work of an artist: "To each of you fathers and mothers I say, just as we see artists fashioning their paintings and statues with great precision, so we must care for these wondrous statues of ours."[29]

John directed parents to make rules for their son and teach the rules by precept and example. He suggested that one parent take the part of the adversary and confront the boy harshly. The other should take the role of advocate, supporting the youth in confronting the first parent. Chrysostom compared the senses to city gates. Different kinds of learning can enter, and parents should beware of evil influences.

Boys were to be taught Bible stories and encouraged to remember and recall them from time to time. Stories and the truths they illustrated were to become something about which it was natural for the boy (and later, the man) to talk.

Chrysostom assumed that parents would arrange the vocational training for their son, but he was concerned about education in morals and personal and social conduct. (John's intended audience must have been primarily the upper socioeconomic class because several of his instructions deal with teaching youths to relate properly to their slaves.) Chrysostom summarized his intent for education referring to Proverbs 1:7:

> Let us then implant in him this wisdom and let us exercise him therein, that he may know the meaning of human desires, wealth, reputation, power, and may disdain these and strive after the highest. And let us bring words of exhortation to his mind: "My child, fear God alone and fear none other but Him."[30]

Augustine of Hippo

Augustine (354-430) was the most important of the Western church fathers because of his significance for both Roman Catholic and Protestant theology and practice. Augustine was born in Tagaste in northern Africa (now Souk-Ahras, Algeria). His family was middle class with his father being pagan and mother, Monica, being Christian. His education took him to Madaura, near his home, and to Carthage to study rhetoric. He soon abandoned the Christian morals Monica had taught him. A spiritual search began with the writings of Cicero. Augustine studied the Bible, but he preferred the dignity of Cicero over the inspired Scriptures. Next his pilgrimage led to Manichaeanism, a synthesis of Zoroastrianism, Buddhism, Judaism, and Christianity. He moved to Rome in 383 and a year later was chosen to teach rhetoric in Milan.

Augustine of Hippo

Lived: A.D. 354-430, native of North Africa, lived in Rome for a time, but spent later life in Hippo in North Africa

Career: teacher of rhetoric in Rome before his conversion to Christianity; later served as bishop of church in Hippo; was one off the foremost of the early Christian theologians

Writing dealing with education: *De Civitate Deo* ("The City of God"

Views related to education:
- the teacher should help the student experience God
- the teacher should take into account the unique characteristics of each student and relate to the students as unique individuals
- Christian education should include the study of Plato, for most Christian doctrines were contained in his writings
- understood the image of God in persons as their rational nature, thus it was to be used as a tool to relate them to God
- distrusted the senses as a means to knowing and urged the use of reason instead
- in the tension between faith and reason, faith must predominate

---

Augustine soon came under the preaching of Bishop Ambrose of Milan. This preaching combined with Augustine's own mystical experience to bring about his conversion to Christianity in 386. He became a catechumen and was baptized by Ambrose. By 388 he had returned to Tagaste and once more devoted himself to study. In 391 Augustine moved to Hippo (now Bona, Algeria), where he became a priest and later bishop. There he established a monastery that later included a school for ministerial training. Augustine died at Hippo in 430.[31]

Augustine's theological and philosophical writings make significant contributions to Christian education. He believed that reason characterizes humans and sets them above other animals, yet this regard for reason did not lead him to elitism. He emphasized the primacy of faith open to the masses. In his polemic *Against Julian,* Augustine argued:

> You, indeed, bar the way for the multitude of the ignorant, whom you say are simple men, busy with other affairs, without instruction, who by faith alone should enter the Church of Christ, lest they be easily frightened by obscure questions . . . let no force of argumentation pluck it [their faith] from them; rather, let them detest every authority and society which tries to convince them of the contrary.[32]

Augustine continued more succinctly in *The Free Choice of the Will:* "Take courage, and go on believing that you believe, for there is no better belief even though the reason for it is hidden from me."[33]

In *The Teacher* Augustine wrote that language, although imperfect, could be used to evoke the "inner light of truth" (12:40). He described the related task of the teacher this way: "The man who teaches me is one who presents to my eyes or to any bodily sense, or even to the mind itself, something that I wish to know."[34] Augustine encouraged the use of gestures and other physical images to facilitate learning.

In *De Catechizandis Rudibus* (The First Catechetical Instruction), Augustine examined the teaching role of Jesus and called teachers to take heart in His example. The teacher was not to protect students from the lure of evil but was to put them on guard against it. The teacher was to have a positive attitude and encourage student participation. The teacher was to become familiar with the student's background to find points of commonality that might enhance learning. This was especially important (or could be more readily implemented) if the student was well educated.

Scripture from creation to the last judgment was the basic subject matter. Instruction was among the priest's highest priorities:

> If you are depressed over having to set aside some other occupation, on which you were already bent as being more important, and on that account are sad and catechize unattractively, you ought to reflect that, . . . it is uncertain what is more useful for us to do, and what is more seasonable, either to interrupt for a while or to stop altogether.[35]

The teacher's attitude helped determine the student's enthusiasm for learning. Augustine thought it better not to teach than to teach ineffectively and without the proper attitude.

For Augustine, understanding was to follow faith. This did not lessen the need to use reason in dialogue with the world. In this way truth could be finally understood without the danger of reliance on the senses.

Notes

1. Eusebius, *Ecclesiastical History,* trans. C. F. Cruse, 9th ed. (New York: Stanford and Swords, 1976), 8.17:345-46.

2. Williston Walker, *A History of the Christian Church,* rev. ed. (New York: Scribner's, 1970), 101.

3. Peter Roberts, *In Search of Early Christianity: The Church United* (New York: Vantage Press, 1985), 44.

4. William Moore and Henry Austin Wilson, "A Sketch of the Life of Gregory," in *The Nicene and Post-Nicene Fathers,* vol. 5 (Grand Rapids: Eerdmans, 1954), 1-8.

5. Gregory, "On the Making of Man," in *The Nicene and Post-Nicene Fathers,* (Grand Rapids: Eerdmans, 1954), 16.9-10:405.

6. Gregory, "The Great Catechism," in *The Nicene and Post-Nicene Fathers,* (Grand Rapids: Eerdmans, 1954), 6:480.

7. Gregory, Prologue to "The Great Catechism," 473.

8. Ibid., 474.

9. Walker, 158-59.

10. John N. Hritzu, "General Introduction," in *Saint Jerome: Dogmatic and Polemical Works,* The Fathers of the Church: A New Translation, ed. Roy J. Deferrari (Washington, D.C.: Catholic University of America Press, Inc., 1965), xv,xvi.

11. Jerome, "Against the Pelagians," in *Polemical Works,* Fathers of the Church, 1:21, 263.

12. Jerome, "Letter 21: To Damasus," in *The Letters of St. Jerome,* trans. Charles C. Mierow, vol. 1 (Westminster, Md.: The Newman Press, 1963), 13:4, 117.

13. Jerome, "Against the Pelagians," 1:22, 264.

14. Jerome, "Letter LII," in *Select Letters of St. Jerome,* trans. F. A. Wright (London: William Heinemann, Ltd., 1938), 207.

15. Jerome, "Letter CCXXV," in *Select Letters of St. Jerome,* trans. F. A. Wright (London: William Heinemann, Ltd., 1938), 419.

16. Jerome, "Letter LIII," in *The Nicene and Post-Nicene Fathers,* trans. W. H. Fremantle, 2d series, vol. 6 (Grand Rapids: Eerdmans, 1983), 11:102.

17. H. De Romestin, "Prolegomena to St. Ambrose," in *The Nicene and Post-Nicene Fathers,* 2d series, vol. 10. (Grand Rapids: Eerdmans, 1983), xv-xvii.

18. Walker, 129.

19. Ambrose, "Three Books on the Duties of Clergy," *The Nicene and Post-Nicene Fathers,* trans. W. H. Fremantle, vol. 10 (Grand Rapids: Eerdmans, 1983), I:1:4, 1.

20. Ibid., "Letter XX," 4:423.

21. Ibid., "Duties of the Clergy," 1:22:100-101, 18.

22. Philip Schaff, "Prolegomena: The Life and Work of St. John Chrysostom," in *The Nicene and Post-Nicene Fathers,* first series, vol. 9 (Grand Rapids: Eerdmans, 1983), 5-16.

23. John Chrysostom, "Concerning the Statues," in *The Nicene and Post-Nicene Fathers,* 1st series , vol 9. (Grand Rapids: Eerdmans, 1983), 15:9, 441.

24. Ibid., 16:4, 446.

25. Ibid., 13:13, 430.

26. *St. John Chrysostom: Baptismal Instructions,* trans. Paul W. Harkins (Westminster, Md.: The Newman Press, 1963), 6:2, 94.

27. Ibid., 10:16, 155.

28. Ibid., 10:30, 160.

29. John Chrysostom, "An Address on Vainglory and the Right Way for Parents to Bring Up Their Children," in *Christianity and Pagan Culture in the Later Roman Empire*, trans. M. L. W. Laistner (Ithaca, N.Y.: Cornell University Press, 1951), 22:96.

30. Ibid., 86:121.

31. Walker, 161-63.

32. Augustine, *Against Julian*, The Fathers of the Church, trans. Matthew A. Schumacher, vol. 35 (New York: Fathers of the Church, Inc., 1957), 5.1.4, 243.

33. Augustine, *The Free Choice of the Will*, The Fathers of the Church: A New Translation, trans. Robert P. Russell, vol. 59 (Washington, D.C.: The Catholic University of America Press, 1968), 1.1.5, 75.

34. Augustine, *The Teacher*, The Fathers of the Church, trans. Matthew A. Schumacher, vol. 49 (New York: Fathers of the Church, Inc., 1957), 11:36, 49.

35. Augustine, *The First Catechetical Instruction*, trans. Joseph P. Christopher (Westminster, Md.: The Newman Press, 1952), 14:20, 46.

10

Women in Education: Ancient Christian Education

Early Christian attitudes toward women reflect the realities of the Greco-Roman world. During this period the place of women in Judaism remained basically unchanged. To understand the role of women in early Christian education (and vice versa), one must remember that Jesus began His ministry and founded Christianity in this social confluence.

The First Century

Jesus challenged the prevailing views of women. He showed little concern when criticized for associating with women. Jesus even engaged women in dialogues that were not only educational but were rabbinic in nature; examples are Jesus' encounter with the Canaanite woman (Matt. 15:21-28 and Mark 7:24-30), His discussion with Martha (Luke 10:38-42), and His conversation with the Samaritan woman at Sychar (John 4:1-26). Two of these educational dialogues fly in the face of socioreligious proscriptions that were not gender related.

Women were among the closest followers of Jesus. The resurrection was first announced to women, and the resurrected Jesus appeared to women. Perhaps the male disciples doubted the women's report because of their disdain for women as witnesses. Apparently the living and resurrected Jesus had a higher estimate of women and their capacity for learning than did His male disciples.

The role of women in the apostolic church is not altogether clear. Many women were among the earliest Christian converts, and women converts were trained in the faith in the same fashion as were men. However, the function of women as educators in the apostolic church (and according to Scripture) is uncertain. The issue is essentially a matter of personal hermeneutics and exegesis.

Ample scriptural evidence exists that women held many significant positions of leadership. In his sermon at Pentecost, Peter included women in a prophetic role in the church and included them in the anointing of the Spirit of God (Acts 2:16-18). Acts 21:9 states that Philip the evangelist had four daughters who were prophetesses. Romans 16:1 mentions Phoebe (as a *diakonos*, translated deacon in the *New Revised Standard Version*) and Mary, Tryphena, Tryphosa, and Persis ("hard" workers in the *New International Version*). In Romans 12:5-8, Paul endorsed no gender distinction in the use of gifts in the church and, in Galatians 3:28, declared that in Christ one is not bound by gender distinctions. On the other hand, Paul shared a different perspective with his protege, Timothy. He regarded women in a much harsher light, requiring of them learning through listening and prohibiting them from teaching (1 Tim. 2:11-14). Paul required silence of the women in church (1 Cor. 14:34) but gave specific direction to Titus regarding the teaching of women:

> Likewise, teach the older women to be reverent in the way they live, not to be slanderers or addicted to much wine, but to teach what is good. Then they can train the younger women to love their husbands and children, to be self-controlled and pure, to be busy at home, to be kind, and to be subject to their husbands, so that no one will malign the word of God (Titus 2:3-5).

Questions many biblical scholars ask regarding this and similar Pauline statements about the role of women in the church relate to how, or to what degree, the apostle may have been influenced by the prevailing male-oriented society of his day or certain localized sociological situations.

The Second and Third Centuries

The *Didache* has only one specific reference to the education of women: parents are admonished to teach their daughters as well as their sons.[1] Otherwise, relatively little is found in the earliest church fathers on the place of women as educators or as the educated. Nevertheless, women equaled and often surpassed men as martyrs in the postapostolic church. However, ecclesiastical power did not consolidate in the women. By accepting the patriarchal societal models of both Hellenism and Judaism, the church chose another course than the egalitarian model of Jesus.[2] Still, some evidence suggests that women were accorded leadership roles that included some teaching responsibilities.[3]

Tertullian (ca. 225) described women as "the gateway of the Devil . . . the unsealer of the forbidden tree . . . the first rebel against the divine law . . ." and blamed them for making the death of Jesus necessary.[4]

Clement of Alexandria (ca. 190) was kinder to women but acknowledged that "a woman is quickly drawn into immorality even by only giving assent to pleasure."[5] He allowed, however, that women were capable of being taught by the church and called for women to be taught equally with men: "They who possess life in common, grace in common, and salvation in common have also virtue in common, and, therefore, education too."[6] Clement almost certainly included women as students in Alexandria.

Women were also among Origen's pupils. Eusebius mentioned several women among Origen's catechumens who suffered martyrdom.[7] Fear of slander regarding his relations with women students, among other factors, motivated Origen to emasculate himself.

Jerome's letters to Laeta (107) and to Gaudentius (128) dealt with the education of daughters as virgins dedicated to Christ. Parents, and in these cases particularly mothers, were responsible for the proper instruction of daughters. Jerome urged Laeta to keep her daughter, Paula, and her attendants away from boys and dedicate Paula to God as Hannah dedicated Samuel. The mother should teach the alphabet using letters carved from wood or ivory; later the mother should guide her daughter's hand as she first learns to write. Her learning should be rewarded with praise and gifts appropriate to her age. Her failures should meet words of encouragement. She should enjoy learning. The mother should teach speech by helping her daughter pronounce the names of persons in Bible stories and by keeping her from poor speech habits. The girl should learn proper behavior and dress.

As the child grew, she was to study the Scripture in a particular order. After all other biblical books have been studied, she could safely deal with the Song of Songs. She should read Cyprian, Athanasius, and Hilary but avoid apocryphal books. She should memorize a Scripture and recite it daily to her parents. Each day was to include the recitation of prayers and singing of psalms at particular hours. She was to learn such skills as weaving and sewing and to develop habits of personal hygiene.[8]

Elsewhere, Jerome evidenced an aversion to women receiving instruction beyond that offered to catechumens. This was one concern as he wrote *Against the Pelagians:*

> But your liberality is so great that, in order to stand well with your Amazons, you have elsewhere written, "Even women ought to have a knowledge of the law," although the Apostle [Paul] preaches that women ought to keep silence in the churches, and if they want to know anything consult their husbands at home.[9]

Jerome chided Rusticus for not being a proper teacher to his wife. He described the woman as the "weaker vessel" and the man as the stronger. Implicit was Jerome's allowance that a woman may teach by the example of her virtue, but he pointed out the misfortune of a man having to learn from his wife.[10]

Like Jerome, John Chrysostom and Augustine had a low view of women and faulted them for many of the sins of men. However, Augustine wrote of the participation of women in the image of God, but only when fulfilling her role of helper.[11] He apparently did not consider women creatures of reason, capable of understanding; a woman could only learn through following the example of her husband.[12]

These latter church fathers gave little place for the instruction of women beyond that which was considered necessary to their functioning as a woman and to salvation. Because of their seductive nature, women should not be trusted with the teaching office of the church. The only teaching role for a woman was motherhood.

Egeria was a female author who lived during the fourth century and kept a diary during pilgrimages to various biblical sites. She may have been a consecrated virgin, but little can be said definitively about her or her education.[13] Her diary includes frequent glimpses of education among fourth-century churches. These descriptions, seemingly addressed to women, are both intriguing and detailed. This is especially true of the latter part of the diary, in which Egeria related particulars of the Jerusalem church's liturgy and educational practices.

Notes

1. *The Didache*, Early Christian Fathers, trans. Cyril C. Richardson (New York: Macmillan, 1975), 4:9, 173.

2. Denise Lardner Carmody, *Women and World Religions*, 2d ed. (Englewood Cliffs, N.J.: Prentice-Hall, 1989), 167.

3. Arthur F. Ide, *Woman: A Synopsis*, From the Dawn of Time to the Renaissance, vol. A (Mesquite, Tex.: Ide House, 1983), 93-94.

4. Tertullian, *Women's Dress*, Fathers of the Church, trans. F. A. Wright (London: George Routledge and Sons, Ltd., 1928), 1:1, 52.

5. Clement, *Christ the Educator,* trans. Simon P. Wood (New York: Fathers of the Church, Inc., 1954), 2:33, 122-23.

6. Ibid., 4:10, 12.

7. Eusebius, *Ecclesiastical History,* trans. Isaac Boyle (Grand Rapids: Baker Book House, 1976), 6.4-5, 223-24.

8. Jerome, "Letter CVII," in *The Nicene and Post-Nicene Fathers,* trans. W. H. Freemantle, 2d series, vol. 6 (Grand Rapids: Eerdmans, 1983), 3-12, 190-94.

9. Jerome, "Against the Pelagians," in *The Nicene and Post-Nicene Fathers,* trans. W. H. Freemantle, 2d series, vol. 6, (Grand Rapids: Eerdmans, 1983), 1:25, 461.

10. Jerome, "Letter CXXII," in *The Nicene and Post-Nicene Fathers,* trans. W. H. Freemantle, 2d series, vol. 6 (Grand Rapids: Eerdmans, 1983), 4:229.

11. Augustine, "On the Trinity," in *The Nicene and Post-Nicene Fathers,* trans. Arthur W. Haddan, 1st series, vol. 3 (Grand Rapids: Eerdmans, 1980), 12.7.10, 158.

12. Augustine, *The First Catechetical Instruction,* trans. Joseph P. Christopher (Westminster, Md.: The Newman Press, 1952), 18:29, 58.

13. Egeria, "Introduction," in *Egeria: Diary of a Pilgrimage,* trans. George E. Gingras (New York: The Newman Press, 1970), 11.

Synopsis
of Part 2

The earliest Christian education resembled Jewish education in nearly every way. The earliest Christians were Jews or Gentiles whose religious sympathies lay with Judaism. A distinctly *Christian* education emerged as the church assumed an identity separate from Judaism.

Christianity's search for permanence and its view of the purpose of human life gave rise to the various expressions and institutions of ancient Christian education. The struggle for survival encouraged the emerging definition of the canon, the creed, and the liturgy, and promoted the institutionalization of the clergy. These were supposed to ensure the continuing presence and purity of the gospel in the face of heresies and persecution.

An important doctrine of persons was developing within the church. Much less agreement existed on the church's doctrine of persons than regarding church survival. It was obvious that God intended for people to live in relationship with Him. What was not so clear was the basic nature of persons. What made them capable of relating to God? What did it mean that people had been created in God's image? How had sin damaged or destroyed the image?

The understanding developed that people (for many of the church fathers—men) were rational beings because they were created in the image of God. This understanding influenced Christian education from that day forward. Its earliest postbiblical manifestation can be found in Alexandria. This made connection with the church's evolving understanding of what it needed to survive. Alexandrian Christians combined the belief that knowledge of and the ability to communicate with the secular world was necessary to the church's continuing influence and existence. The Alexandrian approach has characterized most Christian schools through the centuries.

The Roman imperial government assured the institutional survival of the church by establishing Christianity as the state religion. Augustine exercised far-reaching influence on the development of Christian theology and education. He saw reason as a guard against faulty learning that would come from reliance on the senses. Augustine's approach strengthened the forms of Christian educational curriculum and methodology but also set the stage for the Scholasticism of the Middle Ages.

PART 3

Christian Education
in the Middle Ages

11. Monastic Education

Ascetic Background
Early Desert Fathers
The Monastery and Education
Irish and English Monastic Education
The Cluniac Reform

12. Charlemagne, Chivalry, and the Crusades

The Carolingian Revival
Educational Stages in Chivalry
The Crusades

13. Scholasticism

The Seeds of Scholasticism
Peter Abelard and Conceptualism
Peter Lombard
Thomas Aquinas: The Supreme Scholastic
The Decline of Scholasticism
Strengths and Weaknesses of Scholasticism

14. Medieval Universities

Beginnings of the Medieval University
Abelard
The Corporation
Two Early Models of Universities
Components of the University
The Influence of Medieval Universities

15. Medieval Women and Education

On Being a Medieval Woman
Female Monastic Education
Convent Life
Other Medieval Forms of Female Education
Strengths and Weaknesses of Convents

Synopsis of Part 3

11

Monastic Education

Prior to the end of the fourth century, the Roman Empire, once perceived as invincible, began to show signs of weakness. The empire was divided into eastern and western parts in 286, and these divisions became increasingly important in succeeding centuries. The Eastern portion survived and thrived as the Byzantine Empire until 1453.

Germanic tribes deposed Romulus Augustus, the last Western emperor, in 476. For centuries scholars have analyzed the causes for the decline of the Western Empire. Prominent among the contributory factors was the burden of the ever-increasing army and bureaucracy. In 313 Constantine's Edict of Milan declared that Christians were free to worship without persecution. This reversal in Roman policy also provided for Christians to receive compensation for confiscated property. By the end of the fourth century Theodosius I declared Christianity the legal state religion of the entire Roman Empire. In less than a century, the Christian church changed from a persecuted sect to an established religion.

Because of these laws and the limited economic production of the clergy and religious, some have included Christianity among the causes of imperial decline. The eighteenth-century historian Edward Gibbon, for example, deemed Christianity a major factor in *The Decline and Fall of the Roman Empire*. If the church deserves blame, its share is microcosmic when compared to its macrocosmic efforts for morality, decency, and Christian character in the empire.

The year of 476, more than any other, marks a historical end to the ancient world. The expression *Middle Ages* was coined by historians during the seventeenth century. For purposes of this study, the phrase *Middle Ages* refers to the period in European history beginning in 476 and extending to the death of William of Ockham in 1349.

The term monasticism comes from the Greek *monos*, meaning "alone." Originally monks lived alone in the desert. Although monasticism is not exclusively Christian, increasing numbers of Christian monks dedicated themselves to solitude, primarily for prayer and self-discipline. Eventually these monks banded with other men of similar convictions to form the first monasteries. Almost simultaneously, monastic women called nuns congregated in convents.

The early hermits sought to reach the spiritual condition of Adam prior to his fall; this was believed to require diligent self-discipline. Prayer, meditation, and other disciplines were believed to lead the seeker to the gifts of God.

The purpose of early Christian monasticism was salvation, though monks generally believed in the possibility of salvation outside monasticism. According to ancient monastic accounts, angels appeared to remind some monks that, despite their years in the desert, they had achieved a lower spiritual state than that of some laypersons who lived in the world.

Ascetic Background

Asceticism is the practice of self-denial or even self-punishment for primarily religious reasons. People who follow this life-style are called ascetics.

Greek mystic religions, such as the Pythagorean brotherhood, stressed asceticism. Some ascetic characteristics are found in the practices of the Essenes and Gnostics. Common characteristics of ascetic behavior included denying self of food or sleep for long intervals, wearing rough clothing, exposing the physical body to extreme hot or cold temperatures, refraining from sexual relationships for years or even for life, and whipping or piercing the body with sharp objects.

Some ascetics made a dualistic distinction between spirit and matter. Spirit was held to be pure and good. Matter was evil. Ascetics believed that the body, being matter, was vile and evil, the prison of the spirit or soul. Ascetics reasoned that by inflicting pain on the body and denying innate desires or needs of the body, a person's spirit would be freed.

Such dedicated or detestable behavior, depending on a person's point of view, produced disciplined persons. The perfectors gained followers who were striving to master the ascetic perception of life.

Many early Christians practiced ascetic beliefs. They believed physical life conflicted with spiritual life. To these a denial of physical pleasures led to the possibility of a deeper spiritual existence. Disciplines such as fasting, hard work, and persecution reminded the early Christians of Jesus' life and death on the cross.

In many locations early Christians lived daily with the possibility of martyrdom. Persecution of Christians was common. Anytime a follower denied Christian beliefs, the mission and very existence of the church was thought to be at stake or in question. Therefore, the early church taught its members to endure gladly every form of persecution (1 Pet. 4:12-19).

Some congregations of believers devised what has been termed *schools of martyrdom* to prepare Christians to live and die consistently with their faith. Such instruction was designed to provide acceptable replies to magistrates and to enable a believer to suffer beating with a whip or to die by fire or wild beasts.

Physical exercises and ascetic practices hardened the believer's body, turning attention from the outer person to the inner person. With the same objective, psychological training sought to condition the believer's possible reaction to persecution. In beatings and sufferings, the Christian demonstrated the church's strength and won the admiration of Roman culture.[1]

Early Desert Fathers

In the third century, life was hard for most Christians. They lived amid immorality and vice, and suffered heavy taxation and restrictive laws. There were periods of universal persecution, as during the reign of Decius (ca. 250).

Beginning in Syria and Egypt, many Christians renounced the world and sought solitude in deserts and mountains as "strangers in this world and citizens of the city to come." Under rigorous conditions, thousands chose the life of the Christian hermit. In their minds, they were not embarking upon a new life-style but returning to the apostolic life.

Some hermits achieved notoriety because of competitive degrees of ascetic rigor by such means as wearing weights, going without food and water, among others. Still other hermits became preachers who attracted seekers to the monastic vocation.

The Egyptian **Anthony** (ca. 251-356) is remembered as the father of monasticism. At the death of his parents, Anthony gave away his inherited fortune and turned to the ascetic life. Fifteen years later he became a hermit and lived in a hut on a mountain near the Nile. There, according to stories about him, he struggled through frequent fights with the devil, who in varied ways tried to disrupt Anthony's ascetic practices.

As years passed, followers congregated around Anthony for advice. His followers formed what some scholars identify as the first monastery. Members continued their solitary life but met in a structured way to worship. Although Anthony was illiterate all his life, he was regarded as a man of great wisdom and very loosely represents the beginning of Christian monastic education.

Born in Egypt to heathen parents, **Pachomius** (ca. 292-346) served in Constantine's army for at least one campaign. After military service, he became a Christian and lived the ascetic life on the island of Tabenne in the Nile. Approximately three years later, after studying under an aged hermit, Pachomius organized a monastery and developed a written *rule* to structure the lives of the members. At his death in 346, Pachomius had established nine such monasteries gathering over three thousand monks.

Basil the Great (ca. 329-379) is regarded as the father of monasticism in Asia Minor. He advocated community life but rejected the more extreme asceticism practiced by Egyptian hermits. He introduced the idea of smaller monasteries of no more than forty monks. He valued education and culture in the monastery.

Benedict of Nursia (ca. 480-543) was born into a wealthy family in central Italy. According to the *Dialogues* of Gregory the Great, written about 594, Benedict left home when only twenty to live as a hermit in a cave near Rome. He sought God through prayer and self-torture. Nearby hermits asked him to become their leader, but later his so-called followers tried to poison him, unable to endure his discipline.

In 529 Benedict established a monastery at Monte Cassino, between Rome and Naples. To administer the community, he developed a set of rules consisting of seventy-three chapters and a prologue.[2] This *Benedictine Rule* soon gained acceptance as the standard for other monasteries, and Monte Cassino became the parent monastery of the Benedictine Order.

The *Benedictine Rule* closely regulated the activities of monks. The abbot had absolute authority. The monastery was economically self-sufficient because each monk developed a trade. Article 48 of the *Rule* admonishes: "Idleness is the great enemy of the soul, therefore the monks shall always be occupied, either in manual labor or in holy reading.'' The three main occupations of monks were worship, study, and manual labor. To guard against idleness, Benedict required about nine hours of manual labor daily and an additional two hours of reading from Scripture and other Christian literature. Although Benedict established only twelve small monasteries, his *Rule* preserved his reputation. Benedict is generally considered the founder of Western monasticism, though some would credit John Cassianus or Jerome.

The Monastery and Education

Early monasteries valued manual labor above literary activity. Yet the monastic system required a certain amount of knowledge. To study the sacred writings, monks had to read; to copy manuscripts, they had to write; to comply with worship requirements, they learned to sing; and to set the exact time of the church festivals, some had to calculate the days on the calendar.

The monk took three **vows**, or rules of conduct, upon entering the monastery: chastity, poverty, and obedience. The ideal of *chastity* rejected the importance of human relationships and affections found in homes and families, substituting religious relationships expressed in such spiritual interests as meditation, devotion, and worship. The ideal of *poverty* required the monk to relinquish every economic interest. The monastery was common property. When a person entered the monastery, he sacrificed his goods, property, and claims to inheritance. Thus charity, especially almsgiving, became the highest Christian virtue. The ideal of *obedience* required forsaking rank, distinction, personal interest, individual personality, right of choice, natural human will, and allegiance to other institutions as well as other political and social affiliations for the sake of one's spiritual brothers.[3] All this was done in the name of God.

Limiting human relationships narrowed the approach to moral education. The monastery despised the broadening of culture. Monks aspired to be saints, not scholars; they valued prayers more than poems. Many monks tried to forget what they had learned about poetry, philosophy, and other secular knowledge. Early followers were generally suspicious of the world's knowledge. Memorizing Scripture and the ascetic alphabet produced spiritual knowledge. Monks read to one another during meals to avoid the temptation of bodily pleasure.

Despite its limitations, monastic instruction dominated education in Western Europe from the sixth to the eleventh centuries. Education

during this period was almost exclusively religious. Few other opportunities existed. A study of education in this period illustrates the firm
hold that the church had on society.

At about age ten, boys began monastic schooling. After eight years
of training, they could be admitted to a monastic order. Students who
studied with the intention of joining the order lived at the monastery
and were called *interni*. Parents sometimes gave their children to the
monastery to be educated. Monasteries also received unwanted children.[4]

By the ninth century, monasteries accepted students who wanted to
learn but did not plan to join the order. These *externi* did not live at the
monastery. Both the *interni* and *externi* studied basic subjects: reading,
writing, arithmetic, and religion. Other subjects deemed suitable for
the capabilities of the student were taught as instructors saw fit.

Monasteries also accepted adult Christians. Some of these attended
school while others remained illiterate.

The Scriptorium

The area of the monastery dedicated to the copying of manuscripts
was called the scriptorium. The principal task of those who toiled in
this large room or building was bookmaking and copying Scripture.
Especially in the early development of monastic education, those
unable to perform manual labor were often assigned to the scriptorium.

Most writings that survived the Middle Ages, primarily portions of
the Bible or other sacred books, were preserved by monks. Their work
was highly specialized.

There were at least five stages in the production of books. The first
group of monks prepared the *vellum*, a parchment or animal skin for
binding. A second group copied the manuscripts. In this procedure,
one monk sat at his desk and read aloud while several others sat at their
desks with parchment and pen, writing what they heard—or what they
thought they had heard. A third group corrected any errors they could
find. A fourth group of monks, called illuminators, decorated the
manuscripts with precious stones, colorful pictures, and other designs.
The fifth group placed the finished product in the monastery library,
sold the copies, or traded them for manuscripts in another monastery.
The number of books produced and accumulated depended on such
things as the availability of monks who could write or the focus of
attention desired by the abbot.

Monks who copied Scripture were recognized as having a holy duty.
Frequently a prayer was found on the wall, such as the following

eighth-century entreaty: "O Lord, bless this scriptorium of Thy servants, and all that dwell therein, that whatsoever sacred writings shall be here read or written by them, they may receive with understanding and profit by the same, through our Lord Jesus Christ. Amen."[5]

Ancient Latin texts used only capital letters without punctuation marks or spaces between words. Eighth-century scribes helped the reader by developing a system of small and capital letters and by adding punctuation and spaces between words. After the rise of universities and the invention of movable type, monasteries gave little or no attention to bookmaking.

The Library

The library was a major educational facility in the monastery. Some monastery libraries accumulated hundreds or even thousands of titles, though most libraries were small. The goal was to collect or exchange duplicates produced by the scriptorium.

The library provided a place for the monks to read and study. Monasteries produced many of the finest scholars of the Middle Ages. With few exceptions, the leading thinkers of Western Europe for hundreds of years received their education in monasteries.

Irish and English Monastic Education

During the sixth through the eighth centuries, Western Europe experienced a general period of decline popularly known as the Dark Ages. At this same time, a revival of learning occurred in Irish monasteries, making Ireland more enlightened than her Continental neighbors.

Irish monasteries helped create a more educated population by opening their doors to the laity. Irish scholars of this period, unlike many of their counterparts on the continent, were students of the classics. Unlike Roman clergy, who nearly always used the Latin language, Irish monks maintained interest in the vernacular.

Columba (521-597) was born of royal stock and educated in Gartan, Ireland. He contributed to the excellence of Irish education during the sixth century. With twelve Irish followers, he built a monastery on Iona, an island a mile off the northern coast of Britain. Columba combined an advanced educational program with an evangelistic thrust. He insisted that the monks of Iona support missionary efforts to convert nearby pagan neighbors.[6] Columba died in 597, but his community at

Iona lasted until the Viking invasion of 795. Irish missionaries continued to teach and employ his evangelistic practices in Britain, Gaul, and beyond.[7]

The greatest historian of the early Middle Ages was an English monk named **Bede** (ca. 673-735). He became a student at age seven and studied in the Benedictine monasteries at Wearmouth and Jarrow. Bede wrote commentaries on the works of Augustine, Jerome, and several other saints. He is remembered as the father of English history because of *Ecclesiastical History of the English Nation*. This monumental work sought to reveal the hand of God in historical events. Bede's writing style is characterized by simple, direct accounts, often in story form.

The Cluniac Reform

There were several periods of monastic reform and revival during the Middle Ages. The most significant reform was the Cluniac movement, which began with the founding of the Benedictine monastery at Cluny, France, in 910. The Cluniac monks wanted to discover and revive the best monastic thought of Benedict of Nursia. Yet unlike Benedict, the monks of Cluny sought to integrate monasticism with society. They attempted to eliminate simony, the practice of buying and selling offices in the church, and to enforce the practice of clerical celibacy.

Another contrast to standard Benedictine principles was Cluny's organization. Whereas Benedictine abbeys were constituted independently of each other, Cluny developed a network of up to two thousand monasteries spread across Western Europe.

Five abbots of Cluny (Odo, Maieul, Odilo, Hugh the Great, and Peter the Venerable) provided exceptional leadership to the movement for a period of 211 years. Cluny enjoyed papal support, and when European monasteries experienced difficulty, the abbot at Cluny often responded.

By the twelfth century, Cluny was considered the religious center of Christendom. The largest and finest monastic physical structure in the West was at Cluny. It remained the largest church until the basilica of Saint Peter was completed in the sixteenth century.[8]

Notes

1. S. E. Frost, Jr., and Kenneth P. Bailey, *Historical and Philosophical Foundations of Western Education*, 2d ed. (Columbus, Ohio: Charles E. Merrill Publishing Co., 1973), 111-13.

2. Mehdi Nakosteen, *The History and Philosophy of Education* (New York: Ronald Press, 1965), 144.

3. Kenneth V. Lottich and Elmer H. Wilds, *The Foundations of Modern Education*, 4th ed. (New York: Holt, Rinehart and Winston, 1970), 121.

4. Charles Ashby, *Our Educational Heritage* (Ft. Worth, Tex.: Charles Ashby, 1985), 105.

5. Elias Matsagouras, *The Early Church Fathers as Educators* (Minneapolis: Light and Life Press, 1977), 94.

6. Elmer L. Towns, ed., *A History of Religious Educators* (Grand Rapids: Baker Books, 1975), 69.

7. Nakosteen, 145.

8. Ashby, 101.

12

Charlemagne, Chivalry, and the Crusades

Approximately three hundred years after the barbarians crushed the Western Roman Empire, Charles ascended the throne as sole ruler of the Franks. Nearly thirty years later, on Christmas in the year 800, Pope Leo III crowned him emperor. This act was seen as a restoration of the Roman Empire in the West.

By this time the effectiveness of monastic and cathedral schools had declined. Too often teachers were illiterate, or nearly so. Charlemagne deserved his title "Charles the Great" because he led what some have termed the Carolingian Renaissance.

The Carolingian Revival

Although Charlemagne never mastered the art of writing, he possibly did more than anyone else during the period from 500 to 1000 to improve the quality of education in Western Europe.

The power of the church and popes increased under the rule of Charlemagne. Order and stability in his government contributed greatly to church expansion by military force and missionary activity. In uniting most of Europe for the first time since the Roman Empire, Charlemagne contributed significantly to papal power.

Charlemagne did not follow the ascetic way, but he strongly supported improvements in monastic education. In 787 he declared that bishops and abbots should promote the study of letters. Shortly thereafter, Charlemagne directed the establishment of a school in each monastery or bishopric. Charlemagne assigned officials to enforce his decrees. In 797 the church required town and village priests to maintain schools for teaching children without cost.

Another of Charlemagne's edicts declared that priests would hear prayers in languages other than Latin, Greek, or German. This encouragement of the vernacular influenced the development of Christian education because it made prayer and Scripture available to common people who did not speak Latin, the primary and usually exclusive language of the classroom and church.

Alcuin and the Palace School

After attempting to establish a school with two leaders, Charlemagne chose **Alcuin of York** (735-804) to head his palace school in 782.[1] He had already been a successful student, teacher, and headmaster of the cathedral school of York, England. He brought his library to Charlemagne's court:

> His entire library contained fourteen books—five grammars, three rhetorics, one book from the Bible, one volume of the incomparable Isidore, excerpts from two minor Latin writers, one set of dialogues (unspecified), some notes on Cato, and a lone arithmetic which—from the notation following its name—may or may not have belonged to him.[2]

This was considered a high quality library in 782!

Another indicator of Alcuin's English and Irish educational heritage involved his tolerance of the Greek and Roman classics. Alcuin valued these authors, especially Virgil, though many of Alcuin's contemporaries attributed these pagan writings to the devil.

Five features best describe the teacher Alcuin. First, simplicity, sincerity, and honesty describe his character. Second, his students enjoyed his company and considered him an exciting person. Alcuin presented new ideas and imaginative methods. He made learning fun. Third, he valued individuals; he encouraged each student to identify and pursue his own talents. Fourth, Alcuin reduced complex principles to his students' ability to understand. Fifth, he believed in the ability of his students; he expected them to do well.[3]

Because one of his students was the eager Charlemagne himself, the palace school often followed the itinerary of the student. Charlemagne's traveling court included the king, his family, high-ranking assistants, wives, sisters, and children. Mostly illiterate, his students sought instruction in church matters and, as a whole, favored a broad education.

Alcuin used a conversational method because Charlemagne enjoyed puzzles, riddles, epigrams, and acrostics. Alcuin used positive motivation,[4] avoiding the disciplinary beatings commonly accepted and encouraged during his time.

The palace school attracted scholars and students from all parts of the known world. Representatives of the king's court traveled far to obtain or copy the best available writings. In the process, they developed the Carolingian minuscule handwriting technique that later became a model in printing. Library holdings increased in both Christian and classical titles.

Improved song schools developed voices for choirs in the cathedral worship services. Gregory the Great (ca. 540-604) had placed high priority on music. His musical school, the *Schola Cantorum* in Rome, served for centuries as a reminder of music's important place in instruction and worship. Song schools appeared in cathedral and noncathedral churches. The choirmaster directed the instruction in music and other subjects.[5]

In 804, Alcuin died. The message of reform challenged future generations through his students such as Rabanus Maurus (776-856).

Somewhat later King **Alfred the Great** (871-899) effected educational reforms in England with methods similar to those Charlemagne had brought about on the continent. Alfred gave an eighth of his income to his palace school and other educational causes. He established schools and imported scholars for both old and new schools. Under his influence English common law placed increased emphasis on moral principles. He partially directed the compiling of the *Anglo-Saxon Chronicle,* a prose work about the Teutonic conquests of England.[6] He also ordered the translation of important works from Latin into English, including *Pastoral Care* by Gregory the Great, *Consolation of Philosophy* by Boethius, *Universal History of the World* by Orosius, and *Ecclesiastical History* by Bede.[7]

Feudalism

After Charlemagne's kingdom divided and subdivided several times, there was a general breakdown of authority. The land was divided in an emerging system known as *manorialism.* This system, which tied tillers of the soil to the land, continued with little change into the nineteenth century in parts of Europe.

Feudal society produced three class structures. The *nobility* received grants from the king in exchange for military support. The *clergy* composed the second group. Part of the clergy served under the bishop, who was considered of noble rank. The other members of the clergy took monastic vows and were relegated to the monasteries. Finally, the lowest class, the *peasant* or *serf*, produced crops for his lord. The serf was bound to his lord's land. If the land changed ownership, the serf passed with the land. The system held together with promises of land and service. In some cases, a lord would free a serf. If so, he became known as a "freedman."

Eventually, nobles organized in a system known as *feudalism*. According to this system, each noble received a feud from his lord, who in turn received lands from a lord over him. Lords received their lands in exchange for military support. Peasants (or serfs) worked the land in exchange for the nobles' protection.[8]

At times powerful kings such as Charlemagne managed to integrate power in a central state, but during most of this period there was little central authority.

The Church's Power

The church exercised more power than any other institution in feudalism. In every important event of life, the church demonstrated service and power. The church documented birth by baptism. The priest or another church official performed a couple's wedding ceremony. Finally at death the church officiated again.

The church accumulated massive land holdings over this period. Although clergymen were not expected to participate in physical warfare on the battlefield, they exercised ecclesiastical control with other weapons. Excommunication, for example, removed a person completely from the church and took away opportunity to go to heaven at death. If excommunication failed, a process of interdiction occurred. This action closed churches located on that lord's land, thereby removing all the services of the church from the people. Because of the outcry of the lord's vassals, his submission to the church's power was inevitable.

The church often officiated agreements between lords and serfs. Probably the saddest aspect of this procedure involved the descendants of the man who bargained away his freedom. Records from eleventh-century monks at the monastery of Marmoutier, near Tours, are typical of such transactions of feudalism:

> Be it known to all who come after us, that a certain man in our service called William, the brother of Reginald, born of free parents, being moved by the loved of God and to the end that God—with whom is no acceptance of persons but regard only for the merits of each—might

look favourably on him, gave himself up as a serf to Saint Martin of Marmoutier; and he gave not only himself but all his descendants, so that they should for ever serve the abbot and monks of this place in a servile condition. And in order that this gift might be made more certain and apparent, he put the bell-rope round his neck and placed four pennies from his own head on the altar of Saint Martin in recognition of serfdom, and so offered himself to almighty God. The following are the witnesses who saw and heard what was done.[9]

As this quotation illustrates, a careless act or a desperate move by a family member could seal the fate of all his descendants. The lord gained assurance of future service by binding the serf's children. Under these conditions, a significant number of serfs at death had not traveled more than ten miles from their place of birth.

Were these conditions unchristian? Not according to one eleventh-century scholastic teacher. The following is a portion of a letter from this teacher in response to a monk's request to save his sister from unjust serfdom:

What concern is it of monks—men who have resolved to flee the world, or under what name? Is not every man born to labour as a bird to flight? Does not almost every man serve either under the name of lord or serf? And is not he who is called a serf in the Lord, the Lord's freeman; and he who is called free, is he not Christ's serf? So if all men labour and serve, and the serf is a freeman of the Lord, and the freeman is a serf of Christ, what does it matter apart from pride—either to the world or to God—who is called a serf and who is called free?[10]

Educational Stages in Chivalry

This statement from the eleventh-century sounds strange to modern readers because it reflects the medieval value system of *chivalry*. According to the chivalrous order of values, each person is assigned a placed in society at birth, and that person must accept his or her role. Even the clergy, which in some ways was a "third estate" between nobility and peasantry, had its own distinctions between clerics of noble birth and those of common birth.

Children of the lower class received little formal education. In the home, parents instructed their children to comply with their place in the structure, master certain religious beliefs, learn superstitions and beliefs about their world, and relate with proper manners to equals and superiors. Also the child learned a skill or trade to serve his lord. Usually this was the same labor as the parent's.

Children of nobility needed education to prepare them for their future. The children of the privileged freemen needed to learn methods of government, management skills for large estates, and the military profession. Four basic stages comprised this educational process.

During his first six years a boy remained in his parents' home and learned basic skills. Usually at age seven the boy, known as a "page," served in the manor house of the lord, in the castle of the great lord, or in the court of the king. At this point, the royal lady supervised or educated the young man in a variety of subjects such as religion, music, manners, etiquette of love, rules of honor, basic writing, reading skills, Latin, and the vernacular language. A man provided the page with physical training such as boxing, wrestling, gymnastics, and basic military skills.

Usually at age fourteen, the boy became a personal servant of the lord and his lady. At this stage the young man was called a "squire." He might set the table, work in the house, groom the horse, clean the armor, polish the shield, or accompany his lord at the tournament or in battle. The squire prepared himself for military service by hunting, fencing, swimming, riding, jousting, or falconing. He often learned to play musical instruments like the harp, sing, or play chess.[11]

Any man from any class could gain the title of "knight," but this honor nearly always rested on sons from noble families. At age twenty-one, after advancing through the preliminary stages, a young man could become a knight. This initiation occurred through a feudal ceremony in a church, castle, or palace. Part of the formality included fasting and a night of prayer before an altar where his sword rested. A lecture detailed his duties, and he swore three vows. He vowed loyalty to the church, honor and loyalty to his superiors, and gallantry and loyalty to his lady. Next, he was touched on each shoulder by a sword and proclaimed a knight. Symbolic of his rank, he received a gold chain, sword belt, sword, and spurs.[12]

The ideal knight—as pure, gallant, honorable, just, generous, chaste, humble—was a rare exception. In general, too many knights or nobles were ruthless, selfish, cruel, scheming, and untrustworthy.

The Crusades

When Jerusalem fell to the Turks in 1071, passage by Christian pilgrims to and through the holy lands was hampered or denied. This was important for the practice of penitence. The Turks continued their invasions, and approximately twenty years later, the Byzantine emperor, Alexius Comnenus appealed to Pope Urban II for military aid.

At the invitation of Urban, thousands of noblemen and churchmen gathered at Clermont, France, in 1095 to challenge Europe's leaders to rescue the Holy Land and defeat Islam. Urban's sermon greatly stirred his listeners. He requested them to forsake fighting one another and, instead, to free the Holy Land!

Thousands responded but with different motives. Some sought land and other material gains; many desired adventure and fame; merchants joined the cause to develop potentially profitable markets in distant and nearby lands; and knights, trained to fight, sought added respect for their bloody trade. Regardless of the reasons, a certain restlessness released both response and support. Even those who were unable to go in person sponsored others in their stead. Something was in the movement for everyone.

Religion provided the highest motivation. Some identified the sufferings of Christ as their strongest incentive to act. Others sought the salvation of their souls. The response from both Christian and non-Christian was less than unanimous. Many monks opposed the Crusades. Out on the extended boundaries, where land owned by Christians and Moslems joined, a less than aggressive spirit often prevailed. Many members of the Eastern Church voiced opposition as well.

Yet, the church rewarded those who took up the sword to serve. Faithful crusaders benefited from a promise of plenary indulgence. This decree stated that if a person died "in a state of grace, their sins shriven and pardoned, they could be sure of heaven and be spared any cleansing of sins in purgatory before they went there." [13]

The *Song of Roland* echoes the plenary indulgence theory:

Barons, my lords, Charles picked up for this purpose;
We must be ready to die in our King's service.
Christendom needs you, so help us to preserve it.
Battle you'll have, of that you may be certain. . . .
If you should die, blest martyrdom's your guerdon. . . .
You'll sit on high in Paradise eternal.
The French alight and all kneel down in worship;

God's shrift and blessing the Archbishop confereth,
And for their penance he bids them all strike firmly.[14]

At least eight expeditions to reconquer the Holy Land were attempted.

The first and probably most successful Crusade occurred in 1095, and the final Crusade marked the fall of Acre in 1291. Possibly the most tragic story of the 200-year period of the Crusades was the Children's Crusade of 1212. A sermon by twelve-year-old Stephen of Cloyes, a French shepherd, motivated as many as thirty thousand French children of noble and peasant heritage, many less than twelve years old, to march toward the Holy Land. Some died in route to the sea. When the sea failed to part as promised, disappointment prevailed. Hunger and cold accounted for other deaths. Two merchants offered seven ships. What the children perceived as an answer to prayer, though, resulted in disaster. Two ships wrecked at sea. The other five landed in Algiers only for the children to discover that the merchants had sold them to Moslem slave traders. None arrived in the Holy Land. And legend has it that only one returned to France in 1230.[15]

From a religious point of view, the Crusades failed shamefully. A distorted social balance resulted as thousands relocated either along the way or after the conflicts. More importantly, scores of thousands died in battle or other ways related to the Crusades.

From an economic perspective, the Crusades impoverished nobles and strengthened kings. However, desired trade increased between the East and West, and cities, especially in Italy, grew rich and powerful.

The Crusades produced cultural opportunities and contacts with the East. Centers of scholarship continued to develop and contribute to learning. Intellectual treasures hidden from the West for centuries emerged in abundance. The observational approach to learning practiced during this time in the Moslem world eventually subdued the authoritarian approach that had cradled Christian thought and Western scholarship.[16]

After the Crusades, both manorialism and feudalism declined but did not disappear. The size of many demesnes decreased and the number of serfs grew smaller. The crusades provided an opportunity to practice the system of chivalry. The invention of gunpowder early in the fifteenth century initiated radical changes in the method of warfare and changes in the education of knights.

Notes

1. William Boyd and Edmund J. King, *The History of Western Education,* 11th ed. (Totowa, N.J.: Barnes and Noble Books, 1980), 119.

2. Luella Cole, *A History of Education: Socrates to Montessori* (New York: Rinehart, 1950), 123.

3. Ibid., 127-28.

4. Ibid., 129.

5. Pierre J. Marique, *History of Christian Education,* vol. 1 (New York: Fordham University Press, 1924), 139.

6. Mehdi Nakosteen, *The History and Philosophy of Education* (New York: Ronald Press, 1965), 161.

7. William Boyd and Edmund J. King, *The History of Western Education,* 11th ed. (Totowa, N.J.: Barnes and Noble Books, 1980), 123.

8. Elmer H. Wilds and Kenneth V. Lottich, *The Foundations of Modern Education,* 3d ed. (New York: Holt, Rinehart and Winston, 1961), 132.

9. R. W. Southern, *The Making of the Middle Ages* (New Haven, Conn.: Yale University Press, 1953), 98-99.

10. Ibid., 104.

11. Nakosteen, 165.

12. S. E. Frost Jr. and Kenneth P. Bailey, *Historical and Philosophical Foundations of Western Education,* 2d ed. (Columbus, Ohio: Charles E. Merrill Publishing Co., 1973), 130-31.

13. Rosalind Brooke and Christopher Brooke, *Popular Religion in the Middle Ages* (New York: Thames and Hudson, 1984), 59.

14. Ibid., 60.

15. Jerald C. Brauer, ed., *The Westminster Dictionary of Church History* (Philadelphia: Westminster, 1971), 183-84.

16. Frost and Bailey, 145.

13

Scholasticism

During the ninth and tenth centuries, ecclesiastical abuses increased rapidly as leaders extended the church's influence in defense, government, and real estate. At the dawn of the second millennium, the church held confusing positions on many matters of faith.

By combining philosophy with Christian theology, church leaders created a medieval synthesis which became known as "Scholasticism." With this application of reason to revelation, some church leaders thought that religious beliefs could gain a correct philosophical construction and expression. By the middle of the fourteenth century, Scholasticism defined religion in narrow detail.

Each Scholastic teacher or philosopher regarded himself as a Christian educator. In reality, few Scholastic professors or philosophers displayed legitimate interest in popular education.[1] The teacher stated a problem, and the students compiled arguments for and against solutions. Then, each student logically and rationally proposed his own solution to the problem. In an attempt to find a balanced solution, all arguments were systematically considered and criticized.

Within the period from 1050 to 1350, often called the High Middle Ages, the basic doctrinal framework of the Roman Catholic Church emerged. Thomas Aquinas (1225-1274) was the architectural master of Scholasticism. Since the thirteenth century, his influence on Catholicism has remained significant. In 1879 Leo XIII described Thomas Aquinas as the "safest guide" in solving problems dealing with liberalism. The following year Aquinas was proclaimed the patron saint of Roman Catholic schools.

The Seeds of Scholasticism

The metaphysical argument over universals is older than Plato and Aristotle. Now, more than twenty-three hundred years later, this discussion continues.

Johannes Scotus Erigena (ca. 815-877) is commonly considered the first Scholastic. Erigena, "the greatest intellectual of the Carolingian Renaissance and the one truly original thinker of the Dark Ages,"[2] was an Irish scholar who headed the palace school of Charles the Bald at Paris.

Erigena's knowledge of the Greek language alone qualified him as a unique Western mind of his period. He organized a Neoplatonic system to defend church teachings. Yet, in combating the heresies of his time, he ventured beyond the doctrinal guidelines of the church fathers and orthodox theology.

Similar to earlier apologists, Erigena equated true philosophy with true religion. Arguing primarily from reason, he forced church dogmas to agree with philosophy. His mystic and, in some cases, pantheistic views led him to deny the reality of evil and hell. Later, when thirteenth-century pantheists used Erigena's views to support their beliefs, the church condemned much of his writing.[3]

There was increasing controversy during the eleventh and twelfth centuries between the Neoplatonic realism, which supported reason as man's principal means of knowledge, and nominalist philosophy, which recognized observation and experiment as supreme.

Anselm (1033-1109), the chief realist, was born of a noble family in Aosta, Italy. After studying under his famous teacher Lan'franc, Anselm began preparation toward becoming a Benedictine monk at Bec in Normandy. He served as prior of Bec for approximately fifteen years and then as abbot of Bec for about the same amount of time. In 1093 Anselm became archbishop of Canterbury. In this high position, he differed with the kings over the independence of the English church and with the pope's role in England. As a result, on two occasions, Anselm was exiled from English soil.[4]

Following deductive reasoning and Augustinian principles of faith, Anselm proposed his ontological proof for the existence of God. His use of reason as a method of understanding God departed from tradition. Anselm declared that faith and reason share the same origin, method, and conclusion; yet faith precedes and judges reason.[5] In an effort to harmonize faith and reason, he wrote in his *Monologue on the Method in Which One May Account for His Faith:*

I do not seek to know in order that I may believe, but I believe in order that I may know.

The Christian ought to advance to knowledge through faith rather than come to faith through knowledge.

A proper order demands that we believe the deep things of Christian faith before we presume to reason about them.[6]

Anselm taught and wrote in specific and technical language. He pioneered the dialectic method. Although Thomas Aquinas rejected the validity of Anselm's argument for the existence of God, Descartes (1596-1650) later used a similar argument.

During Anselm's lifetime, the French theologian Roscellinus rejected Anselm's argument, arguing that only individual senses were real; therefore, reason not only preceded faith but also served as a foundation for all knowledge. If this were true, the validity of church dogma and of revealed knowledge would become acceptable truth only when proved by reason. The council of Soissons rejected Roscellinus's philosophical system as heresy and forced him to recant.[7]

These opposing views provided entirely different concepts of religious matters, such as whether the universal church or particular churches best represented the reality and authority of the meaning of "church." The critical inquiry of Roscellinus continued in Abelard, who had studied under Roscellinus at Loches in Brittany.

Peter Abelard and Conceptualism

Abelard (1079-1142) was born in Pattet, Brittany, in France. His father, a knight, desired that his son pursue a military career, but Abelard followed philosophical interests.

Strong characteristics of brilliance and erratic antitraditional behavior were evident early in his life. Abelard relentlessly rejected both the content and method of his teachers. He studied under Roscellinus, a nominalist, and also under William of Champeaux, a realist. In the end, Abelard developed conceptualism, which was philosophically between realism and nominalism but closer to the latter. Whereas both realism and nominalism had claimed to represent Aristotelian logic, Abelard's view was closer, in reality, than the other two. It became a more widely accepted philosophy as well.

Abelard's use of dialectics helped turn theology from mystical meditation toward scientific investigation. Abelard found the essence of Christian teachings in the classics. He stated that there was less difference between the pagan writings and the Gospels than between the Old Testament and the New Testament.

Sic et Non (yes and no), the best example of Abelard's dialectic method, was written as a textbook for his students. In this book, Abelard stated 158 doctrinal propositions, sometimes called "sentences," and for each statement he presented quotations both to support and reject the proposition. The sources of the quotations were the Bible, the church fathers, and other church authorities. This procedure alarmed and embarrassed church leaders. It was a serious blow against authoritative knowledge as exercised by the church. Radical disagreement between the sources cast doubt on the church as the repository of eternal truth. Abelard claimed that the dialectic procedure was intended to stimulate readers and to discover truth. He defended the right of individuals to question all dogma, including church dogma.

Whereas Anselm had earlier expressed ultimate confidence in faith as truth, Abelard began his journey toward truth with the process of doubt. Wisdom for Abelard germinated from frequent questions. He regarded reason as superior to faith and accepted only the matters of faith that were confirmed by reason. His view of faith differed radically from traditional dogma. Abelard stated: "A doctrine is not to be believed because God has said it but because we are convinced by reason that it is so."[8]

Abelard's fiercest opponent was Bernard of Clairvaux (1090-1153). Bernard was a monk and later abbot who gained fame as a preacher. Personally associated with his student, Pope Eugenius III, Bernard traveled across Europe preaching in favor of the antiheretical Second Crusade.[9] Although Bernard was never pope, some have compared his power to that of popes. Because he considered Abelard a threat to the church, Bernard organized the condemnation of Abelard. Despite this condemnation, a modified version of Abelard's teaching appeared in the writings of his student, Peter Lombard.

Peter Lombard

Peter Lombard (ca. 1095-1160) was born in Lombardy in northern Italy. Lombard studied at the universities of Bologna, Reims, and Paris. From approximately 1140, he held a theology chair at the University of Paris. In 1159 he was named bishop of Paris and died shortly thereafter.

At the University of Paris, Peter Lombard studied under Abelard. Lombard could not deny or ignore the conflicts found in Abelard's *Sic et Non*. In contrast to his teacher's resistance to authority, Lombard's reverence for authority made him a friend of the church. His attitude differed from that of Abelard, but he used Abelard's dialectical method. As a scholastic, Lombard employed reason. He contended that God is knowable in a minimum of three ways. In addition to faith and reason, Lombard added the empirical study of God's works.

Although Peter Lombard was a prolific writer, his greatest contribution to scholasticism and medieval education was his four books of *Loci* (sentences). This was a collection of statements from the Bible, the church fathers, and other authorities. Lombard systematically gathered these statements around doctrinal themes: creation, incarnation, redemption, and the sacraments. Lombard cataloged these statements in an attempt to resolve the theological problems that Anselm had raised.

Written between 1147 and 1151, the *Sentences* became the most important theological textbook until the Reformation. An accepted procedure for university students in theology was to prepare a commentary on the *Sentences*. For this reason, Lombard has often been called "the master of the Sentences."

Although he is not considered an original thinker, at the point of instructing Christians about the sacraments, Lombard was the master. Prior to Lombard, the accepted number of sacraments varied from two to twelve. Because seven was considered the number of perfection, the idea of exactly seven sacraments was rapidly and widely accepted by the church. The seven sacraments as taught by Lombard became orthodoxy at the Council of Florence in 1439.[10] Later, the Council of Trent confirmed that action and recognized the sacraments as a means of grace.

The definition of a sacrament that has stood the test of time came after Lombard. Rooted in beliefs of Augustine, Thomas Aquinas defined a sacrament as "a visible form of invisible grace." The three essential parts of a sacrament were *matter*, as in water for baptism; *form*, the correct words; and *ministrant*, the ecclesiastical representative or a person designated by the church.[11] The seven sacraments that Peter Lombard suggested are those that the Roman church follows today: baptism, confirmation, the Eucharist, penance, ordination, marriage, and extreme unction.

Thomas Aquinas: The Supreme Scholastic

Thomas Aquinas (1225-1274) is generally recognized as the greatest Scholastic. With intricate detail, he synthesized Christianity with Aristotelian philosophy. Thomas was born in Aquinas,[12] near Naples, Italy, as the seventh son in his family. At age five his parents placed him in school at the Benedictine abbey of Monte Cassino. As a physically large person, Aquinas moved slowly and acted calmly. He finished with the lowest marks in his class. For these reasons and perhaps others, Thomas was nicknamed "the dumb ox" early in his schooling.

Aquinas

Biographical Facts
- Born near Naples, Italy.
- Gave Benedictine oblate at Abbey of Monte Cassino.
- Was student and teacher primarily at University of Paris.
- Dominican, "the Order of Preachers."

Writings Related to Education
- *Summa Theologica*
- *On the Teacher,* his basic philosophy of education
- Commentaries on books of the Bible
- Commentaries on principal works of Aristotle
- Commentary on Peter Lombard's *Sentences*

Influence on Christian Education
- was the most important scholar and thinker in the Middle Ages
- was mastermind of Scholasticism, a synthesis of Aristotelian logic and church dogma
- is the patron saint of Roman Catholic education.

After studying at the New University of Naples from 1240 to 1244, Aquinas resolved to join the "order of preachers." Thomas' parents wanted a more prosperous life for their son than that of a religious beggar. At age nineteen, he left home to study at the University of Paris and become a Dominican. During the journey to Paris, however, his brothers kidnapped Thomas and imprisoned him for over a year in the family castle. In a variety of ways, the family members attempted to persuade Thomas not to follow a religious vocation. At last, with the assistance of his mother, Thomas escaped and traveled to Paris.[13]

At the University of Paris, Aquinas studied under Albertus Magnus (ca. 1200-1280) also called "the first of the great schoolmen" or "the organizing intellect of the Middle Ages."[14] Much of Albertus's identity hinges on his being the teacher of Thomas Aquinas, but Albertus deserves recognition as a writer of practical books and school manuals. In an age when Aristotle's writings were considered heretical, Albertus, with the help of Moslem commentaries, compiled a comprehensive review of Aristotle's works.[15]

From 1248 to 1252, Thomas continued his studies under Albertus, who by this time had moved to the University of Cologne. In 1250 Thomas was ordained a Dominican priest. After returning to Paris in 1252 he lectured on the Bible and Lombard's *Sentences*. In 1256 he became a master of theology. His most significant teaching occurred at the University of Paris in courses beyond the liberal arts curriculum. In 1257 Thomas wrote *Concerning the Teacher*, which outlines many of his principles of education.

In 1265 he began his masterpiece, *Summa Theologica*. This work attempted to explain Christian theology with the aid of Aristotelian metaphysics and epistemology. This represented a radical departure from what had been the traditional approach to Aristotle. Aquinas stirred bitter conservative voices within the church.

Another reason for the *Summa* was Thomas's intention of writing a textbook to replace Lombard's *Sentences*. This did not become a reality until several centuries after the great Dominican's death. The *Summa* consisted of over two million words. It focused on 512 questions, each subdivided into from one to ten other subsubdivisions. All of this was designed for the Catholic scholars and theology students at a time when Catholics were discouraged from reading the Bible for their own interpretation.

Thomas considered both *faith and reason* epistemologically reliable, and he declared that these two could not conflict because the ultimate source of both was God. As a method of knowing, reason constituted a philosophical base while faith represented a theological foundation. The rational workings of the universe provided an example of Aquinas's theory of natural theology. In his famous proof for the existence of God, Thomas accepted by faith the fact that God exists. Without question, Aquinas presented both faith and reason as viable methods of obtaining knowledge, but he believed that faith was always superior to reason. Conflicts that seemed to exist between faith and reason represented false logic.[16] For Aquinas, education was considered a human right, and the civil government had a responsibility to that end. According to

Aquinas, human laws in no way should contradict divine laws. This represents Thomas's lofty view of the church as supreme in all matters.

Aquinas believed that certain seeds of knowledge existed in all people. God was the initiator of this action, and man without God was incapable of knowledge. The student could acquire knowledge in one of two ways: by a natural cause or by instruction.[17] In Aquinas's thought, all humans desired knowledge and happiness, which were found only by knowing God.

The Thomistic teacher was to lead the student from the unknown to the known. Teaching was an art, and it was impossible without God, the principal teacher.[18]

The educational methodology of scholasticism included a variety of epistemological possibilities. According to Aquinas, reason supported what people had learned by faith, but reason could not overrule revelation.

Thomas Aquinas continued to develop his *Summa Theologica* until about a year before his death. As the result of a mystical experience, Aquinas stopped writing. The experience caused Thomas to describe all that he had written as straw when compared to the heavenly vision.

Aquinas died in 1274 while journeying to the Council of Lyons.[19] His disciples finished the *Summa Theologica,* using his other works.

Thomas Aquinas was the most important scholar of the Middle Ages. His educational influence through the centuries is perhaps best evaluated by his influence on Catholic schooling. As a theologian, he was chiefly responsible for the influence of Aristotelian philosophy on Roman Catholic dogma.

Given the enduring quality of Roman Catholic dogma and polity, Aquinas's interpretation and application of Aristotle remains a cornerstone of Catholicism. Unfortunately, a significant portion of Aristotle's "truth" has been disproved by his own methods. (Vatican II perhaps in a limited way came to a similar conclusion when it modified some schemata as "too scholastic.")

Nevertheless, the educational influence of Thomas Aquinas continues. The most recent Catholic Code of Canon Law in 1983 recommended that seminary students study dogmatic theology "with St. Thomas as their teacher in a special way."

The Decline of Scholasticism

Two scholars contributed to the decline of Scholasticism. Both of these were Franciscans, students at Oxford University, and critics of Thomas Aquinas. The two were **John Duns Scotus** (ca. 1266-1308) and his student, William of Ockham (ca. 1285-1349). After studying at Oxford and Paris, Scotus wrote the customary commentary on Lombard's *Sentences* for his master of theology degree. Scotus was an original thinker during a traditional period of church history. He criticized Aquinas as too theoretical. As an extreme realist, Scotus had a higher appreciation for faith than reason.[20] In fact, he viewed theology as unreachable by reason; therefore, neither faith nor reason needed to prove the other. He became so ridiculously engrossed in teaching against the priority of reason that his students called him *dunce*.

Scotus's greatest difference with Aquinas involved the concept of God. John Scotus considered the *will* of God rather than the intellect as primary. This view became central in the philosophy of William of Ockham, his student. Ockham, unlike Scotus, was a nominalist.

Some have called **William of Ockham** the most influential theologian of the fourteenth and fifteenth centuries, but more scholars have considered him the last of the great Scholastics. Nearly his whole adult life was characterized by critical reaction.

In Ockham's commentary on Lombard's *Sentences* and a series of lectures that followed, church officials found fifty-one heretical statements. Imprisoned by the church in 1324, he remained under house arrest until 1328 when he fled with the leader of the Franciscans. They found refuge in the court of Emperor Ludwig of Bavaria, an enemy of the pope. Later William wrote pamphlets critical of the church, and as a result the pope excommunicated him.

According to Ockham, reason did not validate or disprove faith. Although separate from faith, sense experience along with reason represented the highest form of knowledge.[21] In matters of teaching faith, the acceptability of belief as Christian doctrine was based on the authority of the church.

Instead of developing his own systematic philosophy, William mainly reacted ecclesiastically, politically, philosophically, and educationally to Scholasticism. His influence later led Martin Luther to reject Scholasticism and turn to a more simplistic explanation and teaching of the Scriptures. Also, Ockham's heavy emphasis on sense experience paved the way for modern empirical philosophy.

Believing that God was beyond all knowledge, Ockham rejected Aquinas's proof of the existence of God. At the same time, he dismissed the illumination theory of Bonaventure (1217-1274) and insisted that God could be known only by faith.[22]

William of Ockham is also remembered for an educational method known as *Occam's Razor.* Whereas Aquinas advocated an extrapolative proof, often called "hair-splitting," Ockham stressed simplicity, which must have delighted his students. Ockham advocated the most direct explanation of truth as best; to multiply unneeded hypotheses was a waste of time and energy. Therefore, much explanation could be "shaved" from the argument. His students and critics called this method *Occam's Razor.*[23]

Strengths and Weaknesses of Scholasticism

Scholasticism became a dominant system of thought in the late Middle Ages. Several strengths and weaknesses characterize this philosophy. It provided the Roman Catholic church with a synthesized doctrine of the Christian faith. This stability was an important and powerful ingredient in bringing together the divergent doctrinal ideas of the church fathers. Second, the schoolmen of this period were the principal shapers in the origin and early development of the university movement. Third, the foundation for current Catholic parochial schools can be found in this period. Fourth, during the scholastic period, the production of fine arts reflected the work of the church. Fifth, the preservation of religious and human heritage by the church merits praise. Sixth, the great attention given to the intellectual nature of humans deserves recognition.

The weaknesses of Scholasticism are numerous. First, scholastic thought was used to maintain the status quo. Instead of providing a means for future knowledge, this system celebrated the past. Second, the church's acting as the monopoly of truth, in spite of conclusive evidence of proof from other areas of life to the contrary, caused internal harm to the mission of the church. Third, the intellect of humankind benefited from the scholastic method. However, the intellect of humans, as important as it is, can be developed out of proportion to the other important aspects of living. During this period, the intellect received an abundance of attention while other areas of life suffered.

Fourth, Scholasticism hardly addressed the needs of the common people. Education existed in another language and for another world. Latin was the language of the church and the classroom. During the scholastic period, Greek became important again. Therefore, formal education remained unavailable to the ordinary person.

Fifth, Aristotelianism enslaved the church. The blind acceptance of Aristotle as nearly infallible illustrated historically that the method can distort the message. Sixth, Scholasticism often debated meaningless issues in a serious manner. For example, how important is it to spend several hours theologically discussing the number of angels that can stand at one time on the head of a pin?

Notes

1. Robert Ulich, *A History of Religious Education* (New York: New York University Press, 1968), 72.

2. Hugh Wamble, *History of Christian Thought CHO212* (Nashville: Seminary Extension Department of Southern Baptist Seminaries, 1969), 163.

3. Tony Lane, *Harper's Concise Book of Christian Faith* (Cambridge, Mass.: Harper and Row, 1984), 81-82.

4. James Mulhern, *A History of Education,* 2d ed. (New York: Ronald Press, 1959), 237-38.

5. Lane, 82.

6. B. R. Hergenhahn, *An Introduction to the History of Psychology* (Belmont, Calif.: Wordsworth, 1986), 58-59.

7. Elmer H. Wilds and Kenneth V. Lottich, *The Foundations of Modern Education,* 3d ed. (New York: Holt, Rinehart and Winston, 1961), 126.

8. Ibid., 127.

9. Mulhern, 240.

10. Lane, 87.

11. Ibid., 88.

12. Wamble, 173.

13. Jerald C. Brauer, ed., *The Westminster Dictionary of Church History* (Philadelphia: Westminster, 1971), 50.

14. Elmer L. Towns, ed., *A History of Religious Educators* (Grand Rapids: Baker Books, 1975), 71-72.

15. Ellwood P. Cubberley, *The History of Education* (New York: Houghton Mifflin, 1920), 191.

16. Hergenhahn, 59.

17. E. H. Gwynne-Thomas, *A Concise History of Education to A.D. 1900* (Lanham, Md.: University Press of America, 1981), 59.

18. Towns, 74.

19. Paul Nash, *Models of Man: Explorations in the Western Educational Tradition* (New York: John Wiley & Sons, 1968), 166.

20. Towns, 72.

21. Charles Ashby, *Our Educational Heritage* (Ft. Worth: Charles Ashby, 1985), 129.

22. Mulhern, 242.

23. Kenneth O. Gangel and Warren S. Benson, *Christian Education: Its History and Philosophy* (Chicago: Moody Press, 1983), 115.

14

Medieval Universities

The rise of the universities in the twelfth century is perhaps the highest educational achievement of medieval Europe. Historians often refer to this period as the twelfth-century Renaissance.

With the resurgence of currency and invention of gunpowder, the economic, political, and social shackles of feudalism loosened. Many tillers of the fields moved to the cities. The membership of guilds increased while the importance of the nobility declined.

On the foreign front, the church enlisted thousands to wage war against the Moslems for the Holy Land. At home, inquisitors rode across the lands seeking sacred souls infected with the deadly seeds of heresy. Great Gothic cathedrals towered into the sky in praise to God and as monuments to the arrival of skilled master craftsmen.

Beginnings of the Medieval University

Various factors contributed to the rise of universities in medieval Europe. Among these were Islamic influence, church schools, Scholasticism, and the guild system. The existence of Arab universities before similar European institutions is not mere conjecture. The Egyptian University of Al-Azhar, founded in Cairo around 970, is one of the oldest universities in the world still in operation. Other Arab universities also existed before this time.

Although European scholars before 1000 were fortunate to collect fifty books for their libraries, some educated Arabs held collections of five hundred volumes or more.[1] Early in the ninth century, the Caliph al-Mamum assembled in Baghdad a large number of intellectual treasures that he called his "House of Wisdom." It constituted the accumulation of Islamic thought in script. Even more impressive, al-Hakam

II, an Arab ruler of Cordova, collected six hundred thousand books and other learned materials in his palace and sixty-nine other places.[2]

The organization of medieval European universities was "directly modeled after their earlier Islamic counterparts."[3] The Arabs contributed much to education. They simplified the Roman numeral system with the Arabic numerals used today. Other contributions in mathematics included the foundations of algebra and trigonometry. More directly related to the Middle Ages was their preservation of classical writings, especially Aristotle's. Through Scholasticism, Aristotelian philosophy helped to shape Roman Catholic theology. European scholars rediscovered many works of Aristotle from Arab translations.

A second contributing factor in the origin of the university was church schooling. Although not always directly under the auspices of the church, monastic education excelled in the preservation of chronicles and other knowledge. The Benedictine order from Monte Cassino, the Cluniac reform movement, and the abbey of Bec, in Normandy, served as excellent examples of dedicated monks who recorded intellectual tradition through the Middle Ages.

More important than monastic education in the establishment of medieval universities was the cathedral school. The term *cathedral* comes from a Greek word meaning "seat." These schools existed at the administrative headquarters of the diocese where the bishop presided. Cathedrals became the center of public life with educational activities primarily for training clergy. In general, the bishops who led or supervised the cathedral schools were more receptive to new ideas and influences than the abbots of the monasteries. By the twelfth century, good teachers attracted many students in some of the cathedral schools. Abelard taught several thousand at the cathedral school of Notre Dame in Paris. His teaching attracted the students necessary to establish the university at Paris.

Other diocesan schools included the song school, parish school, and chantry school. The song schools trained boys musically for cathedral worship. Additional training, usually in religion, reading, and writing, was offered by the choirmaster. Some parish priests established schools in their homes and other places. These became known as parish schools. Chantry schools developed later and served in a limited way. The chantry was an endowment for a priest to perform certain activities in the mass. Traditionally, this priest also taught children.

Abelard

Scholasticism and the schoolmen from this period constitute a third factor in the development of the university movement. Abelard is an excellent example. At one time, he lectured using unorthodox content and method to approximately five thousand near the site where the University of Paris originated. Few people in history have possessed such skill in debate and such undisciplined behavior. In a day when teachers were challenged in open debate, Abelard soundly defeated more than one of his teachers. Nicknamed the "indomitable rhinoceros," Abelard taught his students to doubt until logical evidence had been submitted otherwise. His methods created enemies in the church; his success in teaching caused jealousy from his colleagues; and his celebrated love affair with the beautiful and brilliant Heloise resulted in his castration.

Few teachers in history have approached Abelard's popularity. When he walked the streets of Paris, people of all backgrounds, especially women, accompanied him or simply gazed at him through their windows. He disregarded tradition and taught his students to speculate. Abelard did not record his educational methodology, but he created an indelible contrast with the authorities of his time.

Luella Cole has identified six characteristics that distinguished Abelard and his teaching from his contemporaries. First, while traditional teachers approached their students in a solemn, dignified manner, Abelard's lively teaching evoked a response from his students. Laughter, uncommon in the medieval classroom, often burst from students who heard Abelard lecture.

Abelard's Teaching Methods

- Lively presentation
- Blended ideas from various disciplines
- Involved current affairs
- Approached every subject with assurance
- Logical development of ideas
- Passionate defense of truth as he understood it

Second, Abelard blended ideas from one field of study to enhance his teaching in another. For example, if the Song of Songs were his topic, he might discuss current ballads of the troubadours. In other words, he was relevant and interesting. Third, his ideas served as intellectual weapons vividly and dramatically zooming across the war zone of his classroom. A student might not know the topic of the day, but he knew the class would be exciting.

Fourth, Abelard approached every subject with assurance. He expressed his thoughts vividly with assurance and no uncertainties. A teacher's authoritativeness, as Cole correctly points out, breeds popularity; students prefer to disagree with a professor than to find nothing in a lecture that stimulates their reaction. Fifth, Abelard taught systematically and logically from introduction to conclusion. He keenly disproved the complex positions of others. In debate, he was never satisfied simply to defeat his opponent. Abelard deliberately dismantled the opposition unmercifully, idea by idea. Sixth, he passionately shared what he perceived as truth. As gossip stirs in a small town, Abelard sincerely and psychologically got in touch with his audience.[4]

The Corporation

This separation between educators and church authority, which already had appeared in Abelard, was furthered by the formation of the university along the lines of the *guild system* that appeared in Europe shortly after the year 1000. The guild, or *universitatis*, was a corporation formed by a group of merchants or craftsmen, a cathedral chapter, or a community of monks. The primary purpose of this association was protection and security. As the urban areas increased in size, the developing middle class of merchants and professionals needed workers in their trades.

The charter granted to the guild was most often obtained from the pope, emperor, or king. The guild was less dependent on local church authorities than the cathedral or monastery. Craft guilds, nearly free from church control, often helped support priests in exchange for the provision of religious needs to their members. Such a priest often taught school, usually in the vernacular. This became known as the *burgher school movement*; the town supported the school, but the church shared control with the town.[5]

The guild's informal and technical education extended over three distinct stages. In the beginning, the apprentice worked under a master without pay, except for necessities, for seven years. If this proved to be a positive experience, the worker acquired the title of journeyman and began earning limited wages. After three years, the journeyman became a master; he could then own a shop, hire journeymen, and train apprentices. To become a master, the journeyman was required to submit his masterpiece before other members of the guild. Upon their approval, the master became a teacher of others.[6]

The medical university applied this same technique to higher learning. The master taught, and the student prepared his masterpiece, a thesis, as a prerequisite for the profession of teacher. Teachers in theology, law, and medicine organized themselves into guilds. Teachers' guilds played an important part in the development of early universities such as the one at Paris.

Two Early Models of Universities

Two distinct types of universities developed. In southern Europe, universities stressed law and medicine, while northern universities were more closely governed by the church. A contrast between the university at Bologna and the university at Paris is presented in chart 1.

At **Bologna**, the more mature students organized into guilds to protect themselves from exploitation by citizens who sought to charge students high prices for necessities. Since classes met in rented or public places, students often threatened to move the university to another location. This was unlikely at **Paris** because classes had a fixed place to meet in the cathedral or one of the churches. As the number of students increased at Bologna, Paris, and other locations, businesses around the sites grew dependent upon the universities. Places of entertainment and specialty shops appeared early.

Shortly after the inception of universities, both church and state recognized the potential benefits of control by granting charters. In 1200 the French king granted the university at Paris a royal charter. The masters who taught at Paris soon received special rights and privileges. The church actively sought the university's attention as well. The Fourth Lateran Council at Rome in 1215 provided direction in worship, teaching, learning, and curriculum.

A conflict in 1229 between the citizens of Paris and the university scattered professors and canceled instruction for two years. The university resumed in 1231 after intervention by Pope Gregory IX. He issued statutes that created the office of chancellor to administer the university, required professors to take oaths, demanded the sacred

Two Models of Early European Universities

Chart 1

Categories	Southern Model (University of Bologna)	Northern Model (University of Paris)
ORIGIN	• From law school in the 1000's • Italian schools not connected with cathedral or monastic schools	• Primarily from cathedral school • Religious roots
SPECIALIZATION	• Bologna specialized in law • Most other southern European universities specialized in law or medicine but usually included religion	• Nearly all Northern universities specialized in religion but usually included law and/or medicine
STUDENT	• Older, successful professionals • Controlled university by student guilds who hired professors: —punished tardy or absent teachers —used boycotts on professors —granted permission for teacher's absence	• Younger, less professional • Organized into four "nations" 　1. the French 　2. the Norman 　3. the Picard (including the Low Countries) 　4. the English (including Germany and Northern Europe)
PROFESSOR	• Subject to student's legalistic regulations —lecture to begin on time and finish within one minute of bell —posted bond when out of town —deleted difficult material equaled a penalty —fined when less than five students enrolled for a class	• Controlled and administered university by teacher's guilds —charged fees to train students —granted degrees —tried own members for heresy —freedom of speech exceeded the rights of most other people
CURRICULUM	• Seven liberal arts • Nature of curriculum decided by students • Law and/or medicine	• Seven liberal arts • Curriculum decided by teachers • Theology
ORGANIZATION OF FACULTY	• Professors organized into a "college." After passing an examination administered by professors, the master was certified with a license to teach.	• Received license to teach from the chancellor
FAMOUS EARLY TEACHERS	• Irnerlus (c. 1050-1130) • Gratian (c. 1080-1150)	• William of Champeaux • Peter Abelard • Hugo of St. Victor (1097-1141)

language of Latin as the only accepted tongue of instruction, and provided a means for the discipline of scholars. In 1246 Pope Innocent IV claimed papal authority over the university, but serious attempts to enforce this soon dissolved.[7]

In the early 1200s political disputes between Henry II of England and Louis VII of France, combined with other problems in Paris, caused students and masters to withdraw from the University of Paris and establish studies at Oxford and later at Cambridge. These two remained the only such institutions in England and Wales until 1828, when the University College of London appeared.[8]

In England, the Gloucester Grammar School Case of 1410 involved teachers appointed by church officials who sued other teachers for establishing a competitive school and lowering tuition. The court ruled against the church's monopoly rights, declared any qualified person could establish a school at his or her own risk, and reserved the right of parents to choose the school for their children's education. This case served as a precedent and has helped to shape court decisions concerning schools and universities to the present.[9]

A school of medicine at Salerno, begun by Greeks around 1080, may have been the first university in Europe. Greek, Jewish, Arabic, and other sources of knowledge provided the curriculum. In 1224 Salerno merged with the University at Naples.[10]

Another university was founded at Padua about 1222 by scholars from Bologna. Portia, in Shakespeare's *The Merchant of Venice*, had studied law in Padua.[11] Some universities appeared and remained while others appeared and disappeared. By 1500 there were nearly eighty universities in Western Europe.

Components of the University

The medieval university originated in a simple design, yet higher instruction today in many ways resembles its beginnings in the Middle Ages. Any such school by definition concerns teachers, students, curriculum, methods, degrees, and privileges. Although these function together, the distinctiveness of each is presented in this section.

Teachers

Several important schoolmen were mentioned in the previous chapter on Scholasticism, and Abelard was discussed previously as a forerunner of the University at Paris. In addition, two mendicant orders, the Franciscans and the Dominicans, provided the universities with the leading theologians in the late Middle Ages. Both groups of friars ministered outside the cloister.

Francis of Assisi (1182-1226), the mystic, founded the **Franciscans** in 1209. The son of a wealthy merchant, he rejected his inheritance and chose a life of poverty to serve the poor and helpless. He opposed military power and violence but favored discipleship training for women. Francis did not advocate classical scholarship, but he often taught unfortunate people in the vernacular. Francis, the little poor man, wanted to be like Jesus. In the early stage of the university, some of the most important Franciscan teachers were Roger Bacon (1214-1292), Bonaventura (1221-1274), John Duns Scotus, and William of Ockham.

Dominic (1170-1221), a Spaniard, founded the Dominicans in 1216. As he traveled from village to village, Dominic led a small group of barefooted preachers in ministry. The **Dominicans,** more than the Franciscans, served the educated and the wealthy. Whereas previous monastic orders had stressed manual labor, the Dominicans emphasized the intellect and, therefore, taught in Latin. The church largely entrusted the Inquisition to Dominicans. Two important Dominican teachers have already been discussed under Scholasticism, Albertus Magnus and Thomas Aquinas.

Because they begged and did not charge fees to students, the Franciscan and Dominican schoolmen often attracted many students.[12] In general, other professors wore noble gowns and long gloves as they lectured; these sought popularity because their wages depended on students' fees.

Students

Many students wandered from university to university, attended classes as they desired, and worried little about degrees. Since academic qualifications for basic study hardly existed, students could attend several universities before developing skills of reading and writing. This remained true until the Reformation.

Some students left home in their early teens to study and did not return until they were thirty or forty years old. The average age of students at Paris was probably about fifteen. University students were generally older and more mature in southern Europe than in northern Europe.

If unable to read, the serious student attached himself to a master until he could read, write, and speak Latin, which was the learned language of the Middle Ages.[13] Students were classified as local or nonlocal. The term used to describe the place where the local scholar studied was the *studium particulare* while the place to study for nonlocals was called *studium generale*. In time these designations also applied to the geographic region where a graduate could gain a license to teach. By the end of the fourteenth century the terms *studium generale* and university were synonymous.[14] As indicated on chart 1, students and professors from the *studium generale* organized into four nations for power, privileges, and protection.

At the completion of a student's study in the areas of liberal arts and other assignments prescribed by his instructors, he was examined. If successful, he earned recognition as a bachelor of arts. The term *baccalaureus* originated at least as early as the feudal system and meant "beginner." Early in the thirteenth century the amount of time designated at the University of Paris for the completion of these studies was four years.

Curricula and Textbooks

The foundational subjects for medieval instruction consisted of the seven liberal arts. Studies were divided into two groups—the trivium (the three) and the quadrivium (the four). The studies of the trivium (grammar, rhetoric, and dialectic) resemble the humanities in the modern university. These three courses served as prerequisites for the quadrivium (geometry, arithmetic, astronomy, and music). These four required a comprehensive understanding of Latin, which was developed in the trivium.

For the medieval mind, the number seven contained mystical qualities. As the number for perfection, seven indicated completeness. Textbooks presented the seven liberal arts to the learner. Four of the most important textbooks need at least brief elaboration:

- *On the Marriage of Philology and Mercury* by Martianus Capella. This allegorical presentation was written by a pagan from North Africa in the early fifth century. Mercury's bride, the studious maiden Philology, is accompanied by seven bridesmaids. As the wedding ceremony progressed, each of the seven branches were revealed in detail. During the Middle Ages, this served as a textbook for the liberal arts more often than any other.
- *Consolation of Philosophy* by Boethius (ca. 480-524). This Roman

statesman and philosopher influenced medieval education more than Capella. Boethius wrote on a variety of subjects, but his *Consolation of Philosophy* and other philosophical writings helped to retain a limited knowledge about Plato and Aristotle during the Dark Ages. In addition, his music textbook, *De Musica*, was used in universities until the eighteenth century.

- *On the Liberal Arts and Sciences* by Cassiodorus (ca. 490-585) outlined each of the disciplines for monastic education. This writer prescribed the number *seven* for the number of liberal arts, using Proverbs 9:1 as his proof text ("Wisdom hath builded her house, she hath hewn out her seven pillars" [KJV]). Under Cassiodorus's influence, monasteries began collecting and copying manuscripts.
- *Origins* by Isidore of Seville (ca. 560-636) was an encyclopedia combining all worthy knowledge. Other important contributions were Aesop's fables; *On the Education of the Clergy* by Rabanus Maurus (786-856); and the selected writings of Alcuin. Major works in Scholasticism have already been cited.

Methods

The Latin language was used extensively in the medieval universities. Since the cost of books exceeded the means of nearly all students, the teacher carefully read a passage from the textbook and expounded its meaning. Some students attempted to copy the oral reading while others simply listened.

The *lecture* was the principal method of teaching. Usually a lecture lasted two hours, and normally the conscientious student attended three lectures each school day. The study of metaphysics often began at approximately 6:00 a.m. Two kinds of lectures, the ordinary and extraordinary, were delivered. The ordinary lecture was more important because it was read by a master and given in the morning, the preferred time. The extraordinary lecture was presented in the afternoon by students who read notes from previous lectures.

The other method of teaching was debate or *disputation*. An individual or a group of students challenged another person or group in consideration of a thesis. Both parties raised objections and argued differences. In disputations, the professor served as a trainer for his student. This debate often served as a prelude for defending a masterpiece. With the intense competition of debate, the atmosphere produced a sporting spectacle of scholarship.

As discussed earlier, scholastic reasoning in the teachings of Abelard,

Bacon, Aquinas, William of Ockham, and others broke with traditional methods. This form of instruction provided the impetus for modern scientific inquiry.

Degrees and Privileges

Since the Middle Ages the academic assembly in which degrees are conferred has been called a commencement. This term dates back to the early days of the university. When a candidate passed an examination and delivered a lecture, he "commenced" to teach. The bachelor of arts qualified its recipient to study for other degrees. Study for the master of arts usually lasted three or four years.

The master's degree awarded in the Middle Ages gradually became the doctor of philosophy degree of the twentieth century. The current master's degree is relatively new.

The privileges for scholars have greatly changed since the beginnings of the medieval university. In the thirteenth and fourteenth centuries, these included an exemption from taxes, military service, and trial by civil court. Professors have lost such rights and privileges as the right to set prices for necessities, the right to a trial by colleagues, and the right to move the institution. However, they have retained the important right to confer degrees.

The Influence of Medieval Universities

Modern universities resemble their medieval ancestors in organization and degree nomenclature. European universities during the thirteenth and fourteenth centuries helped preserve past knowledge while laying a foundation for future education.

In methodology, the combination of the university movement and scholastic inquiry created the beginning of a break with deductive reasoning. This process gave birth to modern science.

In addition to preserving knowledge and birthing modern science, the universities influenced other important expressions of human life. These institutions produced leaders who addressed critical questions to the coming generations. Many of the arguments against the church raised in later decades by Martin Luther and others originated in medieval classrooms.

The democratic structure and practice of the early universities brought a new factor into European life, in addition to church and state. In this role, some universities criticized the papacy in social, economic, civic, and even religious matters. The university at Paris even assisted in solving the papal schism that resulted in the so-called Babylonian captivity of the church.

The university's democratic model inspired writers and leaders who later penned documents and conceived doctrines in civil government and church polity. The government of the United States and the congregational polity of some Protestant churches demonstrate possible roots from the medieval universities.

To be certain, early universities, in their proud formality but simple essence, displayed numerous weaknesses. Yet, these institutions progressively collated intellectual interests and initiated a perpetual institution that has taken its place in the same company with other builders and shapers of the mind such as the church and state.

Notes

1. Luella Cole, *A History of Education: Socrates to Montessori* (New York: Rinehart, 1950), 151.

2. Richard E. Gross, ed., *Heritage of American Education* (Boston: Allyn and Bacon, 1962), 152.

3. Ibid., 153.

4. Cole, 174-76.

5. E. H. Gwynne-Thomas, *A Concise History of Education to A.D. 1900* (Lanham, Md.: University Press of America, 1981), 65.

6. S. E. Frost, Jr., and Kenneth P. Bailey, *Historical and Philosophical Foundations of Western Education*, 2d ed. (Columbus, Ohio: Charles E. Merrill, 1973), 162.

7. Gwynne-Thomas, 63.

8. James Mulhern, *A History of Education*, 2d ed. (New York: Ronald Press, 1959), 279.

9. Mehdi Nakosteen, *The History and Philosophy of Education* (New York: Ronald Press, 1965), 213.

10. Cole, 141.

11. Pierre J. Marique, *History of Christian Education*, vol. 1 (New York: Fordham University Press, 1924), 83-84.

12. Ellwood P. Cubberley, *The History of Education* (New York: Houghton Mifflin, 1920), 163.

13. Paul Monroe, *A Text-book in the History of Education* (New York: Macmillan, 1913), 124.

14. Robert S. Hoyt, *Europe in the Middle Ages*, 2d ed. (New York: Harcourt, Brace and World, 1966), 325.

15

Medieval Women and Education

Historians have traditionally written about the events of the Middle Ages in the masculine gender. Histories of wars, politics, and the church illustrate male dominance. Constructing a reliable history of female educational accomplishments is difficult because accounts of medieval history have most often been written for men, by men, and in the context of a "man's world."

This chapter briefly introduces female monastic education from the beginning of nunneries to the mendicant orders and presents personalities who were involved in these movements, both female and male.

On Being a Medieval Woman

The subservient role of the woman permeated every expression of medieval life. Her designated inferior rank received validation especially from the church. The majority of early Christian authorities blamed humankind's fall on Eve in particular and woman in a generic sense.

The female's religious leadership role progressively decreased throughout the Middle Ages. For example, the synod of Orleans in 533 abolished the office of deaconess. It ruled: "No woman shall henceforth receive the *benedictio diaconalis,* on the account of the weakness of this sex."[1] Outside of monasticism, the woman's place in the church lacked recognized authority.

The prescribed and accepted domain of medieval women was the home. Throughout the Middle Ages, the church sanctioned procreation and the avoidance of fornication as reasons for marriage. In the twelfth century, Peter Lombard offered additional marital incentives: "reconciliation of enemies, money and the nearest to a mention of love: beauty."[2]

At an early age, the girl's father usually arranged her marriage. Love, attraction, and personal choice were seldom considered as important factors in the parent's choice. Though contrary to modern Western thought, these marriages, more often than not, progressed into a genuine relationship of love and/or endured in a practical fashion. Faced with few other options, the general success of this traditional marriage must be credited to the efforts of women.

Survival, more than pleasure or happiness, was the goal of the medieval woman. Before the age of antiseptic safety, the woman spent a large portion of her adult life either pregnant or nursing children. Serious injury or death often occurred during childbirth. If the woman did not become pregnant, she received the blame. In every way, the typical medieval male looked upon his wife more as his personal property than as his partner. Perceived by the public as having less rational ability and human perfection, women in some cases survived against nearly insurmountable odds.

A double standard of legal rights favored males in cases of adultery, divorce, polygamy, and nearly all other matters. For economic reasons, male children were generally more wanted than females. This was not new in the medieval period because agricultural civilizations have historically expressed this male preference.

Female Monastic Education

In the Middle Ages, the children of peasants, serfs, and other lowly socioeconomic groups nearly always received their meager education from their parents. Such a female could expect her mother's limited instruction in proper behavior as related primarily to manners, religion, superstitions, and housework. The possibility of more educational opportunities for females came almost exclusively to the daughters of the noble and rich. In some cases, tutors visited or lived in the homes of noble families, or a young girl might live for a while under the guidance of a noble woman. In the Middle Ages, however, a woman's best educational opportunity was the convent.

Convent Life

Convents probably appeared first in the Egyptian desert during the early fourth century. Pachomius organized these cloisters with a focus

CHRISTIAN EDUCATION AND THE MIDDLE AGES
Chart 2

	Goals of Education	Woman and Education	Personalities
MONASTICISM	• Save the soul • Disciple physically and morally • Produce saints, more than scholars • Instruct the clergy • Master the ascetic way	• Convents • Best available educational opportunity for women of the age	• Benedict of Nursia • Columba • Charlemagne • Alcuin of York • Alfred the Great
CHIVALRY OF FEUDALISM	• Serve superiors and provide example to lesser ranks • Social instruction • Military readiness	• Educated for homemaking and sometimes to assist absent husband • Directed the progress of young children and often the pages • Trobairitz • Exercised artificial graces	• Charlemagne • William IX, Count of Poitiers • Bertran de Born • Countess of Die
SCHOLASTICISM	• Guard church dogma • Incorporate faith and logic into consistent truth • Develop intellectual discipline	• Women rarely included and most often debased	• Aristotle • Anselm • Peter Abelard • Peter Lombard • Thomas Aquinas
CHRISTIAN MYSTICISM	• Experience union with God • Dogma and authority of institutions often conflicted with mysticism	• Individualistic approach provided welcome place for women	• pseudo-Dionysius • Hildegard • Bernard of Clairvaux • Hugo of St. Victor • Meister Eckhart • Gerhard Groot • Teresa of Avila

CHRISTIAN EDUCATION AND THE MIDDLE AGES
Chart 2

Role of the Teacher	Role of the Student	Curriculum	Methodology
• Train a student (begin about age 10) • Admit to order (begin about age 18) • Model the ascetic way • Provide instruction	• Reproduce the past • Develop a trade for the present • Prepare for the world to come • Deny the body, the enemy of the soul	• Scriptures • Writings of the Church Fathers • Latin Language • Seven Liberal Arts	• Monastic vows —chastity —poverty —obedience • Asceticism • Catechetical • Scriptorium • Seclusion
• Develop virtues, especially courage and service to God, the king or lord and his lady • Prepare the student for his place in society	*Noble Class* • Four stages of chivalry with approx. ages: —Home training (0-6) Pago (7 13) —Squire (14-20) —Knight (21-) • Master the arts of war, religion and love	• "Seven Free Arts" • Influenced the use of vernaculars • Stories and songs	• Tournaments • Battles • Music • Example • Art of listening • Storytelling
• Mental disciplinarian and • Spiritual leader	• Rational and spiritual being • Development of the intellect	• Aristotle • Church dogma • Latin and Greek • *Sic et Non (Yes and No)* • *Four Books of Sentences* • *Summa Theologica (Summary of Theology)*	• Dialectic • Disputation • Synthesis • Reason • Faith
• "The way to God is to descend into one's self." —Hugo of St. Victor • "Reality can never be explained; it can only be experienced."	*Follow Stages* • Purgation • Purification • Illumination • Unification	• Prayers • Sacred literature • Individual perception regarded higher than study and reason	• Asceticism • Intuition • Revelation • Experience • Supernatural (visions and voices) • Prayer

on personal spirituality. Western monasticism for women originated in 412. Caesarius of Arles is credited with the organization of this first group, and his sister Caesaria administered it. In early convents, only virgins and widows were permitted to join. Another significant time of development was the early 530s. Benedict of Nursia, along with Scholastica, his twin sister, founded a convent similar to the earlier ones. Their vows of chastity, poverty, and obedience included what would become part of the standard *Benedictine Rule*. Soon, under the capable leadership of Scholastica, the number of Benedictine convents increased rapidly to rival the number of monasteries.

The convent did not begin as a school, nor did all convents have schools. However, many convents developed a school for girls, and some convents later established infant schools for boys as well. Substantial fees were charged for board and tuition, so expensive in some cases that even the nobles could hardly pay.

Nuns were often the daughters of the aristocracy. A craftsman's daughter rarely studied at the nunnery, and a serf's daughter almost never. Money, more than social class, was the major reason. Despite canon law and monastic rule, nunneries usually required parents to provide land, cash, or something of worth for the girl's dowry.

The church attempted to rule the nunneries, but each abbess often interpreted the rules by her own standards. In the tenth century, an abbess was permitted to rule double monasteries—monasteries of both nuns and monks living in adjacent communities. Such an exception was rare.

The daily Benedictine schedule of activities included prayer, work, and study. Seven worship services occurred daily. The nun arose at 2:00 a.m. for matins in choir, followed by lauds. She was back in bed by dawn and slept three hours. At 6:00 a.m., she said prime. Other services followed during the day. At 7:00 p.m. during winter and 8:00 p.m. during summer, she was directed to bed.[3] Between some worship services, nuns often copied and illustrated manuscripts.

The spiritual quality of personal and corporate worship varied according to the abbess and the women in residence. The *Rule of Saint Clare* required confession twelve times yearly and Communion seven times yearly on special holidays. Some nuns put stones in their shoes and others whipped themselves in hopes of becoming more spiritual.

In the fine arts, some nuns developed outstanding writing abilities. One such case was Herrad, a twelfth-century abbess in Alsace who, with assistance from her nuns, compiled the *Garden of Delights*. It was an encyclopedic collection of knowledge for the full education of the nun—everything a nun should know including history, religion, philosophy, science, and Latin.[4]

Music was a special concern in the convent. During the thirteenth century at the abbey of Las Huelgas, Abbess Berenguela formed a choir with over one hundred nuns and forty children. They sang complex arrangements. Conservatories were available to some nuns as well.

Originally the *Benedictine Rule* required domestic work by all nuns. As the thirteenth century dawned, serious domestic work by nuns was the exception rather than the rule. Larger convents employed cooks, brewers, bakers, priests, bailiffs, porters, and maids.[5] A combination of overexpenditure and incompetent administration partly explains the retarded development of some convents and monasteries.

Medieval monasticism was chiefly a male activity. In thirteenth-century England, six hundred Augustinian and Benedictine monasteries housed fourteen thousand men. At the same time, one-hundred and forty convents were home for three thousand women. The male monasteries were much larger and better endowed.[6]

Roswitha (ca. 930-990), a noble German daughter, distinguished herself as her country's first woman poet and playwright. In classical Latin, she wrote comedy, verse, history, drama, and prose. Her style reflected a highly intellectual person who conversed and wrote of classical and biblical literature. None of Roswitha's writings circulated widely within her lifetime, but later these were translated into English and German. Without much recognition she contributed to the development of the Catholic doctrine of the virgin Mary's Immaculate Conception. Already by the tenth century, Hrotsvitha [Roswitha] (ca. 930-990), the learned Saxon canoness, incorporated many of the popular stories of Mary's life in a verse legend about the virgin. Everything about the events and Mary's behavior demonstrated perfection. She was conceived without sin (the Immaculate Conception).[7]

Hildegard (1098-1179), the tenth child of the Count of Spanheim, was born in the German Rhineland of Bockelheim. At age seven, she entered the Benedictine convent at Disibodenberg under the direct tutorage of Jutta, the abbess. Hildegard read widely and developed competence in Latin, Scripture, music, and other disciplines.

At thirty-eight, she succeeded Jutta as abbess. Shortly thereafter Hildegard began to record visions that had haunted her for years. In her lifetime, this German mystic corresponded with popes, emperors, kings, queens, dukes, counts, and other royal persons.

Hildegard's principal work, *Know the Ways of the Lord,* was written between 1141 and 1151. Ten nuns assisted her in drawing and writing her mysteries about God. She also recorded twenty-six mystical revelations under the title of *Scivas.* The *Book of Divine Works* dealt with revelations and contained an extended explanation of the human body.[8]

Her *Book of Simple Medicine* listed nearly three hundred herbs. She described their medical use and how to pick them. This same theme was continued in *Book of Medicine Carefully Arranged,* which cataloged forty-seven diseases and offered causes and cures for them. According to Anderson and Zinsser:

> She explained that disease came from disruptions to the body's equilibrium and suggested physiological insights centuries ahead of her time, including the circulation of the blood, the ties between sugar and diabetes, nerve action to the brain, and contagion. She commented on the development of the female reproductive system, including descriptions of adolescence from twelve to fifteen and noticed the tendency for women to miscarry or produce defective infants if they conceived before twenty or after fifty.[9]

Hildegard also wrote *Book of Life's Rewards,* a set of allegorical dialogues between vices and virtues. Another area of her creative contributions was music. *Symphony of the Harmony of the Heavenly Revelation* included seventy-seven devotional songs for special feast days.

As an outspoken Christian leader, she sought reform within the church. Corruption in clergy caused her to plead with her audience to consider the Scriptures, not priests, as authority in matters of salvation. She died in Rupertsberg in 1179 but has never been canonized by the Roman Church.

Other Medieval Forms of Female Education

Certainly the convent constituted the most pervasive medieval educational movement for women. Monastic life and education prevailed from the beginning through the end of the Middle Ages though its relative importance has since declined. Other attempts to educate medieval women related directly or indirectly to monasticism.

One of the early monastic leaders who recognized women as spiritual equals was the Irish missionary and churchman Columba. His influence contributed to the later development of double monasteries.

Charlemagne's palace school did not admit women with the exception of his family members and other significant female relatives of his court. Still he insisted that his daughters learn to read, write, and recognize geographical facts.

From the time of the Carolingian churchmen until the end of the medieval period, council after council for monastic reform benefited women less and less. The egalitarianism of English double monasteries faded, and monks moved to other monasteries. In the tenth century, the Cluniac reform movement limited prestige for women in the higher echelons of society. It created no new abbacies for women. The Gregorian reform movement placed even greater restrictions on female education and monasticism.[10]

The chivalric code assumed that females were helpless and inferior. The ideal, educated, polite, gracious, brave, and kind medieval knight who rescued women in distress hardly existed.

Aristocratic daughters were educated to become charming socialites. They learned housekeeping and domestic abilities such as sewing and embroidering. The royal education of the courts differed from the convent. Chivalry gave more emphasis to social graces and less to religious and intellectual development. While the lord of the castle hunted and fought in war, others administrated the estate. This allowed some women the opportunity to practice skills in mathematics, administration, and decision making.

Many women accompanied their **husbands** on the Crusades. Thomas Aquinas in his *Summa Theologica* approved the husband's involvement in the Crusades without the consent of his wife, who could accompany him if she desired. However, the wife's involvement required the husband's consent.[11]

The European **universities** technically consisted of only male students. However, records indicate that as early as the ninth century, women served on the staff of the medical school at Salerno, Italy. During this period, medieval guilds offered a few schools for girls. These perpetuated commercial interests, and taught reading, writing, arithmetic, a modicum of Latin, and religion.[12] An Italian proverb expressed the popular medieval opinion about the education of women: "A girl should be taught to sew and not to read, unless one wishes to make a nun of her."[13]

Peter Abelard became the **private tutor** for the teenager Heloise. Romantic sexual encounters during the tutoring sessions resulted in the birth of a son. This classic love story is preserved in *The Letters of Abelard and Heloise*. Thomas Aquinas wrote that the essence of the female related to her sexual activity while the male's essence centered in reason. With the exception of procreation, he believed that a woman relied on man in nearly every phase of her life. He consequently believed women unsuitable for church leadership. Aquinas encouraged children to love their father more than their mother.[14] Mary, the mother of Jesus, was the only exception in Aquinas's thought.

The mendicant friars demonstrated early interest in the education of women. Before creating the Dominican order in 1215, Dominic founded a nunnery at Prouille. It was an extension of his plan to rid southern France of the Cathars' heretical influence; he preferred to educate young women rather than allow the Cathars to do so. He founded several convents, but, at the time of his death, he warned his followers to disassociate themselves from women.

Dominicans who emphasized education as a priority in ministry feared that sexual temptation would bring about their downfall. Except for mentions of sensuality, Dominican preaching generally avoided the subject of women.

The female arm of the Franciscans, known as "Poor Clares," was founded in 1212 by Clare of Assisi (1194-1253). After this aristocratic woman heard Francis of Assisi preach, she gave much of her inherited wealth to the poor. In forty years as head of the Order of Poor Clares, she established more than sixty-four houses throughout Europe. Her Poor Clares rarely ventured beyond the convent. Scholars have debated whether Clare ever left Saint Damian's convent during her ministry of forty-two years.

Clare's life probably promoted the ideal of the seclusion of women. Pope Boniface VIII issued a document in 1293 prohibiting women from leaving the convent without the local bishop's permission.[15]

Strengths and Weaknesses of Convents

Although the primary purposes of the convent were worship, meditation, and prayer, the nunneries often established schools. Nuns were rarely more than literate. For the few female intellectuals, the convent was a refuge that harbored the most learned women of the Middle Ages. Tradition often stifled the nun's creativity. Yet in literature, music, art, and drama, the medieval woman's most creative expressions originated in the convent. During the Middle Ages, nunneries conveyed the social and religious heritage to a limited number of children, both male and female.

When aristocratic parents failed to find a suitable husband for their daughter, the convent was an alternative to marriage. A few parents granted their daughter's request to remain unmarried and live in a nunnery. When a woman felt a special divine direction in her life toward Christian service, the convent offered her an opportunity to find meaning in vocations unavailable to her in the institutional church. Social service to the elderly was one such ministry.

The convent also provided a place for the nonconformist. Such a person did not seek a religious vocation, nor did she desire marriage. She usually wanted to escape an undesirable situation or to distinguish herself. The convent afforded relief for troubled parents who wanted assistance for their daughters.

Several weaknesses characterized the convent as well. It was often open only to those with money and power. Under this kind of influence, some nunneries became luxurious boarding houses for the daughters of the aristocracy. Also, by the fourteenth century, Latin, the learned language, had virtually disappeared from the majority of convents. This decline contributed to lower intellectual standards. As religious duties waned, internal discipline became lax. Another reason that formal learning for women nearly died was an overemphasis on devotional interests at the expense of academic standards.

In spite of adversity, the nunneries contributed to the status of women. Benefits certainly varied from one convent to another, but, as a whole, convents served as the most constructive educational force for women during the medieval experience.

Notes

1. Ruth A. Tucker and Walter L. Liefield, *Daughters of the Church: Women and Ministry from New Testament Times to the Present* (Grand Rapids: Zondervan, 1987), 133.

2. Frances Gies and Joseph Gies, *Women in the Middle Ages* (New York: Barnes and Noble, 1978), 34.

3. Eileen Power, *Medieval Women*, ed. Moisei M. Postan (Cambridge: Cambridge University Press, 1975), 92-93.

4. Tucker and Liefield, 147.

5. Power, 94.

6. Ibid.

7. Bonnie S. Anderson and Judith P. Zinsser, *A History of Their Own: Women in Europe from Prehistory to the Present*, vol. 1 (New York: Harper and Row, 1988), 216.

8. Ibid., 188.

9. Ibid., 189.

10. Tucker and Liefield, 137.

11. Ibid., 138-39.

12. Mehdi Nakosteen, *The History and Philosophy of Education* (New York: Ronald Press, 1965), 166-67.

13. T. L. Jarman, *Landmarks in the History of Education* (New York: Philosophical Library, 1952), 123.

14. Tucker and Liefield, 164.

15. Ibid.

Synopsis
of Part 3

The church was the most important institution of the Middle Ages. This was especially true in education. In the darkest days, the church carried the candle of enlightenment. Although this fire often flickered, it never completely lost the essential intellectual heritage.

During the late Middle Ages, what was defined as education required a knowledge of Latin, the sacred language of the church and school. Yet Latin did not represent the language of the people. Whatever educational opportunities were available were reserved primarily for the rich and powerful.

In each movement within the Middle Ages, men had greater access to educational opportunities than the women. However, considering all provisions, medieval female education surpassed that offered earlier by ancient civilizations and, in reality, probably exceeded the educational place of women during the Reformation.

At a time in history when education was narrow and limited, persons in the best positions for academic achievement often failed to avail themselves of their opportunities. A considerable portion of the clergy remained illiterate throughout the medieval period. Most early nobles could neither read nor write.

The content of medieval education was predominantly religious. Too much instruction, however, centered in teachings *about* Scripture and the authoritative sayings of the church fathers. Many who copied the Bible and other documents did so because they were unable to survive the physical demands of monastic manual labor. These learned to copy words but gained only a limited understanding of the content.

Extreme contrasts often characterized medieval living. The Christian religion increased in membership but decreased in dedicated followers. Money and power too often motivated ecclesiastical leadership rather than devotion and service. The privileged clergy exercised a double standard of morality. Popes and emperors maneuvered to improve their personal and institutional positions. By the tenth century, the church had so lowered its standards and raised its prices to conceal sins that some have referred to this period as a ''pornocracy'' or rule of harlots.

Two forms of monasticism placed different values on education. The anchorite offered few educational contributions and generally considered additional education as a danger. In contrast, the cenobite, in his or her cloister, developed monastic education as the most influential form of scholarship throughout most of the Middle Ages. Both forms viewed the body as the enemy of the soul and considered this world as preparation for the next.

The monastic vows of chastity, poverty, and obedience renounced three primary social organizations—the home, economic structure, and political stability. Yet, contributions from the monks greatly benefited medieval society. The monk's hard physical work dignified manual labor. As monks cleared lands and drained swamps, living conditions improved for society as a whole. The monasteries sometimes served as asylums and hospitals, giving troubled and helpless people their only hope for survival. Through their scriptoriums and libraries, monks gathered, reproduced, and preserved ancient scholarship. Some of the early ideals of monasticism waned. By the end of the Middle Ages, the monasteries had accumulated more than enough wealth, land holdings, and power to contradict their original desire for solitude, to say nothing of poverty.

Scholasticism lifted the level of scholarship for a privileged few and opened the possibilities for others to study later. In seeking to maintain the status quo, an abundance of intellectual energy escaped on mere trivialities or a play on words. Thomism promoted near idol worship of Aristotle until William of Ockham reduced scholastic appeal.

Of a more positive nature, Scholasticism synthesized Catholic thought, and the Roman Catholic Church has continued until the present as the largest Christian body in the world. Also the scholastic method partially prepared the way for the development of medieval universities.

PART 4

Christian Education in the Renaissance and Reformation

16

Antecedents
of the Reformation

During the centuries immediately preceding the Protestant Reformation, a few Christian leaders attempted church reform. Others sought to free themselves from the ecclesiastical hierarchy to worship as they saw fit. The church attempted to impose its power and to enforce religious uniformity. During the High Middle Ages and continuing through the Reformation, some nonconformists confronted torture and even death for practices that conflicted with the authoritative church. Even when dissenters' lives were spared, the church often punished those who refused to recant by confiscating their homes, lands, money, and other resources.

The power and wealth of the medieval church weakened governments, but the rise of education during the Renaissance of the fourteenth and fifteenth centuries paved the way for the religious and civic changes brought about by the Reformation of the sixteenth century.

The Deplorable Condition of the Papacy

Church leadership during the fourteenth and fifteenth centuries was so corrupt that many saw the necessity for sweeping changes. Popes and higher clergy often lived in palaces with the life-style of princes. The struggle for church power culminated in the papal schism between 1378 and 1417. During these years two or even three rival popes each had claims to legitimacy.

Money controlled the church's agenda. Church coffers swelled because of *simony*, the practice of buying and selling church offices for gain, and the *sale* of *indulgences*, the absolution of sins by payment of money.

Another source of abuse was the sale of *relics*, objects venerated because of their association with a saint or martyr. Someone during the fifteenth century observed that enough pieces of the apostle Peter's body had been discovered to make up thirty skeletons. As saints and martyrs were added, their relics multiplied. Many bishops and princes either bid high prices or manufactured relics. Helena, the mother of Constantine, reportedly found the three crosses of Calvary and identified the true cross by touching a dead man with it and bringing him to life. So precious was this relic that it was cut into bits and bestowed, traded, and sold all over Europe (to such an effort that Calvin later counted pieces of it "to make a full load for a good ship").[1]

The sale of relics became so widespread that the Fourth Lateran Council in 1215 restricted their sale to those authenticated by letters of certification from the Vatican. This created another source of Vatican revenues. This was probably the chief commercial practice of the church just prior to the Reformation.

In about 1245 the scholastic Alexander of Hales proclaimed the church as a *treasury of merit*. This treasury contained an abundant supply of good works from saints whose deeds exceeded the requirements of heaven. The church as both the gatekeeper to purgatory and administrator of the treasury of merit stood as an eternal broker between mortal deeds and immortal escape. As each indulgence was sold, the church acted as a heavenly accountant who transferred good deeds from the repository of the saints to the lowly sinner. Abuse became so rampant that indulgences were sold in advance for sins yet to be committed.

Johann Tetzel (1465-1519), a German Dominican monk, sold papal indulgences in 1517. He proclaimed that a person who purchased an indulgence could free a soul from purgatory. His jingle was: "When the coin in the coffer rings, a soul from purgatory springs." Tetzel provided the immediate occasion that prompted Martin Luther to write his *Ninety-five Theses*.

This drive for wealth adversely affected the spiritual and educational level of the church. By the beginning of the sixteenth century, the church had prohibited the laity from reading the Bible and discouraged priests from using it. Pastoral duties often went unmet, and the Latin liturgy communicated little to the illiterate masses.

During this time in England, a bishop Hooper of Gloucester surveyed 311 English clergy: 168 "were unable to repeat the Ten Commandments. Thirty-one did not know where to find them. Forty could not tell where the Lord's Prayer is to be found and thirty-one did not know the Author."[2]

Papal corruption was also demonstrated by the *Inquisition*. The early Inquisition propelled a crusade against the heretics of southern France known as the Albigenses. To assist in this crusade, the Fourth Lateran Council in 1215 proclaimed that "Catholics who assume the cross and devote themselves to the extermination of heretics shall enjoy the same indulgence and privilege as those who go to the Holy Land."[3]

The Inquisition was most often administered by Dominicans. Inquisitors traveled across the lands bidding heretics to conform and orthodox believers to inform the church of unconventional and unorthodox beliefs and behaviors. In 1280 the penalties for heretical belief or behavior were declared by Nicholas III. The inquisitors prescribed the punishment, and civil authorities applied penalties. A person found guilty of heresy could receive whipping, torture, imprisonment for life, or death by burning at the stake. A defender of heretics or one suspected of heresy and unable to prove innocence could suffer excommunication and/or loss of civil rights.[4] A clergyman could lose his office for serving the sacraments to heretics.

The World in Revival Toward Reform

The Renaissance of the fourteenth and fifteenth centuries brought changes that prepared the way for the Reformation of the sixteenth.

Emphasis on the Individual

The Middle Ages had deemphasized the individual and focused attention on the soul and the church. In contrast, the Renaissance portrayed a change in attitude toward the ascetic bondage of the human body. The Renaissance awakened imagination about the body from a nap of a thousand years.

Mysticism, nominalism, and humanism contributed toward a redefined meaning of human individualism. *Mysticism* sought a direct personal communion with God. *Nominalism*, which developed in the late Middle Ages, emphasized the uniqueness of human experience and opposed traditional religious functions that suppressed individual opinion. The spirit of humanism rejected Scholasticism and the lofty position of Aristotle in the church. *Humanism* focused upon earthly life in the present more than the spiritual life valued by the medieval church for the age to come. Humanism viewed humans inwardly and allowed them to pursue self-understanding. By seeing humans as individuals who could approach God directly, humanism helped to prepare the way for the Reformation.

Fine Arts

The fine arts of the Renaissance displayed and revived the classical ideals of Greece and Rome. A new interest in colors and the human figure brought one of the most creative periods in human development.

Italy's greatest poet was Alighieri Dante (1265-1321). His *Divine Comedy* surveyed medieval thought by telling the story of an imaginary trip through hell, purgatory, and paradise. Francesco Petrarch (1304-1374) wrote over four hundred poems in Italian, and Giovanni Boccaccio (1313-1375) penned *The Decameron*, a collection of one hundred Latin stories set against a background of the Black Death. Also Geoffrey Chaucer's (ca. 1340-1400) *The Canterbury Tales* presented an insightful observation of human nature.

Leonardo da Vinci and Michelangelo were masters of Renaissance art. Michelangelo (1475-1564) is often considered the greatest sculptor in history, but he was also an architect, painter, and poet. He created statues in rich, realistic, and individualistic detail. His statues of biblical characters such as Moses display mastery of human uniqueness.

Leonardo da Vinci (1452-1519) was the Renaissance man par excellence. His paintings of *The Last Supper* and *Mona Lisa* are among the world's most recognized and appreciated works of art. More than a painter, he was one of the most brilliant and versatile personalities in history, distinguished in music, poetry, chemistry, mechanical engineering, and other areas.

Discoveries

The Renaissance brought a new spirit of discovery and commerce. The Crusades initiated interest in exploration, travel, and adventure. Also Marco Polo's (ca. 1254-1324) tales of his expeditions stirred European curiosity.

The greatest age of European discovery occurred from the middle of the fifteenth century to the end of the Reformation. The Portuguese explorer Bartholomeu Dias (ca. 1450-1500) rounded the Cape of Good Hope in 1487-1488. Christopher Columbus (1451-1506) sailed four times to the New World beginning in 1492. Shortly thereafter in 1498, Vasco da Gama became the first European to sail to India. In 1514 Ponce de Leon claimed Florida for Spain. Luther's Reformation was in progress when Ferdinand Magellan (ca. 1480-1521) launched the first successful voyage to circumnavigate the earth in 1519. After his death, the expedition was completed by his crew in 1522.

Scientific Advancements

New scientific discoveries had even greater significance for the church than the discoveries mentioned previously. The English philosopher and scientist Roger Bacon (ca. 1214-1294) helped to revolutionize the perception of man's place in the physical world. His observations of experimental science prepared for the scientific discoveries of the fifteenth and sixteenth centuries.

From its inception, the church had taught that God had placed man on the Earth, the center of the universe; the sun and all other heavenly bodies were believed to revolve around the Earth. Any deviation from the church's assumptions and doctrines, as in other matters, constituted heresy.

Nicholas of Cusa (1401-1464), the German Roman Catholic prelate, philosopher, and mathematician, secretly hypothesized that the Earth rotated and revolved around the sun.[5] However, Nicolaus Copernicus (1473-1543), a Polish astronomer and churchman, developed Cusa's theory more fully in *The Revolutions of Heavenly Bodies*. Aware that his observations directly disputed church dogma, Copernicus delayed publication of his work until the time of his death. While lying on his deathbed, Copernicus was presented a printed copy of his work. Giordano Bruno (1548-1600) speculated that other solar systems with life forms existed; he was burned at the stake. Another disciple of the Copernican theory was Johannes Kepler (1571-1630), who developed laws of planetary motion and contributed to the invention of calculus.

Galileo Galilei (1564-1642) disproved a large number of theories attributed to Aristotle, such as the notion that large heavy objects fall more quickly than lighter ones. Galileo constructed a telescope through which he discovered four moons of Jupiter. This increased the number of known heavenly objects to eleven, not the perfect number of seven as the church taught. The Inquisition so repressed intellectual life that most people refused to look into his telescope because they feared it would be an act of heresy. At seventy years of age, Galileo recanted his findings before the Inquisition. Not until 1984 did the church admit publicly the possibility that Galileo was treated unjustly by the Inquisition court in 1633.[6]

Sixteenth-century Catholic and Protestant leaders condemned early scientists. In his *Table Talk*, Luther called the Copernican theory "absurd." Melanchthon cautioned persons to trust God and not their reasoning abilities. These German educators believed the Copernican theory untrue and contrary to biblical teachings.

Vernacular Literature

The use of modern languages in poetry, song, and other literary works built the foundation for translations of the Bible into the languages of the people. Earlier, medieval troubadours had wandered across Europe singing their songs and telling their stories in the vernacular.

While Christians wanted to worship and read the Bible in their own language, the sad fact was that few people could read in either classical Latin or the vernacular. In 1384 John Wycliffe (ca. 1320-1384), often called "the morning star of the Reformation," initiated the first translation of the entire Bible into English. The English people enthusiastically received Wycliffe's translation, but the church prohibited the common person from reading the Bible in the vernacular. Offenders who were caught with the English Bible often lost their lives.

Printing Press and Other Inventions

The invention of the printing press with movable type by Johann Gutenberg (ca. 1400-1468) in the mid-1400s brought unparalleled benefits. In the history of education, the three most important events are usually considered to be (1) the invention of languages, (2) the invention of writing, and (3) the invention of printing.

The printing press brought rapid changes in many areas of life, including religion and Christian education. Ten Bibles could be printed as cheaply as one could be copied by hand. As a result, biblical knowledge soon became more widely available. Laypersons became less dependent on the clergy for information. Printing even encouraged the adoption of written examinations in the universities. The printing press helped the Reformers multiply the number of informed and determined followers.

Social Changes

A change in the strength of social patterns and institutions contributed to the cause of the Reformation. The invention of gunpowder and development of commerce dealt knighthood a severe blow and gave hope to the common person who was bound by manorialism. Increased trade and travel contributed to the growth of the middle class. In the fourteenth century, the Black Death or bubonic plague devastated Europe's population by at least one-fourth. As the social system revealed signs of collapse, the emerging Renaissance emphasis on freed expression was destined to collide with the church hierarchy. As new opportunities for employment decreased, heavier taxation and impoverishment increased. All this time, church taxes and church abuses accelerated. It is no wonder the common person responded positively to the cries for change from the Reformers.

Nationalism

The power of secular leaders grew. Feudal lords lost some of their power to the emerging national governments. This process was accelerated by the series of battles between the English and French known as the Hundred Years' War (1337-1453). A rising spirit of nationalism inspired opposition to the power of the church. The heads of European states stood to gain large amounts of land, money, and other resources with a reversal of papal power.

During the Renaissance, many civil leaders viewed the Roman Catholic Church as a symbol of foreign tyranny. Martin Luther's call for reform attracted the attention of monarchs. Some consider help from political forces the most important single reason for the success of the Reformation.

The Free Church Principle

As the medieval church grew in numbers, organizations, creeds, and ceremonials, it became more secular and political. The church gave less emphasis to the simple and individual forms of apostolic worship. During the Middle Ages, religious leaders and movements arose that resisted efforts to dictate the believer's conscience. The doctrines of these groups varied, but each desired to worship with a free faith.

These free churches emphasized morality and church discipline in their attempts to maintain a pure congregation. During the ninth century, the predominant church persecuted the Paulicians, in part because of their opposition to the established hierarchy.[7]

Beginning in the twelfth and continuing into the thirteenth century, the Albigenses in southern France opposed image worship, Catholic mass, accumulation of property by the church, and other abuses. Following the declaration of a holy war by Innocent III, the church military murdered thousands of Albigenses and confiscated their lands and resources. The Inquisition that followed burned or destroyed most of those who remained or were unable to go underground.

Marianne Sawicki has observed that the teachings of the Albigenses, such as rejection of the incarnation, are known today only through the accounts of the institution that destroyed them. She also added:

> Albigensian ideas were a symptom of the changing macroeconomic situation in Europe. The traditional means of support for the clergy had been agricultural: the tithes of produce from parish and monastery lands. But the value of these was declining against the new varieties of wealth being produced and enjoyed in the cities.[8]

Peter Waldo and the Waldenses

In the twelfth century, Peter Waldo, a French merchant, gained access to portions of Scripture and concluded that the church of his day was unlike the New Testament church. Waldo responded by giving away his wealth and dedicating himself to a simple life-style. His lay followers, known as "the poor men of Lyons" and later Waldenses, taught biblical principles from house to house.

More like teachers than preachers, these believers traveled in groups of two presenting the teachings of Scripture as authoritative over traditional church doctrines. The Waldenses opposed indulgences, purgatory, masses for the dead, and various other practices of the Church. They taught a simple faith in Christ as found in the Bible and instructed their children in family worship to memorize Scripture.

The Waldenses experienced basically the same fate as their neighbors, the Albigenses. The inquisitors came; hundreds of Waldenses and Albigenses were judged and burned as heretics; their properties were divided among church and civil authorities; many who escaped, including hundreds of women and children, starved or froze to death high in the Alpine mountains. Descendants of the survivors responded to the cries of the sixteenth-century Reformers.

John Wycliffe and the Lollards

In addition to being an excellent translator of Scripture, John Wycliffe (ca. 1320-1384), like others before him, believed that Scripture, not the pope, was authoritative in matters of faith; that salvation came through an individual experience with God; and that the tactics of the institutional church damaged its mission. Being a professor of philosophy at Oxford, he enjoyed a greater opportunity than others to propagate his religious convictions. In relationships between church and civil authorities, he favored the state's right to confiscate the corrupt clergyman's property like any other person's. When the pope summoned him, Wycliffe's association with the English royal family provided protection and allowed him diplomatically to refuse the appearance. Wycliffe died in 1384, but the Church later ordered his body exhumed and burned.

Wycliffe's followers, known as Lollards, fared worse than their leader. They practiced a simple faith based on the will of God as expressed in the Bible. They refused to pray for the dead or worship saints. They wrote evangelistic tracts and distributed them throughout the countryside. Some from the upper classes condemned Wycliffe and his followers for encouraging the poor to seek a better life. The Lollards were severely persecuted in England. Their faithfulness formed the foundation for the free faith movement that continued to develop there during the Reformation. Wycliffe's influence was possibly even greater in Bohemia, where Jerome of Prague, one of Wycliffe's Oxford students, taught John Huss.

John Huss and the Hussites

Born to hardworking peasant parents who sacrificed for their son's education, John Huss (ca. 1369-1415) became an outstanding student at the University of Prague. After becoming a priest in 1400 and gaining the rectorship of the university two years later, Huss was appointed the daily preacher for the Bethlehem Chapel in Prague, where he opposed papal corruption. During the papal schism (1378-1409), when rival popes claimed legitimate election as supreme pontiff, Huss called the papacy an "institution of Satan." His doctrines were similar to those of Wycliffe and the Lollards. Huss was condemned by the Council of Constance in 1415, imprisoned in a small dungeon, and burned at the stake. The Hussites were persecuted, and many lost their lives in Bohemia and Moravia. Their ideas and determination inspired the Reformers.

Girolamo Savonarola

Born into a modest family in Ferrara, Italy, Savonarola (1452-1498) was educated in the Catholic tradition. As a Dominican friar in Bologna, he wrote *On the Contempt of the World* in 1474. After eight years, Girolamo moved to Florence, a city he loved for its beauty and disdained for its sin.

As a spokesman for the poor and oppressed, Savonarola became Florence's most famous preacher. Between 1494 and 1498 as the city's theocratic ruler, Savonarola led a moral reform movement and severely criticized the papacy. His government reformed courts and tax laws, cared for the poor, burned manuscripts, and condemned makeup for women and card playing. Some of his former friends plotted against him, and the city government condemned him. He was hanged and his body burned. This reportedly prompted one unreformed citizen to cry: "Praise be to God, now we can practice sodomy."[9]

Girolamo Savonarola did not advocate the free faith movement. As a Catholic theologian and moral reformer, he was an example of other Catholics who loved God and practiced righteous living. To the Protestant Reformers, Savonarola became a hero. Martin Luther called him the first martyr of the Reformation.[10]

Notes

1. Joseph Gies and Frances Gies, *Life in a Medieval City* (New York: Harper and Row, 1981), 128.

2. Clarence H. Benson, *History of Christian Education* (Chicago: Moody, 1943), 64-65.

3. Hugh Wamble, *History of Christian Thought CHO212* (Nashville: Seminary Extension Department of Southern Baptist Seminaries, 1969), 168.

4. Ibid., 169.

5. Will Durant, *The Story of Civilization, Part V: The Renaissance* (New York: Simon and Schuster, 1954), 529.

6. B. R. Hergenhahn, *An Introduction to the History of Psychology* (Belmont, Calif.: Wadsworth Publications, 1986), 74.

7. Albert McClellan, *Meet Southern Baptists* (Nashville: Broadman, 1978), 8.

8. Marianne Sawicki, *The Gospel in History* (New York: Paulist Press, 1988), 210.

9. Lewis W. Spitz, *The Renaissance and Reformation Movements*, vol. 1 (Chicago: Rand McNally, 1971), 240.

10. Kenneth O. Gangel and Warren S. Benson, *Christian Education: Its History and Philosophy* (Chicago: Moody, 1983), 132.

17

Humanism
and
Christian Education

If Hegel's dialectic were applied to the history of Christian education, the thesis would be the Middle Ages, the antithesis the Renaissance, and the synthesis the Reformation.

D. Campbell Wyckoff has argued that humanism is at least as old as Protagoras (ca. 485-410 B.C.).[1] In his essay *On the Gods,* Protagoras expressed doubt about the reality of Athenian gods. For this, city leaders banished him. Humanistic thinkers through the centuries have quoted his statement as the epitome of their beliefs: "Man is the measure of all things: of those which are, that they are; of those which are not, that they are not."[2]

Renaissance humanists elevated individual human values above those of the church. They studied classical literature and culture and sought to revive ancient learning. Humanists rejected medieval asceticism and rejected scholastic Aristotelianism. Yet there were significant differences among humanists. Many humanists, particularly those in Italy, virtually abandoned Christianity in their passion for ancient culture. On the other hand, most humanists in northern Europe were Christians. These Christian humanists also studied Latin, Greek, and other ancient languages, but they were interested in biblical and patristic studies, as well as Greek and Roman classics. For other general contrasts, see chart 3.

During the Renaissance, humanism profoundly influenced European education by stressing high standards of scholarship. Human values were recognized in relationships between students and teachers. In various ways, Francesco Petrarch, Vittorino da Feltre, Desiderius Erasmus, Juan Luis Vives, and many other educational humanists helped to prepare minds to receive the Reformation.

Francesco Petrarch

Scholars often date the beginning of the Renaissance with the writings of the Italian Petrarch (1304-1374). His early education included scholastic studies and ancient classics. Early in his adult life, Petrarch rose to a minor ecclesiastical role in the church. By opposing the legalism of the Italian universities and recognizing the failure of medieval Scholasticism, he attempted to combine humanism with Christian faith.

Beginning in 1333, Petrarch mastered classical Latin and collected ancient manuscripts, including two orations of Cicero. With two hundred writings from antiquity, his library probably contained more such works than any other in Europe at the time. Petrarch wanted recognition for his achievements, and he is remembered most as a poet. He displayed his "soul of a poet" in efforts to free the human spirit from medieval monasticism and Scholasticism. He said: "I am anti-Aristotle whenever Aristotle is anti-common sense."[3] He cautioned against making religion too intellectual. Instead, he favored personal religion based on the Bible and personal feelings as described by Augustine. Petrarch ascribed as much importance to life on earth as life in the hereafter. Accordingly, he taught that God wanted His children to use and not inhibit their abilities to create a better world on earth.[4]

Vittorino da Feltre

Like Petrarch, the Italian Vittorino da Feltre (1378-1446), whose real name was Vittorino Ramboldini, displayed more interest in religion than most southern humanists. Other than his birth at Feltre, little else is known of his early life. At the age of eighteen Vittorino matriculated at the University of Padua, where he spent twenty years as student and professor. In 1416 he opened the first humanist school in Venice. After six years he returned in 1422 to the University of Padua as professor of Latin literature. Because of the immorality of students, his teaching in Padua lasted only one year.

In 1423 Vittorino returned to Venice, where he became court tutor to the Gonzaga family, the lords of Mantua. During the final twenty-three years of his life, he built the finest school in Europe.[5] Some have praised him as the most important educator of the Renaissance and the "first modern schoolmaster." His school, *Pleasant House,* at one time housed as many as seventy students, and its methods served as a

GENERAL POINTS OF CONTRAST IN
RENAISSANCE HUMANISM
Chart 3

Category of Contrast	Southern Humanism	Northern Humanism
Origin	• Italy	• Northern Europe
Religious Emphasis	• Stressed human concerns over divine; more pagan	• Stressed human worth but in more Christian context
Human Interest	• Individual freedom	• Social reform
Axiological Nature	• More asesthetic and materialistic toward a full & free life	• More ethical and spiritual toward a full & free life
Authorities	• Greek and Roman writers of classical antiquity	• Biblical Greek and Latin; classical writers
Target Audience	• Primarily aristocratic; few had means to achieve desired cultural goal	• Essentially democratic; attempted to improve life for masses of people
Goal of Education	• To exalt human values and develop renaissance man with classical scholarship	• To exalt human values and cultivate a free, moral and responsible society
Church	• Rejected the authoritarian medieval church	• Preserved interest in the church
Goal of Living	• To discover the pleasure of living	• To help produce a better world

contrast to most medieval methods. (See Pleasant House on chart 6 in chap. 21.)

What is known of Vittorino da Feltre and his school has been passed down by the accounts of others. He wrote little, and none of his writings have survived. He is remembered for his effective and creative teaching methods.

Gerhard Groote and the Brethren of the Common Life

Groote (1340-1384) was born into a wealthy family at Deventer, in the Netherlands. His parents died of the plague when he was ten years old, and Gerhard was placed under the care of his uncle. An intelligent student, Groote received instruction in Aachen, Cologne, and other schools. At age fifteen, he entered the University of Paris, and three years later he earned the master of arts.

With inherited wealth, Groote taught, traveled, and studied, enjoying a life of worldly pleasure. At age thirty, a mystic beggar challenged Groote to find fulfillment in his "empty" life. Approximately four years later, at the insistence of his uncle's pastor, Groote became a dedicated Catholic follower of Christ.

Three years later, Groote entered a monastery, and for the next three years he read the mystic writings of Hugo of Saint Victor, Meister Eckhart, and others. Convinced that his lay preaching would serve God more than his living in a monastery, Groote returned to Deventer, where he became a popular preacher. His sermons lasted between two and three hours, and he usually preached twice daily. Using the Bible as his guide, Groote proclaimed that Christians should obey the simple teachings of Scripture. Because he preached against the vices of the clergy, his license to preach was revoked. He embraced educational reform as a means to religious reform. Always concerned for the common people, Groote taught in the vernacular. He translated parts of the Bible into Dutch and ministered faithfully to the sick and aged. Shortly before he became forty-five years old, Groote caught the plague and died.

Groote was a significant Catholic mystic, monastic, reformer, lay preacher, teacher, and Christian thinker. He combined some aspects of mysticism with the popular concerns of humanism.

In the mid-1370s his followers became known as Brethren of the Common Life and were sanctioned by the pope. During the next two centuries in Europe, they established hundreds of elementary and secondary schools. John Cele, Groote's closest friend, became rector of the town school in Zwolle. Because of Cele's excellent administration, this school came to enroll over twelve hundred students. Cele's school became one of the finest in Europe and served as a model for Johannes Sturm at Strasburg and John Calvin at Geneva.

The Brethren of the Common Life formed common communities of twenty or less in what they called "houses." The Brethren often lived and studied together with their students, though some schools maintained separate student dormitories. In the beginning each house was designed for a scriptorium, where the boys became proficient copyists, but as many as sixty houses had installed a printing press by 1490.[6] Unlike the mendicant orders, these lay brethren did not practice begging; all the boys learned a trade.

Many Brethren teachers integrated biblical passages into other subjects. In place of hard punishment for failure, the Brethren teachers rewarded excellence with praise and prizes.

The Brethren of the Common Life virtually disappeared by the middle of the seventeenth century, but their ideals survived through their students such as Thomas à Kempis and Martin Luther. The Jesuits adopted many of the Brethren's ideals while Puritans and Dutch Calvinists adopted others and brought them to the American colonies.

Desiderius Erasmus

Born out of wedlock in Rotterdam, Holland, Erasmus (1466-1536) was separated from his parents at a young age. His father was supposedly a priest and his mother a physician's daughter.[7] Erasmus, one of the most famous students from the Brethren of the Common Life, studied under their tutelage from 1475 until 1484. After living in the homes of guardians, he and his brother were forced by relatives to enter an Augustinian monastery.

Desiderius Erasmus

Biographical Facts
- Born in Rotterdam, Holland
- Educated by Brethren of the Common Life
- Taught at Cambridge, Oxford, and other universities
- Recognized as "the prince of the humanists"

Writings Related to Education
- *Praise of Folly* (1511)
- *The Method of Right Instruction* (1511)
- *Education of a Christian Prince* (1516)
- *Christian Matrimony* (1526)
- *Liberal Education of Boys* (1529)

Influence on Christian Education
- was a constructive critic of the church and Christian education
- was responsible for bringing humanism to England
- advocated advancement in educational opportunities for women
- aided the Protestant Reformation through his writings, especially the satires

---

Besides a few friends among the English humanists, Erasmus related poorly with his colleagues. He disliked them, and many, both Catholic and Protestant, considered him a heretic. With a weak sense of family, homeland, or comradeship, Erasmus devoted himself to Christ and humanistic scholarship.

Erasmus traveled and taught throughout Europe, especially in Germany, France, Italy, England, and Switzerland, where he spent his last years. Unlike Luther, Erasmus believed in reform without revolution. He sought reform by directing the spirit and intellect of the church back to the first century. His goals were similar to Luther's, but their temperaments were different. Erasmus once stated, "My heart is Catholic, but my stomach is Protestant."[8] Luther said that "he but hatched the egg laid by Erasmus. To which Erasmus replied that the egg was but a hen's egg, while Luther had hatched a game cock."[9]

Erasmus is known as "the prince of the humanists." Both Catholics and Protestants sought his allegiance during the Reformation. He refused both because, as he said, a scholar should not be a fanatic or partisan. In a nonviolent fashion, with scholarly satire, he attacked abuses within the Church but refused to support the division of Christianity. Some of his most severe criticisms were directed to churchmen who benefited financially and socially from war.[10] One of Erasmus's Brethren teachers at Deventer once enthusiastically embraced his student and prophesied concerning Erasmus: "You will one day attain the highest summits of knowledge."[11] Not only did Erasmus attain intellectual excellence, he retained with integrity the simple, practical piety implanted in him by the Brethren during his youth.

Erasmus taught and followed the ideal that deeds surpass the importance of creeds and that high moral values benefit society more than correct manners. The primary aim of his educational reform was to develop good, intelligent Christians.

Like other Renaissance humanist educators, Erasmus elevated human importance above medieval conceptions. Not all of his arrows were aimed at Catholicism. He rejected the Protestant doctrine of predestination and criticized much in Protestant preaching as ignorance. For Erasmus, good education created a well-rounded Christian individual who, after learning the meaning of goodness, would *be* good for the good of society.

Although he was more an educational theoretician than practitioner, Erasmus advanced the concept of systematic teacher training. He believed that parents, as primary instructors, spent too little time choosing teachers for their children. He disapproved of teachers who, like the scholastics, paraded their own learning before students. The teacher should build knowledge and character by relating to the child with understanding, using discipline tempered with love.

Erasmus proposed that proper Christian instruction required a knowledge of the Scriptures in Hebrew and Greek and the church fathers in Latin. He said, "I am resolved to die in the study of the Scriptures. In them I find my joy and peace."[12] He knew that the Vulgate contained many errors.[13] He had less interest in metaphysical studies than many other Catholics. He encouraged the study of history and geography to improve understanding of the classics; but, unlike some other humanists, he stopped short of a total endorsement of classical literature. Erasmus also valued learning through play, exercise, and games.

Few satirists have equaled the effectiveness of the "prince of humanists." During the first years of the Reformation, a papal representative in Germany reported to Rome that "the satires of Erasmus were harming the papacy more than the denunciations of Luther. By making people laugh at the Roman system, Erasmus had more effect than the protests of Reformers."[14]

Juan Luis Vives

The birthplace of Vives (1492-1540) was Valencia, Spain, but his most important work was done in England. Although each of his parents had been born into an aristocratic family, neither managed to amass much wealth. Juan's early teacher inspired him to oppose humanism. Between 1509 and 1514, Vives studied at the University of Paris under the scholastic John Dullard.[15] Toward the end of his studies at Paris, Vives read from the writings of Erasmus and became a humanist educator.

In 1519 Vives joined the faculty of the university of Louvain, where Erasmus became his friend. In a letter to Thomas More, Erasmus predicted that Vives's accomplishments would "overshadow the name of Erasmus."[16]

In 1523 at the invitation of Henry VIII, Vives moved to England as tutor to Princess Mary and lecturer at Oxford. At age thirty-two, he married Margaret Valdaura, who was nineteen and the daughter of a good friend. They apparently had a successful marriage.

In 1528 Vives opposed the divorce of Henry VIII from Catherine of Aragon. The king responded by expelling Vives from England. He lived the remainder of his days in Bruges, in present-day Belgium, where he wrote his most important books.

Juan Luis Vives

Biographical Facts
- Born in Valencia, Spain
- Received an early scholastic education, later humanist and sense realist
- Taught at Louvain, Oxford, and Bruges
- Was an English court tutor to Princess Mary

Writings Related to Education
- *Against False Dialectic* (1519)
- *On the Education of Children* (1523)
- *On the Instruction of a Christian Woman* (1523)
- *On Poor Relief* (1526)
- *On Argument and Disagreement in Human* (1529)
- *On the Transmission of Knowledge* (1531)
- *Prayers and Devotional Exercises* (1535)
- *Concerning the Mind* (1538)

Influence on Christian Education
- believed in society's responsibility to rehabilitate and educate the masses
- was most progressive English humanistic educator
- believed in education in the vernacular and sense realism
- was considered by some to be the father of educational psychology
- contributed greatly to the thought of John Amos Comenius and others

---

Vives wrote about a variety of subjects. Vives attacked scholastic thought in *Against False Dialectic* (1519). In *On Poor Relief* (1526), he rejected begging as an inadequate and degrading way of helping the poor. He assigned the community the responsibility of rehabilitating the poor at public expense. With a proper education, he thought, poor persons could become leaders in society. *On Poor Relief,* called "the first scientific work on public charity," displayed Vives' belief in democracy.[17]

Vives resembled Erasmus in many ways. In *On Agreement and Disagreement among Men* (1529), Vives concurred with Erasmus that disputes among states should be settled by arbitration rather than war.

Vives was more democratic than Erasmus and may have been more original and more philosophical than Erasmus.[18]

In 1531 Vives wrote his educational masterpiece, *On the Transmission of Knowledge*. It contains numerous references to Quintilian, who was considered Rome's greatest educator, and it is the most progressive book on education during the Renaissance.[19] Some have considered Vives "the father of educational psychology" because of *On Spirit and Life* (1538) and parts of *On the Transmission of Knowledge*.[20] He was among the first to recommend educating blind, deaf, or mute children.[21] He was an early proponent of school libraries. His insistence on using the inductive method of learning and the vernacular in education influenced John Amos Comenius and the development of sense-realism.

According to Vives, the teacher should discuss the child's progress with parents four times yearly. In the light of the child's gifts and mental abilities, the teacher should recommend future courses of study. Vives taught that a child was to love his teacher like a father. Like Erasmus, Vives placed great importance on teacher's meetings to discuss lesson plans and curriculum.[22]

Religious, natural, and classical studies held the highest place of importance in Vives' curriculum. He stressed the study of history to develop practical wisdom, but he cautioned history teachers not to glorify war. In methodology, he also advocated public over private education, the notebook, the senses as primary in learning, and play as the best source of a child's real inclinations.

At a time when the English considered the Spanish and Catholics to be their enemies, Juan Luis Vives, Spaniard and Catholic, became "the best known English humanist educator."[23] The English *Book of Common Prayer* (1578) drew heavily from his *Prayers and Devotional Exercises* (1535). Yet his contributions have not been widely recognized until recently, perhaps because he was a Spaniard, a Catholic, and a layman. For a list of those whom he influenced, see chart 4.

Other English Humanists

In addition to Erasmus and Vives, several other personalities contributed to the development of English humanism. Thomas More (1478-1535), the son of a London lawyer, was a devout Catholic who became a friend of Erasmus and Vives. More's *Utopia* presented the ideal society from the perspective of the Renaissance. More was

IDEAS OF GREAT EDUCATORS FOUND IN THE WRITINGS OF VIVES

Chart 4

Bacon	Comenius	Locke	Mulcaster	Pestalozzi	Herbart	Froebel
Use of the inductive approach to learning.	Use of the object lesson in teaching.	Initial learning to be approached through the senses.	Use of the vernacular in education.	Virtue of the direct study of nature.	Capitalizing upon the interests of pupils.	Education as a drawing-out process.
Reduction of grammar and other less meaningful ancient studies.	Combination of a practical and a spiritual education.	Memory and habit formation should precede reasoning in early stages of training.	Opposition to tutors.	Graduation of materials suited to pupil readiness.	Rewarding effort.	Development through play and self-activity.
Attacked scholastic wrangling as an outmoded teaching method.	The education of girls.	The importance of proper diet in producing a sound mind and body.	The establishment of public schools.	Love and warmth of the family in school relationships.	Relating experience to apperception and generalization.	Understanding of pupil differences.
	A broadened curriculum.		Parent-teacher conferences.		Education as character-building.	Intervals of relaxation in school.

Source: Richard E. Gross, ed., *Heritage of American Education.* Boston: Allyn & Bacon, 1962, p. 21.

beheaded because he opposed Henry VIII's divorce and break with the pope. Erasmus called More "a man for all seasons." John Colet (1467-1519), another humanist who remained a Catholic, established Saint Paul's School in London with assistance from Erasmus. This was the first of the English humanistic secondary schools. Unlike More and Colet, Thomas Elyot (1490-1546) left the Roman Catholic Church and joined Luther's reform. In 1531 Elyot wrote *Boke Named the Governour,* which presented the moral and cultural idea of humanist education. Elyot's friend Roger Ascham (1515-1568) also joined the Reformers. Ascham's *The Schoolmaster* presented educational methods in the vernacular and advocated the method of double translation in teaching languages. Educational efforts of More, Colet, Elyot, and Ascham contributed to the outcome of the English Reformation.

Notes

1. Iris V. Cully and Kendig B. Cully, eds., *Harper's Encyclopedia of Religous Education* (New York: Harper and Row, 1990), 314.

2. *Webster's Biographical Dictionary* (Springfield, Mass.: G & C Merriam Co., 1970), 1217.

3. Morris Bishop, *The Middle Ages* (New York: American Heritage Press, 1970), 272.

4 R R Hergenhahn, *An Introduction to the History of Psychology* (Belmont, Calif.: Wadsworth Publications, 1986), 70.

5. James Bowen, *A History of Western Education,* vol. 2 (New York: St. Martin's Press, 1975), 225.

6. S. E. Frost, Jr., and Kenneth P. Bailey, *Historical and Philosophical Foundations of Western Education,* 2d ed. (Columbus, Ohio: Charles E. Merrill Publishing Co., 1973), 185.

7. William Boyd and Edmund J. King, *The History of Western Education,* 11th ed. (Totawa, N.J.: Barnes and Noble, 1980), 173.

8. George Faludy, *Erasmus* (New York: Stein and Day, 1970), 195.

9. Kenneth V. Lottich and Elmer Harrison Wilds, *The Foundations of Modern Education,* 4th ed. (New York: Holt, Rinehart and Winston, 1970), 229.

10. Hergenhahn, 71.

11. F. V. N. Painter, *A History of Education,* International Education Series, ed. William T. Harris, vol. 2 (New York: D. Appleton and Co., 1905), 148.

12. Clarence H. Benson, *History of Christian Education* (Chicago: Moody, 1943), 67-68.

13. Kenneth O. Gangel and Warren S. Benson, *Christian Education: Its History and Philosophy* (Chicago: Moody, 1983), 128.

14. Tony Lane, *Harper's Concise Book of Christian Faith* (Cambridge, Mass.: Harper and Row, 1984), 113.

15. Bowen, 388.

16. Robert P. Adams, *The Better Part of Valor* (Seattle: University of Washington Press, 1962), 189-90; quoted in "Erasmus and Vives: Christian Humanists of the Renaissance" (Ph.D. diss., n.p., 1989).

17. Frost and Bailey, 193.

18. Boyd and King, 179-80.

19. Will Durant, *The Story of Civilization: Part VI, The Reformation* (New York: Simon and

Schuster, 1957), 790. Also see Frost and Bailey, *Western Education,* 193; Foster Watson, *Louis Vives* (Oxford: Oxford University Press, 1922), 100.

20. William T. Kane and John J. O'Brien, *History of Education* (Chicago: Loyola University Press, 1960), 208. Also see Steven V. Owen, Robin D. Froman, and Henry Moscow, *Educational Psychology,* 2d ed. (Boston: Little, Brown and Co., 1981), 7.

21. Boyd and King, 181.

22. Juan Luis Vives, *De Tradendis Discipline (Vives: on Education),* trans. Foster Watson (New York: Cambridge University Press, 1913), cxx.

23. E. H. Gwynne-Thomas, *A Concise History of Education to A.D. 1900* (Lanham, Md.: University Press of America, 1981), 85.

18

Martin Luther and Education

Martin Luther's *Ninety-Five Theses* objected to the doctrine and practice of indulgences. Posting theses for debate on church doors was common in Luther's day. Subsequent events, however, led scholars to recognize this act as the beginning of the Protestant Reformation. Luther did not at first intend to divide the church or establish a new church.

The phrase *Protestant Reformation* originated from actions at the Second Diet of Speyer in 1529. Because of divisions between the followers of Luther and Zwingli, the Catholic princes gained a majority and rescinded actions of the First Diet of Speyer in 1526, which had legally recognized Lutheran churches in Germany. The German princes immediately protested and were labeled "protestants." This term came to be applied to the Reformation churches.

To the Catholics, the *reform* efforts were a *revolt* against the one true church. Luther and his followers desired a *restoration* of the apostolic church, but the Catholics viewed these protests as a damaging revolution.[1]

The term *reformation* is at least as old as the thirteenth century, when mystical writers used it to signify a new age of the Holy Spirit within the church. Later humanistic writers applied the term to reform inside and outside the church. Basically, the term meant "to purify a corrupt institution."

Martin Luther

Martin Luther (1483-1546) was born in 1483 near Eisleben, Saxony. His parents were strict, religious, and legalistic free peasants. They named their son after Saint Martin, patron of feasting and reformed drunkards. Hans, a devoted Catholic and an independent religious

---

Martin Luther

Biographical Facts
- Born at Eisleben in Saxony (November 10, 1483)
- Had strict and religious parents
- Received early education in Brethren of the Common Life school at Mansfeld (entered 1501)
- Influenced by scholastic and humanistic teachings at University of Erfurt
- Entered monastery in 1505
- Ordained an Augustinian priest in 1507
- Was professor or theology at University of Wittenberg (1512-1546)
- Posted *Ninety-Five Theses* on October 31, 1517
- Excommunicated in 1520

Writings Related to Education
- "The Letter to Mayors and Alderman of All the Cities of Germany in Behalf of Christian Schools" (1524)
- "Sermon on the Duty of Sending Children to School" (1530)
- *Bible*, translated into German (1521-1534)
- *Hymn Book* (1529)
- *Small Catechism* or *Layman's Bible* (1529)
- *Large Catechism* or *German Catechism* (1529)

Influence on Christian Education
- was primary force in creation of modern German language
- was the leader of Protestant Reformation
- was the major Protestant Reformer in educational issues
- translated both the Old Testament and New Testament into German
- advocated universal compulsory education
- wrote two catechisms
- advocated congregational singing of hymns
- believed purpose of education practical and religious
- believed in responsibility of Christian education—change home and state

---

thinker, worked as a miner to provide a good education for his nine children. In *Table Talks,* Luther said about his ancestry, ''I am the son of a peasant; my father, my grandfather, my great-grandfather were all thorough peasants.''[2] Luther also said, ''My father . . . was a poor miner; my mother carried in all the wood on her back; they worked the flesh off their bones to bring us up; no one nowadays would ever have such endurance."[3]

Martin studied from an early age at the town school in Mansfeld. At age fourteen he studied in Magdeburg, probably in a school operated by the Brethren of the Common Life. After one year, his parents sent him to the School of Saint George at Eisenach, where he remained four years.

Between the ages of eighteen and twenty-two, Luther studied at the University of Erfurt because his father wanted Martin to become a lawyer. Later Luther described his experience at Erfurt as the time when he learned to hate Aristotle. He also said that his greatest discovery there was "the accidental finding of a copy of the Bible, the first complete Bible he had ever seen, in the university library."[4]

Having earned his master's degree, Martin returned to his parents, supposedly to practice law. However, shortly thereafter he joined the Augustinian monastery of Erfurt, surprisingly and without the blessing of his family. In 1507 Luther was ordained a priest. His father, who had disowned him for leaving the study of law, attended Martin's first celebration of mass. Their relationship was to some degree reclaimed.

As an Augustinian friar, Luther spent time in Rome and taught at the University of Wittenberg. In 1512 he earned the doctor of theology degree from Wittenberg. At this time, the university made him a full professor of theology, a position that he retained for the rest of his life.[5]

Three Cardinal Principles
of the Protestant Reformation

Many issues and concerns drew the Reformers of the sixteenth century into conflict with the Roman Catholic Church. Three principles, however, revealed inseparable differences between the Reformers and papacy: justification by faith, supremacy of Scripture, and priesthood of the believer.

Luther's doctrine of justification by faith, though already loosely defined by 1517, was not included in the *Ninety-Five Theses,* nor were the other two principles.

As an Augustinian friar, Luther prayed, fasted, and beat himself in the ascetic tradition to relieve his troubled soul. Twenty years later, he reflected on his pious and diligent efforts by saying, "If ever a monk got to heaven by his monkery, I should certainly have got there."[6]

Luther's beliefs regarding faith developed earliest, it seems, from his study of the Book of Psalms. Commenting on Psalm 106:3 in 1513, Luther stated, "We are not justified by works but just works proceed from the just."[7] In 1515 and 1516 Luther lectured at the University of Wittenberg on the Epistle to the Romans. This study, especially Romans 1:16-17, made an indelible mark on his doctrine of justification by faith.

Secondly, Luther believed the Bible was the supreme authority in Christian living and guidance, not the pope. Because humans are mortal sinners and because church councils are composed of humans, he reasoned, church councils could make mistakes. He also insisted that no church doctrine was valid unless proven by the Scriptures. In 1521 the pope excommunicated Luther and ordered him to appear at the Diet of Worms. When asked to retract his statements, Luther responded that he trusted the Scriptures and his conscience. This led to the Edict of Worms, which declared Luther an outlaw and allowed anyone to kill him without punishment.

Finally, his belief in the priesthood of the believer meant that each Christian as a member of Christ's body had no authority over the conscience of other Christians. Having equal access, each person could approach God directly without a priest. Each person could act as his or her own priest. In addition, belief in the priesthood of the believer denied the superiority of the clergy over the laity.

The sincerity and conviction displayed by Luther and his followers concerning the priesthood of the believer is amazing. Yet, even more astonishing is the fact that Protestants refused to grant freedom of conscience to those who dissented from the Reformer's positions. The result not only pitted Catholic against Protestant, but also one Protestant fanatically in opposition to another.

Educational Principles of Martin Luther

Luther placed primary importance on the Christian home. This constituted the beginning of instruction. He proposed universal education for children of both sexes. In his view, education should be compulsory and state-supported. He revamped education around the theme of faith in God. Its purpose was to develop Christian character in children who, as a result, would better serve God, church, state, and society. Luther was more practical than most humanists, but he shared the humanist idea that education should be well-rounded. Yet Erasmus lamented, "Wherever Lutheranism rules, learning dies."

Although he formulated no systematic philosophy of education, Martin Luther expressed the greatest concern of all the Reformers about Christian education. In several of his writings, Luther magnified the importance of education, but two, *The Letter to Mayors and Aldermen of All the Cities of Germany in Behalf of Christian Schools* (1524) and *Sermon on the Duty of Sending Children to School* (1530), were Protestant manifestos on education.

Luther's *Small Catechism* (1529), later called the *Layman's Bible*, was written over a period of thirteen years and designed for use by the lower clergy and general public. Next to the Bible, the *Small Catechism* has been circulated more than any other book.[8] He had already written a larger catechism called the *German Catechism* (1529), designed especially for pastors and preachers.

From 1521 to 1534, Luther translated the Bible into German. This translation is considered a masterpiece that helped to create the modern German language. In worship, the Reformers emphasized preaching in the vernacular and congregational singing. In 1529 Luther published a hymnbook with forty-three of his songs (thirty-six hymns).[9] His most famous hymn is "A Mighty Fortress Is Our God." Based on Psalm 46, it became the battle hymn of the Reformation.

Luther's schools required the study of Greek and Hebrew. He attributed his biblical language skills to his deliverance from Catholic bondage. The preservation of truth in religion depended significantly on the ability to interpret the original biblical languages. Luther often stated that "he was sure the devil was more afraid of his command of Greek and Hebrew than of whatever measure of the Spirit he had."[10]

To Luther, schools provided a better opportunity for learning than private tutoring. In his view, schools produced leaders who preserved the liberal arts and Christian base of society. Even without the important religious emphasis, schools were essential for preserving society. He proposed that about 40 percent of public funds go to education—more than public officials were willing to invest.

One of Luther's requirements for a schoolmaster was the ability to sing. Each Lutheran school had a cantor. Perceived as coworkers with God, Lutheran teachers were to do more than *train* students to remember lists or merely accumulate facts. In Luther's mind, animals were trained, but only humans could be educated. His educational methods included oral language teaching, a work-study plan to teach trades, the use of catechisms, a variety of learning activities, and other practical approaches. In addition to biblical languages, biblical studies, music, and liberal arts, Luther was ahead of his time in advocating the study of history and science.

Luther influenced Christian education by leading Protestantism, translating the Bible into German, stressing the educational role of the home and state, calling attention to the educational needs of common people, preparing catechisms, and writing hymns for congregational worship. Some of Luther's actions were, of course, unfortunate. Chief among these was his leadership in the peasant's revolt. When the peasants refused to disarm themselves as Luther had requested, he called both the Catholic and Protestant nobility to attack the peasants "like mad dogs." In the end, over 100,000 died, and the Protestant cause lost popularity. This even estranged the peasants and lower classes from Lutheranism, increased the control of civil rulers in religious matters, and hindered the spread of the Reformation.[11]

Luther's German Disciples in Education

Philip **Melanchthon** (1497-1560), Luther's chief assistant, is often called "the founder of the German educational system." Melanchthon was a Christian humanist, educated at the University of Heidelberg. Beginning in 1518 and continuing until his death, he taught Greek and theology at the University of Wittenberg as a layman without a doctorate. He was buried beside Luther at the University of Wittenberg.

Melanchthon organized the German public school system—the first since ancient Rome—along lines harmonious with the church. The state controlled the curriculum and other aspects of teaching; church confessions, on the other hand, controlled the state. Because of his organizational skills, Melanchthon became known as "the German schoolmaster." Yet his greatest contribution was writing textbooks on ethics, physics, religions, history, rhetoric, dialectic, and psychology. His Greek grammar, first written when he was sixteen, passed through twenty-six editions before his death, and his Latin grammar passed through fifty-five editions.[12] His *Commonplaces*, a systematic handbook of Lutheran doctrine, was written in 1521, and by 1529 he had published seven catechetical works. It is not surprising that some consider Melanchthon a greater scholar than Luther.

Johannes **Sturm** (1507-1589), who studied in schools of the Brethren of the Common Life, established the first classical gymnasium in Germany. Based on a humanistic approach, it influenced German secondary education for centuries.[13] Another important German educator was Johann **Bugenhagen** (1485-1558), professor and town preacher at Wittenberg. Bugenhagen more than either Luther or Melanchthon aided the cause of Protestant schools in Germany.

Notes

1. E. Harris Harbison, *The Age of Reformation* (Ithaca, N.Y.: Cornell University Press, 1967), 54.

2. Gustav M. Bruce, *Luther as an Educator* (reprint; Minneapolis: Augsburg, 1928), 56.

3. Ibid., 57.

4. Ibid., 71.

5. Ibid., 83.

6. Harbison, 47.

7. Roland H. Bainton, *The Age of the Reformation* (Malabar, Fla.: Krieger, 1956), 97.

8. Clarence H. Benson, *History of Christian Education* (Chicago: Moody, 1943), 85.

9. H. G. Haille, *Luther: An Experiment in Biography* (Garden City, N.Y.: Doubleday, 1980), 53.

10. Robert R. Rusk, *Doctrines of the Great Educators*, 3d ed. (n.p., 1965), 32.

11. Marianne Sawicki, *The Gospel in History* (New York: Paulist Press, 1988), 236.

12. James W. Richard, *Philip Melanchthon: the Protestant Preceptor of Germany* (New York: Knickerbocker Press, 1898), 136.

13. Kenneth V. Lottich and Elmer H. Wilds, *The Foundations of Modern Education*, 3d ed. (New York: Holt, Rinehart and Winston, 1961), 170.

19

Other
Protestant Reformers
and Movements

Protestantism divided into several groups between 1520 and 1650 for various reasons including the desire to worship as an individual, the need for serious reform in the Church, the educational nature of Renaissance humanism, and doctrinal differences among leaders. Luther and Zwingli differed as early as 1523 over the nature of the Lord's Supper. Zwingli considered the bread and wine to be symbols, but Luther insisted that Christ was literally present in the elements.[1]

Other differences soon developed among Zwinglians. In 1525 and 1526 a group, called Anabaptists by their oppressors, rejected infant baptism for believer's baptism and desired more radical changes in religious practices. The Anabaptists and others of like spirit led the Radical Reformation. In 1536 John Calvin assumed leadership of the reform in Geneva. The other main branch of the Protestant Reformation was the Anglican church, which separated from Rome because of Henry VIII's differences with the papacy.

A brief consideration of these personalities and movements is necessary to better understand the Reformation. The religious and political fallout changed Christian education for centuries.

Huldreich Zwingli

Zwingli (1484-1531) was born near Saint Gall, Switzerland. He was ordained into the Catholic priesthood at age twenty-two. In 1514 after hearing Desiderius Erasmus, Zwingli became his follower. Before Luther posted his *Ninety-Five Theses,* Zwingli preached and appealed for Catholic reform. While a chaplain in the Swiss army, he made three visits to the Vatican, where he saw religious excesses firsthand.

Zwingli's *Sixty-Seven Articles,* which were presented at the first

Zurich Disputation early in 1523, declared his spiritual freedom from the Catholic Church and identified differences with Luther. Catholic statues, monasteries, mass, purgatory, worship of saints, celibacy, and other Catholic beliefs and practices were replaced by Protestant doctrines such as the supreme authority of Scripture; the church as a congregation of the people; Christ as mediator instead of priests; clerical marriage; and free conscience in religious matters.[2]

Zwingli's educational efforts were related to his desire to reform society. The Zurich city council requested that Zwingli write a catechism and confession of faith for the reform. This was Zwingli's *Short Christian Instruction*. In 1523 Zwingli published *On the Education of Youth,* which was more concerned with Christian conduct than with pedagogy for children. In that same year, Zwingli wrote *The Christian Education of Boys,* a treatise on Protestant education.

While serving as chaplain to Protestant forces, Zwingli was killed in 1531. He had prepared the way for other Protestants who would follow his steps away from the Catholic Church.

John Calvin

John Calvin (1509-1564) was born in Noyon, France. His formal education consisted primarily of religion, law, and classical humanism. He studied law at the University of Orleans and theology at the University of Paris. Blessed with a brilliant mind and determined will, John Calvin became a major factor in the Protestant Reformation after his conversion in 1533, especially in the development of a systematic theology.

In 1534 Calvin moved to Basil, Switzerland, and two years later he became the leader of the Protestant pastors in Geneva. After being exiled from Geneva in 1538, Calvin, at the invitation of Genevan leaders, returned and established his theocratic, authoritarian leadership in 1542.

Calvin's major institutional contribution to education was his Geneva Academy, which he established upon his return from exile. The academy was divided into two schools. The private school taught children until about age sixteen, and the public school served as the university.

Controlled by the ministers of the church, the academy employed teachers who agreed to live by the church's confession of faith and monitor the beliefs of students. Teachers who erred in their duties were strictly disciplined by the church. The ideal Calvinistic teacher knew the art of physical punishment; the student needed to know that the instructor's best efforts were mild compared to the burning fires of hell. The following poem illustrates such discipline:

> Who spares the rod with spirit mild,
> He surely hates and harms his child.
> Stripes and fear are right;
> But who disowns their might,
> And trains his son in tender way,
> Unfits him for life's earnest fray.[3]

The teacher's example was to instill in students those habits and values essential to please God—thrift, sobriety, hard work, and responsible behavior. Basically the person who ingrained these concepts into the minds of people and synthesized the expectations into theology was John Calvin. Probably more than anyone else, he deserves credit for instilling adherence to "the Protestant work ethic."

Calvin and Luther agreed on a wide variety of educational practices. They believed the state should financially support compulsory universal elementary education for boys and girls. Parental guidance at home gave children a foundation for school. Calvin's appreciation for the Bible as the supreme authority for all of life was basically the same doctrine as Luther's. Although Calvin rejected the infallibility of popes to interpret Scripture, he insisted that much of his doctrine be considered infallible by his followers. This degree of insistence on infallibility existed to a greater extent in Calvin's writings than in Luther's. Perhaps the doctrine that was most characteristically associated with Calvin is predestination. He believed that God destined some for eternal life and others for eternal damnation. The nature and reward of the afterlife depended on divine predestination.[4]

The writings of John Calvin are more easily read than those of most other Reformers. His *Institutes of the Christian Religion*, first published in 1536, provided a loosely systematic approach for his Protestant teachings. In the *Institutes* Calvin distinguished his theological positions from Luther's.[5] The next year he wrote *Instruction in the Faith*, primarily a collection of catechisms. In 1541 his *Ecclesiastical Ordinances* outlined presbyterian church polity whereby a council of elders governs each local church. Theologians sometimes fail to acknowledge Calvin's political theories and practices of representative and constitutional government. For example, he advocated people's rights to change their own government from within.

Calvin deserves much credit for his theological and social contributions to the Reformation and their continuation through the ages. However, to keep these accomplishments in perspective, the following quote depicts the kind of action that generally follows when church and state unite too tightly:

> He united Church and State to such an extent that moral offenses were punishable by the State. During the first twenty-two years of his rule, fifty-eight people were executed, fourteen witches were burned to death, hundreds were exiled and hundreds more were punished annually for moral offenses. All places of popular pleasure were closed. Dress regulations were severe. Prisoners were tortured to exact confessions of moral offenses.[6]

The followers of Calvin were known by different names across Europe: French Huguenots, Dutch Reformed, English Puritans, Scottish Presbyterians. John Calvin, with his penetrating sermons and disciplined correspondence, significantly influenced the Netherlands, Switzerland, Scotland, England, colonial America, and many other lands for the Protestant cause.

The Radical Reformation

A large part of those who separated themselves from Zwingli beginning in 1525 became known by their enemies as Anabaptists or "rebaptizers." Because this group sought a more thoroughgoing reform than Luther and Zwingli, the Anabaptists constitute the roots of the Radical Reformation.

Anabaptists radically rejected several aspects of sixteenth-century Protestantism. They practiced congregational church polity and replaced infant baptism with believer's baptism, greatly offending both Catholics and Protestants. By sending missionaries, they devised a method to evangelize Europe. Their objective was not so much to reform as to restore the church to the practices of the first century. Anabaptists refused to fight in wars, denounced oaths, advocated separation of church and state, and stressed individual rights. In the opinion of their opponents, these beliefs threatened the order of society.[7]

Anabaptists and other groups labeled "rebaptizers" (Hutterites,

Mennonites, Amish, Baptists, and some Puritans) believed all regenerated Christians were equal in God's sight. For this reason they placed less emphasis on ordination and ministerial education. Their radical theological doctrines helped change governments; their compassionate marriage practices served as a positive example to others; and the blood of their dedicated martyrs, both male and female, served as a reminder of the cost of discipleship.

These beliefs and others brought opposition, persecution, and martyrdom to the Anabaptists, primarily from Catholics, Lutherans, and Calvinists. The stories of Anabaptist martyrdom are vividly recorded in *Martyr's Mirror.*[8] Severe persecution prohibited the establishment of many Anabaptist schools. Therefore, education to these groups mostly meant training in the home and worship.

The English Reformation

Few secular schools existed in England before the Reformation. With monasteries, cathedrals, colleges, hospitals, music schools, and other institutions, the Roman Catholic Church dominated education at the beginning of the sixteenth century.

The English Reformation differed from that of other European Protestant states. **Henry VIII** (1491-1547) became king in 1509. Although his episodes involving wives and other women are legend, his real problem was not women but children: he had no male heir. When Rome would not allow Henry to divorce Catherine of Aragon (1485-1536) in order to marry Anne Boleyn (ca. 1507-1536), Henry proclaimed the Act of Supremacy of 1534, severing the English church from Rome and recognizing the sovereign as head of the English church. By the end of his reign in 1547, Henry VIII had closed about 550 English monasteries and confiscated their property. The seven thousand residents of these monasteries returned to secular life. Most of these monasteries and convents never reopened, a big loss for Catholic Christendom but an even greater loss for educational opportunities.[9] Protestantism came to England in a series of decrees during several decades. In 1558, for example, Queen Elizabeth proclaimed the Acts of Supremacy and Uniformity, which placed the regulation of education under the Anglican Church.

Henry VIII and his successors not only closed schools but also persecuted and martyred scores of men and women who disagreed with them. Until the Act of Toleration of 1689, Congregationalists, Baptists, Puritans, Separatists, and other dissenters suffered.

Notes

1. W. P. Stephens, *The Theology of Huldrych Zwingli* (Oxford: Clarendon, 1986), 46-47.

2. Roland H. Bainton, *The Age of the Reformation* (Malabar, Fla.: Krieger, 1956), 122-25.

3. F. V. N. Painter, *A History of Education,* International Education Series, ed. William T. Harris, vol. 2 (New York: Appleton Century, 1905), 130.

4. Leo Daley, *History of Education* (New York: Monarch Press, 1966), 67-69.

5. Joseph M. Shaw, et al., *Readings in Christian Humanism* (Minneapolis: Augsburg Publishing House, 1982), 332.

6. Daley, 67.

7. William R. Estep, *The Anabaptist Story* (1963; reprint, Grand Rapids: Eerdmans, 1975), 232.

8. George H. Williams, *The Radical Reformation* (Philadelphia: Westminster, 1962), 499.

9. E. Harris Harbison, *The Age of Reformation* (Ithaca, N.Y.: Cornell University Press, 1967), 69-71.

20

The Jesuits
and
Catholic Reformation

Following the revolt of one Protestant group after another, the Roman Catholic Church responded with the Catholic or counter Reformation. Catholic renewal manifested itself in "mystics, missionaries, and educators; in the religious communities which they founded; and in the legislation of the Council of Trent, implemented by a series of reforming popes."[1]

Catholic renewal centered in three interlocking movements: the Council of Trent provided the doctrinal stimulation and evaluation; the Inquisition added ecclesiastical muscle and force; and the Jesuits or Society of Jesus excelled as the teaching and missionary arm of the Catholic Reformation.

In an effort to halt Protestant expansion and growth, Paul III established the Roman Inquisition in 1542.[2] After an early success in Italy, it prevented a wholesale Protestant invasion of Spain. With such results, the papacy turned the Inquisition toward targets in all locations.

The Roman Inquisition operated like the earlier Spanish Inquisition. Inquisitors were to discover and eradicate heretical beliefs by torture. They justified the use of physical pain because they believed there was no salvation outside the Catholic Church.

In some cases, Catholics compromised in an attempt to recover lost territories. The Religious Peace of Augsburg of 1555 stipulated that the ruler of a country or territory could decide the religious affiliation of his or her people. Widespread war resulted. Both Catholics and Protestants persecuted each other by torture or burning at the stake. In the name of religion, thousands lost their lives as the church destructively turned on itself.

In 1545 Pope Paul III called the Council of Trent, which was held in three separate sessions (1545-1547, 1551-1552, and 1562-1563) over a period of eighteen years.[3] The Council of Trent gave comprehensive direction designed to reform the Roman Catholic Church internally. Many conciliar decisions were designed to distinguish the "true church" from Protestant doctrine and practice.

In matters of education, the council gave serious attention to methods of establishing schools, educating priests, and sending missionaries. The council issued a catechism and authorized the creation of seminaries for clerical and lay training.

New religious orders, principally the Jesuits, carried out the dictates of the council. Directions from the Council of Trent served the Roman Catholic Church until the First Vatican Council (1869-1870).

Ignatius of Loyola

Inigo Lopez (1491-1556), youngest of thirteen children, was born in the family castle of Loyola in the Pyrenees. As a part of Spanish feudal aristocracy, Loyola's family owned land but was not very wealthy. In his youth, he was arrested along with several others for disturbing the peace in the city of Pamplona. As a page in the service of Queen Isabella, Loyola learned to read and write, then decided to pursue a military career.

Sometime in early adulthood, Loyola changed his first name to Ignatius. Less than five feet and two inches tall, his assertiveness helped him become an excellent soldier. In 1521, however, his military career ended at Pamplona when a French cannonball injured his legs.[4] A bored convalescent, Loyola turned his attention to reading two books, *The Life of Christ* and *The Lives of the Saints,* provided for him during his sickness. This reading influenced Ignatius to seek a life as a soldier for Christ. Once he was able to travel, he lived in a cave as a religious hermit near Manresa, Spain. There visions further altered his worldly attitude and provided the essence for much of his writing.

In 1522 he began to write *Spiritual Exercises,* a handbook of spirituality that described contemplation and meditation as later adopted by the Jesuits. A year later Loyola attempted to convert Moslems in Jerusalem, but he returned to Spain after discouragement from Franciscans there.

Upon reaching home, Loyola recognized his need for education. After successfully and quickly completing a boy's school in Barcelona, Ignatius studied at Alcala and Salamanca. He met and received encouragement from Juan Luis Vives. With a determined will and vocation,

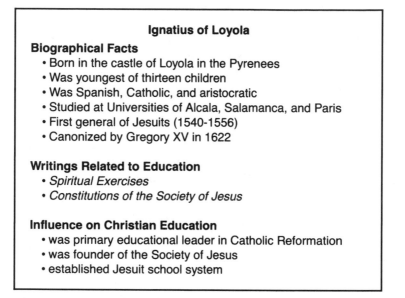

Loyola walked to the University of Paris in 1528, where he studied theology and philosophy and received his master of arts degree in 1534.[5]

While at the University of Paris, Loyola became the leader of a group that later formed the nucleus of the Jesuits. One of about ten or fewer associates was Francis Xavier. In 1534 Loyola's group took a vow to serve Christ in Jerusalem or offer their services to the Pope. After moving to Venice in 1536 and failing to locate in Jerusalem due to war, Loyola and his Company of Jesus received papal approval in 1540.[6]

Loyola did not refer to the new order as Jesuits but preferred to call his group the Company of Jesus or Society of Jesus. However, the popularity of the name "Jesuits" increased during and following the life of Loyola. Organized along military lines, the Jesuits characteristically followed their founder and first general, Loyola.

Members of the society were required to give absolute obedience to the general, but all Jesuits, including the general, were subject to dismissal from the order. A system of surveillance within the order controlled the conduct of members. In addition to the vows of obedience, poverty, and chastity, the Jesuit order demanded a vow of obedience to the pope. Between 1541 and 1556, several expanded editions of Loyola's *Constitutions of the Society of Jesus,* a handbook of rules and other information, appeared. This work and *Spiritual*

Exercises outlined the organization of the new order. Ignatius of Loyola remained the Jesuits' general until his death in 1556. His life as Roman Catholic, mystic, theologian, educator, student, and general caused Gregory XV to canonize Loyola in 1622.[7]

As defenders of Roman Catholicism, the Jesuits surpassed all other orders. Their three primary objectives were to counteract Protestants, provide quality education, and promote missionary expansion. On all three fronts, the Society of Jesus set new marks of Catholic excellence.

The Jesuits and Education

Perhaps the best example of the Jesuits' motto, "All to the greater glory of God," was found in their educational principles. Hundreds of years after the death of their founder, the Jesuits said with assurance: "Give me a child until he is seven, and he will remain a Catholic the rest of his life." The Jesuit system of education deserves consideration because it was one of the most effective in history. The *Plan of Studies,* first published in 1599, addressed nearly every known facet of education. Many Jesuit principles originated with the Brethren of the Common Life, the Christian humanists, and others. Yet, the Jesuits' innovations should not be discounted just because their comprehensiveness overshadowed their creativity. The Jesuits openly appointed committees to pursue the best educational principles regardless of the source.

Jesuit education developed the student's ability to live uprightly in this world and prepare for eternal life with God. Ideally the Jesuit student was to obtain a wealth of sacred and secular knowledge, think logically through complex issues, and persuade others of the truth vividly in verbal and written form. Loyola loved learning, but he cautioned against the sin of worshiping learning.[8] Higher education, his chief means to subdue heresy, was offered to the European middle classes, primarily to Catholics but also to Protestants.[9]

The success of Jesuit schools came not by accident or miracle. Loyola and the Jesuits who followed him gathered the best methods from friend and foe. They meticulously and systematically revised their system. The Jesuits' *Plan of Studies* as printed in 1599 basically governed the establishment and supervision of their schools without modification until 1832.[10]

Probably more than any other single factor, the preparation and dedication of teachers contributed to the success of the Jesuits. Great and specific expectations challenged Jesuit teachers, yet those who taught knew the requirements and received the training necessary to meet these demands.

Teacher training began with the Jesuit who had graduated from the university, excelled in his oral examination, and decided personally to study the art of teaching at the academy for teachers. During the final year of preparation at the academy, the student observed in detail the methods of the master teacher. The student then became a teacher under the supervision of the prefect of studies, who corrected or praised the potential master. The work of the prefect of studies continued after the graduation of his student teacher. During the first two years of teaching, the prefect appeared, usually unannounced, to observe the new teacher's progress. Beginning with the third year, the prefect's appearance in the classroom was limited to one monthly visit to evaluate the teacher. This procedure illustrates the Jesuit zeal for quality control.

Teachers strictly followed the Jesuit prescription of learning in both content and method. With the exception of periodic leaves, the teacher in the lower grades remained with the same group of students each year. This allowed the teacher to know the personal abilities and attitudes of each student. By design, the bond between teacher and student appeared early in their relationship. According to the Jesuits, the teacher should never punish his student. This task belonged to the disciplinarian. If the suggestions offered by the disciplinarian were not followed, the corrector, who was not a Jesuit, intervened. If unacceptable behavior persisted, the student was dismissed from the Jesuit school.

The Jesuit classroom was an intellectual battlefield. Groups of class members competed with each other in dialogue, debate, speeches, and reports. A mental battalion commanded by a class officer for every ten students from one side of the room confronted the opposing group in a bombardment of information, correction, and new information. After wins and losses were counted, the victorious students received awards and medals in school convocations. Where faulty logic was identified in the student's arguments, the teacher continued the approved process to repeat, review, and reward his students. The Jesuit curriculum, which consisted of religion, classics, languages, and other disciplines, provided continuity from the beginning of school through graduation. Students spent about five hours daily in the classroom and about two hours in competitive games and physical exercise.[11]

The Jesuits' system of education consisted of at least three faculties. Usually boys between the ages of ten and thirteen studied with the lower faculty of languages. This faculty was college and became a university when the faculty of arts was added for usually three years of instruction in philosophy, science, and other subjects. The final and most important Jesuit faculty was theology. Designed as a four-year program, this instruction included scholastic theology, biblical literature, church fathers, and canon law. In some places, faculties of civil law and medicine were added.[12]

The remarkable qualitative and quantitative success of Loyola and the Jesuits provides positive examples of Christian education that has influenced every succeeding generation. Beginning in 1540 with the first college established in Paris, Ignatius personally approved the opening of thirty-nine colleges. Probably the one that gained the most praise from him was later renamed the Gregorian University.[13]

By 1584 the Jesuits had established more than 160 colleges.[14] The number of institutions and students increased approximately as follows: 400 colleges by the year 1626; 612 colleges by the year 1710; and 800 colleges and seminaries with 22,589 members by the year 1749.[15] In 1773 Pope Clement XIV dissolved the Society of Jesus and placed their property in the hands of the Roman Catholic Church. This action was reversed in 1814, but substantial harm in the popularity of the Jesuits lingered. The actual success of the order may have been one of the reasons for the temporary papal closure. Much of the credit for the early advancement of the Jesuits belongs to their first and greatest missionary, **Francis Xavier** (1506-1552). His ministry, primarily in the Far East, resulted in several hundred thousand converts for the Christian cause. He also established Jesuit schools wherever possible. For this reason, he is often called "the Apostle of the Indies."

Through the centuries, Jesuit influence has spread worldwide. By 1970, Jesuits in the United States alone operated eighteen universities and ten colleges with an enrollment of 149,456 students; an additional fifty-one secondary schools enrolled 36,982 students.[16] Today the Jesuits continue their mission after the fashion of their founder.

Notes

1. Marianne Sawicki, *The Gospel in History* (New York: Paulist Press, 1988), 230.

2. Roland H. Bainton, *The Age of the Reformation* (Malabar, Fla.: Krieger, 1956), 155.

3. E. Harris Harbison, *The Age of Reformation* (Ithaca, N.Y.: Cornell University Press, 1967), 87.

4. Williston Walker, *A History of the Christian Church,* 3d ed. (New York: Scribner's, 1970), 376.

5. S. E. Frost, Jr. and Kenneth P. Bailey, *Historical and Philosophical Foundations of Western Education*, 2d ed. (Columbus, Ohio: Charles E. Merrill Publishing Co., 1973), 221.

6. Will Durant, *The Reformation*, The Story of Civilization series, part 6 (New York: Simon and Schuster, 1957), 912.

7. *Webster's Biographical Dictionary* (Springfield, Mass.: G & C Merriam Co., 1970), 926.

8. Christopher Hollis, *The Jesuits: A History* (New York: MacMillan, 1968), 75.

9. Ibid., 262.

10. Thomas Hughes, *Loyola and the Educational System of the Jesuits* (New York: Scribner's, 1892), 149.

11. Elmer L. Towns, ed., *History of Religious Educators* (Grand Rapids: Baker Books, 1975), 139.

12. Ibid., 139-40.

13. Ibid., 143.

14. Robert R. Rusk, *Doctrines of the Great Educators,* 3d ed. (n.p., 1965), 53.

15. Tim Dowley, *Eerdman's Handbook to the History of Christianity* (Grand Rapids: Eerdmans, 1977), 414.

16. Towns, 143.

21

Women's Education
in the Renaissance
and Reformation

Ecclesiastical records indicate that women were long considered more susceptible than men to heretical movements. Women experienced more visions and prophecies than men. When charged with identical acts, women were more often burned as heretics than men.

The Beguines was probably the first true women's movement in Western history. It spread throughout Europe, primarily in Germany, the Netherlands, and Italy, between the twelfth and fourteenth centuries.[1] Without papal approval, these mostly poor women fed the hungry, cared for the sick, translated Scripture, and taught their beliefs to others. They took no vows and refused confession with a priest. The Synod of Cologne in 1620 and the Council of Vienna condemned the Beguines as heretics.[2]

Many Waldensian women served as preachers, evangelists, and teachers. They administered communion and baptized believers. When the inquisitors departed Strasbourg in 1212, twenty-three women had been burned at the stake in the same fashion as had fifty-seven men. This is only one example, in a single place within one year. The Taborites, in the tradition of John Wycliffe, were the most radical branch of the Hussite movement. Like the Waldensians and other sects, the Taborites also included women teachers and preachers.[3]

Four Atypical Renaissance Women

The Renaissance did not equally concern men and women. The educational fate of poor males and females changed little during "the rebirth of learning." As had been true in previous centuries, the Renaissance woman's socioeconomic rank most often decided her chances for formal schooling. Yet some women made extraordinary contributions to Christian education. Four women, two English and two Italian, deserve attention: Julian of Norwich (ca. 1343-1413), Anne of Bohemia (1366-1394), Catherine of Siena (1347-1380), and Christine de Pisan (1364-1430).

Several clues toward understanding **Julian of Norwich** and her writings are mystic, Benedictine nun, English, spiritual counselor, teacher, and Neoplatonist. She spent most of her adult life as a recluse in the Norman Church of Saint Julian in Norwich, England. Her *Revelations of Divine Love* and *The Showings* presented her accounts and comments of visions. Julian articulated Christ in a "new vision."[4]

From the aristocratic class but with interest in all persons, **Anne of Bohemia** married Richard II, the king of England. During her lifetime, she assisted and contributed to the translating work of John Wycliffe. Anne read the Bible daily in Bohemian, Latin, and English. In fact, the Scriptures were read aloud to members of her family and her servants. Many lords and ladies followed her model of teaching.[5]

Catherine of Siena was the twenty-third child of Giacomo and Lapa Benincasa. Her birth represented:

neither aristocratics nor lowly serfs, neither intellectuals nor ignoramuses, neither aristocrats nor lowly serfs, neither wealthy nor wanting. . . . As a child she was more precocious and more pious than the average . . . [also] persistent, persuasive, and powerful.[6]

Two events in her life illustrate this diversity. During the plague of 1378 in Siena when thirty thousand persons died, Catherine cared for the sick and dying. In 1376 she convinced the pope to return to Rome from Avignon, France.[7]

She admired the Dominican Mantellate, as these women were called in Siena, but never joined the order. She became the patron saint of Italy.[8] She wrote several books, but two of the most important were *Dialogue* and *Divine Dialogue*.

Christine de Pisan was born in Venice, the daughter of a Venetian mother and Bolognan father who was court astrologer for Charles V.[9] Christine's parents disagreed about her education. Her mother wanted a traditional learning experience for her daughter. Let her be "spinning like other women."[10] Christine's father "was not of the opinion that women grew worse by being educated."[11]

A self-taught journalist, Christine amused and entertained the most prominent nobles of Northern France.[12] She was the first professional female author in France. Her religious and moral writings include "a remarkable series of writings defending, protecting, inspiring, and educating women."[13] Her *City of Ladies* presents an ideal female community with the Virgin Mary as queen. This work has much in common with monasticism.[14] In her *Epistle to the God of Love*, Christine wrote of Jesus' reception of women and how they received Christ.

Education of women was a central issue in the writings of Christine de Pisan. She believed that the "lack of education, not innately inferior qualities, held women back."[15]

Christian Humanists and Female Education

Although they disagreed on aspects of methodology and content, the humanists generally favored education as a right of women. This was true of Erasmus, Vives, More, Elyot, and many other Christian humanists.

Erasmus includes a chapter on the education of girls in *On Christian Matrimony*. To Erasmus, an intelligent woman refined and radiated a Christian home with culture. He defended the educational rights of women for personal distinction and the betterment of society and argued that women should receive equal rights in the secondary schools and universities.

While in England during the mid-1520s, Vives tutored Princess Mary under the patronage of Catherine of Aragon. For Mary, he wrote *On the Right Method of Instruction for Girls* and *On the Education of a Christian Woman*, two of the most important books from the sixteenth century on female education. Vives believed women should read the Scriptures and books about good manners but should avoid writings about love and war. In opposing fragrant perfumes, Vives quoted Plautus: "A woman ever smelleth best when she smelleth of nothing."[16] Vives also warned women against extravagant dress: "It is an old saying and a true: No beast is prouder than a woman well apparelled."[17]

Like Erasmus, Vives considered education a right of women, but he more strictly than Erasmus limited women to working at home. After reading Vives's thoughts on female education, Erasmus wrote Vives a letter; Erasmus considered Vives's treatment of women too severe and expressed hope that his treatment of his own wife was more gracious.[18] Although Vives wrote much about women, most of his instruction falls into the category of education in common, moral, and religious manners.

Luther's Concept of Women and Education

Martin Luther based his view of women on his interpretation of the Bible. In his commentaries on Genesis and the Pauline Epistles, Luther argued that women are less intelligent than men and have an inferior place because of the fall as recorded in Genesis. In 1519 he preached his "Sermon on the Estate of Marriage." A section of *The Babylonian Captivity of the Church* concerns marriage. Consistently in his writings, Luther placed primary importance on the development of a Christian home. This constituted the beginning of religious instruction to Luther.

Luther's marital teachings differed radically from traditional Catholic views. According to Catholic teaching, Celibacy earned heavenly rewards unavailable to married persons.[19] To Luther, celibates approached God the same way as everyone else. God's laws were the same for all, and grace was not earned. Luther's doctrine of the priesthood of believers is helpful in understanding this principle.

The father of Protestantism no longer considered marriage a sacrament, nor did he consider marriage inferior to celibacy. For Luther, the purpose of marriage was more than procreation or remedy for human lust, as Catholicism had generally taught. Although he considered procreation primary, he also emphasized companionship and love for those taking the marriage vows.[20] If, according to his doctrine of the priesthood of believers, each person could approach God in the same way then Protestant ministers could marry.

In 1523 twelve of the forty nuns from the Cistercian Convent of Nimbschem requested that Luther provide a means of escape for them. He did just that when a merchant on delivery to the convent smuggled the nuns out of the convent inside empty herring barrels. One of these nuns was **Katherine von Bora** (1499-1550), "the daughter of a poor aristocratic family from Saxony."[21] Katherine's cloistered experience at Nimbschem resembled Martin's earlier monastic training at Erfurt:

> Seclusion from the world was strictly enforced. Even relatives who visited were separated by a latticed window from the nuns who were accompanied by an abbess. . . . The regulations forbade friendships between the nuns. . . . Silence was the rule . . . and the nuns were required to walk with lowered heads and slow steps.[22]

With the exception of Katherine, these nuns were soon married. Finally, after attempts to match her with another man failed, Luther married her. He had earlier declared himself uninterested in marriage, which disappointed some of his followers. Some church members criticized Luther's marriage claiming that his and Katy's offspring would produce the Antichrist.[23] Yet Luther praised his wife and boasted of their good marriage. His loud and boisterous mannerisms must have inhibited her strong independence. According to Luther, her primary task as a Protestant wife was to care for her husband and family.

In *To the Christian Nobility of the German Nation Respecting the Reformation of the Christian Estate* and other writings, Luther either implied or stressed the need for female education. Supreme in his reasoning was the need for women as mothers and wives to know how to read the Scriptures. He wrote: "Would to God each town had also a girls' school, in which girls might be taught the gospel for an hour daily, either in German or Latin!"[24]

His chief concern for educating women was not so much for the woman's welfare but for posterity. Her personal development remained less important than her role in the home. Luther's view of woman's education was considered progressive in the sixteenth century, yet he cared far more for her "soul" than for her personhood.

According to Luther, the mother was to teach the Bible to the children and instruct them in the catechism and reformed doctrines. This learning at home provided the child with a foundation for the work of the schoolmaster. Under Lutheran leadership, Germany organized public schools for girls long before England.

In the matter of women teaching and preaching at church, Luther stated: "Take women from their housewifery. . . and they are good for nothing." And in a more derogatory manner he wrote, "If women get tired and die of bearing, there is no harm in that; let them die as long as they bear; they are made for that."[25]

To Luther, women lacked biblical qualifications to preach and teach in church. In addition, a woman's soft voice and dull memory disqualified her from such ministries. In some cases, where no suitable man was available, he allowed a temporary exception.[26]

John Calvin and Aristocratic Women

John Calvin's basic views about women resemble Luther's. Calvin's explanations on the subject generally centered on his traditional interpretation of Genesis and the Pauline Epistles. According to Calvin, woman's subjection originated because Eve was created as Adam's "helper." She was made *after* him and *for* him. For Calvin, this account was fundamental for all thoughts about women.

In 1539, John Calvin married **Idelette de Bure** (ca. 1499-1549), an Anabaptist, the widow of Jean Stordeur, a victim of the plague. John and Idelette's marriage lasted until her death ten years later. Several children were born, but each died in infancy. Calvin remained unmarried for the rest of his life.

John Calvin influenced the religion and politics of France and other countries, partly by his correspondence and friendships with aristocratic women. Religion and piety contributed to these connections, but power and money were probably more important.

Of all French noblewomen, **Marguerite of Navarre** (1492-1549) probably most influenced the Reformation.[27] At an early age, she studied under the educated governess Madame Chatillon, learning the biblical languages, Latin, Italian, theology, philosophy, literature, and music. Although she remained Catholic at heart, she defended the Protestant cause. While residing in Paris, she protected the Huguenots. Often called "the prime minister of the poor," she sponsored a variety of educational activities for both women and men.

Her mystic poetry deserves recognition. *The Mirror of the Sinful Soul,* poems based on Psalm 42, was published in 1533. Shortly before dying in 1548, she penned *A Godly Meditation of the Soul,* and after her death, *Heptameron* appeared. Her other writings include *The Primacy of Scripture, Justification of Faith,* and *Doctrine of Election.*[28]

John Calvin considered Marguerite a great hope for the Reformation, but he refused to rely heavily on her influence. In her mysticism, she resembled her Catholic friends, but in the open-door policy of her palace, she identified with Calvin and his Huguenot friends.

Jeanne d' Albret (1528-1572) was the only child of Marguerite and King Henry II of France, her second husband. After her mother's death, Jeanne d' Albret became queen of Navarre. While Marguerite's beliefs may have been in question, Jeanne's were not. She brashly defended John Calvin and the Huguenots, offending Roman Catholics. She and Calvin communicated often about a wide variety of subjects. On Christmas Day 1560, in a public profession of her Protestant faith, she declared Calvinism as *the* religion of Navarre. Religious toleration ceased when Jeanne restricted the use of the crucifix, which she called "idolatrous." Shortly after Jeanne died in 1572, Catholics slaughtered hundreds of Protestants in what is commonly called "St. Bartholomew's Day Massacre."[29]

Renee of France (1510-1575) befriended John Calvin after his exile from Geneva and protected him in her court under the assumed name of Charles d' Esperville. While there, he probably completed the first edition of his *Institutes of the Christian Religion*.

Calvin corresponded regularly with about twenty politically powerful, aristocratic women. Calvin often encouraged these women to hold fast as they faced opposition from religious and other forces.

Calvin confided his beliefs about women in politics to John Knox. Calvin told Knox that "the government of women . . . was a deviation from the original and proper order of nature" but "was to be ranked, no less than slavery, among the punishments consequent upon the fall of man."[30]

Knox, who had suffered bitterly in Scotland under the rule of "Bloody" Mary Tudor, queen of England, and Mary Guise, queen regent of Scotland, attacked the divine right or any other right of placing females in leadership positions. He said this and much more in his tract entitled "The First Blast Against the Monstrous Regiment of Women," printed in 1558.[31]

Women in the Radical Reformation

George Huntston Williams in *The Radical Reformation* has stated that a near equality existed between the Anabaptist "sisters" and "brethren." These women's missionary efforts and martyrdom showed that the doctrine of the priesthood of the believer applied to male and female alike.[32] Other writers have described Anabaptist women as subordinate, inferior, obedient, or silent. Some truth is present in both of these views.

Roland Bainton, a leading Reformation scholar, has credited Anabaptists and their group descendants with insisting that "companionability be the prime ingredient in marriage."[33] Instead of the two-dimensional male and female conception of marriage, theirs was three-dimensional, with Christ as the heavenly bridegroom. Such a marriage became both a physical and spiritual union "conceived in heaven."[34]

Anabaptists considered the family a church in microcosm. The father headed the family as Christ headed the church. Parents saw that their children learned to read and write. Well-constructed letters in *Martyrs' Mirror* show that some wives were better educated than their husbands. Claesken of Workum read aloud for her illiterate husband, and her executioners declared that her good education had seduced her husband into Anabaptism. Claude de Vettre was a pastor's wife whose husband praised her ability to find biblical passages he was unable to locate.[35]

The details of the devoted faith of Anabaptist women have survived partly because of female writers and artists. One example is Margaret Pruss of Strasbourg, who married the Anabaptist Balthasar Beck. In the 1530s, they formed Pruss-Beck Press and printed books by Anabaptist teachers and preachers.

Anabaptist women were martyred by both Catholics and Protestants. Their accounts appear in *Martyrs' Mirror* by T. J. van Braght. About 310 of the 930 Anabaptist martyrs included in this book were women.

Maria of Monjou, a preacher, was executed by drowning at Monschau in 1552. Elizabeth Munstdorp had been married for only a year and was pregnant when she and her husband were martyred in Antwerp.[36] In 1573 the state church imprisoned, tortured, and killed Malyken Wens. In the same year, Maeyken van Deventer suffered arrest and martyrdom for her faith. Elizabeth Dirks of Leeuwarden, who frequently traveled and worked with Menno Simons, was captured in 1549. The policemen must have known her well, because they exclaimed, "We have the right man, we have now the teacheress."[37]

A ballad about the faith and death of Elizabeth is included in the *Ausbund*, the oldest Swiss Anabaptist hymnal. This book dates from 1564 and is still used by the Amish in North America. One writer has paid perhaps the ultimate compliment to Anabaptist women: "The woman in Anabaptistism emerges as a fully emancipated person in religious matters and as the independent bearer of Christian convictions."[38]

Women and the English Reformation

Educational opportunities for women decreased under Henry VIII. He closed and for the most part never reopened many convents, severely hurting women's education. More importantly, his persecution and martyrdom claimed many lives.

These and others spoke against confession, favored the English Bible, and taught a religion considered unorthodox to their family and friends.[39] Henry decapitated Elizabeth Barton and Anne Boleyn, among others; Alice Potkins starved to death.

In Memoriam

As early as 1512, **Agnes Grebill** was burned for her beliefs. Henry's terror also claimed **Ann Audebert, Margery Astoo, Alice Harding, Alice Atkins, Catherine Allin, Petronil Appleby, Margaret Hyde, Anne Askew, Anne Albright, Agnes Stanley, Agnes Edmund,** and **Isabel Morwin** to name a few of the believers.

These women died for their faith during the reign of King Henry VIII of England.

One of the most unusual circumstances involving martyrs concerned the blind Joan Waste (ca. 1500-1556) of Derby. After her conversion to the Reformed faith, she bought a New Testament and paid an old gentleman daily to read the Scriptures to her. By doing this she memorized large portions of the Bible. She also refused to attend mass. For these supposed crimes she was burned at the stake in 1556.[40]

English Protestant sects generally allowed women more authority, expression, and religious freedom than the churches considered orthodox. As a rule, the more radical the sect, the more important the roles assumed by women. Reformation principles had opened the door for women to communicate their revelations and visions.

The Society of Friends, or Quakers, believed that the "inner light" made men and women religiously equal. Kathrine Evans preached with her husband and Elizabeth Leavens. They embraced the proud religious heritage of the Quakers. When Elizabeth Hooten and Elizabeth Williams preached at Oxford, the authorities flogged them and carried them out of town. Anne Austin, Barbara Blaugdone, and Mary Fisher left their families to preach and teach in places as far away as Turkey and Barbados.[41]

Early English Baptist congregations elected women for service, and these women performed their duties at the same time as men. Although most of the women were not ordained, they could teach and preach. They also served as deacons and shared in their church's congregational decision making.[42] During this time, other Baptist women teachers and preachers acted without the blessing of their congregations. Women more often shared leadership roles among General Baptists than among Particular Baptists.

Early Baptist women experienced more freedom than their counterparts in most other religious groups for four reasons. First, their doctrine was based on the Bible, which contains many examples of women in ministry. Second, John Smyth was serving as minister to an Anabaptist congregation exiled in Amsterdam when he organized the group that became known as English Baptists. Third, congregational polity encouraged at least the possibility of female participation. Finally, women constituted over half of the membership of many English Baptist congregations. By their sheer numbers, Baptist women held an advantage.[43]

Catholic Reform and Women's Education

Ignatius of Loyola suffered prolonged criticism because he refused to establish a female branch of the Jesuits. He sought to remove the Jesuits from any chance of a bad reputation that could come from association with females. He often asked his followers to avoid the appearance of wrongdoing toward the opposite sex. While teaching on the matter in a letter to his Jesuits, Loyola advised: "I would not enter upon spiritual conversations with women who are young or belong to the lower classes of the people, except in church or in places which are visible to all."[44] Therefore, Ignatius wanted no part of education for women. He contributed to a halfway house for prostitutes. Many of these women were married, and Loyola sought to reunite them with their husbands after transformation. He called this successful project the House of Saint Martha.[45]

In 1535 **Angela Merici** (1474-1540) established the Ursulines. She desired that nuns move out into society to minister as educators, nurses, and workers with the poor. She wanted nuns to wear everyday clothes and to take reversible vows.[46] The Council of Trent denied these requests with a directive favoring full cloister, which remained the Catholic position on the subject until the late 1890s. According to the Council's argument, religious virgins in the world would be a source of scandal, and Protestant Reformers would ridicule them. If allowed in public, nuns might seduce and corrupt celibate men of the cloth. During the seventeenth century, the Ursulines gained recognition as the leading educators of Catholic girls and served as the model for future teaching orders.[47]

Teresa of Avila (1515-1582) was born in Avila of Old Spain. Her mother died when Teresa was twelve. At this time, Teresa's father placed her in a convent school for the nobility. One of the most celebrated Catholic women of all time, Teresa of Avila, distinguished herself as reformer, author, mystic, and Christian worker. At age twenty-one she became a Carmelite nun.[48] To some she was a saint; to others, a lunatic. During a period of twenty-five years, she established fifteen Carmelite houses.

Of her numerous mystical writings, *The Interior Castle* is her masterpiece. She wrote, "Only a mystic can teach a mystic doctrine, and this teaching is a vital communication. If they, by chance, should write something, that is only a substitute and a reminder."[49] In 1970 Pope Paul IV proclaimed Teresa a doctor of the church, the first woman so honored.[50]

The Englishwoman **Mary Ward** (1585-1642) attempted to establish an order similar to the Ursulines. Afterward she sought to provide domestic education for girls. She believed the primary educator in the family was the woman. Mary tried to provide the female equivalent of Jesuit schooling but met resistance, as had Angela Merici. In 1609 Mary founded the Institute of the Blessed Virgin Mary, a cloistered community for prayer and education associated with the Roman Catholic Church. She insisted that women were not intellectually deficient:

> There is no such difference between men and women that women may not do great things, as we have seen by the example of many saints. And I hope to God it will be seen that women in time to come will do much . . . As if we were in all things inferior to some other creatures which I suppose to be man.[51]

In 1631 the church rejected the efforts of Mary Ward and ordered suppression of her ideas. Like many women before her, she could not change tradition.

Notes

1. Marianne Sawicki, *The Gospel in History* (New York: Paulist Press, 1988), 211-12.

2. Ruth A. Tucker and Walter L. Liefield, *Daughters of the Church* (Grand Rapids: Zondervan, 1987), 161-62.

3. Ibid., 162.

4. Kathleen Parbury, *Women of Grace: A Biographical Dictionary of British Women Saints, Martyrs and Reformers* (Boston: Oriel Press, 1985), 59.

5. Mary L. Hammack, *A Dictionary of Women in Church History* (Chicago: Moody, 1984), 7.

6. Mary L. Coakley, *Long Liberated Ladies* (San Francisco: Ignatius Press, 1988), 21.

7. Igino Giordani, *Catherine of Siena—Fire and Blood,* trans. Thomas J. Tobin (Milwaukee: Bruce Publishing Co., 1959), 4.

8. Bonnie S. Anderson and Judith P. Zinsser, *A History of Their Own: Women in Europe from Prehistory to the Present,* vol. 1 (New York: Harper and Row, 1988), 221.

9. Elizabeth A. Petroff, ed., *Medieval Women's Visionary Literature* (New York: Oxford University, 1986), 303.

10. Frances Gies and Joseph Gies, *Women in the Middle Ages* (New York: Barnes and Noble, 1978), 10.

11. Ibid.

12. Bonnie S. Anderson, *A History of Their Own: Women in Europe from Prehistory to the Present,* vol. 2 (New York: Harper and Row, 1988), 79.

13. Petroff, 304.

14. Ibid., 306.

15. Anderson, 94.

16. Foster Watson, *Vives and the Renaissance Education of Women* (London: Edward Arnold Press, 1912), 77.

17. Ibid.

18. Juan Luis Vives, *De Tradendis Discipline (Vives on Education),* trans. Foster Watson (New York: Cambridge University Press, 1913), lxxxvii.

19. Barbara J. MacHaffie, *Her Story: Women in Christian Tradition* (Philadelphia: Fortress, 1986), 61.

20. Richard L. Greaves, ed., *Triumph Over Silence: Women in Protestant History* (Westpoint, Conn.: Greenwood Press, 1985), 15.

21. Tucker and Liefield, 180.

22. See Richard Friendenthal, *Luther: His Life and Times,* trans. John Nowell (New York: Harcourt, Brace and Jovanovich, 1970), 437; quoted in Tucker and Liefield, 180.

23. Hammack, 96.

24. Edward H. Reisner, ed., *Early Protestant Educators: The Educational Writings of Martin Luther, John Calvin, and Other Leaders of Protestant Thought* (New York: McGraw-Hill, 1931), 41.

25. Will Durant, *The Reformation: A History of European Civilization from Wycliffe to Calvin, 1300-1564* (New York: Simon and Schuster, 1957), 416.

26. MacHaffie, 65.

27. Tucker and Liefield, 186.

28. Nancy A. Hardesty, *Great Women of Faith: The Strength and Influence of Christian Women* (Grand Rapids: Baker Book House, 1980), 53.

29. Tucker and Liefield, 187-88.

30. Ibid., 177.

31. Ibid.

32. George H. Williams, *The Radical Reformation* (Philadelphia: Westminster, 1962), 506-07.

33. Elaine Sommers Rich, *Mennonite Women: A Story of God's Faithfulness, 1683-1983* (Scottdale, Penn.: Herald Press, 1983), 41.

34. Greaves, 57.

35. Ibid., 59.

36. Anderson and Zinsser, 242-43.

37. Greaves, 53.

38. Rich, 22.

39. Anderson and Zinsser, 235.

40. Tucker and Liefield, 191.

41. Anderson and Zinsser, 236.

42. Greaves, 56.

43. MacHaffie, 71.

44. Tucker and Liefield, 201.

45. Ibid., 200.

46. MacHaffie, 64.

47. Anderson and Zinsser, 239.

48. Teresa of Avila, *The Interior Castle,* trans. Kieran Kavanaugh (New York: Paulist Press, 1979), xiv.

49. Ibid., xv.

50. Coakley, 57.

51. Eileen M. Brewer, *Nuns and the Education of American Catholic Women, 1860-1920* (Chicago: Loyola University Press, 1987), 4-5.

CHRISTIAN EDUCATION AND THE RENAISSANCE & REFORMATION
Chart 5

	GOALS OF EDUCATION	WOMEN AND EDUCATION	PERSONALITIES
BRETHREN OF THE COMMON LIFE	• Concentrate in the elementary grades with common people • Rehabilitate impoverished persons • Imitate Christ • Copy Scripture • Establish schools	• Regarded women highly for education • Established the Sisters of the Common Life • Opposed for their acceptance of women by some Catholic orders	• Geert Groote • John Wessel • Thomas á Kempis • Erasmus • Martin Luther • Pope Adrian VI • John Sturn • John Calvin
PLEASANT HOUSE	• Develop good, Christian, moral character • Cultivate well-balanced education in a positive family atmosphere	• Girls studied in their homes under tutors	• Vittrino da Feltre
MARTIN LUTHER	• Develop character and provide Christian service to God, church, state and society • Universal compulsory education with faith in God as the theme	• A lady's primary place was in the home • Provided elementary but not higher education for women	• Martin Luther • Philip Melanchthon • Johann Bugenhagen
SOCIETY OF JESUS	• "All to the glory of God" • Live righteously on earth and prepare for afterlife • Concentrated in higher education	• The Jesuits excluded women from formal education	• Ignatius of Loyola • Francis Xavier

CHRISTIAN EDUCATION AND THE RENAISSANCE & REFORMATION

Chart 5

ROLE OF THE TEACHER	ROLE OF THE STUDENT	CURRICULUM	METHODOLOGY
• Teach and practice Christian principles • Tutor students, especially the loco fortunato	• Seek unification with Christ • Practice love in simplistic life-style	• Studied religion, not as a separate discipline, but in application to all other subjects • Catholic in content • Mystic and humanistic influences	• No vows, no rule • Simplicity, purity • Rewards, prizes, less harsh discipline • Small groups • Vernacular • Promotion of grades at individual pace • Community living
• Live with students and with love win their friendship • Model the lessons for students to observe prior to daily classes.	• Rich and poor children alike are taught • Learn at own individual pace • Boys admitted at age 9-10 and allowed to remain until about 21	• Classical literature • Biblical studies • Seven liberal arts, except medieval logic • Balanced • Physical education	• Humanistic • Instruction in Latin, little use of the vernacular • Praise and encouragement • Games and play • Pleasant surroundings • Physical training • Notebooks
• Parents were the first teachers • Coworker with God • Shema (Deut. 6)	• Learn the content and application of the Bible in well-rounded Christian living • Receive an education, not the ability to verbalize lists	• Biblical studies • Greek and Hebrew • Liberal arts • Music • History & science	• Catechisms • Practical • Work-study plan • Congregational singing • Oral method of studying languages • No harsh discipline • Worship in vernacular
• Follow the Jesuits' "Plan of Studies" • Befriend the student toward Catholic doctrine • Develop the intellect	• Obtain knowledge, think logically, persuade others of the truth in verbal and written form	• Catholic dogma • Theology • Arts • Languages • Classics	• Memorization • Review, repeat, and reward • Military structure • Debate • Teacher training • Competition • Promotion of more able students

Synopsis
of Part 4

Two of the most important milestones in Western history emerged from the fourteenth into the seventeenth centuries. The Renaissance, which means "rebirth of learning," originated in Florence, Italy, in the early 1300s. The origin of the Reformation, the second transitional event, is considered by most to have begun on October 31, 1517, when Martin Luther nailed his *Ninety-five Theses* to the chapel door of the Wittenberg church. In many ways the Reformation was an extension of the Renaissance that focused on religious matters but also influenced every element of society both secular and sacred.

In education, religion, and other aspects of life, the Renaissance produced a revival of humanism, rejecting medieval asceticism and the church's esteem of Aristotle. In general, southern humanism addressed concerns of aristocratic individuals who sought to discover the greatest pleasures of living. Northern humanism, by contrast, developed more interest in social reform, democratic ideals, preservation of the church, and production of a better world. In education, both forms of humanism expressed high interest in a return to classical Greece and Rome. However, the Christian humanists of the Renaissance and Reformation sought an understanding of Greek and Hebrew to interpret the Bible in its original form. Two of the most influential humanists in education were Desiderius Erasmus and Juan Luis Vives.

Certainly many ingredients precipitated the Reformation, but from an educational point of view, four were perhaps the most important. These were: early reformers, humanism, the printing press, and political governments.

In addition to being the leader of the Protestant Reformation, Martin Luther more than the other Protestant Reformers addressed issues in education. His three cardinal principles of the Protestant Reformation have contributed significantly to changes in religion, education, government, society, and nearly every other phase of human existence. Like schools of the Brethren of the Common Life, which trained or influenced many of the Reformers, Luther advocated education for common people, not just aristocrats and clergy. He used the vernacular rather than Latin in teaching, preaching, and congregational singing. Luther's popular catechisms continue to bear Christian witness in many languages.

Luther led the Reformation from his classroom at the University of Wittenberg. By necessity, Luther's form of education was religious. He did not trust the authoritarian church to interpret the Bible. Luther insisted that schools teach Hebrew and Greek so that a person could learn the meaning of the Bible in its original form.

Most of John Calvin's educational principles resemble Luther's. Calvin's Geneva Academy established a theocratic relationship between education, religion, and government. Calvin's theology and educational principles came to the American colonies through the Puritans.

The Anabaptists led the Radical Reformation. Their martyrdom is equaled only by the early Christians. Because they rejected infant baptism for believer's baptism, the Anabaptists experienced the deadly wrath of both Protestants and Catholics. The Anabaptists rejected war for any reason, denounced oaths, advocated the separation of church and state, and stressed the rights of individuals. Lessons from the Anabaptists and other radical groups such as the Mennonites, Baptists, and Puritans encompassed both the cognitive and effective domains of learning. Although they often established schools for their dependents, the educational contributions of these sects were more practical than formal with less emphasis on ordination and ministerial education.

When Henry VIII and other heads of government closed Catholic monasteries and nunneries, educational opportunities for both men and women suffered. The Catholic Reformation stressed the educational plan of the Society of Jesus or Jesuits. Under the leadership of Ignatius of Loyola, this order founded schools, especially for higher education, and sent missionaries to nearly every known part of the earth. The Jesuit system of education was probably the best in history up until its time.

During the Renaissance, aristocratic families often provided teachers for their daughters, but the common people for the most part remained uneducated. Erasmus and Vives favored the education of women, but like most humanists, they directed their attention toward the privileged classes.

Luther promoted respect for women when he affirmed that the ideal state of woman was marriage rather than celibacy, but in some other ways he represented no improvement over the medieval view of women. Luther, Calvin, and other Reformers promoted elementary education for women, but they still considered her place, almost exclusively, to be the home.

Although most women of the Radical Reformation received little formal education, their courage and conviction characterized the true nature of Christian education as well as that of any group before or after them. As they served and suffered in Christian ministry, they magnified the home in companionship with their husbands and in nurturing their children.

PART 5

The Beginnings of
Modern Christian Education

22. John Amos Comenius and Sense Realism

The Life and Career of Comenius
Comenius's Approach to Education
The Four Grades System
Sense Realism

23. European Naturalism and Christian Education

Rousseau
Pestalozzi
Herbart
Froebel

24. The Sunday School Movement

The Birth of the Sunday School Movement
Robert Raikes Pioneered Sunday School Development
The Growth of the Sunday School Movement

25. German Pietists and Christian Education

Spener
Francke
Zinzendorf
Schleiermacher

26. Other Influences on Christian Education

Puritanism
John Wesley and Methodism
John Henry Newman and Higher Education
The Missions Movements
The Salvation Army
Christian Student Movements

27. Women in the Beginnings of Modern Christian Education

Women as Students
Women as Educators

Synopsis of Part 5

22

John Amos Comenius and Sense Realism

The Life and Career of Comenius

Although his life followed closely on the heels of the Reformation, John Amos Comenius (1592-1670) is considered the father of modern education. The name by which he is popularly known is the Latinized version of his real name, Jan Amos Komensky. He was born in Nivnitz, Moravia. He was born into a Hussite family (more specifically the Unitas Fratrem or Moravian Church). At the age of twelve Comenius lost both parents and two of his four sisters, possibly to the plague.

Although the Hussites valued education, Comenius's early education was disappointing because of parental neglect. Four years after the death of his parents, Comenius enrolled in a Unitas Fratrem school in Prerov. He began his formal schooling late but showed great promise. Comenius was encouraged by the rector, John Lanecius, who recognized the youth's potential.

During his three years at the Prerov school, Comenius developed a concern with the way in which the children were taught and dedicated himself to preparation for the Moravian clergy. He received his higher education in Germany at Herborn and Heidelberg. Comenius found the German teachers Johann Alsted, David Pareus, and Johann Fischer to be mentors who encouraged him in his faith and reliance on Scripture for direction in every area of his life, including his educational thought. He became interested in the writings of Wolfgang Ratichius and moved to Amsterdam to study the Dutch educational systems.

After completing his education, Comenius returned to teach at his old school in Prerov. There he composed a Latin grammar and began writing an encyclopedia. Soon after his ordination to the Moravian ministry he married and moved to Fulnek, where he served as minister and master of the church school.

During his pastorate the longstanding tension between the ruling Catholic minority and the Protestant churches broke into open revolt. As part of the Thirty Years War, Spanish Catholic troops captured Fulnek and led Pastor Comenius from the city in exile. His wife and child returned to Prerov, where she soon gave birth to a second child. An epidemic struck Prerov and Comenius's wife and two children died.

John Amos Comenius

Lived: 1592-1670; born in Moravia, but also lived at various times in Poland, Germany, and Hungary; traveled widely

Career: Moravian bishop and educator; educational consultant to various European governments and with some early New England church leaders

Writings dealing with education: *The Great Didactic, The School of Infancy, Orbis Sensualium Pictus* ("The World in Pictures"—an early picture book for children), *Janua Linguarum Reserata* ("The Gate of Language Unlocked"), and other books and pamphlets

Views related to education:
- children to be taught at developmentally appropriate times in their lives
- structure and curricula of education should follow closely studied developmental guidelines
- aim of his educational plan was *pansophia* or "universal knowledge"
- the sources for attaining *pansophia* are nature, art, and God
- the senses must be trusted to inform the learner
- knowledge is a tool for building a better and more peaceful work
- all education must be made more pleasant to more readily effect learning

---

Comenius remarried in 1624 and, in 1625, was sent by the Moravian church to Leszno in Poland. His assignment was to provide a system of resettlement among Moravians who were fleeing persecution. The need for this became apparent when an edict in 1627 was issued that required all Protestants to convert to Catholicism.

Comenius proved to be an incessant worker and was named bishop in 1632. About this time he wrote his most significant books about education, *The Great Didactic* and *The School of Infancy.*

Comenius became well known to the educators of Europe. He petitioned the British Parliament for the funding of a school in which to implement his educational theories. He may have been asked to become the first president of Harvard College. He spent six years in Sweden developing the national school system and continuing his writing. He moved to Hungary in 1650 to direct a school at Saros Patak, where he attempted to apply his philosophy of education. There Comenius wrote a book for children, *Orbis Sensualium Pictus.* It was a simple picture book, but quite a development for its day.

Eventually, Comenius returned to Leszno and then to Amsterdam, where he published various works and catechisms and continued in church ministry until he died.

Comenius's Approach to Education

Comenius believed humans to be the highest of created beings, imbued with the nature of God and made for communion with the divine. He understood learning as a process of discovery beginning at conception:

> Whatever we are, do, think, speak, contrive, acquire, or possess, contains a principle of gradation, and, though we mount perpetually and attain higher grades, we still continue to advance and never reach the highest.
>
> For in the beginning a man is nothing, and has been nonexistent from eternity. It is from his mother's womb that he takes his origin. What then is a man in the beginning? Nothing but an unformed mass endowed with vitality. This soon assumes the outlines of a human body, but has, as yet neither sense nor movement.
>
> Later on it begins to move and by a natural process bursts forth into the world. Gradually the eyes, ears, and other organs of sense appear. In course of time the internal senses develop and the child perceives that he sees, hears, and feels. Then the intellect comes into existence by cognizing the differences between objects; while, finally, the will assumes the office of a guiding principle by displaying desire for certain objects and aversion for others.[1]

For Comenius, persons are rational souls with minds of virtually limitless potential and with an innate desire for knowledge. However, that potential can only be realized (and the human being become a true person) through a proper education. This universal knowledge or *pansophy* was the aim of Comenius's educational structures.

Noting the contrasting ages at which beasts of burden and persons mature, Comenius deduced that God must have given the years of youth to humans for the purpose of education.[2] Thus Comenius encouraged the establishment of common schools. Although he acknowledged the importance of the home in a child's education, he argued that most parents had neither the leisure nor the ability to teach their children properly in the strictest sense. Children of both sexes should be given a *universal education* that would include the arts and sciences as well as languages, morals, and theology.

To Comenius education should be conducted in a more gentle manner than was the practice in most schools of his day. He suggested that the school day last but four hours and that students be taught true comprehension and understanding of truth rather than simply memorizing the opinions of others.[3]

The Four Grades System

In *The Great Didactic*, Comenius refers to nature as an example of how proper learning and teaching takes place and points out specific areas in which the schools of the time had failed. Appropriate educational goals had not been established. The sequence in which many subjects were taught was not the best, and the interrelatedness of the subjects was lost. Students were confused by the variety of teaching methods and lack of guidance regarding the books they were to read.[4]

Comenius gave specific instruction to the teachers of science, arts, languages, and piety. He also advised a form of censorship by which books by "pagans" would be removed from the shelves of Christian schools or the student would be urged to read them with caution.

Comenius divided the first twenty-four years of life into four equal *grades* and suggested an appropriate school for each grade. The first grade was the "school of the mother's knee," the school of infancy. The vernacular school was for childhood, which was the second grade. The Latin school or gymnasium was the third grade, which was during boyhood. Finally, the fourth grade was the university. Only this latter school should take the youth away from home. Comenius wrote, "A Mother-School should exist in every house, a Vernacular School in every hamlet and village, a Gymnasium in every city, and a University in every kingdom or in every province."[5]

The School of Infancy

The school of the mother's knee was to provide a solid foundation on which the child's future education would rest. In this school both parents shared responsibility. Comenius wrote *The School of Infancy* to help parents teach their children. This book calls for parents to become students and purveyors of sound educational practices:

> Let not parents therefore give the instruction of their children alone to preceptors of schools and ministers of the church, since it is impossible to make the tree straight that has grown crooked. . . . But they ought themselves to know how to manage their own treasures that these may receive increases of wisdom and grace before God and man.[6]

Comenius described children as wonderful gifts from God, but gifts that needed to be shaped and trained for life. As Comenius related how children should be taught, he often compared them to aspects of nature—trees and animals, for example. The curriculum for the young child should include, first, instruction in *morals and virtues* (temperance, cleanliness, decorum, respect, prompt obedience, honesty, justice, a work ethic, propriety in speech, courtesy, patience, service, and humility). Second, the child should be exposed to *sound learning*, which included identifying natural objects, telling time, basic geography and astronomy, family relationships and elemental understanding of government; sound learning also included arithmetic, geometry, music, and communication. Third, the child should study theology and doctrine, which Comenius called *piety*. Fourth, the curriculum should include *health*; parents were to see that their child's physical health was preserved.[7] In outlining the curriculum for his school, Comenius cautioned:

> Parents must take care as to the method adopted with infants in these several things. Instruction should not be apportioned precisely to certain years and months (as afterwards in other schools) but generally only. The child's education cannot follow a fixed pattern because all parents cannot observe the order in their homes that is obtained in public schools where no external matters disturb the regular course of things. Furthermore, in this early age all children do not develop at the same time, some beginning to speak in the first year, some in the second, and some in the third.[8]

Throughout the entire curriculum, children were to be taught according to their capabilities; they were to learn appropriate ways of doing things. Comenius stated that when children are first learning to talk, they should be taught simple words with the simple sounds that they could make. But by warning:

> As soon as their tongues begin to be more supple, however, one does wrong to indulge them in this childish way of speaking, since it may cause lisping. Besides, later on when children come to learn longer words, and at length to speak, they will need to unlearn what they had before learned corruptly.[9]

Throughout the curriculum, children were to be taught through the use of objects and situations with which they were familiar. This level of education was to be practical, geared to the child's sensory perceptions. Comenius argued that an appropriate "aid to study in the Mother-School is a picture-book, which should be put straight into the child's hands . . . as sight is the chiefest of our senses."[10] Comenius offered *Orbis Sensualium Pictus* as such a book.

Comenius recommended that the child should move out of the school of the mother, or first grade, at the age of six, give or take a year. Delaying this step unnecessarily would encourage idleness in the child. On the other hand, it would be even worse to push a child who was not ready for such a move. Apparently some parents were overly ambitious in this regard: "Thereby parents who would have a *Doctor* before the time will scarcely have a *Bachelor*, and occasionally may have a *Fool*."[11]

Also important to Comenius was the role of the parents in preparing the child for school attendance. Parents were to be positive and encouraging when discussing the public school with their children. Teachers were not to be portrayed harshly or as persons to be feared but as friends to be loved. The children were to be reminded of the wonderful things to be learned and how this education would help them to become better persons.

The Vernacular School

This public or vernacular school was to broaden the scope of the child's experience, and so, the child's education. As its name suggests, the vernacular school was not to instruct the child in Latin but in the native tongue. Comenius believed that teaching the vernacular was immediately important to the child and foundational to later Latin instruction.

Vernacular school curriculum was to include more than reading, writing, and grammar of the native tongue. Also a part of it was practical arithmetic and geometry, music (basic theory as well as learning folk songs, psalms, and hymns), catechisms, Bible stories and verses, practical ethics, history, geography, astronomy, and mechanical arts and enough principles of economics and government to provide the child a basic understanding of current events.

The vernacular school would prepare students for further study in many areas of life:

> The result will be that those youths who begin the study of Latin or who enter on agriculture, trade, or professional life will encounter nothing which is absolutely new to them; while the details of their trades, the words that they hear in church, and the information that they acquire from books, will be to them nothing but the more detailed exposition or the more particular application of facts with which they are already acquainted.[12]

The vernacular school was to be divided by age into six classes. Each class was to have its own room and its own distinctive textbook, which would include the entire curriculum. These texts were designed to interest but not amuse the child; they were to be written, of course, in the vernacular. Comenius himself wrote six vernacular-school textbooks: *The Bed of Violets, The Bed of Roses, The Garden of Letters, The Labyrinth of Wisdom, The Spiritual Bed of Balsam,* and *The Paradise Park of the Good*.[13]

A day at the vernacular school was to be comprised of four hours for instruction (two in the morning and two in the afternoon) and time for recreation and work. Mornings were devoted to new instruction; afternoons to reiteration, recitation, and copying the previous lesson from the textbook. The copying exercise was for improving penmanship, etching the lesson on the mind, and providing parents with an understanding and evaluation of their child's progress. The teacher was to read the morning lesson aloud, explaining it in as simple terms as necessary; then having the students to read and explain it.[14]

The Latin School

After the vernacular school came the Latin school. "In this school the pupils should learn four languages and acquire an encyclopedic knowledge of the arts."[15] The languages to be studied were Latin, Greek, Hebrew, and the vernacular. Other subjects were dialectics, rhetoric, arithmetic, geometry, music, astronomy, physical science, geography, history, ethics, and theology. Comenius did not assume that such a curriculum would develop experts in each of these fields, but it would provide the basis for higher education in any of them. Comenius considered history "the most important element in a man's education"; it was to be included as part of instruction in every discipline.[16] Each class was to have its textbook which would reflect this objective.

Each subject was to be taught in a deliberate and sequential manner, taking the students from the concrete, which is more easily grasped, to the abstract. As with the vernacular school, Comenius divided the Latin school into six classes oriented to age groups, the sequential nature of the curriculum, and the teaching methodology. The first year was the grammar class because Comenius saw language as foundational to all other learning. The second year was the natural philosophy class, followed by the mathematics class. (Comenius was flexible on the issue of which should come first, natural philosophy or mathematics. He chose this sequence because in his system students would already have, at this stage, an adequate knowledge of arithmetic to help them deal with and organize that which they would learn from their senses in natural philosophy. Also, he felt that there was much to be learned in mathematics that would require some experiential knowledge of the natural world.) The fourth year was the ethics class in which the student would learn how and why people acted morally throughout history. The dialectic class, which was the fifth year, was to engage the student in dialogue with learned persons from throughout history regarding the great issues that confront humanity. The student would bring to the discussion knowledge from all areas of previous education. This was to teach skill in problem solving and would serve as a review of what had already been learned. The sixth year was the rhetoric class. During this year, the student was to receive training in the principles of oratory. Comenius hoped this discipline would develop a hunger for knowledge in areas in which he or she felt lacking.[17]

Comenius suggested four hours of instruction daily. The two morning hours were to deal with the particular area of instruction for that class, and the two afternoon hours were for instruction in history and various activities that would supplement learning.[18]

Comenius developed *Janua Linguarum Reserata* for use in the Latin school. This was a grammar that included a dictionary of selected Latin words and a topically arranged compilation of Latin sentences.[19]

The University

Comenius' concern was primarily for the first three levels of education: the mother school, vernacular school, and Latin school. In the latter part of *The Great Didactic*, however, he offered thoughts on how a university education should be structured. The curriculum was to be comprehensive, making available the deeper study of all areas of learning. Entry into the university was reserved for those who, through examination in the Latin school proved themselves to be the academic elite. Exceptionally gifted university students were encouraged to keep their studies broadly based to gain the ideal of pansophy. The rest were encouraged to specialize in a particular discipline for which they were gifted, such as theology, law, or medicine.

The university library was of great importance, for Comenius expected students to read widely from as many scholars as possible. To facilitate this, the university was to make available what amounted to abstracts and summaries of important works. But Comenius cautioned, "These epitomes should contain the whole author, only somewhat reduced in bulk."[20]

University education was to include lectures and debates dealing with the lectures. A degree would be awarded after successful completion of a public oral examination that covered both the theory and practice of the candidate's field. Comenius observed, "Surely, students who knew that they were to be publicly examined with such severity would be stimulated to great industry."[21]

The educational philosophy and theories of Comenius had many sources. These included, among others, the pain he felt from the loss of his family and the suffering he observed caused by the Thirty Years War. Comenius was convinced that educational reform would bring about a new society—better, more learned, and more peaceful.

Sense Realism

Comenius participated in an important movement known as sense realism. This movement was a reaction to the idealism of Plato. The roots of sense realism date back to the English philosopher Francis Bacon (1561-1626). Bacon, who became lord chancellor under James I, proposed that knowledge is best derived from induction rather than deduction. That is, he believed that a person learns more effectively from collecting and then organizing sensory-perceived data than from abstract reasoning alone.

According to Bacon:

> Man, as the minister and interpreter of nature, does and understands as much as his observations on the order of nature, either with regard to things or the mind, permit him, and neither knows nor is capable of more.[22]

In keeping with this belief, Bacon lamented the prevailing emphasis on the study of words rather than of matter.[23]

Comenius incorporated much of what Bacon had to offer. However, whereas Bacon was most concerned with the natural world, Comenius was also concerned with the supernatural.

Comenius shared with Bacon a concern for universal knowledge and the belief that knowledge (more specifically for Bacon *scientific* knowledge) could bring a better world.

Both Bacon and Comenius innovated the legitimation of sensor experience as a way of learning. From the early church fathers through the Reformation (and especially for the Calvinists), the senses were not to be trusted because through them evil was apt to pollute the mind and the person. Bacon and Comenius not only allowed but encouraged the use of sense experience in learning and instruction.

Sense realism found further expression through the writings of John Locke (1632-1704) and Etienne Bonnot de Condillac (1715-1780). Locke's most important work was his *Essay Concerning Human Understanding*. He believed the mind of a child at birth was a blank upon which all the child's experiences would be written. Such inscription would come primarily through the senses, especially early in life. Although he encouraged reading the thoughts and discoveries of others in education, true learning would come through the senses and experience:

> Knowing is seeing, and if it be so, it is madness to persuade ourselves that we do so by another man's eyes, let him use ever so many words to tell us what he asserts is very visible. Till we ourselves see it with our own eyes and perceive it by our own understandings, we are as much in the dark and as void of knowledge as before, let us believe any learned author as much as we will.[24]

So thorough is Locke in his reliance on observation and experimentation that he is known as the founder of British empiricism.

Etienne Bonnet de Condillac, a French philosopher and priest, concurred with Locke. He contended that the mind was devoid of innate ideas. he did not isolate the mind from the sense organs in describing sensation. Rather he considered sensation to be the process of the sensory organs informing the brain. Condillac divided the process by which sensation led to learning into five steps: (1) observing primary objects, (2) noting the relationship among these objects, (3) observing the intervals between the objects, (4) observing the secondary objects that fill these intervals, and (5) comparing all that has been observed and noted.[25] Condillac further argued that to introduce a derived definition of an object before some sensory experience with it risks compounding an error. On the other hand, after the five steps had been taken, then the individual would be ready to compose a principle relatively free from the structures of another.

The sense realists were important to the development of education in their own right. This is especially true of Comenius. However, as a group they were to have a more far-reaching impact through those who followed in the eighteenth and nineteenth centuries.

Notes

1. John Amos Comenius, *The Great Didactic*, trans. M. W. Keatinge, part 2 (London: Adam and Charles Black, 1907), 2.5, 28.

2. Ibid., 6:6, 59.

3. Ibid., 12:2.5-6, 82.

4. Ibid., 19:2-10, 161-62.

5. Ibid., 27:3, 256.

6. John Amos Comenius, *The School of Infancy*, ed. Ernest M. Eller (Chapel Hill, N.C.: The University of North Carolina Press, 1956), 70.

7. Ibid., 70-75.

8. Ibid., 74.

9. Ibid., 98-99.

10. Comenius, *The Great Didactic*, 28:25, 264.

11. Comenius, *The School of Infancy*, 117.

12. Comenius, *The Great Didactic*, 29:7, 269.

13. E. H. Gwynne-Thomas, *A Concise History of Education to A.D. 1900* (Lanham, Md.: University Press of America, 1981), 105.

14. Comenius, *The Great Didactic*, 29:14-18, 271-73.

15. Ibid., 30:1, 274.

16. Ibid., 30:15, 280.

17. Ibid., 30:4-15., 275-80.

18. Ibid., 30:17, 280.

19. Gwynne-Thomas, 106.

20. Comenius, *The Great Didactic*, 31:8, 283.

21. Ibid., 31:13, 285.

22. Francis Bacon, *Novum Organum*, Great Books of the Western World, ed. Robert M. Hutchins, vol. 30 (Chicago: Encyclopedia Britannica, 1952), 1:1, 107.

23. Francis Bacon, *Advancement of Learning*, Great Books of the Western World, ed. Robert M. Hutchins, vol. 30 (Chicago: Encyclopedia Britannica, 1952), 1:3, 12.

24. John Locke, *Of the Conduct of the Understanding*, The Educational Writings of John Locke, ed. John William Adamson (New York: Cambridge University Press, 1922), 24:227.

25. Gerald L. Gutek, *A History of the Western Educational Experience*, (New York: Random House, 1972), 149.

23

European Naturalism and Christian Education

The eighteenth century is remembered as the Age of Reason or Enlightenment because of the rationalistic and humanistic influences that dominated the intellectual life of Western Europe during that period. The Enlightenment affected most areas of human life and contributed to the American and French Revolutions.

The Enlightenment also had a great impact on educational philosophies and theories. Enlightenment thinkers, unlike staunch Calvinists, believed that, through reason, people could heal their world of its many faults; by applying natural laws discovered by reason, people could perpetually improve and, eventually, establish a utopian society.

Given the assumptions of the Enlightenment, it should come as no surprise that the educational theorists of the eighteenth century adopted and adapted the educational theories of Comenius, Locke, and Condillac. This is best illustrated by the eighteenth-century educational theorists Rousseau, Pestalozzi, Herbart, and Froebel.

Rousseau

Jean Jacques Rousseau (1712-1778) was the son of Isaac Rousseau, a Genevan watchmaker. His mother, Susanne Bernard, died ten months after he was born. He was a sickly child and felt the blame for his mother's death. He learned to read early and soon exhausted the libraries left behind by his mother and her father, who was a minister.

The elder Rousseau became embroiled in legal troubles and fled the country, leaving Jean Jacques in the care of his uncle Bernard. Jean Jacques was sent with Bernard's son to Bossey to study with a Protestant minister, Lambercier. He eventually returned to Geneva, wanting to study for the clergy, but his small inheritance would not afford him such an education. He became an apprentice, first to the town clerk to learn the legal profession and then to an engraver. At sixteen, he ran away from the abuse of this second master.

Living on his inheritance and the generosity of benefactors, he traveled widely. His passion for women was subjugated for a time while he studied for the priesthood, but the bishop did not encourage him to become a priest. He studied astronomy and music; he even composed operas (several of which he burned) and a ballet and offered himself in Paris as a music teacher. He became secretary to de Montaigu, ambassador to Venice and later returned to Paris, where he became acquainted with Condillac and such Enlightenment figures as Diderot and D'Alembert.

In response to the Academy of Dijon, he wrote an essay in 1749 concerning whether progress of the arts and sciences had contributed more to the purification or the corruption of morals.[1] He was surprised by the news the next year that his was the winning essay. The essay made Rousseau well known and encouraged him to continue writing. He lived for a while in Montmorency, where he wrote some of his best known works, including *Emile*, published in 1762.

Rousseau was always the restless spirit. He moved from Protestantism to Catholicism to a general disenchantment with religion. He left several illegitimate children to be raised by others. His later life took him to England and back to Ermonville, France, where he died in 1778. An addiction to the medications prescribed for his health may have contributed to his restlessness.

Rousseau's theories have significantly influenced the history of Christian education, though he led a somewhat profligate life and did not consider himself a Christian. Unlike Christian educators before him, Rousseau believed in the innate goodness of humans. In *Emile*, he wrote concerning the ideal way of educating a young man: "Let us lay down as an incontrovertible rule that the first impulses of nature are always right; there is no original sin in the human heart; the how and why of the entrance of every vice can be traced."[2] The aim of education, then, is to help the child to learn and develop naturally, free from the corrupting influences of society.

In Rousseau's schema, childhood education would take place in five naturally occurring stages: infancy, childhood, early adolescence, late adolescence, and young adulthood. While passing through each stage, the child develops particular characteristics and abilities. The stages of childhood development should determine educational content and method.

Infancy (birth to five years) was to be a time for basic lessons in freedom and responsibility:

> I shall not take pains to prevent Emile hurting himself; far from it, I should be vexed if he never hurt himself, if he grew up unacquainted with pain. To bear pain is his first and most useful lesson. Instead of keeping him mewed up [confined] in a stuffy room, take him out into a meadow every day; let him run about, let him struggle and fall again and again, the oftener the better; he will learn all the sooner to pick himself up.[3]

Education in childhood (five to twelve) was primarily training in the use of one's senses:

> Teach your scholar to observe the phenomena of nature; if you would have it grow, do not be in too great a hurry to satisfy this curiosity. Let him know nothing because you have told him, but because he has learnt it for himself. If ever you substitute authority for reason he will cease to reason; he will be a mere plaything of other people's thoughts.[4]

The child was not to be encouraged to read books, so avoiding the danger of the child's accepting whatever was read without critical thought. Children were incapable of critical thought to any significant degree.

At this point students were to read *Robinson Crusoe*, which tells about life in a state of nature. The teacher should inspire students to learn firsthand how the natural environment functioned, not theoretically but practically. Training in a manual skill was to equip the students to function in nature; students were to develop the ability to cope with reality rather than living in a theoretical state. Manual skill was to be practical—not an art. Rousseau wanted to avoid education in the arts: "The value set by the general public on the various arts is in inverse ratio their utility. They are even valued directly according to their uselessness."[5] At this point, the person's internal and external natural worlds joined.

Rousseau's goal was for the student to be "a worker and a thinker" by the end of early adolescence. During the next two stages, the learner was to become "loving and tenderhearted."[6]

The next stage was late adolescence (fifteen to eighteen). At this time the person was capable of learning about "passions" and human relationships. Rousseau believed that the emotions (sexual emotions, among others) were natural and the means by which the self is sustained. Their destructive character was another result of the corruptive influence of society. Thus the emotions were not to be suppressed and conquered but rather understood and used correctly. Regarding the emotions (particularly the sexual urges that naturally arose in late adolescence), Rousseau believed that the teacher should wait for the student to ask questions. The answers should be forthright, honest, never crude.

Older adolescents were to examine personal and civic relationships. They learned how people think (psychology) and function corporately (sociology and government).

Regarding education about God, Rousseau wrote: "At fifteen [the student] will not even know he has a soul, at eighteen even he may not be ready to learn about it. For if he learns about it too soon, there is the risk of his never really knowing anything about it."[7]

Although Rousseau was suspicious of religious intolerance, he acknowledged that "the neglect of all religion soon leads to the neglect of [a person's] duty."[8] He related what was required of a person in terms of faith to that person's capacity for belief; this included both the adult who had never heard of God and the child who could not yet grasp the abstract.

Early adulthood (eighteen to twenty) was the time when the student learned how different people lived. As throughout all of Rousseau's educational plan, learning took place as the student encouraged the need to learn. This stage of learning was facilitated by travel in which one learned about foreign customs, laws, and languages. It was also at this stage that the student prepared for and entered into marriage.

Although its central character was a boy, the novel *Emile* also included a section on the education of Sophie. In this section as well as in another novel, *The New Heloise*, Rousseau outlined his thinking on the education of girls. This will be examined in a subsequent chapter, but it will suffice here to observe that Rousseau was more protective of girls than of boys.

Rousseau was and remains a controversial figure. His educational, social, and religious philosophies outraged many including the church. Others, however, saw much to be valued in his thought and adopted aspects of Rousseau's philosophies in government and education.

Pestalozzi

Johann Heinrich Pestalozzi (1746-1827) was a Swiss educator, born in Zurich to Protestant parents of Italian descent. He was the son of a surgeon and the grandson of a minister. His father died in 1751, leaving the family in poverty. The young Pestalozzi, his sister, and his older brother (who soon died) were reared by their mother and Babeli Schmid, their woman servant. The devotion of his mother and Babeli apparently had a significant impact on Pestalozzi's educational ideas, for he valued the teaching role of mothers and mother figures.

Pestalozzi was a sickly child and spent most of his time indoors, separated from other children. By the time he started school, he was an impressionable child, easily manipulated by the other children. He spent his summers in Hongg, his grandfather's village parish. There he came to appreciate the natural beauty and the manual labor of villagers and farmers. He learned much from the example of his grandfather.

Although a mediocre student during his elementary and secondary schooling, Pestalozzi blossomed as a scholar at the University of Zurich. He became less introverted and, as a result of an increasing concern for justice, joined the Helvetic Society, a group of scholars committed to social reform in Switzerland.

Pestalozzi at first dreamed of becoming a minister, then a lawyer. Inspired by his summers in Hongg and the writings of Rousseau, Pestalozzi eventually decided to become a farmer. He studied farming with a successful farmer named Tschiffli and, in 1768, bought a farm near Birr. He named the farm Neuhof. After two years of courtship, he married Anna Schulthess in 1769. She bore their only child the next year, named Jean Jacques.

Pestalozzi developed his farm into a school for orphans in 1774. The school incorporated farming activity and a family model of education. The children worked the fields during summer and engaged in handcrafts during winter. Lessons were memorized and recited. The curriculum was well-rounded and included reading, writing, and arithmetic as well as religious training. The aim of the school was to help the children grow in all areas of life. It was organized to take advantage of childhood curiosity and energy.

The school closed after only five years. The demise of the school was attributed (by Pestalozzi as well as others) not to his educational theories but to poor management.

The impoverished Pestalozzi next turned to writing. As early as

1774 he had written *How Father Pestalozzi Instructed his Three-and-a-Half-Year-Old Son*, a record of the early education of Jean Jacques. Over the next seventeen years, however, he wrote for a living and produced several works, developing and explaining his use of Rousseau's philosophy of natural education.

In 1781 he published what became his most popular work, *Leonard and Gertrude*. In this novel he describe how education could reform individuals and society. *How Gertrude Teaches Her Children* (1801) and *Epochs* (1803) had similar themes. He wrote on the mutual impact of society's ethos and education in *On Legislation and Infanticide* (1783). He wrote to defend developmental education in *Researches into the Course of Nature in the Development of the Human Race* (1797). His final book, *Swansong* (1826), was a general defense of his approach to education.

The closing years of the eighteenth century brought turmoil and war to Europe, and Switzerland was not spared. French troops massacred most adults of the village of Stans, leaving many orphans behind. In 1797 Pestalozzi was named head of the government-established orphanage and school in Stans. Pestalozzi again employed the family model of education, but the enterprise dissolved after two years due to the pressure of war.

With the help of friends, Pestalozzi moved to Burgdorf in 1801 to establish a laboratory and training school. He propagated his philosophy of natural education and refined his educational theories. The Burgdorf school lasted nearly four years but was closed when the local government repossessed the facilities.

It was in Yverdon that Pestalozzi experienced some degree of permanence. In 1804 the local government there gave him an old castle. In the castle Pestalozzi essentially reestablished the Burgdorf school. Educators and government representatives from across Europe and the United States visited Pestalozzi's school. Among these were Friedrich Froebel and Johann Friedrich Herbart. Through these and many others, Pestalozzi would have an important influence on education in Europe and the Americas.

Pestalozzi left Yverdon in 1825 after an extended controversy over the management and business affairs of the school. He returned to Neuhof, where he died. His monument reads: "Man, Christian, Citizen. Everything for others, nothing for himself. Blessings be on his name."[9]

Pestalozzi was obviously more concerned about the practice of Christianity than was Rousseau. Although he too denied the idea of original sin, he believed that people had sinned against God and were in need of God's grace. The task of the educator was to develop in persons the natural gifts that, in concert with God's grace, would lead them to reach their potential. Through this genuine religious education, persons could become truly human, something which Pestalozzi believed could reform the world.

The child's education began with the mother (the first of life's intimate relationships being that of mother and infant) and continued through the home and then the school. In the secure relationships that a child finds in the home, moral learning (justice, faith, and love) was more apt to occur. Pestalozzi believed that in family living the child would naturally learn.

According to Pestalozzi, since children were naturally active they should be taught through activity. They should be allowed to observe and express themselves regarding what they observed. This could be applied to instruction in language (expression), arithmetic (counting the objects observed, for example), art, reading, writing, and geography (the child first observing and describing the immediate environment). Students should be assisted in formulating their observations. For instance, after a field trip they would be taught the appropriate names for the objects they had collected. This Pestalozzi did through repetition in singsong chants that firmly planted the lesson in the minds of the children.

In Pestalozzi's scheme of education, learning was much like a journey. Just as a long trip begins with one step, so learning begins with that which was nearest the student. Only after the "near" is understood, the teacher should proceed to the "far." Thus the teacher should move from the known to the unknown, from the simple to the complex.[10]

Pestalozzi went beyond moral and intellectual education. He included both singing and physical education in his curriculum.

The teacher should be patient and loving (a parent figure), and above all, the teacher must be aware of how each student is growing and developing. Pestalozzi called this process of developmental maturation *anschauung*. It was on this that the teacher would construct a planned learning environment particularly suited to the developmental level of the students.

Herbart

Johann Friedreich Herbart (1776-1841) was born in Oldenburg, Germany. His parents separated when he was young, and he was reared by his overprotective mother. She arranged for him to be taught at home and even sat in on some of his classes with him.

Hermann Uelzen was employed to tutor the young Herbart. A university graduate who had studied theology, Uelzen emphasized philosophy and theology more than would normally have been expected of a tutor. However, rather than implementing the usual catechetical approach to instruction, he used the method of philosophical inquiry.

Other than his studies under Uelzen, Herbart's education was rather like that of any other middle-class boy. At the age of twelve he began attending the local Latin school and in 1794 entered the University of Jena, escorted by his mother.

Despite his talent for music and his parents' desire that he study law, Herbart studied philosophy at Jena. There he came under the influence of a Professor Johann Gottlieb Fichte. Fichte, a follower of Immanuel Kant, had adopted a form of idealism. Herbart had already (in Latin school) read and been impressed by Kant, but by 1796 he had begun to move away from Fichte into his own form of realism.

During his university days, Herbart joined with a society called the Association of Free Men. This was a literary society, the antithesis of the popular student drinking club. Most of Herbart's friends were in this circle.

One of his friends, Johann Fischer, was instrumental in Herbart's employment as a tutor in the home of Friedrich von Steiger of Interlaken, Switzerland, in 1797. At first his mother accompanied him but, before their arrival at Interlaken, decided to return to her own home.

Herbart's tutorial contract was for two years, but he was prepared to stay longer because he was aware of the important task ahead of him if he was to remain faithful to the philosophy he had developed and its educational approach. He anticipated spending six to eight hours a day in the classroom as well as time outside the classroom with his charges and in planning and preparation. He would submit to his employer a progress report every two months. However, he soon found need to rethink his old plan and develop a new one. By 1798 he had devised an educational system that remained basically unchanged throughout his life, though he would refine and develop details of it in several of his books.

Energized by the educational system he had developed, Herbart determined to remain with the von Steiger family. During this period he became familiar with Pestalozzi and visited Pestalozzi's school at Burgdorf. However, in 1800 a series of events and the pressure of his parents' wishes led him to return home to Oldenburg. The death of his mother in 1802 freed Herbart to follow his own way in life.

Herbart went to Bremen to study and tutor. There he received his degree in philosophy from the University of Gottingen. He began to lecture on a free-lance basis until he received a faculty appointment to the university in 1805. This appointment was offered after he had refused similar positions in Heidelberg and Landshut.

Herbart remained in Gottingen, where he began his career in writing. After three years, he accepted an invitation to join the faculty of the University of Konigsberg. He was to remain there for most of the remainder of his life—until 1833. There in 1811 Herbart married Mary Drake, the daughter of an English merchant.

Herbart's primary responsibility was to teach a seminar in the science of teaching—pedagogy. He taught by lecturing and required each student to practice teaching with two or three children. The children lived with the Herbarts in their large home. It was a successful seminar, though viewed with some suspicion by critics who saw it as a government subsidy for training private tutors. This experience afforded Herbart the opportunity to teach and experiment; it also filled a home that would otherwise have been childless.

Herbart was a prolific writer. He wrote *General Pedagogy* (1806) and, soon after, *Chief Points of Logic*, *Chief Points of Metaphysics*, and *General Practical Philosophy*. While in Konigsberg, he wrote *Textbook for Psychology* (1816), *Psychology as a Science* (1824), and *Letters on the Application of Psychology to Education* (1831).

Herbart was disappointed that his realism proved to be less popular than the idealism of Fichte and Hegel. He was especially discontented when he was not offered the chair of philosophy at the University of Berlin when it was left vacant due to Hegel's death. Herbart returned to Gottingen in 1833, where he eventually became dean of the philosophy faculty. He continued his writing and teaching until his death in 1841.

Herbart considered personal moral development the basic aim of education. He concentrated on values to be learned from history and literature. These were the heart of the curriculum; other subjects were taught in terms of their relationship to these.

For Herbart the best educated person was not the one who could simply recite facts and quote the thoughts of others. The most highly educated person has the ability to assimilate information and then freely form moral and ethical conclusions and put those conclusions into practice. This arose from Herbart's understanding of what was "natural" to human beings. He wrote:

> All higher mental activity is potentially present, not in brutes, but in children and in savages, and may be regarded as undeveloped talents or as psychic faculties; and the most insignificant resemblances between the demeanor of the savage or child, and that of the educated man, are valued by them as perceptible traces of awakening intelligence, awakening reason, or awakening moral sense.[11]

According to Herbart, education is comprised of three parts: *government*, the teacher-imposed control and self-control necessary to further learning; *discipline*, the development of personal will in the student; and *instruction*, bringing that which is to be learned to the student's attention. These three parts can be seen in Herbart's five steps of teaching:

(1) *Preparation:* the student is prepared for learning by recalling past experiences and concepts.
(2) *Presentation:* the new body of information is made available and explained to the student.
(3) *Association:* the student explores the relationship between the new information and past experiences.
(4) *Generalization:* the student discerns from what was learned in the previous step as a principle.
(5) *Application:* the student experiments with the principle through application in real-life simulations.

In Herbart's system the teacher was an enabler. The task of teaching involved awakening students to what was to be learned as well as assisting them in the analysis and synthesis of information so that they became capable of making independent judgments that were just and moral. Teachers needed to demonstrate independent learning by developing and implementing their own teaching style rather than one that was simply imitative. For teachers to function in this role, they must appropriately apply the tools of psychology. This meant understanding the natural functioning and capabilities of the students' minds and modifying their teaching to reflect this.

Like Rousseau and Pestalozzi, Herbart taught that the child was a "blank slate" (*tabula rasa*) upon which each child should write a lesson from their own experiences, arising out of their own natural abilities and observations. However, in his methodology he insisted on more guided analysis than did the others. Without this, education would have been a loosely connected string of individual observations.

Froebel

Friedrich Wilhelm August Froebel (1782-1852) is best known as the father of the kindergarten. He was the son of a pastor in Oberwiess-bach, Germany. His mother died when he was nine months old. He grew up a lonely, introverted child, isolated from his father and stepmother, whom his father had married when Friedrich was four.

The young Froebel was taught to read by his father and was then enrolled in a local school for girls. In 1793 he was sent to Stadt-Ilm to live with his mother's brother, who enrolled him in a school for boys there. At fifteen he was apprenticed to a local forester. During this apprenticeship he developed an appreciation for nature. After completing his two-year apprenticeship, he enrolled in the University of Jena. He studied subjects auxiliary to forestry until forced to withdraw from the university for financial reasons. He then found employment as a forester.

Although disinherited by his father, he received a small inheritance from his uncle, who died in 1805. With this financial support, he went to Frankfurt to study architecture. Soon after his arrival, he met Anton Gruner, the head of the Frankfurt Model School. Gruner, a disciple of Pestalozzi, offered Froebel a teaching position. Froebel accepted the offer and visited Pestalozzi for two weeks in Yverdon to prepare himself for this new calling.

Froebel found fulfillment in his teaching. He also had accepted the private tutorship of three boys and soon gave up his teaching position to tutor full time. He took his charges to study at Yverdon in 1808. There he determined to develop an approach to education built on Pestalozzi's work but which would be more systematic.

In 1811 he returned his charges to their home and entered the University of Gottingen, convinced that he needed to learn more about the natural sciences. He studied in Gottingen for a year and then enrolled in the University of Berlin for further studies, which were soon interrupted for a time of military service.

He returned to Berlin, where he worked in a museum. After a time, he undertook the education of the children of his recently deceased brothers. He established a school, the Universal German Institute of Education at Griesheim, which he moved to Keilhau in 1817. He married and began writing about education, with his most important writings being *Education of Man* (1826), *Education by Development*, *Pedagogies of the Kindergarten*, and *Mother's Songs, Games, and Stories* (1843).

In 1837 Froebel established the first kindergarten near Keilhau in Blankenburg. He began to lecture widely on this enterprise and even published a weekly newsletter on his activities. Three years later he opened another kindergarten in Rudolstadt. Although the kindergarten in Keilhau failed (Froebel had come to focus his attention on spreading his educational theories—especially those regarding the kindergarten), kindergarten teachers continued to be trained there. In 1848 he established teacher-training schools at Liebenstein and Marienthal, which women primarily attended.

Froebel's wife died in 1839, and in 1851, he remarried. His second wife was Luise Levin, a former student. After Froebel's death, in 1852, Luise became head of the Keilhau school.

In the opening pages of *The Education of Man* Froebel wrote:

> In all things there lives and reigns an eternal law. . . . This all-controlling law is necessarily based on an all-pervading, energetic, living, self-conscious, and hence eternal Unity. . . a quietly observant human mind, a thoughtful, clear human intellect, has never failed, and never will fail, to recognize this Unity. This Unity is God.[12]

This is an important example of how Froebel's deeply held religious beliefs affected his views of education. God was at the very core of the universe and, thus, at the core of education. In fact, just a few lines after the above quote, he stated his goal for education in terms of relationship to God: ''Education consists in leading man, as a thinking, intelligent being, growing into self-consciousness, to a pure and unsullied, conscious and free representation of the inner law of Divine Unity, and in teaching him ways and means thereto.''[13]

For Froebel, education, which was the exposure to the presence of the Divine in the universe, was to begin in childhood. Children were good by nature, thus making their early education particularly important. The teacher was to nurture the child in such a way that the child's innate goodness would unfold and blossom in realized potential. This educational imagery developed from his background as a forester and led to his founding the kindergarten (from German meaning "garden of children").

Froebel believed that play was important to the development of children. It was their "work":

> Play and speech constitute the element in which the child lives . . .
> Play is the highest phase of child-development—of human development at this period . . .
> Play is the purest, most spiritual activity of man at this stage, and, at the same time, typical of human life as a whole—of the inner hidden natural life in man and all things. It gives, therefore, joy, freedom, contentment, inner and outer rest, peace with the world. A child that plays thoroughly, with self-active determination, perseveringly until physical fatigue forbids, will surely be a thorough, determined man, capable of self-sacrifice for the promotion of himself and others.[14]

To help children learn he used play materials that he divided into two varieties: *divine gifts* (objects whose forms were both fixed and symmetrical—spheres, cubes, and cones) and *divine occupations* (objects that the child could mold and change or use to alter other materials—clay, cardboard, sandpaper). By manipulating the gifts and occupations and by participating in other play activities such as singing, dancing, and drama, the child would learn about universal unity and how an individual can influence the universe. The child would also develop socialization skills.

Froebel was concerned that education avoid memorization. Learning should develop the child's creativity and perception. Particularly in the education of a child, the family kept that which was learned at school from becoming extraneous. Froebel sought to unify home and school, especially regarding religious education. Froebel wrote: "If the child has grown up in unity of life and soul with his parents, this unity will not only be maintained but strengthened and intensified during the period of [childhood], provided no disturbing and obstructing causes intervene."[15]

Religious sensitivity was natural to children. They should be encouraged to give expression to their religious observations and feelings. To do otherwise would render them religiously hollow in later life.

This observation is characteristic of what may have been Froebel's greatest contribution education, especially to Christian education. Though he is best known for the kindergarten, he called the world to respect children for what they were and where they were developmentally. They were not miniature adults but children who needed to play and who were capable of experiencing God and His universe in their own way if allowed to do so.

Notes

1. Jean Jacques Rousseau, *Confessions*, vol. 2 (London: J. M. Dent and Sons, Ltd., 1951), 3.

2. Jean Jacques Rousseau, *Emile: French Thought in the Eighteenth Century*, ed. Romain Rolland, et. al. (London: Cassell and Co., 1953), 63.

3. Ibid., 61-62.

4. Ibid., 63.

5. Ibid., 65.

6. Ibid., 66.

7. Ibid., 69.

8. Ibid.

9. Gerald L. Gutek, *A History of the Western Educational Experience* (New York: Random House, 1972), 198.

10. Gerald L. Gutek, "Johann H. Pestalozzi," *A History of Religious Educators*, ed. Elmer Towns (Grand Rapids: Baker Book House, 1975), 244.

11. Johann F. Herbart, *A Textbook in Psychology*, trans. Margaret K. Smith (New York: D. Appleton and Co., 1897), 39.

12. Friedrich Froebel, *The Education of Man*, trans. W. N. Hailmann (New York: D. Appleton and Co., 1899), 1.

13. Ibid., 2.

14. Ibid., 54-55.

15. Ibid., 237.

24

The Sunday School Movement

The Sunday School is the best known institution of Christian education among Evangelicals today. It is so much a part of Christian education that it seems almost normative. Many presume it has always existed, but such is not the case. In fact, the Sunday School is relatively new.

The Birth of the Sunday School Movement

Although the Christian church established schools of biblical and catechetical instruction from its earliest days, the Sunday School traces its roots back only to the late eighteenth century. At that time England was shifting from an agrarian to an industry society. This Industrial Revolution, as it is known, was fueled by inventors and inventions: James Hargreaves invented the spinning jenny in 1764; James Watt invented the steam engine, and Richard Arkwright patented the spinning machine, both in 1769; and Edmund Cartwright invented the power loom in 1783. England soon became a textile center. America provided cotton. British mines produced coal to fuel the steam engines that powered the machinery. All of this led to the rapid industrialization and urbanization of England.

The capitalism of the Industrial Revolution made the fortunes of some and increased the wealth of others. However, for most of the growing urban lower class, conditions were miserable. Housing, clothing, nutrition, and sanitation available to the urban poor were wretched. For most poor families even the children were forced to work in the factories.

These children labored in conditions that were, by any measure, unhealthy and unsafe. Young workers were frequently maimed and killed. They worked in these sweatshops as many as twelve hours a day, six days a week. Childhood, much less a public elementary education, did not exist for them. Small wonder, then, that on Sundays, their only free day, these children ran wild in the streets and often became involved in crime. All this perpetuated the poverty-crime-prison cycle into which these children were born.

Robert Raikes Pioneered
Sunday School Development

The poverty-crime cycle was particularly true in Gloucester. Among the citizens of Gloucester who were disturbed by what they saw was Robert Raikes (1736-1811), a native of the city. Both of his grandfathers, Richard Drew and Timothy Raikes, were ministers. His father, Robert, Sr., was a newspaper publisher who campaigned against secrecy in the House of Commons and various ills of society including the living conditions of the poor. The wife of Robert, Sr., died, leaving him with two daughters. At the age of forty-six he married Mary Drew (twenty-one at the time), who would give birth to Robert, Jr. By the time of the birth of his son, the elder Raikes was a man of moderate wealth and publisher of the *Gloucester Journal*.

Information regarding young Robert and his early education is scant. He and his seven siblings were christened at Saint Mary de Crypt Church, where he probably attended school. When he was fourteen he enrolled at the cathedral school. Raikes studied there a short time before being apprenticed to his father to learn the publication craft. His father died in September of 1757, and Robert was freed from his apprenticeship a month later. He took over his late father's newspaper and the leadership of the family, seeing to the education and marriage of each sibling. At thirty-one Raikes married Anne Trigge of nearby Newnham. They had ten children, of whom eight survived to adulthood. The Raikes family was close, and the children became well placed in marriages and diverse vocations.[1]

Raikes, like his father, was a crusading editor. He championed the poor, who were unable to afford the rising cost of wheat. He was concerned about the penal system and prisons. He was a frequent visitor to the local prisons and became involved in training prisoners in basic literacy. These and other public stands and activities led to his being known in Gloucester as "Bobby Wild Goose."

Raikes looked with concern and compassion on the children whom he saw running about the streets of Gloucester on Sundays, uncontrolled and uncontrollable. He solicited the help of the rector of Saint John the Baptist Church, Thomas Stork, in dealing with the problem.

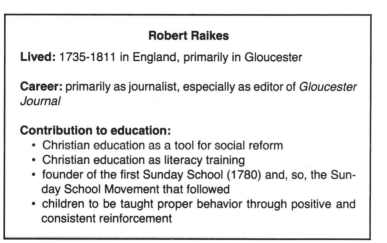

Robert Raikes

Lived: 1735-1811 in England, primarily in Gloucester

Career: primarily as journalist, especially as editor of *Gloucester Journal*

Contribution to education:
- Christian education as a tool for social reform
- Christian education as literacy training
- founder of the first Sunday School (1780) and, so, the Sunday School Movement that followed
- children to be taught proper behavior through positive and consistent reinforcement

The First Sunday School

Raikes felt that education was an effective tool in battling vice and moral degeneration. He determined to develop an experimental school to test his theory. However, he was legally barred from doing so. Until the passage of the Enabling Act in 1779 persons outside the Church of England were prevented from having schools. In 1780 he and Stork enlisted children from the lowest rung of the socioeconomic ladder in Gloucester in their first Sunday School. It met in Sooty Alley in the kitchen of a Mrs. Meredith. (Sooty Alley was near the city prison in an area of Gloucester heavily populated by chimney sweeps.)

Raikes's first students included boys and girls from six to fourteen years old. They were expected to develop proper personal hygiene habits. Many were reluctant to attend the school. Some were brought by their parents hobbled with heavy weights, logs, or shackles bound to their ankles. Discipline was strict. Those who misbehaved were immediately taken by Raikes to their parents, whom he expected to immediately punish their children. Raikes would then return the children to the school.

The primary aim of Raikes's school was literacy training. However, the students were also given some Christian education. They were taught to read from the Bible, and they memorized catechisms and were taken to worship services. Writing was not taught.

Raikes developed a schedule for his schools that began at 10:00 a.m. and ended at 5:00 p.m. A two-hour instruction period was followed by a one-hour lunch break. The afternoon session included catechetical instruction and worship attendance.

Raikes was personally involved in the first Sunday School and others that he established later. However, he also employed women as teachers. He and Thomas Stork selected four women as the first teachers. They were paid a shilling a day. Also, some of the older and more gifted students were usually given the responsibility of tutoring and teaching some of the others.[2]

The first Sunday Schools met with mixed success in developing discipline among the students. Students in the first Sunday School were so boisterous that Mrs. Meredith quit, the school closed, and the students were transferred to another school. Nevertheless, Raikes was generally pleased with the accomplishments of the Sunday Schools. In a letter to William Fox he wrote:

> A clergyman from Painswick called on me this afternoon, expressed his surprise at the progress made there. Many boys can now read, who certainly have no other opportunity that what they derive from their Sunday instruction. This he assured me was the fact. I hear the people of Forest Dean have begun to set this machine in motion among the children of the colliers, a most savage race. A person from Mitchel Dean called upon me a few days ago to report their progress. "Sir," said he, "We have many children now who, three months ago, knew not a letter from a cart-wheel, (that was his expression) who can now repeat hymns in a manner that would astonish you."[3]

Overcoming Difficulties

The Sunday Schools remained obscure until Raikes touted them in a letter to the *Gentleman's Magazine* in 1783. The idea was welcomed by some, condemned by others. Among those opposed to Sunday Schools were the Church of England and British government. It was condemned for giving the laity and poor too much control and authority. It was considered divisive and threatened to deny the wealthy a virtually endless source of underpaid labor. On the other hand, many supported Raikes's idea and became friends of the Sunday School. Some were of the British establishment and gentry. For the most part, they were supportive of Raikes's efforts to improve society. John

Wesley was one of the few clergymen who favored the Sunday School. While on a preaching mission to Bingley, Yorkshire, Wesley visited a Sunday School and was impressed with its work. He determined to make the Sunday School an important element in what became known as the Methodist movement.

Another early supporter of the Sunday School was **William Fox.** Born in 1736, the same year as Raikes, near Gloucester in the village of Clapton, Fox had little opportunity for education in his childhood. Nevertheless, he became a successful businessman. He was converted as an adult and eventually united with a Baptist church in London.

Fox became concerned with the plight of the poor. He was particularly aghast that so few were capable of reading the Bible. After moving back to Clapton, he tried various approaches to dealing with his concern for the poor. In 1785, while attending a monthly Baptist meeting (held at the King's Head Tavern in Poultry), Fox suggested that they work together to give the poor more access to the Bible by teaching them to read. Some discussion resulted as to whether or not such an effort should include those outside the Baptist fellowship. Fox was convinced that the task would require as many as possible become involved. The group decided to call for a meeting that would take place the following August. During the intervening June, Fox and Raikes exchanged the letter cited earlier. In the letter they also expressed mutual admiration, commitment, and encouragement.

At the August meeting it was decided that the best approach to teaching the poor to read would be through Sunday Schools. They agreed to form a society for the establishment of Sunday Schools throughout England. A letter was circulated inviting others to join in their undertaking. On August 30 the first Sunday School society was established, the society for Promoting Sunday Schools throughout the British Dominions later known as the Sunday School Society.

Through the influence of its supporters and the goodwill it generated, the concept of the Sunday School overcame the efforts of its detractors. The popularity of Sunday School was broad based. It included many from the laity and an increasing number of clergy. Records vary regarding the number of students enrolled in the growing movement. Although some reports claim an enrollment of 500,000 by 1796, more modest estimates put the number at 400,000 by Raikes's death in 1811 and at 1,250,000 by 1831.

The Sunday School Society was an important influence in the growth of the movement. It provided financial support for hiring teachers. However, by 1794 most Sunday School teachers were volunteers.

The Growth of the Sunday School Movement

As the Sunday School movement gained momentum other groups formed for its support. One of these, the Sunday School Union, was begun in 1803 and would eventually overshadow the Sunday School Society. The Sunday School Union began publishing books for use in the schools. Among its publications were a promotional booklet, *An Introduction to Reading* (in two parts and with accompanying teaching helps), a catechism, a list of Bible verses, "The Sunday School Teacher's Magazine" (beginning in 1813), and songbooks for teachers and students. The Union was also concerned with the improvement of teaching. It sponsored and participated in various experiments in instructional enhancement.

In North America schools were held on Sunday well before 1780. Many of those who had settled in the New World came with deeply seated religious convictions. It was only natural that their concern for their children's literacy would join with a like concern for their children's religious training. John Wesley may have begun something akin to a Sunday School in Savannah, Georgia, in 1737. Similar institutions sprang up in Ephrata, Pennsylvania, in 1739; in Bethlehem, Connecticut, in 1740; and in Philadelphia, Pennsylvania, in 1744. The purpose of these schools was explicitly and implicitly religious and denominational. They were linked directly to and sponsored by churches. They also discontinued after a brief period in which they experienced scant approval. Finally, they focused on children already in the church fellowship. All these characteristics set these schools apart from what Raikes established.[4] Nevertheless, they did, in a sense, prepare the way for the arrival of the Sunday School movement in the United States.

Little education was available in the South of the early United States. **William Elliot** of Virginia, in 1785, started a school much like those of Raikes. It met in his home on Sunday nights for the purpose of teaching his children and those of his servants, slaves, and neighbors. Similar schools were begun in 1786 by Francis Asbury and in 1790 by the Methodist Conference of Charleston, South Carolina. Due to increasing interest in Sunday Schools in Pennsylvania, The First Day or Sabbath School Society was established in Philadelphia in 1790. It included various denominations and had a similar educational purpose to the Sunday Schools of Raikes and The Sunday School Union.[5] Other similar societies soon formed. Still, some were concerned that the Sunday School would sap the strength and diminish the authority of the church. Also, considerable opposition existed in the new nation to anything with British origins. Soon some churches allowed Sunday Schools to meet in their buildings.

Sunday Schools in the United States were to remain relatively free of denominationalism. This was, for the most part, by mutual consent. Most denominations were reluctant to adopt Sunday Schools, and most Sunday Schools and their sponsoring societies wanted to remain free of denominational control.

The American Sunday School Union was formed in 1824. It arose out of the efforts of the Philadelphia Sunday and Adult School Union and that organization's national aspirations. Six years after it began, the American Sunday School Union set for itself the goal of planting Sunday Schools throughout the Mississippi Valley what was then the western frontier of the nation. Their hope was to complete this task in two years. Their hopes were not realized in the time allotted, but some measure of success was achieved. Through this effort, the Sunday School became an important part of the missionizing of the American West and brought some education where, at first, none would have been. So effective was the Sunday School at this point that some state legislatures in the West considered allowing Sunday Schools to suffice for public education. The Sunday School was also an integral part of the Union's plan to keep the interior of the nation primarily Protestant.

Although the Union and various denominations and churches developed close ties, the Union was determined to remain free of doctrinal controversy. As a means to this end, its constitution held that only laity could serve on its Board of Managers. Equally determined to use Sunday Schools as a tool of their own missionization and doctrinal propagation, several denominations established their own Sunday School unions and societies. Like the Union, these denominational societies published materials for use in their Sunday Schools.

The individuals who brought the Sunday School to the Mississippi Valley took on the role of missionaries and circuit riders. They traveled from place to place, mostly by foot, organizing schools along the way. This organization included selling the locals a Sunday School library.

The Sunday School movement in the United States had, to this point, been westward. This would soon change, however. The eastern seaboard was becoming urbanized, mostly due to the influx of European immigrants. The increase in population density led to a decrease in living conditions and an increase in crime. Many of the new immigrants were Roman Catholic. This disturbed many who were fearful of what they termed "papist" and foreign influences. To deal with this, the Sunday School Union encouraged the development of mission Sunday Schools in cities. Nevertheless, the anti-Catholic bias and bigotry worked against the Union's drive to establish urban Sunday Schools.[6]

Another opportunity arose for the Sunday School to influence a significant segment of early nineteenth-century American society. It was to be found among blacks—slave and free. The young nation found itself deeply divided over the issue of slavery. Even those who opposed slavery did far too little to educate blacks. During the Sunday School Union's campaign in the Mississippi Valley, efforts were made to teach the blacks there. However, for the most part, blacks were ignored for fear of criticism. Sunday Schools were established by black denominations such as the African Methodist Episcopal and African Methodist Episcopal Zion Churches. In most Southern states, teaching the black slaves was prohibited by law, although plantation schools existed such as that begun by William Elliot. The antieducation laws became even more rigorous in the face of slave rebellions. Sunday School was at least partially blamed for the Southampton Insurrection in Virginia in 1831. This attitude grew after John Brown's raid on Harper's Ferry in 1859. The leader of that rebellion, Nat Turner, had been taught to read in a Sunday School. Sunday School missionaries from the North were often viewed with suspicion and called agents of abolition by people in the South. By the late 1850s individuals involved in the Union spoke more openly against slavery. However, corporately, the Sunday School Union did little to combat slavery, and this apathy was reflected in the Sunday School at large. One exception was an incident of civil disobedience staged by the Sunday School children of Oberlin, Ohio, in 1859. This action was in support of their Sunday School superintendent, who had been arrested for aiding escaped slaves.[7]

Very early in the nation's history, many were concerned with religious liberty. Through the efforts of James Madison and support of some religious groups such as Baptists, the Constitution included a Bill of Rights—its first ten amendments. The first amendment includes this sentence: "Congress shall make no laws respecting the establishment

of religion or prohibiting the free exercise thereof.'' The meaning of
this was, and continues to be, a matter of great debate. However, a
''wall of separation'' (as Thomas Jefferson called it) arose between
church and state. This led to the churches being relieved of control and
responsibility for public education. The churches, through the Sunday
School, remained a viable influence on education in the United States.

Growth of the Sunday School in the United States was similar to
what it had enjoyed in Britain. By 1832, 8,268 Sunday Schools were
affiliated with the American Sunday School Union. They were spread
among twenty-seven states and the District of Columbia. The number
of Sunday School Union schools grew to approximately 65,000 (located in thirty-six states and the District of Columbia) by 1875.[8] In
1889 it was claimed that at least ten million persons were enrolled in
American Sunday Schools. If those claim were true, Sunday School
enrollment in the United States amounted to one-sixth of the total
population at that time.[9]

Notes

1. Frank Booth, *Robert Raikes of Gloucester* (Nutfield, Redhill, Surrey: Robert Denholm House, 1980), 33-40.

2. C. B. Eavey, *History of Christian Education* (Chicago: Moody, 1964), 225.

3. John C. Power, *The Rise and Progress of the Sunday Schools: A Biography of Robert Raikes and William Fox,* 2d ed. (New York: Sheldon and Co., Publishers, 1868), 76.

4. Elmer Towns, ed., *A History of Religious Educators* (Grand Rapids: Baker Book House, 1975), 226-28.

5. Eavey, 231-32.

6. Robert W. Lynn and Elliot Wright, *The Big Little School: Two Hundred Years of the Sunday School,* 2d ed. (Birmingham, Ala.: Religious Education Press, 1980), 59-60.

7. Ibid., 61-65.

8. Anne M. Boylan, *Sunday School: The Formation of An American Institution, 1790-1880* (New Haven: Conn.: Yale University Press, 1988), 31-33.

9. Gerald E. Knoff, *The World Sunday School Movement: The Story of a Broadening Mission* (New York: Seabury Press, 1979), 3.

25

German Pietists
and Christian Education

Soon after the Reformation, Protestant theologians became increasingly concerned with defining orthodoxy. This new Protestant Scholasticism was at times denounced for excessively intellectualizing religion. Those who advocated a devotional Protestantism became known as Pietists. This new movement, Pietism, injected a particular flavor to education in the denominations and churches it touched and to which it gave birth.

Spener

Philipp Jacob Spener (1635-1705) is known as the father of German Pietism. He was born in the village of Rappoltsweiler in Alsace, a province on the German-French border ceded to France in 1648 by the Treaty of Westphalia. Spener's was a devout Lutheran home. Both his family life and the Christian devotion of the Countess von Rappoltstein proved to be important in the religious development of Spener.

At age sixteen Spener entered the nearby University of Strasbourg, where he studied theology under orthodox Lutherans. However, at Strasbourg, Spener was also exposed to a concern for the form and quality of the catechetical instruction of children, a concern not found in most Lutheran circles to the degree it existed there. At Strasbourg, he also came under the influence of the mysticism of Johann Arndt and the Puritanism of Lewis Bayly, author of *The Practice of Piety*.

Spener studied and taught at Strasbourg until he left for Basel, Switzerland, in 1659. In Basel he studied Hebrew and, eventually, the teachings of the Waldenses. Spener also developed an interest in the preaching of Jean de Labadie, a French mystic. Spener's continued his

education in Tübingen, Germany, where he was awarded his doctorate
and married in 1663.

In 1666 Spener became pastor of a church in Frankfurt on the Main,
a German commercial and cultural center. He worked to improve the
quality of the catechetical instruction. Four years later, after his arrival
in Frankfurt, he began meeting in his home with a group of people who
shared his concern for deepening personal faith. He named this group,
and others like it that would develop later, *Collegia Pietatis*. Thus
encouraged in his concerns, Spener wrote, in 1675, *Pia Desideria, or
Heartfelt Desire for a God-pleasing Reform of the True Evangelical
Church. Together with Several Simple Proposals Looking Toward This
End.*

Pia Desideria began with an explanation of what Spener viewed
as failures that had led to a decline in the church. He pointed out
the failures of the civil authorities, clergy, and laity. He took governments to task for abusing what he considered their God-given authority
and position. They often obstructed the divine justice they were
to promote. Spener accused the clergy of being uncommitted to a
servant ministry. He was dismayed at the materialism, blatant personal
ambition, and ungodliness exhibited by some pastors. Despite poor
governmental and ecclesiastical leadership, Spener held laypersons
accountable for giving themselves to such sins as drunkenness, ava-
rice, and litigiousness. He warned that this situation provided a poor
witness to Jews and Catholics.

Yet Spener had hope, based on his understanding of God's promises
in Scripture. In the second and third parts of *Pia Desideria*, he
explained this hope and outlined a reform program. He called for Bible
reading in church and home. He encouraged the formation of small
groups in order to enable ministers to know their parishioners better
and minister to them more effectively. Through these groups,
laypersons would become more involved in priestly functions.

Spener was aware that his proposals required pastors who "are
themselves true Christians and then, have the divine wisdom to guide
others carefully on the way of the Lord."[1] The schools and universities
required to educate such a clergy would be as concerned with the
student's spiritual development as with the academic:

> The professors could themselves accomplish a great deal here by their
> example (indeed, without them a real reform is hardly to be hoped for)
> if they would conduct themselves as men who have died unto the world,

in everything would seek not their own glory, gain, or pleasure but rather the glory of their God and the salvation of those entrusted to them, and would accommodate all their studies, writing of books, lessons, lectures, disputations, and other activities to this end.[2]

Spener suggested that professors be well acquainted with the individual needs and gifts of their students. Such knowledge would enable them to tailor instruction to fit each student. Although Spener recognized that disputations could degenerate into practices of futility and emptiness, he allowed that they could be useful if controlled. He recommended that disputations be in German rather than Latin to prepare the future ministers to explain the gospel in terms understandable to the average person and defend the faith in areas with significant Jewish populations.

Spener continued to stress pastor theology:

> Just because theology is a practical discipline and does not consist only of knowledge, study alone is not enough, nor is the mere accumulation and imparting of information. Accordingly thought should be given to ways of instituting all kinds of experiences through which students may become accustomed to and experienced in those things which belong to practice and to their edification. . . . It would also be desirable if students were given concrete suggestions on how to institute pious meditations, how to resist the lusts of the flesh . . . Studying alone will not accomplish this.''[3]

In 1686 Spener left Frankfurt for a ministry as court chaplain in Dresden. There his influence continued as the growing Pietist movement brought him many disciples, among them August Hermann Francke. In Dresden, however, he met considerable opposition, particularly from the universities in Leipzig and Wittenberg. He accepted the pastorate of Saint Nicolas Church in Berlin, where he served until his death in 1691.

Francke

August Hermann Francke (1663-1727) was one of Spener's devotees, but he contributed even more to education than Spener. Francke was born into a devout family. His father was an influential and well-to-do lawyer. Even in childhood the young Francke was exposed to the writings of the early German Pietists. A precocious child, his early education consisted of private instruction and then the gymnasium. When only fourteen years old, he enrolled in the University of Erfurt. He also studied at Kiel and received his degree at the University of Leipzig, where he taught for two years beginning in 1685.

While in Leipzig, Francke participated in a Bible study group called the *collegium philobiblicum*. Because of the influence of this group he left the university for a time and sought the guidance of Spener. He became a committed Pietist and, in 1689, returned to his teaching position at Leipzig. However, his Pietism led to some conflict with university administrators and faculty. In 1690 he left Leipzig to pastor in Erfurt. A year later he was compelled to move again because of tensions with the university in Erfurt. He assumed a pastorate in Glaucha, where, thanks to the influence of Spener, he was invited to teach without salary at the nearby University of Halle.

Much of Francke's ministry in Glaucha focused on education. He was concerned that many of the parents there cared little for the proper education of their children. This led Francke to establish a school in 1692 for these children of poverty. This school was supported by donations and endowments from the townspeople, as was the *Armenschule*, an orphan school which Francke founded in 1695. The schools flourished with enrollments quickly growing to over one hundred in the orphan school and six hundred in the elementary school. In 1697 Francke opened the *Lateinschule*, or Latin school, which made a college preparatory education available to children of all socioeconomic levels. For the children of the wealthy and nobility, Francke created the *Paedagogium Regium*, a boarding school that included about seventy boys as students. Francke was also involved in training teachers. Living in a university town, Francke made use of the resources at hand. He offered needy university students meals (at the *Freitisch*, or "free table") in exchange for their instruction in his *Armenschule* and *Lateinschule*. In 1705 he established a school for teachers, the *Seminarium Praeceptorium*.

The curriculum of the *Paedagogium* differed from that of Francke's other schools. Because children of the nobility were destined for lives of greater privilege and broader experience, they were given a more diverse education. They were taught in German but also learned another language or two (French and either Italian or English). They learned the finer points of etiquette and business and received more instruction in the social sciences than their counterparts in the *Armenschule* and *Lateinschule*.

As a Pietist, Francke insisted that his schools be deeply religious, cultivating a devotion of the heart, not simply of the mind. Children were taught hymns and the catechism so that they could apply the inherent truths to their lives. Prayers were not memorized, but children learned to pray in their own words. Discipline was stringent, but love was the guiding principle. Physical punishment was rare. Francke considered the home as an integral facet of a child's education. However, in the parents' absence, the school was to function as a substitute. Classes were kept relatively small. This helped teachers know their students better and improved instruction.

Francke later became vice-chancellor of the University of Halle, a position in which he clashed with rationalist faculty. Ill health curtailed his preaching and teaching in his later years in Halle.[4]

Francke's influence on European Christianity in general and European Christian education in particular has proven significant. He effected change directly as he championed Pietism before seats of power. His impact has also been felt through the leadership of his students and disciples. One of these was Count Nikolaus von Zinzendorf.

Zinzendorf

Nikolaus Ludwig Zinzendorf (1700-1760) was born into the German nobility in Dresden, Saxony. His father was an official of the Saxon court. Jacob Spener, a friend of the elder Zinzendorf, was named godfather of the young Nikolaus. Soon after Nikolaus's birth, his father died. His mother remarried, and he was reared a devout Lutheran Pietist by his grandmother. At age ten he enrolled in Francke's *Paedagogium* in Halle. Zinzendorf found his days at Francke's school to be most difficult with too much time given for work and not enough allowed for play. He disdained Francke's educational methods, comparing them to slavery. Nevertheless, he studied at the *Paedagogium* until 1716, when he entered the University of Wittenberg to study law.

Zinzendorf left Wittenberg in 1719 to broaden his experience through travel. Two years later he returned to Dresden where he entered governmental service and, in 1722, married Erdmuth Dorothea von Reuss. Although he had developed an appreciation for traditional Lutheranism, Zinzendorf still remained committed to Pietism. He supported a Pietist church on his family estate, Bethelsdorf, which he had purchased from his grandmother. By 1722, Berthelsdorf had become a sanctuary for Moravians fleeing persecution in Bohemia. There Zinzendorf founded a school for the poor and orphans. At Berthelsdorf the Moravians founded the village of Herrnhut (Lord's Watch) and began to intermingle with Lutheran Pietists. In 1727 these two main groups and some other minor ones merged into a reformed Moravian church (formally known as the *Unitas Fratrem*) under the spiritual leadership of Zinzendorf. Zinzendrof's personal fortune would prove to be crucial to the survival of the church.

Zinzendorf was eventually ordained a bishop by the Moravians. After his banishment from Saxony under accusation for proselytizing, Zinzendorf devoted himself to traveling and writing. In 1740 he published *Plan of a Catechism for the Heathen*, supporting Moravian mission efforts. (Early Moravian missions included work among the Eskimos of Greenland and among native Americans. George Washington was impressed by Moravian missions among Native Americans.) Zinzendorf's travels took him across Europe and to the West Indies, North America, and England. In England he met John Wesley, whose life had been significantly altered by the witness of Moravians. Zinzendorf also influenced the legitimization of the Moravians by the British Parliament. His banishment from Saxony was rescinded in 1747, but he continued to spend much time in England during this remaining years. His last days were spent in Herrnhut, where he died in 1760.

Zinzendorf's school at Berthelsdorf was the first of many Moravian schools. The earliest of these were for Moravians only, but other schools were opened to a wider public as their renown increased.

Zinzendorf stressed the importance of recognizing the unique personhood of each child. He affirmed the value of play in childhood development, perhaps in reaction against his days in the *Paedagogium* in Halle. He gave children the freedom to act like children. Even though he wrote the catechism *Pure Milk* to help mothers train their children, Zinzendorf was not concerned that the child simply learn to recite dogma; rather, he sought to lead children to a life freely devoted to God and to develop the ability to express this devotion in their own words. He affirmed children in their childhood by reminding them that Jesus was once a child.

Zinzendorf gave special attention to the education of adolescents. He was aware of the "in-between years"—years when the youth was neither child nor adult, yet both child *and* adult. He reminded youths of Jesus' own adolescent development, assuring them that Jesus had struggled with the same issues and temptations that frustrated them. He also encouraged them, when confused and in need of a sympathetic ear, to seek out a *Kinder-Vater*, an adult in the community trained to counsel youth.[5]

Zinzendorf was careful to include the entire community in education. He developed a plan for parental education and organized the community into educational units (called "choirs") along developmental and gender lines.

Zinzendorf published a hymnal and a special Bible. He wrote many hymns expressing his personal devotion and responding to events in his Christian pilgrimage. Most of his hymns centered on "the Lamb," that is, on the person and work of Christ. Zinzendorf believed that Christians integrated spiritual truths in their lives through repeated hymn-singing. His special edition of the Bible was abridged to include passages believed to speak specifically to Christians and translated into a simple and up-to-date vernacular.[6]

Schleiermacher

Pietism also influenced Christian education through Friedrich Ernst Daniel Schleiermacher (1768-1834). Although he is best known for his contributions to theology, hermeneutics, and philosophy, Schleiermacher also contributed significantly to the philosophy of Christian education. He was born in Breslau, which is Poland now. His father, Gottlieb Schleiermacher, was a minister in the Reformed Church serving as a chaplain with the Prussian army. At age fifteen he enrolled with his older sister, Charlotte, in a Moravian school in Niesky. In his two years of study in Niesky, Schleiermacher was deeply affected by Pietism but also developed an appreciation for classical literature. In 1785 he entered the Moravian seminary at Barby, where he studied another two years. Schleiermacher felt stifled by the mild asceticism of the Moravians and by their censorship of some classical literature. As a result, he left Barby in 1787 to study two years at the University of Halle. Although enrolled as a theology student, he was free to examine the classics. While in Halle, Schleiermacher was swept up in the movement toward the philosophy of Professor Immanuel Kant of Königsberg, and by the Romanticism of the day. Upon leaving Halle, Schleiermacher spent two years with an uncle in Drossen studying and contemplating his vocation. He finally chose the ministry and, in

1790, became a certified clergyman of the Reformed Church by passing the required theology examinations.

Later that same year Schleiermacher was hired as a teacher by a noble family in Schlobitten. After three years in that position, he taught for one year in a boys' school and then served as a pastor in Landsburg. From 1796 to 1802 he was a hospital chaplain in Berlin, where he came into immediate contact with some of the most progressive and influential thinkers of the day. Personal problems, including an extended infatuation with the unhappily married wife of a local minister, required that he leave Berlin and accept a pastorate in Stolpe. In 1804 he returned to the University of Halle to serve on the theological faculty. The Napoleonic wars interrupted Schleiermacher's teaching career in Halle. In 1807 he returned to Berlin, where he taught and lectured. The following year he married Henrietta von Willich, a nineteen-year-old widow of one of his friends. In 1810 he was appointed to teach theology in the newly formed University of Berlin. He remained there until his death in 1834, writing and lecturing extensively.

Schleiermacher was concerned for the development of the inner person. He saw that education, despite certain advancements, had fallen prey to old dangers. "Hence, our judicious and practical education of to-day is but little distinguished from the ancient mechanical article, and that little is neither in spirit nor in working."[7] Rather than helping, new forms of education only hindered, for "at the very outset the youthful spirit, instead of enjoying free play and opportunity to see world and man as a whole, is restricted by alien ideas and early accustomed to a life of prolonged spiritual poverty!"[8]

Schleiermacher determined that education should engender in persons appropriate relationships with governments, God, other persons, and themselves. A comprehensive theory of education would address the beginning and ending points of the educational process, who is responsible for education, whether education is to support or revise the status quo, the universality of education, and what extent (if at all) the student should be made aware of concepts and forces alien to those of the teaching institution. Schleiermacher tied education closely to ethics. Education should be mindful of the present (leading the individual to enjoy success at every stage in life rather than seeing each stage as preparing for the next) as well as the future (keeping in mind the adult that the child will one day be). Further, education must be appropriate to the community in which the child lives.[9]

Schleiermacher's philosophy of education grew out of his theology.

In *The Christian Faith*, he set piety as the essence of the church. By "piety," he meant a self-consciousness consisting of two elements: "the one expresses the existence of the subject for itself, the other its co-existence with an Other."[10] He related these elements to feelings of *freedom* and *dependence*, which he felt to be mutually inclusive. They were coexistent and reciprocal:

> Neither of the two members will ever completely disappear. The feeling of dependence predominates in the relation of children to their parents, or of citizens to their fatherland; and yet individuals can, without losing their relationship, exercise upon their fatherland not only a directive influence, but even a counterinfluence. And the dependence of children on their parents, which very soon comes to be felt as a gradually diminishing and fading quantity, is never from the start free from the admixture of an element of spontaneous activity towards the parents.[11]

The objective of Christianity in general (and Christian education in particular) was to nurture both of these elements. Schleiermacher related the feeling of "absolute dependence" to "God-consciousness." (Schleiermacher even expressed the need for redemption in terms of "God-forgetfulness," thus setting the development of God-consciousness at the heart of the redemptive process.)[12] This was one of the most obvious effects of Pietism on Schleiermacher's philosophy of Christian education. It was to be an integral part of the church's efforts to bring people into a right relationship with God. This goal could be accomplished by requiring persons to memorize and assent to creeds and catechisms. Neither should they be discouraged from freely using their God-given intelligence. Rather, they should be led to a keen awareness of the presence and importance of God in their lives. Further, Christians should learn to live freely in healthy relationships with themselves, others, and God. Each of these relationships, in terms of both their inner and outward experiences, would naturally derive from (support) and inform the others.

Since Schleiermacher emphasized relationship in his theology and philosophy, it comes as no surprise that he stressed the importance of the family in Christian education. The home was to function as a partner with the church and government to educate children. The home, however, had primary responsibility. After all, it was in the family that the individual first experienced relationships on an intimate basis. Parents were to teach by example. Their faith was to be contagious rather than something forced upon the child. Religious instruction in the home was to include worship and develop in the child a positive disposition toward faith, the church, and education as well as personal discipline.

Schleiermacher was concerned that the home and church not shirk responsibility by relying on the public schools to teach religion. The purpose of the public schools, as instruments of the state, was to teach, in terms of the inner person, morals (rather than faith), mathematics, science, and other subjects not taught by the church school. It was imperative that the government provide for public schools and that they be maintained separate from the church. Public schools should serve all citizens, regardless of age or social status. Church schools completed the well-rounded system of education. They were to provide instruction in the traditions of the faith and understanding of the Bible.[13]

Notes

1. Philipp Jacob Spener, *Pia Desideria* in *Pietism*, ed. G. Thomas Halbrooks (Nashville: Broadman, 1981), 252.

2. Ibid., 253.

3. Ibid., 260.

4. Gary R. Sattler, *God's Glory, Neighbor's Good: A Brief Introduction to the Life and Writings of August Hermann Francke* (Chicago: Covenant Press, 1982), 97-98.

5. T. F. Kinloch, "Nikolaus Ludwig Zinzendorf," *A History of Religious Educators*, ed. Elmer L. Towns (Grand Rapids: Baker Book House, 1975), 207.

6. Ibid., 203-04.

7. Friedrich Schleiermacher, *On Religion: Speeches to Its Cultured Despisers*, trans. John Oman (New York: Harper and Row, 1958), 136.

8. Friedrich Schleiermacher, *Soloquies*, trans. Horace L. Friess (Chicago: The Open Court Publishing Co., 1926), 60.

9. Tom F. Kinloch, *Pioneers of Religious Education* (London: Oxford University Press, 1939), 107-08.

10. Friedrich Schleiermacher, *The Christian Faith*, English Translation of the Second German Edition, trans. H. R. Macintosh (Edinburgh: T. & T. Clark, 1960), 13.

11. Ibid., 15.

12. Ibid., 54.

13. Schleiermacher, *On Religion*, 203-04.

26

Other Influences
on Christian Education

The beginnings of modern education was affected by many persons and movements not mentioned in the previous chapters. This chapter presents some of these: Puritanism, John Wesley and Methodism, John Henry Newman and the Oxford Movement, various missions movements, William Booth and the Salvation Army, as well as some Christian student movements.

Puritanism

Although Henry VIII (1509-1547) formally separated the Church of England from the Roman Catholic Church in 1534, the struggle to define the nature of Anglicanism only began during his reign. Puritanism arose in the struggle to *purify* the English church of such "papish" influences as clerical garb. Queen Mary (1553-1558) banished many Protestant leaders in her attempt to reimpose Roman Catholicism, but these leaders fled to Switzerland and Germany only to return, following her death, zealous to teach Reformed doctrine and practice. The Puritan movement was increasingly influenced by Calvinistic doctrine, including the authority of Scripture and the priesthood of believers. This influence continued during the long reign of Elizabeth I (1558-1603) and throughout the seventeenth century.

Some Puritans, such as Thomas Cartwright (1535-1603), wished to remain within the Anglican Church. Others, including Robert Browne (1550-1633), became Separatists, establishing churches distinct from the Anglican Church. Both the Puritans and the Separatists endured heavy persecution.

Persecution eventually paved the way for the propagation of Puritan and Separatist principles. Fleeing oppression in England, many Puritans and Separatists emigrated to the Netherlands and North America. The educational thought of John Calvin had a special impact on the Puritans and Separatists. This "educational Calvinism," was the foundation for the Puritan system of education in colonial New England.

The Puritans taught doctrine as did most other Christian groups—through the use of catechisms. Their stress on the authority of Scripture made literacy training important. Also, their goal of establishing a theocratic state made universal education a priority.

The Puritans accepted the Calvinistic interpretation of total depravity. This belief carried over to their view of children. Out of concern for the souls of little ones, Puritan ministers sometimes preached sermons particularly for and to children. The aim of these children's sermons was to replace childhood vanity with "early piety."[1]

John Wesley and Methodism

Another force that affected the development of education during this time was Methodism. John Wesley (1703-1791), the founder of Methodism, was the son and grandson of ministers. He and his brother, Charles, studied at Oxford and were ordained to the ministry of the Church of England. They accompanied Oglethorpe to the North American colony of Georgia and busied themselves in mission efforts there. Charles returned to England due to poor health, and John returned because of a failed romance.

Upon arriving back in England, John became involved in a Pietist society organized by Peter Boehler, a Moravian. In 1738, during a meeting on Aldersgate Street in London, John became convinced that salvation came only through faith in Jesus Christ. He called this his conversion, and it profoundly changed his life.

Seeking to learn more about others who shared his conviction, John visited Herrnhut to learn from Zinzendorf and the Moravians, although he never aligned with them. Wesley's determination to organize the rule and conduct of the Christian life resulted in his followers being called "Methodists." Although Wesley never left the Church of England, Methodism gradually separated and formed a separate church.

Wesley was an acquaintance and supporter of Robert Raikes. Wesley and Methodism aided the growth of the Sunday School movement in England and the United States.

Wesley was concerned with the spiritual nurture of children and based his approach to education on principles of sense realism and universal education. (It was particularly with universal education in mind that he endorsed the Sunday School.) He wrote that the education of children should be a special priority in a Methodist society. He wrote several teaching manuals and tracts for children. Wesley valued the home in the Christian education of children. Through the efforts of the church, Sunday School, and home, children could learn of God's grace and develop the personal spiritual discipline to live in that grace.[2]

Wesley was concerned that a child's Christian education continue until adulthood. To this end he established Methodist schools to supplement the training of the child by the home and Methodist society. Many of these schools were established and centered on a well-rounded curriculum that included health and physical education, instruction in Christian faith, and development of the intellect. These schools were for Methodist children exclusively, and Christian nurture at home was necessary for the child's enrollment to continue.[3]

John Henry Newman and Higher Education

John Henry Newman (1801-1890) contributed to Christian education, especially higher education, by struggling to define the place of faith and religion in a scientific and industrial age. He was born in London in 1801, the first child of John Newman, a banker, and his wife, Jemima. At age seven, John Henry was enrolled in a private boarding school of some renown. In the summer of 1817 he entered Trinity College of Oxford University and graduated three years later. He was a gifted student. His relative youth and immaturity resulted in some problems with his examinations during his final year, but he was appointed a fellow of Oriel College in 1821.

His father had expected John Henry to enter the legal profession, but his son chose to study toward ordination in the Church of England. John Henry was ordained to the diaconate in 1824 and the priesthood a year later. He served successively the parishes of Saint Clement and Saint Mary, while continuing to function as an academic. He became involved in the Oxford Movement, a fellowship concerned about perceived wrongs in the Church of England; Newman and others wrote tracts calling for church reform. Newman finally converted to Roman Catholicism in 1845 and received ordination in 1847.

Newman returned to England soon after his ordination. By this time, the need for a Catholic university in Ireland had become apparent. Irish Catholics had suffered two centuries of persecution. This persecution had abated but not disappeared. In 1851 Newman was invited to become the first rector of the Catholic University of Ireland in Dublin. Upon his arrival in Dublin in 1852, Newman presented a series of lectures which were the basis for his most significant book on education, *The Idea of a University*. He worked diligently to develop the university and continued writing and lecturing. He soon became discouraged and physically drained. He first offered his resignation in 1857, but it was not finalized until 1859. The university continued without Newman but was absorbed by the Royal University of Ireland in 1879 and the National University of Ireland in 1908.[4]

Newman continued to write and would prove to have significant impact on the Roman Catholic Church in a variety of areas, particularly doctrine and ecclesiology. Pope Leo XIII appointed Newman to the cardinalate in 1879. In his last years, Newman's health gradually declined until his death in 1890.

In Newman's day a scientific revolution resulted in theology being excluded from undergraduate studies in many universities. In these schools an emphasis on practicality and professional training left little, if any, room for the liberal arts. This was bothersome to Newman, who felt that a student's education needed the moral influence of theology. Newman believed that, if a university wished to be true to its mission, it would include theology in its curriculum. Theology should take its legitimate place alongside other branches of knowledge and should not be intrusive in its relationship with the other disciplines:

> Far indeed am I from having intended to convey the notion, in the illustrations I have been using, that Theology stands to other knowledge as the soul to the body; or that other sciences are but its instruments and appendages, just as the whole ceremonial of worship is but the expression of inward devotion. This would be, I conceive, to commit the very error, in the instance of Theology, which I am charging the other sciences, at the present day, of committing against it. On the contrary, Theology is one branch of knowledge and Secular Sciences are other branches. Theology is the highest indeed, and widest, but it does not interfere with the real freedom of any secular science in its own department.[5]

Newman supported the practice of undergraduate instruction in theology for lay students by lay faculty. Such instruction was not to instill dogma but to develop religious knowledge. A student thus equipped (as well as with a general knowledge of history, literature, and philosophy) and capable of integrating the various academic disciplines, was better equipped for life regardless of career or location. However, he was concerned that students with this level of religious knowledge realize their limitations and not attempt to deal with the finer points of theology. (Newman had a similar misgiving regarding ecclesiastics who intruded into other fields).[6]

Newman believed that university education should prepare students for *all* of life, not only for the narrow demands of one profession. He was not opposed to professional education, but he called for a liberal education to be the foundation of a university education, after which a student would engage in professional studies.[7]

The Missions Movements

Throughout history, Christian education has had ties with Christian missions. This tradition continued during the beginnings of modern education with Protestants as well as Roman Catholics. This era was not only one of great changes in education, but also one of exploration and discovery. Franciscans, Dominicans, Augustinians, and Jesuits accompanied explorers such as Vasco da Gama, Columbus, and Pedro Cabral. As these explorers opened new worlds to European trade and commerce (as well as to European domination and colonialism), missionaries spread the gospel and Christian education. They established church schools that taught doctrine and literacy. They established libraries and universities. Among the latter were universities in Lima and Mexico City, both of which were founded in the sixteenth century, a century before Harvard University was established. Further, these missionaries reduced many indigenous languages to writing and published books using the new languages.[8]

Roman Catholic mission strategy in Asia in the sixteenth and seventeenth centuries included Christian education. By 1700 Catholic missionaries had founded a college for girls and two universities (a Jesuit College in San Jose and a Dominican College in Santo Tomas) in the Philippines. As was the case with Roman Catholic missionaries to the Americas, these also busied themselves with studying indigenous cultures and languages.[9]

Moravians and other early Protestants incorporated Christian education in their mission enterprise. Missions underpinned the development of the Sunday School in the United States. Earlier, Protestant ministers had accompanied Dutch traders on voyages to the East Indies, ministering mostly to the colonists but also working among indigenous peoples. Missions organizations developed among Anglicans. Again, their priority at the outset was ministry to colonists. However, as time passed, evangelization, education, and other ministries among indigenous peoples became more important.

William Carey (1761-1834) ushered in a new era in Protestant missions. An English Baptist, Carey was a cobbler and pastor. He was largely self-educated and became an authority in botany and an expert linguist (fluent in Hebrew, Greek, Latin, Dutch, Italian, and French). In 1792 he began urging British Baptists and others to become engaged in foreign missions; the next year he sailed for India, where he served until his death.

Until Carey, missions were tied to the state church of the colonizing nation. Carey hoped that his mission would eventually be self-sustaining. That was never realized, but many societies in England and the United States arose for the support of missions as a result of Carey's efforts. Some focused on foreign missions, others on home missions. Many of these societies promoted their work by publishing educational tracts and pamphlets. Missions education had become an important part of their task.

The Protestant missionaries—before and after Carey—involved themselves in the Christian education of their charges. Teaching was done in mission churches and schools. However, their educational enterprises on mission fields were not so extensive nor as organized as were those of the Catholics.

The missions reawakening among Protestants in the nineteenth century made necessary missionary-training institutes. Already universities and colleges with theology faculties, as well as seminaries, trained aspiring missionaries. Some, however, felt that missions opportunities should be made available not only for the highly educated. Such groups and individuals came to support schools like the East London Institute for Home and Foreign Missionaries, established in 1870, and similar Bible schools and missionary colleges in Europe and, especially, in America.[10] The emphasis in these schools was, and continues to be, vocational training with narrowly designed curricula and little emphasis on liberal arts.

The Salvation Army

The Salvation Army developed in the mid-1800s out of the life and work of its founder, William Booth (1829-1912). Booth had been expelled from the Methodist Church in England and based his movement on revivalism and missions. Booth recognized the importance of basic education but observed that the current system of education was not producing moral persons or persons who held manual labor in high esteem. He wrote, "Our Education tends to overstock the labor market with material for quill-drivers and shopmen and gives our youth a distaste for sturdy labor."[11] Booth felt that education should reform persons and make them able to provide for themselves and their families. To neglect this would be to "enable a starving man to tell his story in more grammatical language than that which his father could have employed."[12] Booth, then, was placing education at the heart of social reform, at which he and his followers labored so intently. This intensified and particularized the social-reform educational aims of Raikes's Sunday School movement.

Booth described how the Salvation Army would work for social individual reform through the establishment of "colonies." In preparation for living in these settlements, people would be taught such virtues as patience, honesty, as well as how to live in relation to others, and the rules of the community. They would also be taught a trade and "economies they would have to practice."[13]

The Salvation Army soon developed training schools for its officers. Booth founded the first Salvation Army School for Officers' Training in 1880. It was open only to women. Within the year Booth opened a similar school for men in his own house. From the beginning these schools were faithful to Booth's call for practical education. (They also continued Booth's military pattern, with the training school students being called "cadets.") The Salvation Army training schools, like the Bible schools, had a relatively narrow curricula. Focus was basic theological education as well as teaching in the rules of the organization and skills necessary to fulfill the Salvation Army's functions (evangelism and social work). Because of the background of many of their converts, these schools included instruction in basic etiquette.[14]

Christian Student Movements

Various Christian student movements had an influence on Christian education during the latter part of this era. Among these were Young

Men's Christian Association (1844), Young Woman's Christian Association (1855), and World Student Christian Federation (1895). These and others were ecumenical and worked through their own structures. Many other denominationally based and missions-oriented student groups existed. Most of these student organizations wanted to add Christian dimension to the education of the students they involved. Although they were, in a sense, adjunct to the campuses on which they were active, they were educational institutions in themselves. They trained students for effective church leadership roles and published materials in support of their training efforts. Missions-minded student groups were active in missions education as a significant part of missions support.[15]

Notes

1. Sandford Fleming, *Children and Puritanism: The Place of Children in the Life and Thought of the New England Churches 1620-1847* (New Haven, Conn.: Yale University Press, 1933), 97.

2. C. A. Bowen, *Child and Church: A History of Methodist Church-School Curriculum* (New York: Abingdon, 1960), 27.

3. David I. Naglee, *From Font to Faith: John Wesley on Infant Baptism and the Nurture of Children* (New York: Peter Lang, 1987), 228-37.

4. Americo D. Lapati, *John Henry Newman* (New York: Twayne Publishers, 1972), 74-75.

5. John Henry Newman, *The Idea of a University* (Oxford: Clarendon Press, 1976), 427-28.

6. Ibid., 303-306.

7. Ibid., 145.

8. J. Herbert Kane, *A Concise History of the Christian World Mission: A Panoramic View of Missions from Pentecost to the Present*, rev. ed. (Grand Rapids: Baker Book House, 1982), 64-65.

9. Ibid., 62-63.

10. C. B. Eavey, *History of Christian Education* (Chicago: Moody, 1964), 336-38.

11. William Booth, *In Darkest England and the Way Out* (Chicago: Charles H. Sergel and Co., 1890), 99.

12. Ibid., 100.

13. Ibid., 187.

14. Harry Edward Neal, *The Hallelujah Army* (Philadelphia: Chilton Company, 1961), 42-43.

15. Donald G. Shockley, *Campus Ministry: The Church Beyond Itself* (Louisville: Westminster/John Knox, 1989), 12-36.

27

Women in the Beginnings of Modern Christian Education

The role of women in education changed rapidly during the dawn of modern Christian education. This shift, though not universal in any sense, was the result of necessity and of a growing appreciation for women as persons. It was both a result of and a contributor to a growing enlightenment regarding the role and potential of women in society and women's rights.

Women as Students

Comenius declared that education was to be available not only to all classes but also to both sexes:

They [women] are formed in the image of God, and share in His grace and in the kingdom of the world to come. They are endowed with equal sharpness of mind and capacity for knowledge (often with more than the opposite sex), and they are able to attain the highest positions, since they have often been called by God Himself to rule over nations . . . Why, therefore, should we admit them to the alphabet, and afterwards drive them away from the books? Do we fear their folly? The more we occupy their thoughts, so much the less will the folly that arises from emptiness of mind find a place.[1]

Comenius was not, however, in favor of arousing the inquisitiveness of girls. He was concerned that they learn those things necessary for them to be good wives and mothers. Further, he hoped that a well-educated girl would become a woman who could make intelligent and moral decisions in life.[2]

As Comenius described the structure and curricula of his system of education, he seldom referred specifically to "girls," although he sometimes mentioned "children." He most often used nonspecific terms such as pupils or students and the gender-specific boy. This may simply reflect the writing style of the time. By making a higher level of education available to girls, Comenius showed himself to be progressive for the time. His use of the feminine imagery (mother school or school of the mother's knee) were not evidences of feminism, but only images of domesticity referring to the importance of the home and both parents in childhood education.

Rousseau was less advanced in his view of women in education than in his views on education in general. He used the fictional female character Julie as the major educational figure in *The New Heloise*. At the close of the section in which she described her role as the teacher of her children (part 5, letter 3), Julie admitted her dependence on the wisdom and insight of her husband to educate her children. When Prince Louis Eugene of Wirtemberg inquired of Rousseau how to educate a daughter in the mode of *Emile,* Rousseau again evidenced more conservatism. He recommended that the girl be taught by a governess who need not herself be educated but who must evidence common sense. Rousseau thought the father, not the mother, should retain control of the girl's education. He wrote:

> Feminine judgement is admittedly not reliable enough, and maternal love is blind. If the mother were appointed judge in default of the father, either the governess would not trust her or she would be more concerned about pleasing the mother than about bringing up the child properly.[7]

Rousseau favored more control with girls than with boys. In describing the appropriate way in which girls should be taught, he often used words such as "rules" and "control," evidencing a further distrust of the feminine mind and ability to learn than on the level of men.

The European naturalists (Pestalozzi, Herbart, and Froebel) did not extensively treat the education of girls separate from that of boys. Although they used masculine terms to speak of pupils, there is little evidence that their language was deliberately exclusive.

Pestalozzi and Froebel used feminine imagery in their educational schemas. They used women as teachers, in part because men were away fighting the Napoleonic wars. Yet the writings of Pestalozzi and Froebel demonstrate a sincere appreciation for the potential of women as teachers.

Women were important in the birth and growth of the Sunday School movement. In the earliest Sunday Schools, Robert Raikes employed women as paid teachers. As the movement spread, many women supported it as a means of bettering society. Others continued to serve as teachers and missioners of the Sunday School unions.

The German Pietists were concerned for the education of young girls. August H. Francke wrote that girls should be educated if for no other reason than moral and social betterment.[4] Zinzendorf, too, stood for equal education for girls. He and his daughter established a boarding school for girls in Pennsylvania in 1742.[5] He segregated the sexes and used the young Jesus as a model, even for teaching girls. He emphasized goodness, a virtue of the young Jesus as a *child,* not simply His goodness as a *boy.*

George Fox (1624-1691), founder of the Quakers, had a relatively high and egalitarian view of women. He once told a meeting of English Quakers:

> Faithful women, who were called to the belief of the Truth, being made partakers of the same precious faith, and heirs of the same everlasting gospel of life and salvation with the men, might in like manner come into the possession and practice of the gospel order, and therein be helpmeets unto the men in the restoration, in the service of Truth, in the affairs of the Church, as they are outwardly in civil, or temporal things; that so all the family of God, women as well as men, might know, possess, perform, and discharge their offices and services in the house of God.[6]

This spirit of gender equality led American Quakers to establish Swarthmore College in Philadelphia in 1869. It provided for the higher education of both sexes.[7] Swarthmore College was named for the estate of the Fell family—early supporters of George Fox—in Ulverston, England.

Quakers even included women leaders and allowed them to speak and preach in their meetings. Elizabeth Fry, a Quaker, helped establish a school in Newgate Prison, London, in 1817. The school was opened to teach children of inmates but soon included the children's mothers as well. The school was loosely structured but included literacy training (using the Bible as the text), sewing, and other activities.[8]

Women as Educators

Early Methodism gave women positions of leadership. Wesley was at first reluctant to allow women to preach, fearing this would identify

Methodists with Quakers and because it appeared to contradict some biblical passages. Later, Wesley changed his mind, in part because of the success of some women evangelists. Methodist women were more widely involved in the leadership of study groups and classes in which they expounded portions of Scripture. These classes were often far removed from small, intimate groups meeting in the parlor of a home. They sometimes reached the large proportions of the class led by Sarah Crosby in 1761. Her class included over two hundred regular attendees.[9]

In Methodist Schools

Women were also leaders in many Methodist schools. Around 1760 Molly Maddern, whose husband taught at Wesley's school in Kingswood, managed a nearby school for girls. In 1763 Sarah Ryan and Mary Bosanquet established a Methodist school in Leytonstone. This school for orphans was located in "The Cedars," a house Bosanquet had inherited. The student body was normally comprised of about twenty students, most of whom were girls. The students wore uniforms, and discipline was strict but lovingly given. Subjects of instruction included basic education as well as practical and vocational skills. Life at the school included a weekly meeting of the entire school family in which teachers and students discussed matters of discipline and correction. Some criticized the school as a sort of convent because of its communal organization and strict discipline. However, the school, Mary Bosanquet, and Sarah Ryan enjoyed the support of John Wesley. Many other Methodist schools were established on the Leytonstone model.[10]

Wesley recommended a particular curriculum for the education of women. His *Female Course of Study, intended for those who have a good Understanding and much Leisure* was an intense course for laywomen. The course was to last for several years and require five to six hours of daily study. It included a great deal of Bible study, but also such subjects as grammar, arithmetic, geography, and history.[11]

In Missionary Education

Missionary movements of the eighteenth and nineteenth centuries provided additional educational opportunities for women. Although women were usually given second-class treatment and prohibited from preaching they proved effective missionaries. Women were especially instrumental in founding and developing societies for missions support and education.

In many countries, the mission schools were the only schools available to indigenous girls. This opened the door for women to serve as educational missionaries, and mission schools, both elementary and secondary, proliferated and flourished. Higher education was eventually made available in some areas. The first Christian college for women in Asia, Isabella Thoburn College (named after a Methodist education missionary to Lucknow, India), was established in India in 1887.[12]

As mission societies grew under the leadership of women and as more women were sent as missionaries, concern arose for appropriate training for female missionaries. Missions training schools were often open to women as well as men, but some believed that women needed separate training. Annie Armstrong, who founded the Woman's Missionary Union (WMU) of the Southern Baptist Convention, believed this way. She founded the WMU in 1888 and served without pay as its executive secretary until 1906. Armstrong was convinced that the education of Southern Baptist women missionaries should be under the aegis of the WMU. Others felt that such could better be done at a coeducational seminary. Armstrong argued that to train women missionaries at a seminary would lead to training them for the pastorate. To her this would be unbiblical. Armstrong's opponents prevailed in the dispute, and Armstrong resigned as a result.[13] The Woman's Missionary Union Training School was established in 1907 by the Southern Baptist Convention, although as an arm of and adjacent to The Southern Baptist Theological Seminary in Louisville, Kentucky.

In Schools for Girls

From the seventeenth century through the nineteenth, women gave other evidences of an increasing role in education. Anna Maria van Schurman (1607-1678) was widely sought as an expert in several languages and taught philosophy and history at the University of Utrecht in the Netherlands. In 1661 Francoise d'Aubigne (1635-1719), wife of Louis XIV of France, established a church-sponsored school for girls whose families were unable to afford them an education. Henriette Campan (1753-1822) established a system of schools for girls in France and wrote many books on education, among them *De'l Education* (1824). Saint Madeleine Barat (1779-1865) founded the Society of the Sacred Heart of Jesus and provided the impetus for the primary aims of the order, one of which was education. In Germany,

Bertha von Marenholtz-Bulow was one of the primary disseminators of Friedrich Froebel's theories of education. In 1850 Frances Buss of England (1827-1894) set up the North London Collegiate School for Girls, which would be a model for subsequent British secondary education for girls. Buss and Emily Davies (1830-1921) accomplished the admission of women to the previously all-male universities in England. In Germany, Helene Lange, Franziska Tiburtius, Minna Cauer, and Frau Kettler began a movement in the late nineteenth century to qualify women for admission to universities and to encourage universities to accept women as students.[14]

In England a movement began, despite religious and traditional barriers, toward more educational opportunities for women. In the 1840s Queen's and Bedford Colleges for Ladies were founded. In the 1880s faculty wives in Oxford organized women's lectures. Parliament passed the Education Acts of 1870 and 1876, which indirectly influenced the improvement of women's elementary and secondary education. By the end of the nineteenth century, women were earning degrees not only from those colleges and universities established particularly for them, but also from Oxford, Cambridge, and other previously all-male institutions.[15]

Notes

1. John Amos Comenius, *The Great Didactic,* trans. M. W. Keatinge (London: Adam and Charles Black, 1907), 68.

2. Ibid., 68-69.

3. Jean Jacques Rousseau, *Memoir on the Education of the Prince of Wittenberg's Infant Daughter Sophie* from *The Minor Educational Writings of Jean Jacques Rousseau,* trans. William Boyd (New York: Columbia University Press, 1962), 80.

4. Gary R. Sattler, *God's Glory, Neighbor's Good: A Brief Introduction to the Life and Writings of August Hermann Francke* (Chicago: Covenent Press, 1982), 52-53.

5. A. J. Lewis, *Zinzendorf the Ecumenical Pioneer: A Study in the Moravian Contribution to Christian Mission and Unity* (Philadelphia: Westminster, 1962), 174.

6. George Fox, *George Fox: An Autobiography,* ed. Rufus M. Jones (Philadelphia: Ferris and Leach, 1909), 536-37.

7. Elfrida Vipont, *The Story of Quakerism: Through Three Centuries* (London: The Bannisdale Press, 1960), 225.

8. Ibid., 190-91.

9. Earl Kent Brown, *Women of Mr. Wesley's Methodism* (New York: The Edwin Mellen Press, 1983), 23-26.

10. Ibid., 52-59.

11. Ibid., 51.

12. Ruth A. Tucker, *Guardians of the Great Commissions: The Story of Women in Modern Missions* (Grand Rapids: Zondervan, 1988), 139-43.

13. Ibid., 104.

14. Joan Macksey and Kenneth Macksey, *The Book of Women's Achievements* (New York: Stein and Day, 1976), 65-72.

15. Philippa Levine, *Victorian Feminism 1850-1900* (London: Century Hutchinson, 1987), 27-30.

Synopsis
of Part 5

Modern Christian education originated in the Renaissance and Reformation. The Renaissance and Reformation brought a willingness to rethink old approaches in many fields. Led by Comenius, Christian educators encouraged the use of the senses to inform the rational self. This served both to heighten the hunger for knowledge and to satisfy that hunger. It supplied a means to help persons understand and experience their relationship as part of creation.

This new thought recognized the natural self as being legitimate and important but not to the exclusion of the rational self or even on a par with it. This required Christian education to provide a curriculum and method by which persons could exercise their best as both natural and rational beings, while avoiding excesses.

Educators of the day increasingly saw their students as trustworthy, both as observers of nature and as spiritual beings. This optimism is surprising, considering the suffering caused by wars and revolutions of the day. This optimism gave rise to important movements in the history of Christian education. One of these was the Sunday School movement. Raikes's vision for the potential of the rowdy children of Gloucester (and, to be sure, his impatience with them) inspired him to start the first Sunday Schools. A similar spirit aroused others who aided the movement's growth throughout England and beyond. Another example was Comenius, who provided much of the flavor and spirit of the era. His educational principles exhibited trust in people and affirmed persons as educable beings. He believed this despite the tragedies in his life and in the life of his nation and church.

Comenius and others presented in this part are examples of modernity, though they lived two or three centuries ago. What makes

Comenius *modern?* He broke away from the educational approaches of the Middle Ages. His proposals continue today in spirit and form. Structures Comenius suggested for education remain in place today, though the details and labels may have changed. Much of what he suggested sounds as though he were advising churches, schools, and parents today. Pestalozzi, Wesley, and others also influence Christian education even today.

PART 6

Americans and Christian Education

28

Christian Education in Colonial America

Pious colonial parents normally taught prayers, Scripture, and hymns to their children at home. Sizeable settlements nearly always built a house of worship. In areas with sparse populations, churches met in homes. A traveling minister usually preached on a regular or occasional schedule. He conducted funeral services, marriage ceremonies, and baptisms as need arose and time permitted.

Schoolteachers who crossed the Atlantic found simple facilities—often nothing more than a one-room log schoolhouse. Sometimes the teacher also served the community as preacher. He boarded in homes and received few, if any, wages. Books and teaching materials were scarce. The basic curriculum was the "four R's": reading, 'riting, 'rithmetic, and religion.

In most cases, few children had the opportunity to study and those only in winter. During other seasons, they worked on the family farm or elsewhere. If circumstances permitted, the elite sent their children for refinement to England or Continental Europe. The methods and content of colonial education differed because of varieties of climate, religion, vocation, and background. A distinct type of education developed in each of the three colonial regions.

The New England Colonies

Many colonists came to American in search of religious freedom. Puritans in New England settled primarily to avoid harsh treatment from the English church. The Calvinistic dissenters of the Massachusetts Bay Colony required that their children learn to read the Bible.

Of the four New England colonies, only Rhode Island practiced religious liberty. Massachusetts, Connecticut, and New Hampshire maintained a Puritan religious establishment. This was, of course, inconsistent with their requests in England, because the once-persecuted Puritans persecuted others.

In Puritan thought, a literate religious society produced good citizens, but ignorance corrupted society. The typical Puritan believed that he was conceived in sin to live a disciplined and difficult life. A sinner by nature, he deserved the rod to correct his evil ways. Since no room existed for error, the good child behaved like an adult. Good or bad, however, his eternal destiny was predetermined by God.

One-room town schools provided elementary education in the vernacular for boys and girls at various ages and stages of learning. In the beginning attendance was not compulsory. A teacher's preparation and proficiency varied. Usually the town schoolteacher was less qualified than the Latin grammar schoolteacher who had the task of preparing young men for college. The dame school, which was imported from England, featured another type of teacher. As the woman of the house worked, she listened to the recitations of children who gathered in her house. In any of these schools, a child who failed to master the assigned lesson according to the proper catechetical method was often severely disciplined.

The legal foundation for education in the New England colonies began with the Mayflower Compact of 1620. In this agreement the Puritans professed their obedience to just and equal laws. Concern for education in these colonies was soon evident in laws passed by the General Court of Massachusetts in 1642. Five years later that Massachusetts legislature enacted a law placing educational responsibilities on towns and requiring educational opportunities for the youth. The Massachusetts laws of 1642 and 1647 led the way for legislation in other colonies. All New England colonies except Rhode Island enacted some form of school legislation and collected taxes for education.[1]

Three books provided the basic curriculum for students in colonial New England: the *Hornbook,* the *New England Primer,* and the *Bay Psalm Book*.

The child's first primer was the *Hornbook*. It was a single piece of parchment, covered by a transparent substance and connected to a handle. The alphabet, the Lord's Prayer, and other religious doctrine were written or printed on the parchment.

In 1690 the first edition of the *New England Primer* by Benjamin Harris appeared. By 1700 the *Primer* had replaced the *Hornbook* in many places. The *Primer,* called New England's *Little Bible,* contained names of the Old and New Testament books alphabetically arranged, the Lord's Prayer, "An Alphabet of Lessons for Youth," the Apostles' Creed, the Ten Commandments, and other religious contents. The *New England Primer* also illustrated each letter of the alphabet with a rhyming couplet with a moral lesson. The examples in chart 6 illustrate the design.

Examples from the
New England Primer
Chart 6

A. In Adam's Fall We sinned all.	R. Rachel doth mourn for her first born.
F. The Idle Fool Is whipt at School.	S. Samuel anoints whom God appoints.
J. Job feels the Rod Yet blesses God.	Y. Youth forward slips Death soonest nips.[2]

In 1640 Stephen Day of the Massachusetts Bay Colony printed *The Bay Psalm Book,* the first book written and printed in the colonies. It consisted largely of a collection of psalms which were selected by several ministers. Henry Dunster's revision of the book in 1651 appeared in twenty-seven editions throughout the colonies and also in England.

The Southern Colonies

Virginia, Maryland, North Carolina, South Carolina, and Georgia were the Southern colonies. Most residents of this region followed the Anglican religion, but more diversity existed there than in the New England colonies. For instance, colonists came to Virginia chiefly for economical reasons. Whereas the Puritans dissented from the Church of England, the Virginians were mostly Anglicans who considered education a duty of parents, not the church or state.

Colonial education in the South followed one of two patterns. The rich plantation owners employed private tutors for their children or sent them to England. Because of the distance between plantations, schools were impractical in the land of tobacco, sugar, indigo, and cotton. The second type of education was apprenticeship schools where poor children and orphans received basic training to develop work skills.

The Society for the Propagation of the Gospel in Foreign Parts, organized in 1701, placed three hundred missionaries in the colonies, most of these in the South. For the purpose of evangelization, this society attempted to teach Indians and blacks how to read and write. This assistance was not always received well by the whites. For example, in 1740 South Carolina passed a law that prohibited such education for blacks.[3]

The Middle Colonies

Residents of the Middle Colonies (New York, New Jersey, Pennsylvania, and Delaware) were more diverse than the New England Puritans or the southern Anglicans. Anglicans, Lutherans, Presbyterians, Quakers, Roman Catholics, Jews, Dutch Calvinists, and others settled the Middle Colonies. This ethnic, linguistic, and religious diversity greatly affected education.

These groups generally supported education but refused to allow any denomination or sect to control the content and methodology of schools. Consequently, each religious group established its own school, the local minister was often the teacher as well. These parochial schools served children in the middle colonies until the mid-1830s.

English and Dutch traditions influenced education in this region. However, Pennsylvania Quakers had their own peculiar social, moral, and religious ideas about education. The abolitionist movement in America was led by itinerant Quakers such as John Woolman (1720-1772). In his *Journal*, first published in 1774, he detailed efforts for other classes and races. Quakers provided instruction for blacks or integrated many of their schools by 1700.

Perhaps the most important Quaker school for blacks was the "African School" that Anthony Benezet (1713-1784) established in Philadelphia. After becoming a Quaker in London about 1727, Benezet moved to Philadelphia in 1731. There he openly opposed slavery, attempted to educate blacks, improved the living condition of Indians, and headed a school for poor girls.[4]

German Moravians stressed infant schools, and the Presbyterians from Scotland and Ireland initiated grammar schools in the Middle

Colonies. Other parochial schools provided basic education with their own particular religious emphases.

Colonial Higher Education

Higher education in the American colonies progressed little during the first two centuries. A select few were educated for leadership. Enrollments were small, and curriculum was narrow. Teaching was more concerned with character building than research. Local and colonial grants supplied funds. America's first colleges were generally fashioned from English tradition.

Colonial Colleges and Religious Affiliation
Chart 7

Foundation Date	College	Colony	Religious Denomination
1636	Harvard	Massachusetts	Puritan
1693	William & Mary	Virginia	Anglican
1701	Yale	Connecticut	Congregational
1746	Princeton	New Jersey	Presbyterian
1754	King's College (Columbia)	New York	Anglican
1756	College of Philadelphia (University of Pennsylvania)	Pennsylvania	None
1764	Brown	Rhode Island	Baptist
1766	Rutgers	New Jersey	Reformed Dutch
1769	Dartmouth	New Hampshire	Congregational

Harvard College, named in honor of John Harvard, was established in 1636. This Massachusetts minister contributed money and approximately four hundred books to the young institution. The townspeople expressed gratitude to Harvard by changing the name of their community from Newtowne to Cambridge, the name of the English university that Harvard had attended.

Henry Dunster, a graduate of Cambridge, was Harvard's first president. For almost ten years he was the school's sole professor. A core curriculum was directed toward preaching ministers but was available to all qualified students, yet well over half of Harvard's colonial graduates were clergymen. Dunster's forced resignation occurred in 1654, when he expressed doubts concerning the doctrine of infant baptism.

At the institution's founding, only males who had mastered Latin and Greek were admitted. The specific purpose of Harvard College was "to advance learning, and perpetuate it to posterity, dreading to leave an illiterate ministry to the churches, when our present ministers shall die in the dust."[5]

The College of William and Mary was also established to educate ministers. In 1693 the English monarchs provided a grant with the intention of supplying the church of Virginia with a "seminary of the ministers of the gospel" and promoting "true philosophy and other good and liberal arts and sciences."[6] In addition to religion, this second colonial college provided instruction in etiquette and manners for Southern society. The William and Mary School of Law, the first such higher school in the colonies, educated Thomas Jefferson, John Marshall, and other architects of American democracy.

In 1701 the General Assembly of Connecticut consented to a request from a group of ministers who wanted a college in Connecticut to train ministers. At first the school moved from place to place. In 1720 the financially troubled college gained a permanent home in New Haven, Connecticut. The name was changed to Yale College when Elihu Yale, a wealthy merchant, gave a large sum of money.

Nine colleges began instruction in colonial America. Most had only one building. All owed allegiance to a Protestant faith except the College of Philadelphia, later the University of Pennsylvania (see chart 7).

◆ ◆ ◆ ◆ ◆ ◆ ◆ ◆ ◆

Religion permeated elementary and higher education in early colonial America, though religious domination diminished somewhat during the eighteenth century.

The three colonial regions had differing religious traditions, and these differences were reflected in educational differences. The Puritans of

New England educated their children uniformly, whether in a private setting at home or in public schools. Wealthy plantation owners in the southern colonies hired private tutors, who often lived in the same house with the children they taught. Religion in the middle colonies was more diverse with Catholics, Jews, and various Protestant groups. Many denominations and residents there established private and parochial schools.

Notes

1. Gerald L. Gutek, *Education and Schooling in America*, 2d ed. (Englewood Cliffs, N.J.: Prentice-Hall, 1988), 10.

2. Sheldon S. Cohen, *A History of Colonial Education, 1607-1776* (New York: John Wiley and Sons, 1974), 62.

3. Rosemary Radford Ruether and Rosemary Skinner Keller, *Women and Religion in America,* The Colonial and Revolutionary Periods, vol. 2 (San Francisco: Harper and Row, 1983), 26-27.

4. Warren Button and Eugene F. Provenzo, Jr., *History of Education and Culture in America,* 2d ed. (Englewood Cliffs, N.J.: Prentice-Hall, 1988), 45.

5. Calvin Grieder and Stephen Romie, *American Public Education,* 2d ed. (New York: Ronald Press, 1955), 88.

6. Raymond E. Callahan, *An Introduction to Education in American Society: A Text with Readings,* 2d ed. (New York: Alfred A. Knopf, 1960), 119.

29

Religion in Nineteenth-Century American Education

America experienced an intellectual revolution in the nineteenth century. The English Industrial Revolution had begun in the middle of the eighteenth century, sparked by scientific discoveries. Many decades before Darwin's *Origin of Species* (1859), the scientific spirit of the Enlightenment was influencing American life in the home, church, and school. Yet religion persisted as a formative ingredient in nineteenth-century American education, though religious influence varied from place to place.

Legal Foundations

The Constitution of the United States, ratified in 1788, did not directly address education. Colonists preferred the control of education be left with local landowners rather than a centralized political power. This slowed growth of national influence on education. Support and control of education, during the early days of the American republic, was more a local or state concern than a national responsibility.

The Dartmouth College case developed because of differences between college trustees and the New Hampshire legislature. In 1816 the governor changed Dartmouth College, privately owned and operated, into Dartmouth University, which was state-controlled by trustees appointed by the governor.

After the New Hampshire Superior Court ruled in favor of the university and governor, the case reached the United States Supreme Court. Daniel Webster successfully represented his alma mater.[1] Webster argued that the charter was a contract: the legislature had neither right nor power to violate the charter. Webster maintained that this was also true of every college in America. After a delay of eleven months, Chief

Justice John Marshall wrote the majority opinion, using Webster's argument as the main point of the Supreme Court decision.[2]

The court defended the sanctity of charters and protected corporate businesses as well. The legal position of private colleges was enhanced when the Supreme Court ruled that states could not take over private colleges without permission of the trustees. The case further implied that state universities were constitutional and that education was "an object of national concern, and a proper subject of legislation."[3]

Another milestone in the history of American higher education was the opening of America's first state university, the University of Virginia, founded in 1825 under the leadership of Thomas Jefferson (1743-1826). Jefferson's views on education were influenced by the Enlightenment; they clashed with religious tradition and threatened denominational colleges such as Yale and Princeton. While Jefferson wanted more sciences and modern languages in the curriculum of higher education, church schools preferred theology and classical languages.

In response to the reform movement, which supported the need for practical studies and the reduction of "dead languages," the Yale faculty in 1828 issued the Yale Report. This rather paternalistic document confessed that changes were needed gradually but not immediately. Concerning scientific studies, the Yale Report did not suggest the elimination of specialized studies but concluded that such studies had no place in the undergraduate college.[4] According to Robert E. Potter, the Yale Report was perhaps "the greatest influence in stabilizing the college curriculum during the middle third of the nineteenth century."[5] The Yale Report was very popular. With the rejection of attempted reforms at Harvard College and the University of Virginia, the Yale Report demonstrated the staid nature of American higher education before the Civil War.

The German university became the model for American graduate schools. After the founding of Johns Hopkins University in 1875, many liberal arts colleges reorganized as research-oriented universities. A more secular direction generally replaced the more religious orientation structure that had characterized college classrooms before the Civil War.

Protestantism in the Public Schools

A new working class emerged with the growth of factories in New England and the Middle Atlantic states. Aided by improved rail and water transportation, cities like Boston and New York grew over 300 percent from 1820 to 1850. The rapid growth of cities brought slums, poverty, crime, and deplorable family conditions.

Many factory owners would only employ whole families, paying lower wages to women and children. An average workweek consisted of six thirteen-hour days. This left little time for schooling. In the 1830s, two-fifths of New England factory workers were less than sixteen years old.[6]

Eventually federal child-labor laws prevented children from working during their school-age years and protected them from cruel exploitation. As families moved into the cities, they often left behind the concept of the one-room schoolhouse, which had allowed local and religious control of education. Most factory workers, especially between 1828 and 1860, were apathetic toward educational issues. Yet in places such as Boston and Philadelphia, organized workers called for a public system of tax-supported schools operated by the state. Education offered to the common people free of charge would strengthen the economic base for a democratic society.

During the nineteenth century, American public schools reflected their Protestant roots. Especially in New England the public or common schools would have died an early death without the confidence of Protestants. Founders of common schools early included Protestant orthodoxy and the work ethic. Puritans who settled New England contributed most of what was valuable for America's future educational development.

The common school movement of the nineteenth century, although never common to all people, deserves recognition as a major contributor to American educational, social, and cultural history. Publicly controlled and supported, the common schools provided many American children with a practical education emphasizing moral values.

Horace Mann (1796-1859) of Massachusetts is considered the father of the public school. Although he favored the use of the Bible in schools, Mann wanted to free public education from religious control while emphasizing citizenship and character building.

Not all religious groups embraced the public schools. Many Roman Catholics and Lutherans rejected the principles taught in common schools and continued to educate their children in private schools. Parochial schools grew after the Civil War because more immigrants came to America from predominately Catholic countries such as Spain and Italy. Catholics consisted of about 1 percent of the American population in 1800, but by the middle of the 1880s they numbered in excess of eight million.[7]

Catholic opposition to public schools grew amid charges of Protestant prejudice and bigotry. Catholics disapproved of hymns, prayers, and textbooks resembling Protestant worship. They criticized reading from the King James Bible as being "anti-Catholic." Many Protestants denounced Catholics as "foreigners" seeking to implant papal power in the United States.[8]

John Carroll (1735-1815), the first Catholic bishop in America, effectively led Catholics in valuing Christian education and establishing parochial schools for both males and females. He also founded Georgetown College in 1791 and later became the first archbishop of Baltimore.

While some arguments between Protestants and Catholics about the public schools remain unsettled, few doubt their value for American society. The common schools redirected the role of the Sunday School from basic education to Bible study. Public schools gradually absorbed the work of infant schools, which had provided some education and religious instruction to children of working mothers. In the 1830s the term *primary department* developed in New York. Public schools largely set aside Joseph Lancaster's monitorial system, which used better students to help the weaker.

An examination of nineteenth-century American textbooks validates the Catholic accusation that Protestant thought greatly influenced the formation of the American mind. **William Holmes McGuffey** (1800-1873), a Presbyterian minister and educator from Pennsylvania, wrote and illustrated the most influential grade school textbooks. His *Eclectic Readers* sold over 120 million copies. He preserved the stereotype of the true American as pious, patriotic, and Protestant. Samuel G. Goodrich (1793-1860), another Protestant minister, also typified the ideal American as Protestant. He authored over one hundred children's books under the pseudonym Peter Parley.[9]

Revivalism and Christian Education

The movement created by **Jonathan Edwards** (1703-1758), with the assistance of additional preachers, is commonly called the Great Awakening. Environmental conditions, low moral actions, and religious practices substantially contributed to the period of revivals, especially from 1720 to 1750.

The Great Awakening resulted in the founding of denominational colleges, including Princeton, Brown, and Dartmouth. Revivalistic preaching emphasized that believers experience conversion. Unlike most preachers who followed him, Edwards's sermon delivery was not sensational. Although he preached in monotone, scores professed the Christian faith. "Sinners in the Hands of an Angry God," his most renowned sermon, illustrated his motivational tactic of fear.

Edwards disagreed with the revivalists who prescribed an emotional experience to validate personal faith. Taking a more traditional position, Edwards viewed religious experience as subject to critical judgment.[10] Displaying a keen intellect and sensitive spirit, Edwards sometimes studied more than thirteen hours daily. Yet he said that the purpose of the minister was not to "store the head but stir the heart."[11]

A Second Great Awakening occurred during the first quarter of the nineteenth century on American college campuses and through frontier camp meetings. Under the preaching of Timothy Dwight (1752-1817), president of Yale and grandson of Jonathan Edwards, revival swept the campus at New Haven.

In 1808 the Protestant theological seminary movement began with the opening of Andover in Massachusetts. By 1855 an accepted pattern of theological education was in place: after four years of college, the male ministerial student completed three years of seminary. By 1900 there were more than 150 theological schools in the United States.[12]

Although having no seminary education, **Charles G. Finney** (1792-1875), considered the most renowned revivalist of the nineteenth century, conducted revivals and camp meetings across much of America. He served as president of Oberlin College (1851-1866) and taught revival theology.

The frontier revival, which lasted until about 1850, inspired the formation of new schools, especially by Presbyterians and Congregationalists. Methodists and Baptists, rather than *requiring* theologically trained ministers, ordained men who expressed a call from God regardless of their education. Frontier camp meetings increased the Sunday School and stirred the hearts of Christians toward foreign missionary service and support.[13]

The Bible school movement grew out of revivalism. From the standpoint of Christian education during the final one-third of the nineteenth century, the work of **Dwight L. Moody** (1837-1899), the famous lay preacher from Northfield, Massachusetts, deserves most attention. Although backing formal education, Moody gave thousands of men and women the opportunity to study in his Bible schools. Never claiming to be a scholar, he had little time or interest in technical study of the Bible; study in the original languages did not interest him. His interpretation of Scripture was simple and unsystematic, yet seldom offensive.

Moody first established the Northfield (Massachusetts) Seminary for girls in 1879, followed by the nearby Mount Hermon School for boys two years later. His most celebrated Bible school, the Bible-Work Institute of Chicago Evangelization Society (now called Moody Bible Institute), began operation in 1886.

Moody's pedagogy brought practical solutions to the spiritual needs of people. He used various methods of popular education: Sunday Schools, YMCA's, chautauquas, extension classes, and correspondence schools. In addition Moody published his sermons and other writings. As a catalyst for the Fleming H. Revell Company and the Moody Press, he is entitled to recognition as a significant publisher of evangelical materials. By the end of the nineteenth century, Revell advertised itself as "the largest American publisher of religious books."[14]

Nineteen-century American population statistics indicate that church membership in America grew from 10 to approximately 40 percent. Without question, revivalism contributed more than its share to this growth.[15]

William Rainey Harper and the University of Chicago

By sponsoring lectures, Cambridge University in England popularized extension education in the nineteenth century. Following this idea, the Chautauqua movement, under the auspices of the Methodist church, attracted many in America during the last quarter of the nineteenth century and the first quarter of the twentieth century.

The Chautauqua movement began in 1874 with the establishment of a normal school on Lake Chautauqua in western New York state.[16] This movement spread biblical studies and popular education using organization and management similar to a Sunday School. William Rainey Harper (1856-1906) began his career as a teacher and administrator at Chautauqua Lake, but he went on to become the first president of the University of Chicago in 1891. Harper was able to turn his educational ideas into reality because John D. Rockefeller (1839-1937), the Baptist industrialist, used much of his massive wealth to found the University of Chicago. Harper's modifications and innovations in

American higher education in general and Christian religious education in particular remain influential today.

Harper popularized correspondence studies. During the first decade of operation, the University of Chicago enrolled nearly three thousand correspondence students. There were students from every American state, and 87 percent of the enrollees were teachers in schools and/or churches.

Harper considered his pragmatic, scientific method as *the* way and not *a* way to study the Bible. By practicing a ''higher criticism'' of the Bible, he valued the teacher as a research scholar who did not always interpret Scripture literally. For this and other reasons, he received loud and prolonged criticism from his predominately conservative and fundamentalist Baptist constituents as well as other critics. Harper was intensely interested in publishing biblical research. The University of Chicago possibly had the first university press in America,[17] though Johns Hopkins makes the same claim.[18]

In 1903 Harper founded the Religious Education Association, which many consider his most important contribution to Christian religious education. Responding to his call for a convention of religious educators, more than three thousand leaders from the United States and other countries attended the first meeting in Chicago. Most of Harper's forty-six books and other writings are in the area of biblical language studies. In nineteenth-century history in the area of Christian education, this scholar led in innovative methods of scientific Bible study.

William Rainey Harper and Dwight L. Moody were acquaintances. Although generally on opposite ends of the theological and educational spectrums, each admired the results of the other. In eclectic fashion, they represent American diversity at the close of the nineteenth century.

Notes

1. Richard Hofstadter and Wilson Smith, eds., *American Higher Education: A Documentary History*, vol. 1 (Chicago: University of Chicago, 1961), 41.

2. Robert E. Potter, *The Stream of American Education* (New York: American Book Co., 1967), 173.

3. Ibid., 174.

4. John S. Brubacher and Willis Rudy, *Higher Education in Transition: A History of American Colleges and Universities, 1636-1976*, 3d ed. (New York: Harper and Row 1976), 105.

5. Potter, 182.

6. Ibid., 190-91.

7. James C. Carper and Thomas C. Hunt, *Religious Schooling in America* (Birmingham, Ala.: Religious Education Press, 1984), 2; Kenneth S. Latourette, *The Great Century in Europe*

and the United States of America, A.D. 1800-A.D. 1914, A History of the Expansion of Christianity, vol. 5 (New York: Harper and Brothers, 1941), 230, 255.

8. Warren H. Button and Eugene F. Provenzo, Jr., *History of Education and Culture in America*, 2d ed. (Englewood Cliffs, N.J.: Prentice-Hall, 1988), 140-41.

9. Sidney E. Ahlstrom, *A Religious History of the American People* (New Haven: Yale University Press, 1972), 642.

10. Dewitte Holland, Jess Yoder, and Hubert Taylor, eds., *Preaching in American History: Selected Issues in the American Pulpit* (Nashville: Abingdon, 1969), 116-17.

11. Roland Bainton, *Yale and the Ministry* (New York: Harper and Brothers, 1957), 34.

12. James W. Fraser, *Schooling the Preachers* (New York: University Press of America, 1988), 11.

13. Edith C. Magruder, *A Historical Study of the Educational Agencies of the Southern Baptist Convention, 1845-1945* (New York: Columbia University Press, 1951), 12-13.

14. Allan Fisher, "D. L. Moody's Contribution to Christian Publishing," *Christian History* 25 (1990):32.

15. Fisher Humphreys, ed., *Nineteenth Century Evangelical Theology* (Nashville: Broadman, 1981), 11.

16. Joseph E. Gould, *The Chautauqua Movement: An Episode in the Continuing American Revolution* (New York: State University of New York Press, 1961), 5.

17. Thomas W. Goodspeed, *William Rainey Harper: First President of the University of Chicago* (Chicago: University of Chicago, 1928), 141.

18. N. R. Kleinfield, "How Six Press On," *New York Times Book Review* 21 (October 1979):11.

30

Pragmatism and Education

Pragmatism (sometimes called experimentalism, instrumentalism, or progressivism) was a major break with traditional philosophies. It developed in America during the nineteenth century, when great value was placed on visible results. The meaning of life for Americans became increasingly defined by measurable accomplishments in the present rather than in their foreign heritage or unknown future. Truth from a pragmatic viewpoint was tentative and open-ended. As problems were solved, Americans became even more scientific and practical. From the mid-1800s until the present, America has continued, in religion, education, and nearly all other aspects of life, to operate pragmatically.

Roots of Pragmatism

Heraclitus (ca. 540-470 B.C.), the Greek philosopher, wrote: "All things flow; nothing abides. One cannot step twice into the same river. Into the same rivers we step and do not step; we are, and we are not." Everything is constantly in a process of change.

The English scientist Francis Bacon (1561-1626) favored the inductive method of thinking and employed science as a social pursuit. Other Europeans who significantly influenced American life and education were John Locke, Jean Jacques Rousseau, Johann Heinrich Pestalozzi, Johann Friedrich Herbart, and Friedrich Wilhelm Froebel, who focused attention on the student in unconventional ways.

Following the European Enlightenment, more emphases in science and mathematics gradually entered the curriculum of American schools. An academy, cofounded by Benjamin Franklin, stressed a practical curriculum. Some of the skills and subjects not included in previous formal schools were carpentry, shipbuilding, engraving, printing, painting, cabinetmaking, farming, and carving. A self-educated man, Franklin called attention to the need to study science, invention, and technology.[1]

The frontier spirit fostered the pragmatic temper. The frontiersman's interest was oriented toward the future, not the past. His job had to be done. His problems had to be solved. Acquainted with a relatively fixed heritage, new Americans suddenly noticed a rapid change in laws, governments, and social institutions.

Early Americans were judged less by their claims of ancestry than by their abilities to function—the ability to get things done. Ideas alone did not change living conditions on the frontier. A valid method was one that yielded observable results.

The independent nation needed an organized educational system. A variety of plans was offered. Though these ideas differed greatly, there were common points:

- Education met the needs of a self-governing polity;
- Education reflected the needs of a developing nation that included vast expanses of frontier land and abundant supplies of natural resources;
- Education was useful rather than classical or ornamental; and
- Education was American rather than European.[2]

With exceptional interest, intellectuals discussed Charles Darwin's *The Origin of Species*. Evolution was soon the topic of conversation with scholars everywhere. *The Origin of Species* contributed significantly in at least three ways:

> First, the conception of evolution in which species arise and disappear implies that reality is not a static, closed system, but a dynamic process of change and development. . . . Second, the evolutionary view brings man and all his cultural achievements within a natural process of development, and thus cuts the ground from the theory of special creation and the "two-world" outlook associated with it. . . . Third, the pragmatists rejected the notion that evolution applied to the body of man, but not to his mind.[3]

Founders of Pragmatism

Charles Sanders Peirce

Born in Cambridge, Massachusetts, Charles Sanders Peirce (1839-1914) received his formal education at Harvard. He taught two years at

Harvard and approximately five years at Johns Hopkins. Peirce coined the term *pragmatism*, but he is relatively unknown because he published little: he wrote *The Grand Logic* and edited *Studies in Logic*.

William James and John Dewey are better known, but Peirce contributed more original thought to the philosophy than they. James and Peirce were associates at Harvard, and Dewey was Peirce's student at Johns Hopkins. Peirce's pragmatism was based in physics and mathematics, Dewey's in biology and social science. James's was in psychology. Of the three, James wrote with more religious motivation.

William James

The most outstanding psychologist-philosopher in the last quarter of the nineteenth century was William James (1842-1910). His father was a theologian and his older brother, Henry James, was a novelist. William James's philosophy of religion, more than Peirce's or Dewey's, was directed to the existence of God.

James objected to the concept of absolutes. He did not believe in a single truth "out there." In his system each person selected a belief from his possible options. The selection that "worked best" was truth to James. Credited with causing Americans to accept pragmatic thought, James viewed a concept or object as worthless if there were no results.

In 1902 James published *Varieties of Religious Experience*, which developed from his Gifford Lectures at Edinburgh. This was a major contribution in the development of psychology of religion as a discipline. While on the faculty at Harvard, William James undertook the first formal study of psychology in the United States. He taught that creative teachers who applied psychological principles improve the quality of education.

The "new psychology" as found in James's *Principles of Psychology* (1890) stimulated Dewey to "formulate the instrumentalist role of the inseparability of thought and action, knowing and doing; ideas were seen no longer as objects of contemplation but as instruments of action."[4]

Two of William James's students, Edward L. Thorndike (1874-1949) and G. Stanley Hall (1844-1924), became influential in the development of American education. Thorndike concentrated in the stimulus-response psychology, while Hall is known as the father of the child study movement, because of his work in child development.

John Dewey

Born in Vermont before the Civil War, John Dewey (1859-1952) was still alive during the Korean War. The man who doubted absolutes witnessed more change than anyone else who lived before him. After graduating at the head of his class with a major in philosophy at the University of Vermont, Dewey studied under G. Stanley Hall at Johns Hopkins. Over a period of forty-six years, Dewey taught at the University of Michigan, the University of Minnesota, the University of Chicago, and Columbia University. He is credited as the author of at least forty-six volumes.

John Dewey viewed education as a social process seeking social ends. In *My Pedagogic Creed*, Dewey wrote: "Education ... is a process of living and not a preparation for future living."[5] In Dewey's thinking, education should be a natural growth for the child. The student was guided by the community. Active participation was the most effective method for a student to learn democracy. According to Dewey, social studies and social activities were the subject matter and concern of education.[6]

According to David H. Roper, Dewey's neopedagogy included five basic tenets: (1) child-centered education; (2) education through intrinsic motivation; (3) education through activity; (4) education as reconstruction of experience; and (5) social-centered education.[7]

As a critical naturalist, Dewey accepted natural knowledge as the total of everything, therefore, the Divine Being was not responsible for creation.[8]

In 1894 John Dewey moved from the faculty of the University of Michigan to become head of the department of philosophy at the University of Chicago. Shortly thereafter, the department of pedagogy (later education) was established with Dewey as chairman. In 1896 he and his wife founded the Laboratory School at the University of Chicago. Dewey associated the scientific school with the departments of philosophy, psychology, and education. Until his departure in 1904 he operationalized his experimentalist education. Children learned primarily by using their senses and solving problems. Two of Dewey's books detailing his work at the Laboratory School are *The School and Society* (1898) and *The Child and the Curriculum* (1902).

Dewey's *Democracy and Education* (1916) has been called the most influential book ever written on American education. He believed schools should teach the principles of democracy with democratic methods and projects. Francis W. Parker (1837-1902) and others credited Dewey with being the father of the Progressive Education movement. His impressions of progressive education are presented in *Experience and Education.*

John Dewey has probably influenced the direction of American education more than any other individual. He studied American society and viewed education as one phase of society. His efforts for practical application of democratic principles in schools led Dewey to conclude that the only way the child could adequately prepare for social life was to engage in social life. Seeking to reform society, Dewey's writings and actions provided the impetus for the Progressive Education movement that ran its course during the first half of the twentieth century.

Pragmatism and Religious Education

For centuries education had been subject centered. The teacher was the authority and most eminent person in the classroom. The pragmatist thought the opposite idea was the best for the educative process. Instruction was to be child-centered. The teacher was a corporate problem-solver.

According to the pragmatist, the classical curriculum of antiquity and the Middle Ages had little place in the new world. In this tradition, an educated person taught and wrote in an archaic language. In the new American world, the more practical person needed a new kind of educational experience. This demanded methodologies that stressed "doing," "getting things done," and "bottom-line results." An identified problem needed a solution, and instruction that solved America's problems was highly valued. "Learning on the job" became an important American method, especially on the frontier.

In religious education the Sunday School movement of the twentieth century has experienced change as a result of the progressive education emphasis. Sunday School teachers especially with preschoolers and children, have in many settings turned more attention to the child and less to biblical content. Often the claim is made that more application has been the result. For example, when a typical preschool child walks into the Sunday School room, he or she may choose from several areas of interest for participation such as nature, music, or homeliving.

Vacation Bible Schools have characteristically *involved* children in arts and crafts designed to illustrate Bible stories. These schools are often organized to produce evangelistic *results* or decisions from the children. Other examples include an increase in *activities* connected with youth work.

Churches often organize Bible study groups to *solve the problems* of their members. Bible classes that *meet needs* are usually well attended, and this produces *results* for the church. Although some churches desire more pragmatic activities than others, the tools for measuring results have changed during the last century. Some believe this pragmatic approach is short on Christian depth and content. Curriculum planning has also changed noticeably in church educational programs. Under a more practical arrangement, lessons are grouped in units with projects to support the basic content.

John Dewey's progressive movement has influenced all phases of American education. Seeking numerical results, many churches have "baptized" his ideas. Whether this action is best, only time will indicate.

Notes

1. Gerald L. Gutek, "Historical and Philosophical Foundations," in *An Introduction to the Foundations of Education*, ed. Allan C. Ornstein (Chicago: Rand-McNally, 1977), 164-65.

2. Ibid., 164.

3. John L. Childs, *American Pragmatism and Education: An Interpretation and Criticism* (New York: Holt, Rinehart and Winston, 1956), 18-19.

4. Patricia A. Graham, *Progressive Education: From Arcady to Academe* (New York: Teachers College Press, 1967), 6.

5. James W. Noll and Sam P. Kelly, *Foundations of Education in America: An Anthology of Major Thoughts and Significant Actions* (New York: Harper and Row, 1970), 237.

6. Ibid., 238-39.

7. David H. Roper, "John Dewey," *A History of Religious Educators*, ed. Elmer L. Towns (Grand Rapids: Baker Book House, 1975), 320.

8. Ibid., 315.

31

Horace Bushnell
and Christian Nurture

In 1979 sixteen Protestant, Catholic, and Jewish scholars of religious education were asked to identify the most important books ever written in the discipline. The book most often listed was *Christian Nurture* by Horace Bushnell (1802-1876).[1]

Bushnell's basic proposition in *Christian Nurture* was that "the child is to grow up a Christian, and never know himself as being otherwise."[2] Evangelical revivalists rejected Bushnell's thesis as unorthodox or heretical. Bushnell rejected the conservative theology of nineteenth-century New England, including sensationalism, revivalism, the total depravity of man, and what he called "ostrich nurture." Instead, Bushnell proposed a Christian family environment, infant or household baptism, and the "organic unity of the family."

The Life of Horace Bushnell

Horace Bushnell was born in 1802 in Bantam, Connecticut. His father was a Methodist of Huguenot descent and an agricultural and manufacturing background. His mother had been reared Episcopalian from a Huguenot background. Both parents rejected the Calvinistic doctrines of predestination and the total depravity of man.

Others described the Bushnell home as comfortable but simple. Horace's warm, industrious, and intelligent mother influenced him more than anyone else in his early years. He characterized her as:

> The only person I have known in the close intimacy of years who never did an inconsiderate, imprudent, or in any way excessive thing that required to be afterwards mended. . . . She was a good talker, and was often spoken of as the best Bible teacher in the congregation, but she never fell into the mistake of trying to talk her children into religion.[3]

In 1820 Horace professed faith in Jesus Christ and joined the New Preston Congregational Church, where his parents had been members since his birth. Three years later, Bushnell entered Yale College, where he studied until he graduated in 1827. His friends described Bushnell as handsome, sportful, musical, and original. Independent thought characterized his entire life. He refused to enter recitation contests at Yale, because he found them unreal and awkward. However, if a true question were raised, Bushnell became eager to address the issue. In religious matters, he expressed doubts about religion based on emotion.[4]

After graduation from Yale, Bushnell taught at Norwich, Connecticut. Describing himself as unsuited for classroom teaching, he soon moved to New York City to practice journalism.

Between 1829 and 1831, Bushnell served as a tutor at Yale and studied law. During this time many students at Yale experienced revival. In 1831 Bushnell made a new decision of conversion to Christ. This was, in his words, "a simple and profound desire to be and do right, rather than to have a personal relationship with God."[5]

The year 1833 was a very busy one in the life of Bushnell. In February, he became pastor of the North Congregational Church in Hartford, Connecticut, where he served for twenty-six years. This was the only church that he served in his ministry. In May 1833 Bushnell was ordained into the gospel ministry. In September of that same year, Mary Apthorp of New Haven became his wife.

Horace and Mary were the parents of five children. In 1837 an infant daughter died. In 1842 their only son died at age four. Concerning this event Bushnell said: "I have learned more of experimental religion since my little boy died than in all my life before."[6]

In 1859, due to declining health, Bushnell retired as pastor. From that time until his death on February 17, 1876, he was active in publishing books, pamphlets, and sermons.

Bushnell's Concept of Christian Nurture

The genesis of *Christian Nurture* appeared in Bushnell's article "Revivals of Religion" in 1836, but *Christian Nurture* was presented to the public only in 1846. Various changes were made in the contents of the book until the final edition was printed in 1861.

The thesis of *Christian Nurture,* that "the child is to grow up a

Christian and never know himself as being otherwise,'' was amplified by Bushnell in this statement:

> The aim, effort, and expectation should be, not, as is commonly assumed, that the child is to grow up in sin, to be converted after he comes to a mature age; but that he is to open on the world as one that is spiritually renewed, not remembering the time when he went through a technical experience, but seeming rather to have loved what is good from his earliest years.[7]

Through the ''organic unity of the family,''[8] Bushnell proposed that the primary medium by which the grace of God could be transmitted was through the Christian family. Bushnell opposed the concept of ''instantaneous conversion'' but understood true conversion as a growth process begun in a Christian environment from infancy and articulated at home and church by example.[9]

Bushnell did not offer his theory of Christian nurture as a mechanical formula for reaching sinless perfection, nor did he say that parents were perfected by the process of Christian nurture. He encouraged parents to serve as living examples and to speak with their children on occasions about parental faults and weak points.

Bushnell on Revivalism

In the early years of Bushnell's ministry at North Church, he led revival meetings and urged his congregation to profess Jesus Christ as Savior.[10] In neither a pragmatic nor a spiritual way were the results at North Church a positive revival of religion. The following numbers substantiate the claim: ''in 1834, only forty-one came into the church on profession of faith; in 1835, only four; and, in 1836, twelve.''[11] Because of his unsuccessful attempts to lead North Church in revival, Bushnell confessed, ''The most disheartening impediment to the Christian minister . . . is the thought that religion depends only on revivals.''[12] In another criticism of revivals, Bushnell created the analogy of the ostrich:

> The ostrich, it will be observed, is nature's type of all unmotherhood. She hatches her young without incubation, depositing her eggs in the sand to be quickened by the solar heat. Her office as a mother-bird is there ended. When the young are hatched, they are to go forth untended, or unmothered, save by the general motherhood of nature itself. Hence the ostrich is called sometimes the ''wicked,'' and some-

times the "stupid" bird. . . . she is both heartless and senseless; too heartless to care for her young, and too senseless to maintain a motherhood as genial even as that of the sand.[13]

Bushnell on the Family

In 1836 Bushnell rejected revivalism and turned to the idea of Christian nurture. This concept placed heavy emphasis on the home as the primary place of nurture. Citing biblical examples such as Paul's baptism of the household of Stephanas (1 Cor. 1:16) and the Philippian jailer's family (Acts 16:31-33), Bushnell defended both infant baptism and infant church membership as important aspects of the restoration of the "organic unity of the family."

He argued that, in organic families, one generation is the natural offspring of another. At birth an exerting power over the infant exists. With no capacity of will, the child forms impressions from his or her surroundings. As character forms from nurture, the child grows in the likeness of the parents, especially the mother.[14] Bushnell concluded his description of the organic unity of the family by writing to parents "Your character is a stream, a river, flowing down upon your children, hour by hour."[15]

Bushnell on Character Formation

According to Bushnell, parental modeling is the heart of Christian nurture. His theory required Christian parents to provide a living example. Parental duties in Bushnell's theory built on the premise that like begets like: "It is not what you intend for your children, so much as what you are, that is to have its effect."[16] Simply stated, the life of the parent flows into the life of the child.[17] Constantly in Bushnell's writings, this theme occurred. As he stated in *Christian Nurture,* "Examples are the only sufficient commentaries."[18]

Bushnell argued that preparation for the important task of parenting was necessary. The mother provided the key to salvation for the child. The impressions given by the godly mother strictly enforced the idea that parents taught religion not by doctrine but by the reality of their lives. Bushnell believed that the love of the mother revealed the love of Christ.

Even though Bushnell stressed parental qualifications, he was aware that not all parents were Christians. Therefore, he warned against a father's injustice and a mother's impatience. Also he discouraged too much prohibition. One of his related statements created this message:

"Thou shalt not do this, nor this, nor this, til, in fact, there is really nothing left to be done."[19] Bushnell advised parents to forbid a minimum of things but to soundly enforce the forbidden.

According to Bushnell, parental faultfinding and being hard to please too often focused on trivia. His countersuggestion was for parents to seek ways to praise children. Hard feelings and displeasure should be resolved as soon as possible. Holding resentments and grudges created pain in relationships. Parents should administer after much thought and with a gentle voice.[20]

Bushnell identified certain Christian vices. One was sanctimony: "a saintly, or over-saintly air and manner."[21] Another bigotry; he judged that "no class of children . . . turn out worse, in general, than the children of Christian bigots."[22] He viewed Christian fanaticism as disastrous. Bushnell described a fanatic as:

A man who mixes false fire with the true, and burns with a partly diabolical heat. . . . He scorches, but never melts. He is most impatient of what is ordinary and common, and does not sufficiently honour the solid works and experiences of that goodness which is fixed and faithful. This kind of character makes a fiery element for childish piety to grow in.[23]

Judging and condemning were termed censorious habits. These people were "a large class of disciples who think it a kind of duty, and a just acknowledgement of the fact of human depravity, to be seeing always dark things."[24] This kind of behavior, according to Bushnell, lowered confidence and esteem in children, while confident parents helped create faith in children.

To aid the nurturing process, Bushnell devoted over one hundred pages of *Christian Nurture* to practical matters in the faith process including physical nurture, play, family government, and family worship.

In his theory of Christian nurture, providing and feeding children was an important physical and spiritual activity for parents. Good manners in children, he claimed, promoted self-government. While animals had no manners, a child's positive manners displayed good religious training. Bushnell praised personal neatness and dress as another form of physical nurture. Parents should not overdress or "doll up" their children "to tickle a certain weak and foolish pride in the parents."[25]

Bushnell devoted a chapter in *Christian Nurture* to "Plays and Pastimes, Holidays and Sundays." In *Work and Play*,[26] another of his books, he dealt with theories introduced in *Christian Nurture*. He conceived the play of children as the symbol and interpreter of Christian liberty because enhancing the joy of children was one of the first duties of Christian parenting. Parents should place special emphasis on the birthdays of children. This helped to develop a higher self-esteem in children.

Biblical passages such as 1 Timothy 3:4 guided Bushnell's understanding of family government. Parental authority was from God and genuine only as long as it agreed with God's purposes. Family discipline, rightly administered, contributed to an obedient, pious child.

The parent was warned not to oppress a child. Discipline was best administered in private to spare the child's self-respect. Bushnell charged parents to *trust* their children: "Nothing wounds a child more than to see he is not trusted."[27]

Finally, family worship was usually considered positive for children, especially family prayers and Bible reading. With the concept of modeling in mind, Bushnell said: "The great difficulty in faith, after all, is to be faithful."[28] He illustrated this by saying that God will not honor the prayer of the man who prays for holiness and gets off his knee to defraud his neighbor.

Bushnell's Contributions to Christian Education

Horace Bushnell is often called the father of the Christian Education movement in America. George Albert Coe wrote: "If it is necessary to give a date to mark the transition to the modern conception of Christian training we could not do better than to name ... the first issue of Horace Bushnell's *Christian Nurture*."[29]

In *Christian Nurture* Bushnell compared his ideas on Christian conversion with the position of Baptists and other conservative Christians. According to Bushnell, Baptists believed that each child reached the moment or age of accountability; conversion occurred instantaneously and completely at some point in each child's life. Bushnell, on the other hand, believed in an organic connection of character. Conversion, in Bushnell's view, was not a sudden encounter in the child's life but a gradual spiritual birth in the child.

Bushnell characterized himself as "sound in ethics and skeptical in religion."[30] He credited nature for his soundness, and Calvinistic theology was his explanation for being skeptical about religion. As a theologian, Horace Bushnell was a self-professed liberal. Some of his critics doubted whether a person with Bushnell's views could be Christian. According to Bushnell, his critics propagated a religion that "men are to grow up in evil, and be dragged into the church of God by conquest."[31]

In conclusion, *Christian Nurture* served as a theological divide with the extreme individualism of older Puritanism. The modeling process by parents in *Christian Nurture* placed a heavier emphasis on the home. Bushnell was far ahead of his time in advocating a religious relationship that was psychologically positive for the child. Excessive emotionalism, he said, was not a positive contributing factor in a child's development.

Bushnell's educational philosophy was saturated with experimental and naturalistic thought. He proposed that proper education could solve human problems, even religious problems. He claimed that morally good parents nearly always produced morally good children. Certainly, proper education and good parents provided a greater opportunity for children. However, more often than admitted by Bushnell, such circumstances do not produce results as good as desired.

Although Horace Bushnell spent the most of his life as a pastor and theologian, he deserves recognition as an educator for primarily two reasons: (1) he guided the attention of the church toward children; and (2) he magnified the responsibility of the Christian family.

Notes

1. C. F. Melchert, "What Should I Read?" *Religious Education* 74 (July-August 1979): 442-44.

2. Horace Bushnell, *Christian Nurture* (New York: Charles Scribner and Co., 1861), n.p.

3. Randolph C. Miller, *Education for Christian Living* (Englewood Cliffs, N.J.: Prentice-Hall, 1956), 9.

4. William R. Adamson, *Bushnell Rediscovered* (Philadelphia: United Church Press, 1966), 17-18.

5. Ibid., 19.

6. Mary B. Cheney, *Life and Letters of Horace Bushnell* (New York: Scribner's, 1903), 105.

7. Bushnell, 4.

8. Ibid., 56.

9. Ibid., 8-10.

10. William A. Johnson, *Nature and the Supernatural in the Theology of Horace Bushnell* (Lund: CWK Gleerup, 1963), 108.

11. Ibid.

12. Ibid.

13. Ibid., 40.

14. Sheldon S. Cohen, *A History of Colonial Education, 1607-1776* (New York: John Wiley and Sons, 1974), 67.

15. Bushnell, 74.

16. Horace Bushnell, *Views of Christian Nurture and Subjects Adjacent Thereto* (Hartford: E. Hunt, 1849), 6.

17. Perry G. Downs, "Christian Nurture: A Comparative Analysis of the Theories of Horace Bushnell and Lawrence O. Richards" (Ph.D. diss., New York University, 1982), 101.

18. Bushnell, *Christian Nurture,* 241.

19. Ibid., 193.

20. Ibid., 195-96.

21. Ibid., 170.

22. Ibid., 171.

23. Ibid.

24. Ibid., 172.

25. Ibid., 189.

26. Horace Bushnell, *Work and Play* (New York: Scribner's, 1881), n.p.

27. Bushnell, *Christian Nurture,* 216-17.

28. Ibid., 252.

29. Elmer L. Towns, ed., *A History of Religious Educators* (Grand Rapids: Baker Books, 1975), 278.

30. Wayne R. Rood, *Understanding Christian Education* (Nashville: Abingdon, 1970), 14.

31. Bushnell, *Christian Nurture,* 21.

32

The Education
of Women
in Early America

Like their European ancestors, the early American woman fulfilled primarily two nurturing responsibilities: she bore many children and managed the home for her husband. Since so much was to be done, her excellent work was usually rewarded with more work. For most women, few hours remained for other activities.

Colonial formal education for females hardly existed. Secondary and higher education provided an opportunity for males only. Tutors often taught sons and daughters of the wealthy. Despite their limitations, dame schools assisted the process of learning in the home. In their spare time, some Colonial schoolmasters instructed girls.

Mary Fisher (1623-1698) and other Quaker women served as ministers in Colonial America. Anne Austin was probably the first Quaker missionary to America. At least four female Quaker ministers were martyred before 1776. Mary Dyer (ca. 1604-1660) was hanged in Boston for her beliefs. At Quaker meetings both men and women spoke "the word" from the Lord, this in spite of ancient beliefs and biases against women. In addition, Quakers did not ordain any of their ministers whether male or female.

Since Colonial days, Quaker women have continued to lead ministries. Excellent examples include Lucretia Mott (1793-1880), who led efforts for moral and social reforms, and Hannah Whitall Smith (1832-1911), who served as teacher, preacher, and evangelist.[1] With the exception of a few other women such as Anne Hutchinson (1591-1643), who was expelled from the Puritan church in 1638 for teaching that direct access to God's grace was possible without assistance from a minister or a church, most Colonial female ministers were Quakers.[2]

In 1787 Benjamin Rush (1745-1813), an early advocate of formal female education in America, wrote an essay entitled *Thoughts Upon Female Education*. He sought to change educational practices so that women who became mothers might enlighten their sons. A signer of the Declaration of Independence, Rush founded the Young Ladies' Academy of Philadelphia.[3]

Women in Evangelistic Ministries

From the beginning of the Sunday School movement, boys and girls received biblical instruction from male and female teachers. Women probably realized the value of the Sunday School for churches before the men did. According to Martin Marty, the early Sunday School movement was "often opposed by ministers not simply because it was new or was a threat to established ways of doing things but because it was often in the hands of women."[4]

Organized in 1824, the American Sunday School Union was largely a lay movement. The Union encouraged women to teach other women. Materials were developed for mothers who met weekly to discuss problems related to parenting. Clifton E. Olmstead credited the Union: "Undoubtedly this woman's movement within the church was a forerunner of the broader movement which would develop later in the century to call for equal rights for women in other fields."[5]

Baptist women actively participated in missions movements. In 1800 Mary Webb (1779-1861), although confined to a wheelchair, formed the Boston Female Society for Missionary Purposes, the first of several such organizations established by and for women in America. The Women's Union Missionary Society developed in 1860 as women from six different denominations created the interdenominational movement.[6]

Ann Judson (1789-1826) accompanied Adoniram, her husband, to Burma. They were the first American Baptist foreign missionaries. Together they translated the Bible into the Burmese language and taught it to the people.

Charlotte "Lottie" Moon (1840-1912) spent nearly forty years as a Southern Baptist missionary to China. This aristocratic Virginian taught the Bible to Chinese girls until the Boxer uprising of 1900. At this time, opposition to female education and other causes forced her to direct attention to other evangelistic work. Sarah Osborn (1714-1796) taught school and led revivals.

Phebe Palmer (1807-1874), a lay preacher in the Holiness movement, led revivals in the United States and other countries.

Congregational hymn singing greatly stimulated the revivalist movement. Fanny Crosby (1820-1915), the blind American Methodist
hymnist wrote over eight thousand hymns including "Blessed Assurance" and "Pass Me Not, O Gentle Savior." These women and many
others contributed to the spirit of revival in America during the
eighteenth and nineteenth centuries.

Female Seminaries

The "female seminary" movement originated in the eighteenth
century, after the Americans declared independence from English rule.
Especially between 1821 and 1836, from Georgia to New England and
west to the frontier, female seminaries offered women an entrance to
formal education. Located primarily in the North, these early female
academies greatly enhanced educational opportunities for women.

In 1821 Emma Willard (1787-1870) founded the Troy Female
Seminary in New York, sometimes called "the first woman's high
school in America." For the remainder of her life she sought to
improve educational quality and opportunity for women. Her efforts
did not return void, because her influence helped form several important schools for women including Vassar, Elmira, and Mary Sharp.[7]

Equally or more importantly, Willard trained women to teach in
American schools. Like colonial educators, she promoted salvation
and Christian service also. She added courses such as foreign language, philosophy, history, and literature, disciplines previously reserved for men. During her lifetime, she witnessed an increasing
acceptance of women in the teaching profession; by 1846, 56 percent of
all teachers in Connecticut were women, and by 1857 the total had reached
71 percent. In 1850, 70 percent of Vermont's teachers were women.[8]

Another pioneer in women's education was Mary Lyon (1797-1849)
of Massachusetts. The daughter of an humble but devout Puritan
farmer, she advanced educational opportunities for deprived but capable females from *all* social classes. Unable to pay for her own education, she begged for the schooling expenses of others. Although her
funds were limited, her standards of excellence in curriculum exceeded
the expectations of even Emma Willard.[9]

In 1837 Mary Lyon established the Mount Holyoke Seminary, the
forerunner of Mount Holyoke College. According to Lyon, education
was for social and religious service. She encouraged students to become missionaries, especially in foreign lands.[10]

Catherine Esther Beecher (1800-1878) founded several schools for women including Hartford Female Seminary in Connecticut and Western Female Institute for Women in Cincinnati. Her distinguished family included her father, Lyman Beecher, a Presbyterian preacher; her sister, Harriet Beecher Stowe, the author of *Uncle Tom's Cabin;* and her brother, Henry Ward Beecher, a famous preacher.[11] Catherine recruited and trained girls from the East to teach the uneducated masses in the West. In 1852 she formed the American Woman's Education Association, which promoted higher education for women by founding schools; and it also informed the public of the need for better schools and trained teachers. Beecher encouraged women to become "saviors of society" within the humble and sacrificial model of Christ.[12]

Oberlin College and Coeducation

Female colleges developed first in the South. Church groups led in establishing such schools as Wesleyan Female College in Macon, Georgia, which in 1836 became the first college to confer higher degrees on women. Shortly thereafter, Alabama Baptists founded Judson College in Marion, Alabama.

In the nineteenth century critics of coeducation questioned the value of higher education for women. They asked: Would a man love a learned wife? Did God intend for a woman to advance beyond her domestic duty in the home? Were women equipped mentally and physically to meet the challenges of higher education? Did not Eve lead Adam into original sin and, therefore, did she not serve as the best example of the inferiority of her sex? What great works of art, lines of literature, or inventions had women ever produced?

A proponent of coeducation and equal education in America was Mary Wollstonecraft (1759-1797). An Englishwoman, she argued that mental differences of the sexes were caused by social environment. She believed that equality of opportunity in many areas—political affairs, legal training, employment, social status, and overall education—would show women to be as capable as men.[13] This fact was later proved with the emergence of intelligence tests.[14]

In America the concept of coeducation was accepted more easily in the West than in the more traditional East. From its inception in 1833 Oberlin College in Ohio admitted both women and blacks. In 1841 Oberlin became the first college in the country to award the bachelor of arts degree to a female who was under the same program requirements as a male. Although in a few cases boys and girls had been educated together in academies and seminaries, Oberlin marked the beginning of higher coeducation in America. Fifty years later, Oberlin had graduated 133 women and 850 men.[15]

Two of these graduates were Lucy Stone (1818-1893) and Antoinette Brown Blackwell (1825-1921). As a sign of her individuality, Lucy Stone retained her maiden name in marriage. This woman suffragist became a writer for other women's causes as well.

After beginning her ministry as a Congregationalist, Nettie Brown later joined the Unitarian Church. She was the first *ordained* woman minister in America, probably in the world. Upon completing the bachelor of arts, she applied for studies toward a theological degree at Oberlin. The theology department refused admittance but allowed her to attend classes. After completing the requirements for a theological degree, she was not permitted to graduate. Finally in 1908, Oberlin awarded her an *honorary* degree.[16]

Without question, Nettie embodied persistence. She wrote ten books, and, in 1920, a few months prior to her death at age ninety-six, Nettie voted. Her efforts as a leader of the women's suffrage movement had borne fruit.[17]

Oberlin drew even more criticism for admitting blacks than for educating women. One graduate stated: The schools which our students taught were characterized as "nigger" schools—the churches where they preached were "nigger" churches.[18]

In 1862 at Oberlin, Mary Jane Patterson became the first black woman to earn a bachelor's degree in the United States. She taught in Philadelphia and the District of Columbia until her death.[19]

In some states before the Civil War, whites were not permitted by law to teach blacks to read and write. This was considered a statutory crime.[20] In Florida the sale of slaves funded the state's early *public* education system. These and other barriers possibly explain why only twenty-eight blacks earned college degrees in America before the Civil War.[21]

As abolitionist, social reformer, and advocate of women's rights, Sojourner Truth (ca. 1797-1883) helped to pave the way for black women to receive an education and a better life. Though illiterate all her life, this former slave mastered biblical stories and preached the cause of freedom for blacks throughout America.[22]

Amanda Smith (1837-1915), another former slave with limited formal schooling, became a powerful evangelistic missionary. She attended gospel meetings led by Phebe Palmer and maintained friendship with Frances Willard. Whether in America or abroad, Smith became an effective Holiness preacher.

Another former slave, Lulu Fleming (1862-1899) was valedictorian at Shaw University and later graduated from Pennsylvania Woman's Medical College. Following her studies, she became a pioneer missionary to the African Congo.

Harriet Ross Tubman (ca. 1820-1913), known as the conductor of the Underground Railroad, helped over three hundred fugitive slaves to freedom. Remembered today as the black emancipator, she also promoted the formation of black schools after the Civil War.

◆ ◆ ◆ ◆ ◆ ◆ ◆ ◆ ◆

By the dawn of the twentieth century, educational opportunities for American women had multiplied from Colonial beginnings. Although the quality and availability of female education never completely equaled that for men, a foundation for better preparation in the twentieth century was laid. When given a chance for education and ministry, nineteenth-century women generally prevailed.

Notes

1. Edward T. James, Janet W. James, and Paul S. Boyer, eds., *Notable American Women 1607-1950,* vol. 3 (Cambridge: The Belknap Press of Harvard University Press, 1971), 314-15.

2. Rosemary R. Ruether and Rosemary S. Keller, *Women and Religion in America,* The Colonial and Revolutionary Periods, vol. 2 (San Francisco: Harper and Row, 1983), 165.

3. Charles W. Hackensmith, *History of Physical Education* (New York: Harper and Row, 1966), 337.

4. Leon McBeth, *Women in Baptist Life* (Nashville: Broadman, 1979), 105.

5. Clifton E. Olmstead, *History of Religion in the United States* (Englewood Cliffs, N.J.: Prentice-Hall, 1960), 292.

6. Ruether and Keller, 244.

7. Robert F. Hessong and Thomas H. Weeks, *Introduction to Education* (New York: Macmillan, 1987), 119.

8. Joel Spring, *The American School, 1642-1990,* 2d ed. (New York: Longman, 1990), 123.

9. Ruether and Keller, 238-39.

10. Hessong and Weeks, 120.

11. Ibid.

12. Edward T. James, Janet W. James, and Paul S. Boyer, eds., *Notable American Women, 1607-1950,* vol. 1 (Cambridge: The Belknap Press of Harvard University Press, 1971), 123.

13. John S. Brubacher and Willis Rudy, *Higher Education in Transition: A History of American Colleges and Universities, 1636-1976* (New York: Harper and Row, 1976), 64.

14. Minette Drumwright, *Women in the Church: A Study Guide* (Nashville: Seminary Extension Department of the Seminaries of the Southern Baptist Convention, 1978), 111.

15. James H. Fairchild, *Oberlin: The Colony and the College 1833-1883* (New York: Garland Publishing, 1984), 184-85.

16. James, James, and Boyer, 159.

17. Robert S. Fletcher, *A History of Oberlin College: From Its Foundation Through the Civil War* (Oberlin, Ohio: Oberlin College Press, 1943), 293.

18. Richard Hofstadter and Wilson Smith, eds., *American Higher Education: Documentary History,* vol. 1 (Chicago: University of Chicago, 1961), 433.

19. Kenneth V. Lottich and Elmer Harrison, *The Foundation of Modern Education,* 4th ed. (New York: Holt, Rinehart and Winston, 1970), 27.

20. Brubacher and Rudy, 74.

21. John D. Pulliam, *History of Education in America,* 2d ed. (Columbus, Ohio: Charles E. Merrill, 1976), 96.

22. Ruether and Keller, 11.

Synopsis
of Part 6

The search for freedom of religious experience and expression caused many Europeans to settle in the New World. Opportunities for elementary and secondary education in Colonial America existed predominately through a combination of factors related to family, faith, and finances.

Although there were regional variations, religious themes shaped Colonial homelife and schooling. This trend extended into higher education as well. Nine Colonial colleges opened between 1636 and 1776, eight of these with partial or total religious funding.

From the birth of the republic until the dawn of the twentieth century, a variety of Christian concerns continued to direct much American education. For example, the public school movement, characteristic of education in the United States, would not have survived without Protestant support.

Revivalism produced personal conversions and assisted in establishing hundreds of denominational colleges, universities, and seminaries. A pragmatic intent diversely directed Christian education movements all the way from Dwight L. Moody's Bible schools to William R. Harper's higher criticism at the University of Chicago.

Before the end of the nineteenth century, female colleges and seminaries had trained a comparatively small number of American women to serve as teachers, preachers, and missionaries. Yet, this progressive trend has continued until today. These institutions together with the gradual acceptance of coeducation solidified the foundation of female education in America.

Directly opposed to revivalism, Horace Bushnell, in *Christian Nurture,* emphasized the importance of the family in religious conversion. This book provided the impetus for the religious education movement and the professional development of many Christian educators in the twentieth century.

PART 7

Christian Education
in the Twentieth Century

33. Christian Educators of the Twentieth Century—I

George Albert Coe
William Clayton Bower
Luther Allan Weigle
J. M. Price
E. J. Chave
Hugh Hartshorne
Gaines S. Dobbins
Edna Baxter
Paul Vieth
Rachel Henderlite
Randolph Crump Miller

34. Christian Educators of the Twentieth Century—II

Findley B. Edge
D. Campbell Wyckoff
Sara Little
Paulo Freire
James Michael Lee
John H. Westerhoff III
Gabriel Moran
James Fowler
Thomas H. Groome

35. Movements in Twentieth-Century Christian Education

Vacation Bible School
Church Day-Care Centers and Kindergartens
Christian Education as a Profession
Ministry of the Laity/Lay Renewal
Private Schools
The Women's Movement

Synopsis of Part 7

33

Christian Educators
of the
Twentieth Century—I

The twentieth century has witnessed a ground swell in Christian education. Many persons are worthy of mention because of their contributions to this surge. This chapter and the following chapter identify some of these persons. The list is not all-inclusive, and readers should study others who have contributed to their own perspectives and faith traditions.

George Albert Coe

A driving force for the scientific study of religion and religious education in the early twentieth century was George Albert Coe (1862-1951). He was also one of the founders of the Religious Education Association (REA).

Coe was born into a minister's family in Mendon, New York, in 1862. He was educated at the University of Rochester, Boston University, and the University of Berlin. He taught philosophy at the University of Southern California from 1888 to 1891 and Northwestern University from 1891 to 1909. In 1909 Coe moved to New York City, where he taught psychology and education at Union Theological Seminary for thirteen years. He left Union to become professor of education in the Teachers College of Columbia University, where he served until his retirement in 1927.

Coe wrote many books and articles and found time to write Christian education curriculum materials for use in churches. He lectured widely to learned societies and schools. *Religious Education,* the journal of the REA, published his last article in 1951, the year he died.

Coe's interest in and impact on Christian education were varied. He was concerned that Christian education be both doctrinal and ethical.

He believed that the church had failed by making Christian education a purveyor of dogma and facts rather than a transmitter of a Christian life-style characterized by deliberate and conscious obedience to God. He defined Christian education as "the systematic, critical examination and reconstruction of relations between persons, guided by Jesus' assumption that persons are of infinite worth, and by the hypothesis of the existence of God, the Great Valuer of Persons."[1] Coe's emphasis on the moral development task of Christian education is evidenced even in the titles of many of his books: *Education in Religion and Morals* (1904), *A Social Theory of Religious Education* (1917), *The Motives of Men* (1928), *Educating for Citizenship* (1932), and *What Is Religion Doing to Our Consciences?* (1943).

Coe was convinced that, since moral development was an important task of religious education and that persons were by nature religious, religious education should be made a part of general education. These beliefs helped motivate Coe to form the REA and were the basis for his address to its first session in 1903.

In later life, Coe moderated what had been perceived as his "radical" or "liberal" call for scientific study of religious education. He still valued science as a tool, but he deemphasized science in favor of deeper emphasis on piety rising from personal relationship with God in Christ.[2]

William Clayton Bower

Bower was born in 1878 in Wolcottville, Indiana, and attended Tri-State College in Angola, Indiana; Butler College in Indianapolis; and Columbia University in New York. He pastored Disciples of Christ churches in New York and California before moving to Lexington, Kentucky, in 1912 to teach religious education in the College of the Bible and in Transylvania College. After fourteen years, Bower joined the faculty of the University of Chicago Divinity School. He retired in 1943 and moved back to Lexington, where he taught parttime in Transylvania College and the University of Kentucky.

Bower was an early contributor to *Religious Education* and helped shape the young REA. He was widely published and remained active in writing and the affairs of the REA as late as 1960. He died in 1982.

Bower's contributions to Christian education came through teaching, writing, and organizational activities and were primarily in the fields of curriculum development, experiential education, sociology of education, and moral and spiritual development. Among his books are *A Survey of Religious Education in the Local Church* (1919), *The Educational Task of the Local Church* (1921), *The Curriculum of Religious Education* (1925), *Religious Education in the Modern Church* (1929), *Character Through Creative Experience* (1930), *Christ and Christian Education* (1943), *Church and State in Education* (1944), *Protestantism Faces Its Educational Task Together* (with Percy Roy Hayward in 1949), and *Moral Values in Education* (1952).

Bower held that experience is one basis for the curriculum. Guided and controlled experience would enable the curriculum to remain person-centered and assist the learner in the process of self-realization.[3] As he described his theory of curriculum, he stated his dependence on Rousseau and his contemporary John Dewey.[4]

In 1946 the Kentucky State Department of Education began exploring the creation of a moral and spiritual development curriculum for public schools. Two years later Bower was asked to chair an advisory committee to develop such a curriculum. Bower agreed with Coe that the moral development aspect of religious education should be employed in general education. Bower had already researched in the area and had written *Character Through Creative Experience* (1930) describing the relationship of religion to the formation of morals in scientific terms and stating that the differences in religions had "rootage in the differing economic, social, intellectual, aesthetic, and ethical experiences of these groups."[5] Thus, Bower seemed uniquely qualified to lead a program of moral education in public education, while maintaining separation of church and state. He described the process and the product of the committee's work in *Moral and Spiritual Values in Education*.

Luther Allan Weigle

Weigle taught at Yale Divinity School for thirty-three years (1916-1949), serving as Horace Bushnell Professor of Christian Nurture (1916-1924), Sterling Professor of Religious Education (1924-1929), and dean (1929-1949). He was born into the home of a Lutheran pastor in Littleston, Pennsylvania. Educated at Gettysburg College and Lutheran Theological Seminary in Gettysburg, Pennsylvania, he went on to earn a Ph.D. at Yale. His first teaching position was at Carleton College in Northfield, Minnesota. There he wrote his most popular book, *The Pupil and the Teacher.*[6] Weigle left Carleton for the position at Yale.

Weigle contributed in a broad range of areas related to Christian education. *The Pupil and the Teacher* was an instructional handbook commissioned by the Lutheran Publication Society, used as a textbook by the International Sunday School Association. It was the second in a series of four volumes. In it, Weigle introduced Sunday School teachers to their roles and a basic theological, spiritual, and developmental understanding of the students. (The specific developmental understanding dealt with early, middle, and later childhood and early and later adolescence.) He provided the teacher guidance about principles and methods of instruction as well as lesson planning and group dynamics. Describing the true teacher as an evangelist, he wrote: "The work of the teacher thus centers around **pupil's personal decision** [Weigle's emphasis] to accept the love of God as revealed in Jesus and to live as God's child."[7]

The Pupil and the Teacher was well-received, eventually being translated into Chinese, Japanese, Portuguese, and Spanish. It was issued in new revisions and editions. It sold over a million copies, going out of print by 1950.[8] Weigle later wrote *Talks to Sunday School Teachers* (1920) as a supplement to *The Pupil and the Teacher*. With Henry H. Tweedy he also wrote *Training the Devotional Life* (1919). This book provided instruction on helping children learn the various forms and contexts of worship. It encouraged the development of well-rounded worship, including all its elements and involving the whole person. Tools for worship included prayer (which Weigle and Tweedy viewed as the key to worship), Bible reading, music, and memorization of worship materials. Children were to be taught to worship in their homes as well as churches and church schools. Another of Weigle's books related to Christian education was *Jesus and the Educational Method* (1939), which grew out of a series of lectures. It is basically a Christian educator's response to Albert Schweitzer's writings on the historical Jesus.

Weigle was an early leader in the development of an accrediting body for theological higher education in North America. He was involved in the birth of the American Association of Theological Seminaries, now known as the Association of Theological Schools (ATS). He was also a member of the American Standard Bible Committee (of the International Council of Religious Education), which led in the publication of the *Revised Standard Version* of the Bible. *Bible Words That Have Changed In Meaning* (1955) and *Bible Words in Living Language* (1957) Weigle's books are related to his work on this committee.

Weigle was a resource for missionaries interested in Christian education. He was involved in a significant missions consultation in China in 1935 sponsored by the National Committee for Christian Religious Education in China.[9]

During Weigle's last years at Yale and under his leadership, the Divinity School developed the Yale Studies in the History and Theory of Religious Education. Books resulting from this series have been described as among the most important published works regarding Christian education in America.[10]

J. M. Price

John Milburn Price was born in 1884 in rural western Kentucky in the Marshall County town of Fair Dealing. He was the youngest of six surviving children born to a Civil War veteran and his wife. The Prices were a devout Baptist family. J. M. attended the Southern Normal School (now Western Kentucky University) in Bowling Green, Kentucky; Baylor University in Waco, Texas; Brown University in Providence, Rhode Island; and The Southern Baptist Theological Seminary in Louisville, Kentucky.

Price had served as Sunday School evangelist in the Blood River Baptist Association in Kentucky before beginning seminary. After his graduation, he struggled with three career options: to serve as full-time Sunday School secretary for the Kentucky Baptist Convention; to be an educational missionary to China; or to establish and organize a School of Christian Pedagogy at the fledging Southwestern Baptist Theological Seminary in Fort Worth, Texas. He opted for the challenge in Texas.[11]

Under Price's leadership, the school he established grew from one student in 1915 to become the largest school of religious education in the world. It was the first such school among Southern Baptists. Price's efforts to establish the credentials of religious educators as professionals was evidenced in part by the growth of the school and the degrees it offered: Diploma in Religious Education (1915), Bachelor of Religious Education (1919), a three-year Master of Religious Education (1920), and a Doctor of Religious Education (1923).[12] Price retired from Southwestern Seminary in 1956 and then served for a time as visiting professor at Hardin-Simmons College and Howard Payne College (both in Texas and now universities).

In 1932 Macmillan published *Introduction to Religious Education* by Price, L. L. Carpenter (Limestone College, Gaffney, South Carolina) and J. H. Chapman (Howard College, now Samford University, Birmingham, Alabama). This book included chapters by various scholars on foundations, principles, and institutions of religious education and was intended as a college or seminary textbook. In Price's chapter entitled "Leadership in Religious Education," he argued that religious education needed trained professions just like business and government. He encouraged pastors to recognize the role of religious educators and urged awareness of the legitimacy of the educational director or minister of education as a vocational role.[13] An update of this work, *A Program of Religious Education,* was edited by Price, Carpenter (by this time on the faculty at Baylor University), and A. E. Tibbs (of Baptist Bible Institute, now New Orleans Baptist Theological Seminary). Price later joined Carpenter, Chapman, and Tibbs in writing *A Survey of Religious Education* (1940; second edition 1959).

Price, as a founder (in 1935) of the National Association of Administrators of Schools and Departments of Religious Education and Social Work, worked for the recognition of religious education as a profession. This organization evolved into the American Association of Schools of Religious Education, now recognized by the United States Department of Education as a national accrediting body; it later merged with ATS.[14]

In the second edition of *A Survey of Religious Education,* Price wrote, "No system of education is complete that does not include the religious element, and no system of religion is adequate that does not involve education."[15] In his call to develop religious education as a profession and interrelate religion and education, Price did not wish to overobjectify religious education. He stated that the "educational process cannot control or supplant the operation of the Holy Spirit in the heart and mind of the individual . . . teaching can stress but cannot impart."[16]

Price wrote several books intended for training lay workers in the local church. One of the most popular of these was *Jesus the Teacher* (1946). Others, such as *Formative Factors in Christian Character* (1959) and *The Unfolding Life* (1963), introduced lay workers to developmental and social issues in religious education in the local church.

E. J. Chave

Ernest John Chave was born in 1886 in Woodstock, Ontario, Canada. He attended McMaster University in Toronto, receiving an A.B.

(1906) and a Th.B. (1910). He later studied at the University of Chicago, where he received an M.A. (1920) and Ph.D. (1924). Chave served as minister in Baptist churches in Vancouver, British Columbia, and Sioux Falls, South Dakota, before joining the faculty of the University of Chicago Divinity School as professor of Religious Education in 1926.

Chave's doctoral dissertation dealt with developmental issues confronting children. This concern for children continued in his later writing career. In 1925 he published *The Junior: Life Situations of Children Nine to Eleven Years of Age,* a popularization of his doctoral dissertation. *Personality Development in Children* (1937), was published for use as a college and seminary textbook also useful among well-informed laypersons. In these books, Chave wrote that teachers should be aware of the myriad forces that daily mold and shape the children who were their students. He also pointed out the challenges facing the teacher of a handicapped child, warning that "the handicapped child is not necessarily a maladjusted one, but the problems he faces may lead to maladjustments unless he is wisely guided."[17] In this light Chave called for educators to recognize the rights afforded disabled children by a White House Conference seven years earlier.[18]

Chave believed that religion was a fluid force in the lives of persons that arose out of the events and issues surrounding them more than from ancient traditions that may have very little relevance to contemporary life: "Once religion was chiefly fears and wonderings, mimetic acts and emotional displays, with few simple beliefs and fixed ceremonies, but today theologians and philosophers struggle to find adequate statements of ideas and ideals."[19] Chave wrote this in his most influential book on religious education, *A Functional Approach to Religious Education.* In it, Chave defined religious education as "a systematic, planned procedure for making religion meaningful and operative in individual and collective living."[20] After Chave's death in 1961, Stewart G. Cole wrote the following tribute in *Religious Education:*

> For professor Chave, sound religion was a natural value experience of growing persons, ensuring the individual a richly meaningful adjustment in the art of living. It was the job of religious education to help people of whatever faith or folk background to cope with their respective life situations, to enlist attitudes and understandings which inspired adventurous participation in the life process, and to conserve the consequent values and convictions for the enrichment of their fellowmen.[21]

Chave influenced religious education in other ways and by other means. He wrote *Supervision of Religious Education* in 1931. It was intended for religious education professionals and was broad in scope, including chapters on recreation, tests and measurements, denominational and agency work, as well as some basic issues in the field. *Measure Religion: Fifty-two Experimental Forms* (1939) provided a collection of forms by which one could objectively analyze and evaluate aspects of worship, church administration, knowledge of the Bible and theology, religious instruction, and so forth. It was an important early tool for the statistical analysis of religious education.

Chave was also important in developing the Religious Education Association. He chaired various committees of the REA and served as its president.

Hugh Hartshorne

Born in 1885 in Lawrence, Massachusetts, Hartshorne attended Amherst College (A.B., 1907), Yale University (M.A., 1910), Yale Divinity School (B.D., 1911), and Columbia University (Ph.D., 1913). He taught religious education at Union Theological Seminary in New York for ten years beginning in 1912. He was ordained in 1913 as a Congregational minister. From 1922 to 1924 he taught at the University of Southern California, but he returned to New York in 1924 to serve as a research associate in the Character Education Inquiry of the Teachers College, Columbia University. He joined the faculty of Yale Divinity School in 1929, serving as researcher and professor of religious education and related fields until his retirement in 1954. He was active in the affairs of the REA, contributing to its dialogues and publications and serving as director in 1930 and president from 1935 to 1939. He influenced Christian higher education outside his immediate place of service and faith community. The Northern Baptist Convention in 1944 recruited him to lead a survey of theological education, which resulted in *Theological Education in the Northern Baptist Convention* (1944-1945, coauthored with Milton C. Froyd). It was an analysis of the status, needs, and possibilities for seminaries of the Northern Baptist Convention.

Hartshorne was a student of George A. Coe and was inspired by his mentor to further explore the issue of moral development and character education. Writing in *Childhood and Character: An Introduction to the Study of the Religious Life of Children*, Hartshorne defined religious education as:

the process by which the individual, in response to a controlled environ-ment, achieves a progressive, conscious, social adjustment, dominated by the spirit of brotherhood, and so directed as to promote the growth of a social order based on regard for the worth and destiny of every individual.[22]

Although he wrote widely for a variety of audiences, Hartshorne seldom ventured far from his premise regarding the task of religious education. In 1915 he wrote, "Christian worship is fundamental to Christian character."[23] Along with Elizabeth R. Pendry, he wrote *Organizations for Youth: Leisure Time and Character Building Proce-dures* (1935). The book described numerous Christian organizations (YMCA, YWCA), non-Christian organizations (Boy and Girl Scouts, 4-H, Boys Clubs, Camp Fire Girls, Junior Red Cross, DeMolay) that could be utilized by churches, communities, and families as resources for giving moral direction to their youth in or out of schools. It lists Protestant, Catholic, and Jewish youth programs.

Hartshorne sought to improve the effectiveness of church school (Sunday School). Using the latest scientific technique to gather his data, he researched the structures and modes of church school adminis-tration found among churches in a variety of settings. In 1933 he reported his findings in *Church Schools of Today*, a valuable guide for churches and church schools seeking their own model of administration.

Gaines S. Dobbins

Dobbins was born in 1886 in southwestern Mississippi to a farming family that included seven children. His father was a Methodist, his mother a Baptist. He was a rebellious and widely read adolescent; at sixteen he had read Rousseau's *Emile* and determined to become a journalist.[24]

Dobbins was educated at Mississippi College, a Baptist college in Clinton, Mississippi, where he was converted in 1906, two years before his graduation. He earned two degrees at The Southern Baptist Theological Seminary (Th.M. in 1913 and Th.D. in 1914) and an A.M. at Teachers College of Columbia University. He later attended Peabody College and the University of Chicago, where he studied under John Dewey and George A. Coe. From 1915 to 1920, Dobbins was an editor at the Sunday School Board of the Southern Baptist Convention. In 1920 he moved to Louisville, Kentucky, where he taught at The Southern Baptist Theological Seminary for thirty-six years. He had been brought to the seminary as professor of Sunday School Pedagogy and Church Efficiency, areas later known as church administration and Christian education. He believed that churches could function more efficiently and still remain faithful to the New Testament; indeed, they would improve efficiency by adhering to New Testament patterns. In *Can a Religious Democracy Survive?* (1938) he acknowledges, however, that the drive for efficiency can jeopardize the personal freedom that Baptists in the past have defended.

Dobbins once wrote that in all of his classes and writings he had attempted to stress that the message and method of New Testament teaching on church administration "call for maximum use of lay leadership."[25] *A Ministering Church* (1968), a popular textbook for college and seminary church administration classes, he described church administration as central to the role of pastor as *episkopos*. Dobbins argued, "Not every man can at once be an eloquent preacher, a skillful pastor, a brilliant teacher, an outstanding evangelist, a notable scholar; but every man called of God can faithfully 'care for God's church.' "[26]

Dobbins also wrote books to help laypersons improve teaching among all age groups in local churches. His approach was student centered, intended to help teachers develop Christian commitment and witness. *The Improvement of Teaching in the Sunday School* presents five possible types of aims a teacher might have: information (knowledge of the facts), inspiration (emotion that touches and motivates a person's innermost being), determination (conscious and overt commitment to act upon knowledge and inspiration), application (following through on what was determined), and consecration (character comprised of a pattern of application).[27]

Dobbins influenced church administration, instructional methodology, worship, and religious journalism. Through his students and his writings, Dobbins has been the most influential leader in shaping Christian education and church administration among Southern Baptists. The department he organized is now the School of Christian Education and awards one diploma and three degrees (M.A., M.Div. in Christian Education, and Ed.D.). Dobbins's students have become ministers, missionaries, editors, and teachers in diverse settings. He published over thirty books and hundreds of articles for denominational curriculum and professional journals. He lived to be ninety-two and continued to write until the year before he died.

Edna Baxter

Edna Baxter was a Methodist educator who made important contributions to curriculum development, childhood education, teacher training, and teaching methodology in theological higher education. She was born in 1890 in Nichols Township, New York, and, at the age of nine, moved with her family to Athens, Pennsylvania. She was educated at Folts Mission Institute in Herkimer, New York, where, after her graduation in 1915, she taught Bible until 1919. She studied at Boston University (B.R.E., 1921); Northwestern University (M.A., 1923); and Garrett Theological Seminary (B.D., 1927; M.Div., 1972; University of Chicago; Yale University; Union Theological Seminary; Columbia University; and the School of Drama and Speech in London.

Baxter served as area director of education for the Methodist Episcopal Churches in Lake and McHenry counties in Illinois, while studying at Northwestern University. She based her master's thesis on her activities on that role. In 1926 she moved to Hartford, Connecticut, where she served at Hartford Seminary as professor of religious education until her retirement in 1960.

Baxter's ministry as area director of religious education, during her years at Northwestern, convinced her that a seminary education for religious educators should include "supervised experience with people beyond the academic classroom to [properly prepare them] for this work."[28] This, together with her concern that the children of seminary students attend a nursery school, led her to organize a laboratory school at the seminary. The school was open to children of seminary faculty, students, and visiting missionaries and to children from the community. The school curriculum was designed to teach both children and parents. Most teachers were seminary students who were expected to relate directly with the children and parents and meet with Professor Baxter for weekly evaluation and planning sessions.[29]

Baxter was committed to training to improve lay leadership, especially children's Sunday School teachers. This commitment was reinforced through the years by concerns shared by her students' supervised experience. She became aware of lay teachers' need for more knowledge of the Bible and the development of Christianity. She included these topics in her courses. In 1939 she wrote *How Our Religion Began*,[30] intended for younger and middle adolescents and their teachers. The book was a comprehensive introduction to the history of the Bible and concepts and practices arising out of the Bible. This book included a discussion of complex theories of multiple authorship of the Pentateuch, together with study questions and activities at the end of each chapter and an appendix of helps for teachers. She later published *The Beginnings of Our Religion* (1968), designed less with the adolescent in mind and more for their teachers and other laity; it provided more transition into the New Testament and no helps for the reader or the teacher.

In 1960 Baxter published *Teaching the New Testament,* written for children, adolescents, and their teachers. In popularized extensive information on the New Testament and its setting Baxter made teachers aware of developmental issues affecting their charges and suggested learning activities such as drama, model construction, and creative worship. She also wrote *Learning to Worship* to equip ministers and laity alike to be effective worship educators with children. Her concern was that "whatever children learn about worship and prayer comes largely (if at all) from parents or church teachers. Too often such worship is highly abstract and symbolic."[31]

Paul Vieth

Vieth was a professional Christian educator active in educational ministries in the local church. His greatest contributions to Christian education were in character development, creative teaching in the church, and developing objectives in Christian education.

Vieth (1895-1978) was born in Warrenton, Missouri, in 1895. He attended Central Wesleyan College (A.B., 1917), Columbia University, and Yale University (B.D. 1924; Ph.D. 1928). From 1917 to 1920, he was field secretary for the Missouri Sunday School Association and served as minister and director of religious education from 1922 to 1925. He served on the staff of the International Council of Religious Education for six years and moved to Yale University Divinity School in 1931. At Yale he was professor of religious education and director of field work (1931-1939) and Horace Bushnell Professor of Christian Nurture (1939-1963).

Vieth believed that Christian education should change persons. He stated that the primary goal of church school teaching was "to help the pupil to discover for himself what constitutes Christian conduct under particular circumstances."[32] In *The Church School*, Vieth defined Christian education as "education **into** [Vieth's emphasis] the Christian life."[33] The cognitive learning that could take place in Christian education was not to be ignored, but the character-building or *disciple-making* role was even more important.

In 1930 Vieth published two books arising out of his work as the executive director of the curriculum development arm of the International Council of Religious Education. The books, *Objectives in Religious Education* and *The Development of Curriculum of Religious Education*, dealt with the development of a well-rounded and cohesive church religious education curriculum through establishing comprehensive, clearly stated goals that reflect what the church means by "religious education." The objectives provided guidelines for the International Lesson Committee of the Council and its constituent denominations, but they also helped Christian educators and churches in general to rethink the intent of their educational ministries. The objectives reflect Vieth's concern for the affective dimension of Christian education, including not only the development of Christian character but also a "deep appreciation and love for the Bible"[34] and "an acquaintance with and appreciation of religious culture as recorded in the fine arts."[35]

Vieth valued worship as a means to reach the objectives of religious education. He wrote, "Communion with God in worship is the heart of religious experience."[36] and elsewhere he added, "The most characteristic activity in which Christians engage as groups is worship."[37] He related the goal of helping persons to grow in their relations with God to worship; for this reason he believed that worship and Christian education support one another.

In 1946 Vieth and William L. Rogers, director of the Religious Film Association, coauthored *Visual Aids in the Church*. Motion pictures, slides, and filmstrip projectors had not long been used in churches. Vieth and Rogers were encouraged that these teaching aids were being used, but they believed that the potential of these aids was not yet being realized for a lack of guidance.[38] The authors included a history of the technology of visual aids, including mentions of Comenius's *Orbis Sensualium Pictus* and the *New England Primer*. Vieth and Rogers dealt with bulletin boards, chalkboards, charts, diagrams, dioramas, models, projected media, and field trips. The authors described the worth of the media and outlined how churches could more effectively use media.

Rachel Henderlite

In 1905, Rachel Henderlite, the daughter of a Presbyterian minister, was born in Henderson, North Carolina. She earned degrees at Agnes Scott College in Atlanta, Georgia (A.B., 1928), New York University (M.A., 1936), and Yale University (Ph.D., 1947). She taught briefly at Synodical College (a Presbyterian junior college in Holly Springs, Mississippi), Montreat College in North Carolina, and Harding High School in Charlotte, North Carolina, before accepting a position as professor of religious education at Presbyterian School of Christian Education in Richmond, Virginia, in 1944. From 1959 to 1965 she served as director of curriculum development for the Board of Christian Education of the Presbyterian Church in the United States. In 1965 she became the first woman ordained by the PCUS and began teaching at Austin Presbyterian Theological Seminary in Texas, where she retired in 1971.

Henderlite had written her dissertation on *The Theological Basis of Horace Bushnell's Christian Nurture* and, in 1955, published *A Call to Faith,* writing that Christian education was at the core of the purpose of the church. As a "body of those being redeemed" the church has a basic task of teaching and learning together:

> Although the proclamation of the church is clear and can be clearly and confidently made, nevertheless none has been able to grasp the whole meaning of it. The truth of God and the truth about God stretch far beyond the ability of men to understand it. There will be continually a need to explore its fuller meaning and significance for man. And so the members of the church will need to explore the truth together, seeking to clarify the nature and requirements of the Kingdom of God. Those who are more mature will lead those who are less mature, and all will grow together in the knowledge of God.[39]

Henderlite recognized that Christian education and general education had much in common: (1) both were "responsible for the transmission of knowledge"; (2) both had "certain skills to teach"; and (3) both felt responsibility for personal growth and for changes in behavior and attitudes."[40] However, she argued that "Christian education is basically different from general education."[41] She believed that Protestant Christian education had failed to recognize the limitations of progressive education and behavioral psychology in considering the Holy Spirit's function relating to persons.[42] She lamented that Christian education had been too strongly influenced by both Liberalism and Fundamentalism; Liberalism regarded the Bible as a mere "source book for human experience," whereas Fundamentalism placed its own interpretation of the Bible over the Bible itself, thus binding people. Henderlite concluded that "the church's method of Bible study should ensure the openness of the student to confrontation by the Spirit and the willingness of the student to wrestle with the Spirit" until the student were overcome."[43]

Randolph Crump Miller

Miller (1910-) was born in Fresno, California. His father was an Episcopal priest who made education a priority in his parish. Miller was a church-school teacher even during his high school and college years. He studied at Pomona College (A.B., 1931) and Yale University (Ph.D., 1936). Intending to follow in his father's footsteps, he was ordained a deacon in 1935 and a priest in 1937. After receiving the Ph.D., Miller taught philosophy of religion at Church Divinity School of the Pacific in Berkeley, California. While there, he taught courses in religious education and pastored a mission church. Both experiences awakened his intense interest in religious education.

Miller began his writing career during his sixteen years at Berkeley. He first wrote *A Guide for Church School Teachers* (1943), a practical book for churches. With Henry H. Shires, he edited *Christianity and the Contemporary Scene* (1943), dealing with various issues confronting the contemporary church; Miller himself wrote the chapter on "Christian Education Today."

Miller sought to link the content of Christian education with the method in *The Clue to Christian Education* (1950). He outlined various doctrines and theological issues, expressing them in contemporary adult terms, then "translated these great themes in terms of the experiences and capacities of children."[44]

In 1952 Miller joined Yale Divinity School as professor of Christian education, assuming the Horace Bushnell Chair of Christian Nurture at Yale the following year. He continued in this position until he retired in 1982.

Miller was active in the Religious Education Association. He was acting editor (1956-1957), editor (1958-1978) of the REA journal *Religious Education* and was executive secretary of the REA from 1982 to 1985.

Miller's theology of Christian education was highly influential among mainline Protestants. He believed that theology should provide the basis for the content, method, and goals of religious education and that it should determine the roles of pupil and teacher. In *The Theory of Christian Education Practice*, he observed that Christian education was rapidly becoming recognized as a theological discipline: "Theology and educational theory can be in dialogue, with insights from both fields commingled in an overall educational theory suitable for Christian education."[45] He acknowledged that theology is often expressed by the faith community in terms of doctrines, worship, and value systems. However, he proposed that Christian education be centered in the Bible as "the primary source of our believing and our teaching as Christians,"[46] while helping students learn to think for themselves and thereby discover their own uniquely personal relationship with God and ways that this relationship can be lived out.

Notes

1. George Albert Coe, *What Is Christian Education?* (New York: Scribner's, 1929), 296.

2. Gaines S. Dobbins, *Great Teachers Make a Difference* (Nashville: Broadman, 1965), 85-86.

3. William Clayton Bower, *The Curriculum of Religious Education* (New York: Scribner's, 1925), 35-36.

4. Ibid., 51-52.

5. William Clayton Bower, *Character Through Creative Experience* (Chicago: The University of Chicago Press, 1930), 233-34.

6. Broadman W. Kathan, "Six Protestant Pioneers of Religious Education: Liberal, Moderate, Conservative," *Religious Education* LXXIII (Special edition, September-October 1978): S141-S142.

7. Luther A. Weigle, *The Pupil and the Teacher* (New York: Hodder and Stoughton, 1911), 195.

8. Luther A. Weigle, "Toward Christian Unity," in *Glory Days: From the Life of Luther Allan Weigle*, comp. Richard D. Weigle (New York: Friendship Press, 1976), 29.

9. *Education for Service in the Christian Church in China: The Report of a Study Commissions, 1935*, (Shanghai: The National Committee for Religious Education in China, 1935), 3.

10. Kathan, S-142.

11. Clyde M. Maguire, *J. M. Price: Portrait of a Pioneer* (Nashville: Broadman, 1960), 57.

12. Kathan, S-144.

13. J. M. Price, "Leadership in Religious Education," *Introduction to Religious Education*, ed. J. M. Price, et. al. (New York: Macmillan, 1932), 237-53.

14. Maguire, 108-11.

15. J. M. Price, "Nature and Scope of Religious Education," *A Survey of Religious Education*, 2d ed. (New York: Ronald Press, 1959), 5.

16. Ibid., 7.

17. Ernest J. Chave, *Personality Development in Children* (Chicago: University of Chicago Press, 1937), 252.

18. Ibid., 256-57.

19. Ernest J. Chave, *A Functional Approach to Religious Education* (Chicago: University of Chicago Press, 1947), 2-3.

20. Ibid., 126-27.

21. Stewart G. Cole, "In Memoriam," *Religious Education* LVI:6 (November-December 1961):402.

22. Hugh Hartshorne, *Childhood and Character: An Introduction to the Study of the Religious Life of Children* (Boston: Pilgrim Press, 1919), 6. Two years earlier Hartshorne presented this definition in an article in *Religious Education*.

23. Hugh Hartshorne, *Manual for Training in Worship* (New York: Scribner's, 1915), 2.

24. Austin C. Dobbins, *Gaines S. Dobbins: Pioneer in Religious Education* (Nashville: Broadman, 1981), 13-23.

25. Gaines S. Dobbins, "The Seminary and Religious Education," *Review and Expositor* LIII:2 (April 1956):185.

26. Gaines S. Dobbins, *A Ministering Church* (Nashville: Broadman, 1960), 33.

27. Gaines S. Dobbins, *The Improvement of Teaching in the Sunday School* (Nashville: Convention Press, 1943), 57-59.

28. Edna M. Baxter, *Ventures in Serving Mankind: An Autobiography* (Allison Park, Penn.: Pickwick Publications, 1984), 19.

29. Ibid., 20-21.

30. Ibid., 24.

31. Edna M. Baxter, "Foreword," *Learning to Worship* (Valley Forge, Penn.: Judson, 1965), vii.

32. Paul H. Vieth, *How to Teach in the Church School* (Philadelphia: Westminster, 1935), 13.

33. Paul H. Vieth, *The Church School: The Organization, Administration, and Supervision of Christian Education in the Local Church* (Philadelphia: Christian Education Press, 1957), 17.

34. Paul H. Vieth, *Objectives in Religious Education* (New York: Red Label Reprints, 1930), 265.

35. Ibid., 276.

36. Ibid., 112.

37. Paul H. Vieth, "Editor's Introduction," *The Art of Group Worship*, ed. Robert Seneca Smith (New York: Abingdon-Cokesbury, 1938), 7.

38. William L. Rogers and Paul H. Vieth, *Visual Aids in the Church* (Philadelphia: Christian Education Press, 1946), v.

39. Rachel Henderlite, *A Call to Faith* (Richmond, Va.: John Knox, 1955), 120.

40. Rachel Henderlite, *Forgiveness and Hope: Toward a Theology for Protestant Christian Education* (Richmond, Va.: John Knox, 1961), 42-44.

41. Rachel Henderlite, *The Holy Spirit in Christian Education* (Philadelphia: Westminster, 1964), 15.

42. Ibid., 26-27.

43. Ibid., 80.

44. Randolph Crump Miller, *The Clue to Christian Education* (New York: Scribner's, 1950), 201.

45. Randolph Crump Miller, *The Theory of Christian Education Practice* (Birmingham, Ala.: Religious Education Press, 1980), 161.

46. Ibid., 197.

34

Christian Educators
of the
Twentieth Century—II

Findley B. Edge

Findley Bartow Edge (1916-) was born in Albany, Georgia, and educated at Stetson University (A.B., 1938), The Southern Baptist Theological Seminary—where he was a student of Gaines S. Dobbins—(Th.M., 1942; Th.D., 1945), and Yale University (M.A., 1955). During his school years he pastored churches in Apopka, Florida, and in Simpsonville, Kentucky.

After receiving his doctorate, Edge taught religious education at Southern Seminary. In 1956 he was named Basil Manly Professor of Religious Education and retired from that position in 1984.

Many of Edge's contributions to Christian education relate to the theme of his dissertation, *Religious Education and the Problem of Institutionalism*. He related the development of Christian education to the cycle of institutionalization and a counterreaction seeking freedom, creativity, and growth. Institutionalization results "when the spirit of religion is subordinated and it becomes primarily a matter of form or external observance."[1] According to Edge, all church history (including Southern Baptist history) witnesses this cycle. He urged Southern Baptists to avoid the pitfalls of institutionalism that would rob them of their historical distinctives, particularly their belief in freedom and the priesthood of believers. He called for a creative, self-evaluating, experience-based system of Christian education.

Edge continued his warning against institutionalized religion in *A Quest for Vitality in Religion: A Theological Approach to Religious Education* (1963). Edge argued that going to church has become "the accepted thing to do" in the Bible Belt. Southern Baptists experienced excellent numerical growth during the 1950s, but they failed to confront important ethical issues.[2] Edge warned the Southern Baptists' success may eventually result in their demise because congregations had been weaken by the influx of many unregenerate church members. This brought a decline in commitment and discipline (in the broadest sense) and, hence, to the demise of the church as an authentic body of Christ.

Edge continued this discussion in *The Greening of the Church* (1971). This book grew out of reaction to the earlier work and Edge's experiences studying and experimenting with Christian renewal movements including the Church of the Savior in Washington, D.C. He called laypersons to awaken to a renewed sense of mission and reclaim their rightful place as ministers in their own right. The church's ministry of education should revise its self-image. Edge suggested that a church think of itself as a school for training ministers. In his climactic chapter entitled "The Local Congregation as a Miniature Theological Seminary," Edge argued that clergy should act as equippers and enablers, emphasizing the *call* or *vocation* of laypersons to exercise *gifts* within the church. Churches should promote the development of community and self-directed learning among adults, especially in small groups.

Edge has continued to maintain his emphasis on the ministry of the laity. In 1983 he wrote, "The laity cannot fulfill their ministry by proxy. They cannot pay someone else to carry out their calling."[3] He wrote *The Doctrine of the Laity* for the Southern Baptist annual doctrinal study in 1985.

Edge wrote about improving teaching in the Sunday School in *Teaching for Results* (1956) and *Helping the Teacher* (1959). However, in both his teaching and writing careers his most distinctive impact was in calling for Christian education to be involved in church renewal through training and equipping the laity as ministers.

D. Campbell Wyckoff

Wyckoff was born in Geneseo, New York, in 1918 and earned three degrees from New York University (B.S., 1939; A.M., 1942; Ph.D., 1949), where his major field was religious education. He worked with the Presbyterian Board of National Missions (1942-1947) as an area director of youth ministry and then in a general administrative position. In 1947 he was appointed professor of religious education at New York University, where he served until 1954, when he became professor of Christian education at Princeton Theological Seminary. He taught at Princeton until his retirement in 1983.

Wyckoff's leadership has been important to Presbyterians and other denominations in Christian educational theory and curriculum development as well as youth ministry. His influence has been extended through his teaching, writing, and leadership in REA, various Presbyterian agencies and boards, and the Association of Theological Schools.

Wyckoff's first book, *The Task of Christian Education* (1955), was developed for use by ministers and lay teachers in the church. He described the aims of Christian education in terms of nurturing persons to total commitment to relationship with God and living the logical outcome of that relationship. For Wyckoff this would involve faithfulness to the faith traditions and the Bible while reverencing the uniqueness of individual personality as it is transformed through its unique relationship with Christ and expressed through each person's experiences. "This means that [the Christian personality] comes into being as, through the Holy Spirit, God in Christ becomes the definitive reality in life to the child, youth, and adult."[4] Wyckoff held that the aim of the church (and, so, of Christian education) was to transform the individual and society. In *The Task*, he dealt more with the transformation of the personality, while in *The Gospel and Christian Education* he dealt more with transformation of culture. He viewed education as "the bridge between a culture and the new supplies of persons that its society keeps producing."[5] While expressing reservations regarding use of the term *gospel*, Wyckoff nevertheless stated that all facets of Christian education—theory, methodology, administration—should be structured with "the gospel of God's redeeming work in Jesus Christ as its guiding principle."[6]

Wyckoff saw the need for Christian educators to be more deliberate about the curriculum of Christian education. He included both home and church in the curriculum and recognized that, while planning is important to curriculum development and implementation, "much of education is unplanned, since its raw materials are gathered in all of a person's relationships."[7] He was careful to make the distinction between *curriculum* (all that describes how education is allowed and encouraged to happen) and *curriculum materials* (media used as tools of the curriculum).

Writing in 1982, Wyckoff called for a renewal of ministry to youth. A ministry to youth should be one of depth and sensitivity to the cultural, developmental, and relational issues with which adolescents must deal. Those who would minister to youth should be well informed on these issues and should be willing to acknowledge their own limitations, using all resources at hand to help youth. Youth should be given opportunities to exercise their own autonomy and call to mission. Wyckoff identified the goal of youth ministry this way: ''The goal is to help youth and persons in youth ministry gain insight into self and community in relation to church and culture, in tension with God's vision of community.''[8] This expressed Wyckoff's professional and practical concern for youth ministry in local churches that began early in his career. Wyckoff wrote *In One Spirit: Senior Highs and Missions* (1958) as a practical help for professional and lay youth ministers seeking to develop youth with a sense of mission and commitment to missions.

Sara Little

Sara Pamela Little was born in 1919 in Charlotte, North Carolina, and was educated at Queens College in Charlotte (A.B., 1939), Christian Training School—now Presbyterian School of Education—in Richmond, Virginia (M.R.E., 1944), and Yale Divinity School (Ph.D., 1958). From 1944 to 1950, Little was assistant to the regional director of Christian education for the Synod of North Carolina. In 1951 she joined the faculty of the Presbyterian School of Christian Education, where she taught until 1976. In 1973 she began teaching at Union Theological Seminary in Richmond, where she retired in 1989.

Little, a widely respected Christian educator and scholar, has lectured around the world to professional groups of many denominations. She has also led in the REA—particularly through her service on the editorial board of *Religious Education* and as writer and contributor to that publication.

Little's most important early work was *The Role of the Bible in Contemporary Christian Education* (1961). In it she wrote that Christian education cannot function separate from theology any more than it can function independently of educational theory and philosophy. It must function as an integrative discipline. She suggested that it is God's revelation—as contained in the Bible—that forms the character of the curriculum of *Christian* education. Even when the focus is a specific biblical text, the curriculum of Christian education will necessarily pay heed to the message of the entire Bible and to life experiences of the learners.[9]

Little remains committed to a dialogical approach to Christian education, but remains equally certain that Christian education should maintain a confessional flavor while respecting and affirming the freedom of the student.[10] For Little, religious instruction is a component of Christian education that enables the student to become a part of the faith community. This instruction develops an understanding of that community as well as the ability to decide and believe the religion of the community—that which sets that community apart from others.[11]

Little has given practical expression in her approach to Christian education through other books. *Learning Together in the Christian Fellowship* (1956) is practical and oriented toward helping teachers and leaders in the local church. She indicates that developing community enhances the learning situation and is definitive for the church as a community. She offers concrete examples of and suggestions for methods of teaching, describing their aims, strengths, and weaknesses. *The Language of the Christian Community* was published in 1965 as part of the Presbyterian Covenant Life Curriculum. It is a study book intended to help youth and their leaders deal with ways faith communities—especially those of the Reformed tradition—have expressed themselves and their beliefs. Little's concern to involve youth in church life is further expressed in *Youth, World, and Church* (1968), written for both professional and lay workers. She describes the youth of the church as young laity and challenges youth to live—as should the adults of the church—as faithful stewards of their gifts.[12]

Paulo Freire

In 1921, Paulo Freire was born in Recife, Brazil. His family was middle class, but the Great Depression left the family in poverty. He was educated at the University of Recife, where he studied law, philosophy, and psychology of language, graduating with a Ph.D. in 1959. He worked for governmental welfare and educational agencies and became involved in Brazil's National Plan of Adult Literacy. Influenced by Karl Marx's writings on alienation and Maritain's *Education at the Crossroads* as well as his own experiences as a hungry child and working with the poor, Freire concluded that education should awaken oppressed persons to their plight and help them find ways to free themselves. He was imprisoned in 1964 for his teaching and writing on this kind of education and eventually expelled from Brazil. He worked with Chilean educational agencies for five years and taught for a brief time at Harvard University. He was an educational consultant for the World Council of Churches before returning in 1980 to Brazil, where he became professor of education at the Catholic University of Sao Paulo in 1981.

In *Pedagogy of the Oppressed*, Freire criticized what he called that "banking" method of education in which the teacher was set above the student as possessor of knowledge the students needed but did not have. "Projecting an absolute ignorance onto others, a characteristic of the ideology of oppression, negates education and knowledge as processes of inquiry."[13] Freire concluded that both teacher and student can function in both roles.

Freire's impact can be found in two words that he added to the vocabulary of Christian education: *conscientization* and *praxis*. According to Daniel Schipani, " 'Conscientization' can be defined as the process in which persons achieve a deepening awareness, both of the sociocultural reality that shapes their lives and their capacity to transform that reality."[14] In using the term *praxis*, Freire was dealing with the polarity existing between theory and practice. For education to liberate it must involve both: "But it must be emphasized that the praxis by which consciousness is changed is not only action but action *and* [Freire's emphasis] reflection."[15]

Freire has been influential in reawakening Christian educators to their revolutionary and dangerous task if the gospel of Jesus Christ is to be the core and content of their educational enterprise. Many contemporary Christian educators (Thomas Groome being one of the more important) have used Freire in developing their own approaches. Freire has also given an educational framework based on and for Liberation Theology, one of the most important theological movements of the late twentieth century.

James Michael Lee

Lee was born in New York City in 1931 and educated there, being reared and confirmed in the Roman Catholic Church. He attended Catholic schools and received degrees from Saint John's University (A.B., 1955), and Columbia University (A.M., 1956; Ed.D., 1958). He taught in New York City high schools from 1955 to 1959. From

1959 to 1960 he taught at Seton Hall University in South Orange, New Jersey; Hunter College in New York City; and Saint Joseph College in Connecticut. In 1962 he joined the University of Notre Dame in Indiana as professor of education.

After the demise of the graduate program in religious education at Notre Dame, he joined the education faculty at the University of Alabama in Birmingham (UAB) in 1977. In Birmingham he founded Religious Education Press; under his creative leadership, Religious Education Press has become the most important publisher of religious education in North America.

Lee's impact has been felt beyond his specific contributions as a publisher. He has had important things to say as an editor and author, particularly regarding religious instruction.

Lee's most important contributions have been in religious instruction. (There are three functions of religious education: religious instruction, religious counseling, and administration of religious education activities.) Lee's three most significant books are *The Shape of Religious Instruction* (1971), *The Flow of Religious Instruction* (1973), and *The Content of Religious Instruction* (1985); these three share the same subtitle: *A Social Science Approach*. Lee was concerned that too little attention had been given to linking religious instruction to social science theory. This deficiency left religious instruction at the mercy of educational fads. He proposed that social science be the means by which religious instruction could develop a well-informed, culturally viable theory and practice.[16]

Although Lee believed that theology was important to religious education, including religious instruction, he argued that theology could not provide objective verification.[17] Social science, on the other hand, was oriented toward the quantitative treatment of data and providing replicable research, open to public scrutiny.[18] He added that religion, not theology could not "necessarily generate acts of religion or even religious content."[19] For Lee only through the social sciences could religious instruction understand and develop strategies to change the student's observable religious behavior.[20]

Lee edited books on guidance and counseling as well as religious education. *The Religious Education We Need: Toward the Renewal of Christian Education* (1977) was intended as a tool to help Christian educators develop visions for their own futures in Christian education and offered practical suggestions to enhance their personal ministries. *The Spirituality of the Religious Educator* (1985) focuses on "the ways in which religious education activity decisively affects the spiritual development of the religious educator as religious educator."[21] Its perspective on spirituality is broad and considers a wide variety of understandings of spirituality. It reflects Lee's own contribution to the ecumenical examination of religious education.

John H. Westerhoff III

A widely published author and editor, John Henry Westerhoff III is an important participant in contemporary discussions on Christian education. He was born in Paterson, New Jersey in 1933, and educated at Ursinus College (B.S., 1955), Harvard Divinity School (M.Div., 1958), and Columbia University (Ed.D., 1974). He was ordained to the clergy of the United Church of Christ (UCC) in 1958 and pastored UCC churches in Maine and Massachusetts from 1958 to 1966. Westerhoff served as editor for the United Church Board of Homeland Ministries from 1966 to 1974, when he became professor of religion and education at Duke Divinity School. He served as editor of *Religious Education* for ten years beginning in 1977 and was ordained into the Episcopal priesthood in 1978. Besides his current duties as a professor at Duke, he serves as priest at a chapel and is active as an editor, writer, leader, and thinker in the REA and the Association of Professors and Researchers in Religious Education (APRRE).

Although he has addressed many issues in religious education, Westerhoff's primary contribution has been to present socialization as a model for Christian education. He wrote, "No one has faith who has not been in part educated to it by others . . . That was done in the context of participation in a local congregation."[22] He stated this model more clearly in relation to the church as a faith community in *Will Our Children Have Faith?* (1976). In presenting this model Westerhoff asked that more attention be given to the church as a faith community and to Christian education as a means by which persons are enculturated into that community. This means that the focus of Christian education will be to develop means to bring students to awareness of, dialogue with, and deliberate personal investment in and expression of the liturgical, historical, and ethical traditions of the faith community. He contends that, if Christian education is based on an instructional model, its result will be *religion* (acceptance of propositional knowledge): if based on a socialization model, the result of

Christian education is more likely to be *faith* (reorientation of a person's life).

Westerhoff explains, refines, or expresses his approach in *Learning Through Liturgy* (Gwen Kennedy Neville as coauthor, 1978), *Liturgy and Learning Through the Life Cycle* (William H. Willimon as coauthor, 1980), *Bringing Up Children in the Christian Faith* (1980), *The Spiritual Life: Learning East and West* (John D. Eusden as coauthor, 1982), and *Building God's People in a Materialistic Society* (1983) as well as in numerous articles in professional journals.

Gabriel Moran

An important contributor to contemporary Roman Catholic theology and religious education, Gabriel Moran was born in Manchester, New Hampshire, in 1935. He was educated at the University of New Hampshire and Catholic University of America (B.A., 1958; M.A., 1962; Ph.D., 1965). He is a part of the Roman Catholic order of Christian Brothers and has taught in high schools in Providence, Rhode Island (1958-1961); De LaSalle College (1962-1965); Manhattan College (1956-1970); and New York Theological Seminary (1970-1979). Since 1979, he has been professor of religious education at New York University.

Moran argues that theology (especially a theology of revelation) is the most important element in a theory for religious education. Theology does not stand alone but is at the source, for it deals with revelation in which the person participates, not simply observes. Moran believed that "Christian revelation is a personal communion of knowledge, an interrelationship of God and the individual within a believing community."[23] (Moran outlined his understanding of the relationship between theology and religious education in *Catechesis of Revelation*, published in 1966.) In *Design for Religion* (1970), Moran acknowledged the contributions of those who had espoused experience-centered education, but he expressed doubt that they had really understood the dilemma of procedure ("experience or a set of beliefs") posed by such a system.[24] Moran wishes to engage this struggle, understanding that Christian theology is wider than the dogma held by any one faith tradition and that revelation is found in human experience. Thus, he calls for an ecumenical education "that will be concerned with the world man lives in"[25] and takes into account the breadth of human religious and doctrinal expressions. To do otherwise would stifle the freedom and curiosity of the individual and lead eventually to "denial of the human person."[26] For Moran, this would do further violence to the essence of the Christian faith[27] as well as the personal nature of Christian revelation.

James Fowler

Although James Wiley Fowler III has not developed a philosophy or theory of Christian education, his research and writing regarding faith as a developmental issue have profoundly influenced dialogue within the Christian education community.

He was born in Reidsville, North Carolina, in 1940, into the family of a Methodist pastor. He was educated at Duke University (B.A., 1962), Drew Theological Seminary (B.D., 1965), and Harvard University (Ph.D., 1971). He served as associate director of Interpreters House from 1968 to 1969. He next taught applied theology and directed a research project on faith and moral development at Harvard Divinity School. In 1976 he became professor of theology and human development at Boston College and, in 1977, moved to his present position as professor and director of the Center for Faith Development at the Candler School of Theology of Emory University in Atlanta, Georgia.

Fowler's interest in faith development gave rise to his coauthoring *Life Maps: Conversations on the Journey of Faith* (1978) and *Trajectories in Faith* (1980) before publication of his influential book *Stages of Faith: The Psychology of Human Development and the Quest for Meaning* (1981).

In *Stages of Faith*, Fowler begins with a theological position similar to that of Paul Tillich and Richard Niebuhr: faith, as a universal factor in human experience, transcends religion and dogma. If faith is a human universal, a person's capability for faith and growth in faith can be outlined in developmental stages such as those Piaget identified for the cognitive person, Erikson for the psychosocial person, and Kohlberg for the moral person.

Fowler proposes that faith development be understood in seven stages (the earliest, being informal):

1. Undifferentiated Faith (infancy)
2. Intuitive-Projective Faith (early childhood)
3. Mythic-Literal Faith (school years)

4. Synthetic-Conventional Faith (adolescence)
5. Individuative-Reflective Faith (young adulthood)
6. Conjunctive Faith (mid-life and beyond)
7. Universalizing Faith.[28]

Fowler's work has influenced many areas of ministry and has evoked responses and reactions in books and journals in a variety of professions and faith traditions. Likewise, *Stages in Faith* touched on so many concerns of Christian educators (theology, the nature of faith, developmental studies, psychology of religion) that it sparked a dialogue which continues wherever Christian education is studied.

Thomas H. Groome

In 1945 in Dublin, Ireland, Thomas Henry Groome was born into a Roman Catholic family. His father participated in the Irish Revolution earlier in the century and was active in national politics, even running for president of Ireland. (He was narrowly defeated.) The younger Groome was educated at Saint Patrick's College (M.Div., 1968), Fordham University (M.A., 1973), and the Teacher's College of Columbia University and Union Theological Seminary in New York (Ed.D., 1976). He taught theology and religious education at Catholic University of America in 1975 and took his present position as professor of theology and religious education at Boston College the following year.

Groome's most significant contribution to Christian education has been his approach to Christian education as defined in book *Christian Religious Education: Sharing Our Story and Vision* (1980). Groome calls his approach "shared praxis" and develops it (as both an educational theory and an educational methodology)[29] on a broadly based synthesis of current and historical, theological, philosophical, and educational thought. For Groome, it is essential that the individual become a participant in the past, present, and future of the faith community. He defines Christian religious education:

> political activity with pilgrims in time that deliberately and intentionally attends with them to the activity of God in our present, to the Story of the Christian faith community, and to the Vision of God's Kingdom, the seeds of which are already among us.[30]

Groome's shared praxis is a form of experiential education influenced by the Hebrew call to "know" as well as Groome's understanding of the nature of faith, faith development (he relies on Fowler at this point), and the need of persons for freedom and empowerment. He recognizes his dependence on Freire, having been especially influenced by *Pedagogy of the Oppressed*.[31]

Groome describes shared praxis in terms of molding six components (present action, critical reflection, dialogue, the "story," the "vision," and present dialectical hermeneutics) into five movements:

1. Naming Present Action—in which participants describe what they do corporately and individually as the faith community in reaction to the lesson content;

2. The Participants' Stories and Visions—in which the participants begin to critically reflect on what led to the "present action" and what was expected to come of it;

3. The Christian Community Story and Vision—in which Groome would rely on Scripture, tradition, and history communicated through a variety of possible media to urge the participants toward growth and change (Groome writes, "toward maturity in Christian faith");

4. Dialectical Hermeneutic Between the Story and Participant's Stories—in which participants can discover how their stories compare to, contrast with, rise out of, and are part of the Story of the Christian faith community;

5. Dialectical Hermeneutic Between the Vision and the Participants' Visions—in which participants are challenged to discover ways in which their hopes and future actions can be a part of or *are* a part of the hopes and future actions of the Christian faith community and will, indeed, be part of the birthing of that community.[32]

Not all Christian educators have agreed on the worth of Groome's work, but he, like Fowler, has inspired a great deal of interest. Quoted on the jacket of *Christian Religious Education*, D. Campbell Wyckoff wrote that, "Groome's is the first complete statement of a theory of Christian education in recent years" and that Coe's *A Social Theory of Education* "is the only comparable book in the field." Perhaps Groome's most lasting contribution to Christian education will be in the pattern he sets for developing his own approach to Christian education.

Notes

1. Findley B. Edge, *Religious Education and the Problem of Institutionalism* (Th.D.: The Southern Baptist Theological Seminary, 1944), 3.

2. Among the ethical issues with which Edge was concerned at this time and later on in his career and would remain somewhat of an activist (writing letters, organizing groups of people with like concerns, etc.) were racism, peacemaking, and the fundamentist takeover that marked the Southern Baptist Convention beginning in the mid-1970s.

3. Findley B. Edge, "A Search for Authenticity," *Modern Masters of Religious Education*, ed. Marlene Mayr (Birmingham, Ala.: Religious Education Press, 1983), 53.

4. D. Campbell Wyckoff, *The Task of Religious Education* (Philadelphia: Westminster, 1955), 166.

5. D. Campbell Wyckoff, *The Gospel and Christian Education: A Theory of Christian Education for Our Times* (Philadelphia: Westminster, 1959), 29.

6. Ibid., 171.

7. D. Campbell Wyckoff, "The Curriculum and the Church School," *Religious Education: A Comprehensive Survey*, ed. Marvin J. Taylor (New York: Abingdon, 1960), 99.

8. D. Campbell Wyckoff, "Afterword," *Religious Education Ministry with Youth*, ed. D. Campbell Wyckoff and Don Richter (Birmingham, Ala.: Religious Education Press, 1982), 244.

9. Sara Little, *The Role of the Bible in Contemporary Christian Education* (Richmond, Va.: John Knox, 1961), 163-65.

10. Sara P. Little, "Religious Instruction," *Contemporary Approaches to Christian Education*, ed. Jack L. Seymour and Donald E. Miller (Nashville: Abingdon, 1982), 42.

11. Ibid., 42-48.

12. Sara Little, *Youth, World, and Church* (Richmond, Va.: John Knox, 1968), 29.

13. Paulo Freire, *Pedagogy of the Oppressed*, trans. Myra Bergman Ramos (New York: The Seabury Press, 1970), 58.

14. Daniel S. Schipani, *Conscientization and Creativity: Paulo Freire and Christian Education* (Lanham, Md.: University Press of America, 1984), ix.

15. Paulo Freire, "Education, Liberation, and the Church," *Religious Education* LXXIX:4 (Fall 1984):527.

16. James Michael Lee, "To Change Fundamental Theory and Practice," *Modern Masters of Religious Education*, 297.

17. James Michael Lee, *The Shape of Religious Instruction: A Social Science Approach* (Dayton, Ohio: George A. Pflaum Publisher, 1971), 115-28.

18. Ibid., 138-39.

19. James Michael Lee, *The Content of Religious Instruction: A Social Science Approach* (Birmingham, Ala.: Religious Education Press, 1985), 9.

20. Harold W. Burgess, *An Invitation to Religious Education* (Birmingham, Ala.: Religious Education Press, 1975), 127.

21. James Michael Lee, "Introduction," *The Spirituality of the Religious Educator*, ed. James Michael Lee (Birmingham, Ala.: Religious Education Press, 1985), 1.

22. John H. Westerhoff III, "A Socialization Model," *A Colloquy on Christian Education*, ed. John H. Westerhoff III (Philadelphia: United Church Press, 1972), 82.

23. Gabriel Moran, *Catechesis of Revelation* (New York: Herder and Herder, 1966), 13.

24. Gabriel Moran, *Design for Religion: Toward Ecumenical Education* (New York: Herder and Herder, 1970), 24-25.

25. Ibid., 27.

26. Gabriel Moran, *Vision and Tactics: Toward an Adult Church* (New York: Herder and Herder, 1968), 130.

27. Moran, *Design for Religion*, 97.

28. James W. Fowler, *Stages of Faith: The Psychology of Human Development and the Quest for Meaning* (San Francisco: Harper and Row, 1981), 113 *ff*.

29. Thomas H. Groome, *Christian Religious Education: Sharing Our Story and Vision* (San Francisco: Harper and Row, 1980), 137.

30. Ibid., 25.

31. One may wonder about the impact of stories of oppression at the hands of England told by Groome's father and the Irish nation and what may have sensitized Groome to Freire and issues Freire surfaced.

32. Groome, 207-23.

35

Movements in Twentieth-Century Christian Education

Christian education has grown and diversified during the twentieth century. Not every movement or issue has confronted (or been confronted by) each faith community in the same way. Some have been more directed toward Christian education in the local church, while others have been more related to the academic community. This chapter gives a sampling of each with observations regarding their implications and effects. Readers should further research these and other significant movements and draw their own inferences. Developing a more objective treatise on how these currents and movements may or may not fit together is one for all of us, but will best be done by someone, as Robert Frost put it, "ages and ages hence."

Vacation Bible School

Although the nineteenth century saw several attempts to maximize the church's influence on children during summers it was not until the early twentieth century that this idea began to take hold. Robert G. Boville was executive secretary of the New York City Baptist Board of Missions at the turn of the century. He had a concern, similar to that of Raikes in Gloucester, that children of New York be given religious instruction during their idle summers to keep them out of trouble and develop patterns for productive and upright adult living. Boville had been impressed by earlier attempts by churches in Montreal and by Epiphany Baptist Church in New York City.

Boville used vacationing students from local colleges and seminaries. Using students from Union Theological Seminary as faculty leaders (among them was Harry Emerson Fosdick), he opened in 1901 five Vacation Bible Schools that enrolled about a thousand children. The schools included time for worship, religious instruction, crafts, and recreation. By 1903 there were seventeen such schools in New York City, and schools were soon begun in Philadelphia and Chicago. By 1907 there were forty-five Vacation Bible Schools in a number of cities, and the movement developed to the point that Boville founded the National Committee on Daily Vacation Bible Schools,[1] which spread the concept around the world.

By 1917 the association was renamed International Association of Daily Vacation Bible Schools; by 1922 these schools numbered 5,000 worldwide, the vast majority in North America.[2] By 1949, nearly fifty years after Boville's first schools, International Council of Religious Education reported 62,161 schools involving 546,517 faculty volunteers and 4,045,598 pupils.[3]

As the movement grew, it was adopted and adapted by many churches, denominations, and missions agencies. In 1907 the International Association of Daily Vacation Bible Schools became an affiliate of the newly organized International Council of Religious Education. The schools were known by names such as Vacation Bible Schools (VBS) and Vacation Church School. Schools took on a variety of forms both in content and structure. Many churches have used VBS as a means to expand their ministries of Bible teaching, missions education, and evangelism. Some focus on other areas and include programs of sex education and prevention of substance abuse. Some last four to six weeks, others are of shorter duration.

Although VBS no longer carries the immediate connotation of a "mission" enterprise, it is sometimes used as a tool in missions settings. Missions agencies often employ college students as "summer missionaries" who serve mostly as VBS workers. Most schools now last one week, although the two-week VBS flourished in many denominations as late as the early sixties. Most schools are closely graded by age or school grades and have access to ample VBS materials published by denominational and nondenominational publishers.

Cultural and demographic shifts have brought change in the already multifarious forms of Vacation Bible School. The age groups have increased to include, in various places, preschoolers, adolescents, and adults. Often, adolescents are used as teachers as were college and seminary students under Boville. Churches and denominations that hold fast to the basic aims and goals of the first Vacation Bible School have found themselves challenged to develop new and original approaches and curricula.[4]

Church Day-Care Centers and Kindergartens

Until well into the twentieth century, child care was considered the responsibility of parents or the extended family. Only the most unfortunate and indigent children or the children of immigrants became wards of the state and/or were given to the care of a nonfamily agency, such as an orphanage or settlement house. Children in need of such care and their families were often stigmatized.

More recently attitudes toward child care have changed as both parents—or the only parent—are employed. The shift in attitudes is only one element in the growth of churches providing day-care services and/or kindergartens. Since the 1950s more and more public school kindergartens are available to build children's basic educational skills. This growth has led many parents in areas without public school kindergartens to expect churches or other organizations to provide these services. Further, parents in both situations often look for ways to boost their children's readiness for kindergarten through day-care centers that provide for at least some educational structure as well as the opportunities for a child to interact with nonfamily peers on a regular and organized basis. Others simply want to expose their children to Christian principles and the church.

Various factors have motivated churches to provide day-care and kindergarten ministries. One impetus has been to provide a ministry to families that need it or want it. Another is that churches have become aware of the often unused resources and high investment in their educational buildings and space; this has been especially important in a time of increasing construction costs and interest rates and critical to churches saddled with a heavy building debt and facing decreasing membership. Churches have also seen the operation of a day-care center and/or kindergarten as an opportunity to evangelize children and their parents. Children of the church who are enrolled in the center or kindergarten are further integrated into church as a way of life.

As recently as 1984 an estimated 70 percent of all day-care centers in the United States were located in churches.[5] As churches have become increasingly involved in the provision of day-care centers and kindergartens, they have realized the need for persons trained in preschool education. Further, governmental regulations often require that at least the director of the church day-care center and/or kindergarten have a minimum of a bachelor's degree in education.[6] Many seminaries now offer courses and degrees preparing persons for service in these church ministries.

Christian Education as a Profession

Throughout history some persons have functioned, by some definition, as professional Christian educators. Most of these were trained either as clergy or as educators. A movement began earlier in this century to establish Christian education (or religious education) as a profession distinct from theology or education, yet related to them both. This movement can be expressed in terms of the following areas: academic training (professional study), specific vocational identity, professional societies, parish ministry, and ordination.

In this century numerous seminaries and university graduate programs have established more closely defined and expanded programs in Christian education. Although some programs have met untimely deaths, most schools have strengthened their religious education programs. At first, seminaries offered few courses in religious education and expected students preparing to be professional Christian educators to study the same disciplines as those preparing for the pastorate. Then a department of religious education was established offering a "certificate" or "diploma" in religious or Christian education. As the department grew, students were given access to bachelors or masters degrees, but not distinct from theology. Eventually schools offered degrees specifically in Christian education. Finally, schools offered doctoral work and degrees in Christian education. Current seminary catalogs illustrate the proliferation of degrees open in Christian education.[7]

Curriculum offerings have expanded. In some of the larger schools students training as Christian education professionals specialize in a specific area of Christian education, such as administration, foundations of education (history and philosophy), or developmental studies. Of course, curriculum and degree changes are expected to meet requirements of the accrediting agencies. Standards of the Association of Theological Schools (ATS) for accreditation of master's degrees require that programs include "the opportunity for acquiring the varied understandings required by the religious educator, for supervised practice in educational ministry, and for the personal and spiritual growth."[8]

What is a Christian educator? John L. Elias suggests an understanding that calls for awareness of the three "publics" that confront religious educators: the academic community, the church, and the general public.[9] The first two of these provide the most help in understanding the development of specific professional identity among Christian educators.

At the turn of the century many in the academic community became concerned that religious education was neglecting the scientific study of education. William Rainey Harper, George A. Coe, and others were concerned that religious education was so devotionally oriented that it neglected the insights of John Dewey and other educational thinkers. Concerned leaders formed the Religious Education Association (REA) in 1903.

The REA was originally comprised exclusively of Protestant Christians but changed over the years (as its self-understanding changed) to become the ecumenical society it is today, numbering among its members Christians (Protestant, Evangelical, Catholic, Orthodox) and Jews. Over the years the REA has provided forums for dialogue on issues of concern to professional religious educators: the nature of religious education, the relation of religious education to science, religious education as a discipline, ethnic religious education, and so forth. REA sponsored dialogue takes place in national meetings and through its journal *Religious Education* (begun in 1906). The Association of Professors and Researchers in Religious Education (APRRE) was established in 1969 and now meets concurrently with the REA and is a joint publisher of *Religious Education*. Its affiliation with APRRE has strengthened REA's ties with the academic community, but REA is also concerned for religious education in the local church or synagogue. Both REA and APRRE have served as points around which Christian educators in the academic community develop professional identity.

Although the REA has always included them among its number, Christian educators in local churches have their own established professional societies and interest groups. Many denominationally oriented regional and national associations have developed out of the need for mutual support, dialogue, and establishment of professional standards or guidelines within the faith community.

Christian educators in local churches have also seen their professional identity change through the titles accorded their positions through this century. In some denominations and churches the earliest identifiable Christian educator was known as a "hired Sunday School superintendent.'' As Christian educations became recognized as a profession (if not quite *clergy* in some fellowships), he or she became known as Director of Religious Education (or Christian Education). This title is still maintained in some churches and denominations, especially to designate a layperson with educational administration responsibilities or to indicate whether the person has a master's degree or has been ordained. Current titles for Christian educators in local churches include director of religious education or Christian education (DRE or DCE), minister of education, associate pastor in education, and titles indicating specialized ministry to a specific age-group or in a specific area.[10] The possibilities are as numerous as the churches which Christian educators serve.

Separate from the issue of titles, but not unrelated, is that of ordination. Faith communities have differed and continue to differ widely in their understandings of both ordination and the role of the Christian educator. Some churches have called out their Christian educators from among those already ordained. Others perceive ''clergy'' almost exclusively in pastoral terms and, so, consider the Christian educator a layperson or as someone between clergy and laity. Many of these perceptions have begun to change. Some churches have modified their stances on the meaning of clergy to include those outside the pastoral ministry and have chosen to ordain as clergy their Christian education professionals. This has been controversial, particularly among churches in which ordination of women is a matter of debate.

Ministry of the Laity/Lay Renewal

Ministry of the laity refers to involvement of laypersons throughout the ministry structures of the church. Some understand this to mean that laity are coequal with the clergy. The concept is not new. Some believe New Testament teaching rejects the clergy-laity polarity. Some theologians and educators throughout history have stressed the importance of lay ministry in the church. During the twentieth century John R. Mott, Findley B. Edge, and other Protestants have rediscovered the Protestant heritage of priesthood of the believer, while Vatican II has involved laity in liturgical and catechetical leadership. The Southern Baptist Convention established 1988-1989 as ''The Year of the Laity,'' though a Convention resolution in 1988 weakened its historically firm position on priesthood of the believer and formalized a shift toward pastoral authority.

As churches across the denominational and theological spectrum have dealt with redefining the role and function of the laity (and clergy), they have been challenged to rethink their approaches to education in the local church. Edge wrote in *The Greening of the Church* (1971) that the educational task of the church committed to lay ministry could be expressed in terms of "a miniature seminary." In *The Doctrine of the Laity* (1985), Edge outlined eleven areas in which lay ministers must be trained: Bible knowledge, doctrines, church functions, church history, missions, Christian ethics, witnessing, teaching, visitation, counseling, and administration.[11] Such an understanding requires that Christian education be an *equipping* ministry, rather than mere catechesis, enculturation, or indoctrination.

This movement holds other implications for Christian education. To educate and equip the laity for ministry will, as Freire put it, empower them, and clergy (Christian educators among them) will experience, in some terms, a loss of power. Further, this shift in power will make more imperative Thomas Groome's challenge that Christian religious educators understand the role of the teacher as "fellow-pilgrim."

Private Schools

Private schools have been part of Christian education throughout its history. For instance, the Roman Catholic Church has long maintained parish schools in the United States.[12] Since 1950, however, private schools have grown significantly, many located in churches and identified as "Christian" schools. Until 1980 diverse forces influenced this phenomenon: religious fundamentalism, right-wing politics, and the rejecting of the Supreme Court desegregation order by white racists. The curricula and character of these schools has been debated, including whether or not the schools and their curricula are, in fact, Christian. This calls into review the essence of Christian education, especially that part of Christian education not related to catechesis.

Three Supreme Court decisions in the first half of the century set the stage for the conflict to come. In *Gitlow vs. New York* (1925), the court ruled that rights guaranteed by the First Amendment are among those protected from intrusion by all states by the Fourteenth Amendment. In *Pierce vs. Society of Sisters,* the court upheld the right of parents to enroll their children in parochial rather than public schools. In *McCollum vs. Board of Education* (1948), the court ruled that public

school participation in "released time" programs of religious education was unconstitutional.[13]

A series of Supreme Court decisions in the 1950s and 1960s against
racial segregation and required religious exercises gave increased impetus to the Christian school movement. The court ruled in *Brown vs.
Board of Education* I (1954) and *Brown vs. Board of Education* II
(1955) that racially segregated public schools, though claiming to be
equal, were inherently unequal and, therefore, unconstitutional. Despite these rulings, racial segregation remained a fact in many areas of
the United States. Federal troops were required to enforce the integration of the schools in Little Rock, Arkansas, in 1957. Federal marshals
and a federalized National Guard enforced the integration of the
University of Mississippi in 1962. Racist policies were often justified
and encouraged through the preaching and educational "ministries" of
many (though not all) churches. Although students had been bused to
enforce racial *segregation* for many years, when the Supreme Court
began ruling (in *Swann vs. Charlotte-Mecklenburg Board of Education*
in 1971 and in other cases) that busing was a legitimate and constitutional tool for enforcing racial *segregation* racists, communities, and
churches argued that the issue was community schools.

Concurrently, the court ruled in *Engel vs. Vital* (1962) that it vio-
lated the Constitution for a public school to use "official" prayers (in
this case one composed by a group of clergy) for its students to recite.
Abingdon School District vs. Schempp and *Murray vs. Curlett* (1963)
declared public school-sponsored prayer and devotional Bible reading
unconstitutional. These rulings enabled persons who opposed racial
integration to claim for themselves a moral and spiritual "high
ground"; they justified their racist "Christian" schools through a
rhetoric of concern for the religious education of their children, the
quality of education in general, and the removal of religion from the
public schools. In many cases these schools were established in or by
churches to protect their tax-exempt and tax-deductible status. Further, many churches found that hosting such a school could ease their
financial burdens.

Some of these segregationist schools have ceased to exist. Many are
no longer explicitly racist but maintain implicitly racist policies. Some
have shifted their agenda from racism to fundamentalist civil religion.
Others have shifted their agenda toward a legitimate concern for
quality education. Systems of these schools have developed in a few
areas, and specific curricula have been published.

Although exceptions exist, most of these schools have provided a substandard education. They point to high standardized test scores achieved by their students compared with those in the public schools. However, such a raw comparison fails to take into account a number of factors: students come from a more enculturated class (the culture bias of the SAT and ACT is well documented). Their students tend to receive more family educational support than other students; these schools, unlike public schools, can select their students and do not have to accept students with learning disabilities and other academic handicaps. They also drain resources from the public schools.[14]

The Women's Movement

The role of women in America has changed dramatically during the twentieth century. First, the women's suffrage movement gained for women the right to vote. During World War II many women ignored sexual stereotypes to work in defense plants and serve in the armed forces. More recently, the feminist movement is building on these earlier experiences. Women are increasingly aware of their abilities and potential. More women are seeking higher education, working outside the home, and leading in areas formerly reserved exclusively for men. This cultural shift has affected American society in many areas.

Just as the women's movement has changed the face of American society, it has also influenced Christian education. Additional influences have been the rise of Liberation theology and the reemphasis on ministry of the laity. These factors have opened doors for women to serve in a variety of Christian education roles as both laity and clergy.

The role of women as lay Christian educators was once very limited. Opportunities were restricted to those areas considered "appropriate for a woman": Sunday School workers and teachers (of anyone, except for adult males), women's missionary society volunteers, and so forth. Some churches still restrict women to these duties, but many now encourage women to serve as God has gifted them individually, thus creating almost limitless possibilities.

Women are also finding more opportunities for service as Christian educators identified as clergy. These, too, are exploring the gamut of options in Christian education. For some time women have been accepted as missionaries and as Christian educators (with preschoolers, children, and adolescents), but now they find themselves following other avenues of ministry. Most women find their opportunities to follow God's call to clergy limited only by their own and their faith community's willingness.

Women have experienced a growing and resulting need for education in service as Christian educators, whether as laity or clergy. This has caused churches to rethink the content, curriculum, and methods of Christian education at all levels. Since education throughout history has been male dominated and male oriented, Christian educators have begun to explore such issues as learning styles (Do women learn differently than do men? What are the differences?), gender-inclusive language, and liturgy. The concern is how these issues can inform the curriculum, content, and method of Christian education so that all students can be more effectively equipped.

The number of women enrolled in theological seminaries or teaching on their faculties has increased significantly. Many are enrolled in degree programs that would have not been open to them forty or fifty years ago. Some seminaries and graduate schools of religion offer courses and degrees in women's studies.

The effect of the women's movement on men in Christian education has been varied. Some have found themselves threatened by the "empowerment" of women in Christian education, but others have themselves been empowered and have found callings to serve as Christian educators in roles heretofore considered the domain of women.[15]

Notes

1. Gerald E. Knoff, "Fifty Years and a Future," *International Journal of Religious Education* XXVII 5 (January 1951):6.

2. R. E. F. Aler, *Vacation Bible School* (Nashville: The Sunday School Board of the Southern Baptist Convention, 1923), 7.

3. Knoff, 7.

4. Freda A. Gardner, "Vacation Church School," *Harper's Encyclopedia of Religious Education*, ed. Iris V. Cully and Kendig B. Cully (San Francisco: Harper and Row, 1990), 677.

5. Eileen W. Linder, "The Churches and Day Care," *The Christian Century* CI 14 (April 1984):427.

6. Whether or not the government (local, state, or federal) has the right or license a *church* day-care center or kindergarten is a matter of continuing debate, constitutionally and otherwise. Another constitutional issue related to church day-care centers and kindergartens are tax credits for child care and tuition credits and vouches in areas with or without public kindergartens.

7. A listing of Christian education degrees available would still include diplomas and certificates in Christian education, but would also include B.R.E., M.R.E., M.A., M.Div., M.Div.-C.E., D.Min., D.R.E., Ed.D., and Ph.D.

8. Robert L. Conrad, "Professional Study," *Harper's Encyclopedia of Religious Education*, ed. Iris V. Cully and Kendig B. Cully (San Francisco, Harper and Row, 1990), 513.

9. John L. Elias, *Studies in Theology and Education* (Malabar, Fla.: Robert E. Krieger Publishing Co., 1986), 17-28.

10. Dorothy Jean Furnish, "Director of Religious Education," *Harper's Encyclopedia of Religious Education,* ed. Iris V. Cully and Kendig B. Cully (San Francisco: Harper and Row, 1990), 190.

11. Findley B. Edge, *The Doctrine of the Laity* (Nashville: Convention Press, 1985), 146.

12. The Roman Catholic Church has almost always used the parochial school in the United States as a means of general education as well as Christian education.

13. "Released time" is a system by which students in public schools are "released" to attend religion courses being taught on the school grounds by sectarian teachers. Students choosing not to attend these classes are placed in study halls.

14. David Nevin and Robert E. Bills, *The Schools that Fear Built: Segregationist Academies in the South* (Washington, D.C.: Acropolis Books, 1976), 85-88.

15. Nelle Morton, "Feminism Movement," *Harper's Encyclopedia of Religious Education,* ed. Iris V. Cully and Kendig B. Cully (San Francisco: Harper and Row, 1990), 258.

Synopsis
of Part 7

Christian education has expanded and diversified in the twentieth century. It has been influenced significantly by the scientific study of education in general. Some see this as a benefit for Christian education; for others it has been a bane. Most faith communities have seen the need to place greater emphasis on their efforts in education. The spectrum of Christian education today has widened because diverse faith communities are contributing to it. An assortment of educational philosophies, theories, and approaches operate within each faith community and cross the lines that distinguish one community from another.

Certainly the emergence of Christian education as a distinct profession has been a unifying theme regardless of denominational and church affiliation. The Religious Education Association and, of late, the Association of Professors and Researchers in Religious Education have been catalysts to this end.

Harold W. Burgess provides the structure by which to understand the main themes (or theoretical approaches) of twentieth-century Christian education and theorists that group around them: (1) the traditional theological, theoretical approach ("primarily concerned with communication of a divine message"); (2) the social-cultural approach ("Practices generated within this theoretical approach are typically oriented to life through social activity."); (3) the contemporary theological theoretical approach ("focuses on an organic relationship between religious education and the Christian community"); and (4) the social-science theoretical approach (more concerned with theories of instruction and learning that are not based on a theology but into which a theology can be inserted as content).[1] Burgess identifies several persons not dealt with in this book as representative of these approaches. Those in this book with whom Burgess deals and the approaches by which he groups them are:

- Social-cultural theoretical approach—George A. Coe, William Clayton Bower, Ernest J. Chave
- Contemporary theological theoretical approach—Randolph Crump Miller, Gabriel Moran, D. Campbell Wyckoff, Sara Little
- Social-science theoretical approach—James Michael Lee

Of course, grouping and labeling persons always carries a certain risk. Admittedly, that is also the case when one identifies the most important persons and/or movements in any era or discipline. Historical perspective can make all the difference in interpreting the lifework of persons as well as their eventual impact and that of others on a given area. It may be too soon to judge the long-term importance of Mary C. Boys' *Educating in Faith: Maps and Visions* (1989) and Timothy A. Lines' *Systemic Religious Education* (1987), though both appear to contribute much to contemporary dialogue on the nature and direction of religious education.

Recent movements in Christian education are also hard to evaluate. With the increased diversification of Christian education, currents do not equally affect all faith communities. Some movements in Christian education are still in their infancy and have not yet revealed their mature character. Christian education among ethnic minorities and cross-cultural Christian education, for example, must develop more in order to be dealt with as a field of study; this will enable ethnic majorities and ethnic minorities to teach, inform, and appreciate each other in order to fulfill the liberating nature of the gospel. Paulo Freire has attempted to lay a base for this in Third World context as has Olivia Pearl Stokes among African-Americans.[2] For Christian educators to be equipped to deal with these and other issues will require that they become even more broadly educated and informed.

The scientific study of Christian education and religious education in the twentieth century has answered many questions. As happens when any science makes new discoveries, it has unearthed many new questions and underscored old ones. Marianne Sawicki put it well when she wrote:

These are tough and perhaps daunting questions. However, the endurance of the gospel through almost twenty centuries of teaching gives us cause to hope. Ultimately our hope is in the promise of Jesus that a rather foolishly parental God is even now taking over on this planet and straightening things out. Our survey of these centuries persuades me that it is so.[3]

Notes

1. Harold W. Burgess, *An Invitation to Religious Education* (Birmingham, Ala.: Religious Education Press, 1975), 15.

2. Olivia Pearl Stokes, "Education in the Black Church," *Religious Education* LXIX 4 (Summer 1974):443-45.

3. Marianne Sawicki, *The Gospel in History: Portrait of a Teaching Church: The Origins of Christian Education* (New York: Paulist Press, 1988), 291-92.

Bibliography

Anderson, Bonnie S. and Judith P. Zinsser. *A History of Their Own: Women in Europe from Prehistory to the Present*, Vols. 1&2. New York: Harper and Row, 1988.

Bruce, Gustav M. *Luther as an Educator*. Reprint. Minneapolis: Augsburg Press, 1928.

Bushnell, Horace. *Christian Nurture*. New York: Charles Scribner and Co., 1861.

Button, Warren and Eugene F. Provenzo, Jr. *History of Education and Culture in America*, 2nd ed. Englewood Cliffs, New Jersey, 1988.

Carper, James C. and Thomas C. Hunt. *Religious Schooling in America*. Birmingham, Alabama: Religious Education Press, 1984.

Cole, Luella. *A History of Education: Socrates to Montessori*. New York: Fordham University Press, 1924.

Cully, Iris V. and Kendig B. Cully, eds. *Harper's Encyclopedia of Religious Education*. New York: Harper and Row, 1990.

Eavey, C.B. *History of Christian Education*. Chicago: Moody Press, 1979.

Frost, S.E., Jr. and Kenneth P. Bailey. *Historical and Philosophical Foundations of Western Education*, 2nd ed. Columbus, Ohio: Charles E. Merrill Publishing Co., 1973.

Gangel, Kenneth O. and Warren S. Benson. *Christian Education: Its History and Philosophy*. Chicago: Moody Press, 1983.

Groome, Thomas H. *Christian Religious Education: Sharing Our Story and Vision*. San Francisco: Harper and Row, 1980.

Gross, Richard E., ed. *Heritage of American Education*. Boston: Allyn and Bacon, 1962.

Gwynne-Thomas, E.H. *A Concise History of Education to A.D. 1900*. Lanham, Maryland: University Press of America, 1981.

James, Edward T., Janet W. James and Paul S. Boyer, eds. *Notable American Women 1607-1950*, Vols. 1-3. Cambridge, Massachusetts: The Belknap Press of Harvard University Press, 1971.

Lottich, Kenneth V. and Elmer H. Wilds. *The Foundations of Modern Education*. 4th ed. New York: Holt, Rinehart and Winston, 1970.

MacHaffie, Barbara J. *Her Story: Women in Christian Tradition*. Philadelphia: Fortress Press, 1986.

Matsagouras, Elias. *The Early Church Fathers as Educators*. Minneapolis: Light and Life Press, 1977.

Mayr, Marlene, ed. *Modern Masters of Religious Education*. Birmingham, Alabama: Religious Education Press, 1983.

Miller, Donald E. *Story and Context: An Introduction to Christian Education*. Nashville: Abingdon Press, 1987.

Nakosteen, Mehdi. *The History and Philosophy of Education*. New York: Ronald Press, 1965.

Ruether, Rosemary R. and Rosemary S. Keller. *Women and Religion in America, The Colonial and Revolutionary Periods*. Vols. 1-3. San Francisco: Harper and Row, 1983.

Sawicki, Marianne. *The Gospel in History*. New York: Paulist Press, 1988.

Towns, Elmer L., ed. *A History of Religious Educators*. Grand Rapids: Baker Books, 1975.

Tucker, Ruth A. and Walter L. Liefield. *Daughters of the Church*. Grand Rapids: Zondervan, 1987.

Ulich, Robert. *A History of Religious Education*. New York: New York University Press, 1968.

Index

FIRST MONETARY COURSE AND SEMINARY